T0347245

Climate-Resilient Development

The concept of resilience currently infuses policy debates and public discourse, and is promoted as a normative concept in climate policy making by governments, non-governmental organizations, and think tanks.

This book critically discusses climate-resilient development in the context of current deficiencies of multilateral climate management strategies and processes. It analyses innovative climate policy options at national, (inter-)regional, and local levels from a mainly Southern perspective, thus contributing to the topical debate on alternative climate governance and resilient development models. Case studies from Africa, Asia, and Latin America give a ground-level view of how ideas from resilience could be used to inform and guide more radical development and particularly how these ideas might help to rethink the notion of 'progress' in the light of environmental, social, economic, and cultural changes at multiple scales, from local to global. It integrates theory and practice with the aim of providing practical solutions to improve, complement, or, where necessary, reasonably bypass the UNFCCC process through a bottom-up approach which can effectively tap unused climate-resilient development potentials at the local, national, and regional levels.

This innovative book gives students and researchers in environmental and development studies as well as policy makers and practitioners a valuable analysis of climate change mitigation and adaptation options in the absence of effective multilateral provisions.

Astrid Carrapatoso is an Assistant Professor at the Department of Political Science at the Albert-Ludwigs-Universität Freiburg, Germany.

Edith Kürzinger is a freelance consultant, coach and trainer on sustainability issues with a background in development research (German Development Institute – DIE), development policy (Federal Ministry for Economic Cooperation and Development – BMZ) and project management (GTZ).

Routledge Studies in Sustainable Development

This series uniquely brings together original and cutting-edge research on sustainable development. The books in this series tackle difficult and important issues in sustainable development including: values and ethics; sustainability in higher education; climate compatible development; resilience; capitalism and de-growth; sustainable urban development; gender and participation; and well-being.

Drawing on a wide range of disciplines, the series promotes interdisciplinary research for an international readership. The series was recommended in the *Guardian*'s suggested reads on development and the environment.

Institutional and Social Innovation for Sustainable Urban Development
Edited by Harald A. Mieg and Klaus Töpfer

The Sustainable University
Progress and prospects
Edited by Stephen Sterling, Larch Maxey and Heather Luna

Sustainable Development in Amazonia
Paradise in the making
Kei Otsuki

Measuring and Evaluating Sustainability
Ethics in sustainability indexes
Sarah E. Fredericks

Values in Sustainable Development
Edited by Jack Appleton

Climate-Resilient Development
Participatory solutions from developing countries
Edited by Astrid Carrapatoso and Edith Kürzinger

Theatre for Women's Participation in Sustainable Development
Beth Osnes

Urban Waste and Sanitation Services for Sustainable Development
Harnessing social and technical diversity in East Africa
Bas van Vliet, Joost van Buuren and Shaaban Mgana

Sustainable Capitalism and the Pursuit of Well-Being
Neil E. Harrison

Climate-Resilient Development

Participatory solutions from developing countries

**Edited by Astrid Carrapatoso
and Edith Kürzinger**

LONDON AND NEW YORK

First published 2014
by Routledge
2 Park Square, Milton Park, Abingdon, Oxon OX14 4RN

and by Routledge
711 Third Avenue, New York, NY 10017

Routledge is an imprint of the Taylor & Francis Group, an informa business

© 2014 selection and editorial material, Astrid Carrapatoso and Edith
Kürzinger; individual chapters, the contributors

British Library Cataloguing in Publication Data
A catalogue record for this book is available from the British Library

Library of Congress Cataloging-in-Publication Data
Climate resilient development : participatory solutions from developing
countries / [edited by] Astrid Carrapatoso and Edith Kürzinger.
   pages cm. – (Routledge studies in sustainable development)
Includes bibliographical references and index.
1. Environmental policy – Economic aspects – Developing countries.
2. Climatic changes – Economic aspects – Developing countries.
3. Sustainable development – Developing countries. 4. Economic
development – Environmental aspects – Developing countries.
I. Carrapatoso, Astrid. II. Kürzinger, Edith.
HC59.72.E5C554 2014
338.9'27091724–dc23   2013011306

ISBN: 978-0-415-82078-3 (hbk)
ISBN: 978-0-203-38598-2 (ebk)

Typeset in Times
by HWA Text and Data Management, London

Contents

Figures

Tables

Contributors

Luís Artur is a Lecturer and Researcher at Eduardo Mondlane University in Maputo, Mozambique. His main professional interest is on the interface between different actors in disaster response contexts, disaster risk management, and local adaptation to climate change. He holds a PhD in Disaster Studies and an MSc in Development Sociology from Wageningen University in The Netherlands and a BSc in Agronomy from Eduardo Mondlane University in Maputo, Mozambique.

Marie-Ange Baudoin has a degree in Political Science and a DESS in Development Studies from Université Libre de Bruxelles. She obtained a PhD in Environmental Sciences in 2012. She is currently a BAEF Post-Doctoral Researcher at the University of Colorado's Consortium for Capacity Building. She specializes in climate change adaptation and disaster risk reduction for African countries.

Astrid Carrapatoso holds a PhD in Political Science and presently works as an Assistant Professor at the Albert-Ludwigs-Universität Freiburg, Germany. She was previously a Research Fellow at the University of Auckland, New Zealand, and at the National Europe Centre at the Australian National University in Canberra, Australia. Her research focus is on international climate policy making, inter-regional climate cooperation, EU–Asia relations, and sustainable development.

Sampson E. Edusah is a Senior Research Fellow and Director of the Bureau of Integrated Rural Development (BIRD). He coordinated the NUFFIC-funded NPT/GHA/278 Project at the College of Agriculture and Natural Resources (CANR) at Kwame Nkrumah University of Science and Technology (KNUST) in Kumasi, Ghana, from 2005 to 2012. He holds a Doctoral Degree in Development Studies from the University of Bradford, UK, where he worked as an Assistant Lecturer from 1998 to 1999. His areas of specialization include small-scale industry, natural resources, livelihoods, and project management.

Thomas Grammig has been working as an engineer in technical assistance projects since 1985. His PhD thesis in Anthropology, published in 2002 as

'Technical Knowledge and Development', from the EHESS in France was a seminal work, which defined communication structures in industrial projects. He has implemented Montreal and Kyoto Protocol projects for German companies and development co-operation agencies, such as GIZ-Proklima.

Ciara Kirrane has a degree in Social Science and works as an Environmental Justice Policy Officer with Trócaire in Ireland. Founded in 1973, Trócaire is the official overseas development agency of the Catholic Church in Ireland. She currently leads Trócaire's advocacy on climate justice. Previously, she was responsible for the coordination of a research project on climate change and resilience, and from 2009 to 2012 spent time conducting fieldwork in Malawi, Kenya, and Honduras.

Edith Kürzinger holds a PhD in Economics. Since 2006, she has been a freelance trainer and consultant on change management in development co-operation and a resource person and publicist on sustainable development issues. As a Research Fellow of the German Development Institute (DIE) in Berlin/Bonn, she studied development issues of emerging economies and advised the Federal Ministry for Economic Co-operation and Development (BMZ) from 1983 to 1993. As Deputy Head of BMZ's Environment and Climate Division, she worked on the implementation of the UNCED decisions and UNFCCC negotiations. As a Team Leader in GTZ (1996–2006), she developed and disseminated a wide variety of management tools; the PREMA© concept and training modules have boosted resource efficiency and profitability in companies in Africa, Asia, Europe and Latin America, and are actually disseminated by PREMAnet e.V., a German NGO, and local partners.

Pauline Lacour is a Post-Doctoral Fellow at the University of Grenoble's CREG Research Unit. Her research is specialized in international economics and environmental economics. She focuses on the environmental content of economic relations between Japan and China, and is interested in environmentally friendly technology transfers.

Lars Otto Naess holds a PhD in Environmental Sciences and is currently a Research Fellow in the Climate Change Team at the Institute of Development Studies in Brighton, UK. His current research interests include social and institutional dimensions of adaptation to climate change, policy processes on climate change and agriculture at national and sub-national levels, the role of local knowledge for adaptation to climate change, and adaptation planning in the context of international development. Much of his recent work has focused on Africa, particularly Tanzania, Kenya, Malawi, and Ethiopia.

Gala Bhaskar Reddy is an Indian Forest Service officer with over 32 years' experience in forestry, food security, and participatory livelihood-focused watershed development programmes. He held team leader positions in DFID-funded WORLP and WFP-funded food security and participatory tribal development projects. He has an MSc and further certificates from the Indian Forest College, OTTA, Wolverhampton, KILA, Trichur and ASCI, Hyderabad, India. He has been actively engaged in action research over the past 13 years.

Niranjan Sahu has 22 years' experience in teaching, extension, research and development. He worked in DANIDA-assisted CWDP and DFID-funded WORLP programmes. He holds an M. Tech in Agricultural Engineering with a specialization in Soil and Water Conservation from IIT, Kharagpur; Overseas General Management from Ramboll, Denmark; a post-graduate certificate in Business Management from XIM, Bhubaneswar; and a post-graduate diploma in Social Work and Human Resources Development.

Cliona Sharkey works as a Policy Officer at Trócaire in Ireland. Her academic background is in European Union studies, human rights, and development management. She has worked in both the inter-governmental and non-governmental sectors, at the UN headquarters in New York, and at the Council of Europe in Strasbourg. In the NGO sector, Cliona worked for a number of years coordinating development projects in Southern Africa. Before taking up her current role, she spent three years as the Climate Change and Food Security Policy Officer with CIDSE, an international network of development agencies based in Brussels, Belgium.

Jean-Christophe Simon is a Senior Economist at IRD (UMR 201) and Senior Research Fellow at EDDEN Institute (CNRS, University of Grenoble). His research focuses on developing and emerging economies' current sustainable development challenges, particularly looking at economic tools to make climate and environmental policies compatible with economic competitiveness.

Mareike Well holds a degree in Political Science from the University of Freiburg in Germany, and the Institut d'Etudes Politiques d'Aix en Provence in France. During her studies, she also worked for GIZ Indonesia and now focuses her research on environmental and forest governance in Indonesia as well as on climate change issues in EU–Asia relations.

Amy Woodrow-Arai has a degree in International Politics and Development. She worked with the Native Spirit Foundation which promotes the protection of indigenous rights and celebrates indigenous cultures through the arts. In this context, she co-organized the Native Spirit Film Festival in 2011. Currently, she works at the Gaia Foundation supporting communities to strengthen self-governance, revive indigenous knowledge, and protect Sacred Natural Sites in response to threats from the extractive industries.

Foreword

This book is an outcome of one of EADI's Working Groups' sessions (proceedings) that took place during the General Conference of the European Association of Development Research and Training Institutes (EADI), which was jointly organized with the British Development Studies Association (DSA) at the UK's University of York on 19–22 September 2011. EADI is the leading professional network for development and regional studies in Europe. Its membership includes a wide range of development research and training organizations, think tanks, national bodies, and researchers throughout Europe. EADI's 21 Working Groups cover a wide range of development issues, from aid policy to urban governance, from industrialization strategies to environment and development, the theme covered by the Working Group that presents its York Conference papers and discussions with this volume. The other organizer of the York Conference, the DSA, connects and promotes the development research community in the UK and Ireland. At the York Conference, some 700 scholars and development practitioners from about 40 countries exchanged their ideas and discussed their experiences based on research and case studies drawn from many developing countries struggling to cope with the challenges posed by economic development, political transformation, climate change, and other pressures on the ecosystems and livelihoods, especially of the poor.

EADI congratulates the convenors of the Working Group on environment, climate change and sustainable development and editors of this volume, Astrid Carrapatoso and Edith Kürzinger, for taking up, together with their Working Group, the title of the conference 'Rethinking Development in an Age of Scarcity and Uncertainty: New Values, Voices, and Alliances for Increased Resilience' and building this into a timely publication. The papers presented and discussed during the Working Group sessions in York were enhanced and updated by both the authors and the editors, making this volume a very valuable contribution to the understanding of the complex interrelationships amongst the challenges of climate management, development of livelihoods, and resilience to external shocks from natural disasters and increasing climate variability.

This book shows that climate policy may have reached an impasse with the failed climate summits since Copenhagen 2009, which proved unable to produce a new global agreement on limiting greenhouse gas emissions that would commit major polluters, including the emerging economies, to reasonable reduction efforts. This is an example of the general trend that was visible at the York Conference and has also become apparent in other fora. After many decades in which OECD countries claimed to be the model for the developing world, 20 years after the Earth Summit in Rio de Janeiro, we may have finally entered into a world that leaves behind the North–South divide and opens the space for global learning from the best examples that can be found in whatever country and region to manage the long and arduous transition towards achieving sustainable, climate-resilient development for all.

Jürgen Wiemann
Vice President
European Association of Development
Research and Training Institutes (EADI)

Acknowledgements

This book would not have been possible without the help of a great many people. First, it would not have counted on the necessary *matière brut* if not for the motivation of the EADI Secretariat (Thomas Lawo, Susanne von Itter) to organize a substantive input into the EADI global conference in York in 2011, rather than closing the EADI Working Group on Environment, Sustainable Development and Climate Change. Second, we thank the contributors, many of whom we met at the York conference, who so positively took up our repeated questioning, criticism, and suggestions – and presented papers included in this volume of which we are very proud. Third, our thanks to the editorial team at Routledge for accompanying us in the production process: to Khanam Virjee for showing interest in York in our topics, and particularly to Charlotte Russell for her constant support and encouraging attitude. Fourth, we would like to express our deepest gratitude to Joyce Miller and Jürgen Wiemann: to Joyce for her amazing job in proofreading and skilled editorial work, which gave us continuous support and valuable hints on content during the final phase when we were pulling everything together; to Jürgen for the valuable comments when critically reading all of the contributions, which helped to significantly improve the texts. We would also like to acknowledge the team of motivated young research assistants at Freiburg University who helped in the final editing of this book: Anna Leiber, Verena Lais, Vanessa Guinan-Bank, and Felix Idelberger – thanks for all the efforts. And finally, our thanks go to Mareike Well who supported us significantly in the final phase of the book, which we deeply appreciated. The collaboration that has resulted in this book, our research, and our understanding of climate-resilient development have considerably benefited from discussions with the book's contributors, colleagues from the university, and a wide range of practitioners.

Last, but by no means least, we would like to thank our partners and families for their continuous support and for patiently accompanying us throughout this long process.

Abbreviations

AC	air conditioner
AFC	Agriculture Finance Cooperation
AOSIS	Alliance of Small Island States
APD	assistant project director
ARD	Agriculture Research for Development
ASEAN	Association of Southeast Asian Nations
ASEF	Asia–Europe Foundation
ASEM	Asia–Europe Meeting
ATTAC	Association pour la taxation des transactions financières et pour l'action citoyenne (Association for the Taxation of Financial Transactions and Civil Action)
BAT	best available technology
BATNA	best alternative to a negotiated agreement
BAU	business as usual
BCM	Bilateral Cooperation Mechanism on Forests
BMU	Bundesministerium für Umwelt, Naturschutz und Reaktorsicherheit (Germany) (Federal Ministry for Environment, Nature Conservation and Nuclear Safety)
BMZ	Bundesministerium für wirtschaftliche Zusammenarbeit and Entwicklung (Germany) (Federal Ministry for Economic Cooperation and Development)
BRICS	Brazil, Russia, India, China, South Africa
BSH	Bosch/Siemens Hausgeräte
CACHET II	Carbon Capture and Hydrogen Production with Membranes
CANR	College of Agriculture and Natural Resources (Kwame Nkrumah University of Science and Technology, Kumasi, Ghana)
CBDR	common but differentiated responsibility
CBDRM	community-based disaster risk management
CBEEX	China Beijing Environment Exchange
CBT	capacity-building team
CC	climate change
CCA	climate change adaptation

CCS	carbon capture and storage
CDI	Centre for Development Innovation
CDM	clean development mechanism
CER	certified emission reduction
CeRPA	Centre Régional de Promotion de l'Agriculture (Regional Centre for Agricultural Promotion)
CFCs	chlorofluorocarbons
CGIAR	Consultative Group on International Agricultural Research
CH-EU-BIO	Development of Co-firing Power Generation Market Opportunities to Enhance the EU Biomass Sector Through International Cooperation with China
CIAT	Centre international pour l'agriculture tropicale (International Center for Tropical Agriculture)
CIC	change implementation committee
CIDA	Canadian International Development Agency
CIFOR	Center for International Forestry Research
CIG	common interest group
CLIMA	Directorate General for Climate Action
CLIMATECOST	the full cost of climate change
CLRC	cluster-level resource centre
CO_2	carbon dioxide
COACH	Cooperation Action with CCS China–EU
CONAIE	Confederación de Nacionalidades Indígenas del Ecuador (The Ecuadorian Confederation of Indigenous Peoples)
CoP	conference of parties
CORDIS	Community Research and Development Information Service
CPSW	Council of Professional and Social Workers
CRD	climate-resilient development
CTC	climate technology centre
CYG	Certificados Yasuní de Garantía (Yasuní Guarantee Certificates)
DAC	development assistance committee
DANIDA	Danish International Development Agency
DFID	Department for International Development (UK)
DG	directorate general
DHO	Dutch Network for Sustainable Higher Education
DIE	Deutsches Institut für Entwicklungspolitik (German Development Institute)
DNA	designated national authority
DRR	disaster risk reduction
DSA	Development Studies Association
EADI	European Association of Development Research and Training Institutes
EC2	Europe–China Clean Energy Centre

ECOFUEL	EU–China Cooperation for Liquid Fuels from Biomass Pyrolysis
EFR	environmental fiscal reform
EIA	environmental impact assessment
ENVforum	Asia–Europe Environment Forum
EoCM®	PREMA®-Environment-oriented Cost Management
ERU	European emission reduction unit
ETS	emissions trading scheme
EU	European Union
EUA	European Union Allowance
EU ETS	European Emissions Trading System
EUGeoCapacity	Assessing European Capacity for Geological Storage of Carbon Dioxide
FC	Forestry Commission
FDI	foreign direct investment
FGD	focus group discussion
FRELIMO	Frente de Libertação de Moçambique (Mozambique Liberation Front)
FYP	five-year plan
G-77	Group of 77
GCF	Green Climate Fund
GD	Guangdong
GDI	German Development Institute (see DIE)
GDP	gross domestic product
GE	green economy
GEF	global environment facility
Gerando	Gestão de Risco à Nivel da Comunidade (Community-Based Disaster Risk Management)
GHG	greenhouse gas
GHG2E	greenhouse gas recovery from coal mines and unmineable coalbeds and conversion to energy
GIZ	Gesellschaft für Internationale Zusammenarbeit (Society for International Cooperation)
Gt	gigatonne
GTZ	Gesellschaft für Technische Zusammenarbeit (Society for Technical Cooperation)
GWP	global warming potentials (relative to CO_2)
HCFCs	hydrochlorofluorocarbons
HDI	human development index
HDR	Human Development Report
HFCs	hydrofluorocarbons
HPMP	HCFC-22 Phase-Out Management Plan
HPPD	High-Level People-To-People Dialogue
HRM	human resource management
IA	implementing agency

IAR4D	Integrated Agriculture Research for Development
ICARDA	International Center for Agricultural Research in the Dry Areas
ICARE	China–EU Institute for Clean and Renewable Energy
ICDP	Integrated Conservation and Development Project
ICR	international climate regime
ICRA	International Centre for Development Oriented Research in Agriculture
IDID	Initiatives pour un Développement Intégré et Durable (Initiatives for Integrated and Sustainable Development) (NGO)
IEA	International Energy Agency
IGO	intergovernmental organisation
INGC	Instituto Nacional de Gestão de Calamidades (National Disaster Management Institute)
INGO	international non-governmental organisations
INRM	Integrated Natural Resource Management
IPCC	Intergovernmental Panel on Climate Change
ISO	International Organization for Standardization
ITT	Yasuní Ishpingo Tambococha Tiputini
ITTO	International Tropical Timber Organization
IUCN	International Union for the Conservation of Nature
KBK	Kalahandi, Bolangir and Koraput
KfW	Kreditanstalt für Wiederaufbau
KNUST	Kwame Nkrumah University of Science and Technology
KP	Kyoto Protocol
LAIC	land–atmosphere interactions in China
LCA	life cycle analysis
LDC	least developed country
LDCF	least developed country fund
LPG	liquefied petroleum gas
LST	livelihood support team
M&E	monitoring and evaluation
MDG	Millennium Development Goal
MEA	multinational environmental agreements
MLF	Multilateral Fund (of the Montreal Protocol)
MLNR	Ministry of Lands and Natural Resources
MoFA	Ministry of Food and Agriculture
MOST	Chinese Ministry of Science and Technology
MOVECBM	monitoring and verification of enhanced coalbed methane
MP	Montreal Protocol
MRV	measurement, reporting and verification
MT	megatonnes
NAMA	nationally appropriate mitigation action
NAPA	national action plan for adaptation

NDRC	National Development and Reform Commission (China)
NEA	National Energy Administration
NGO	non-governmental organisation
NIC	newly industrialised countries
NPO	non-product output
NPT	The Netherlands Programme for the Institutional Strengthening of Post-Secondary Education and Training Capacity
NRM	natural resources management
NSDP	net state domestic product
NSDS	national sustainable development strategy
NUFFIC	The Netherlands Organisation for International Cooperation in Higher Education
NZEC	near-zero emissions coal
ODA	official development assistance
ODP	ozone-depleting potential
ODS	ozone-depleting substances
OECD	Organisation for Economic Co-operation and Development
OST	open space technology
OWDM	Orissa Watershed Development Mission
PD-DRDA	project director – district rural development agency
PD-WS	project director – watersheds
PFCs	perfluorocarbons
PIA	project-implementing agency
PIC	project implementation committee
PPP	polluter pays principle
PPP	purchasing power parity
PRA	participatory rural appraisal
PREMA®	Profitable Resource Efficiency Management
PSU	project support unit
PUR	polyurethane foam
PV	photovoltaic
R&D	research and development
RE	resource efficiency
REDD(+)	Reducing Emissions from Deforestation and Forest Degradation
RENAMO	Resistência Nacional Moçambicana (Mozambican National Resistance)
Rio+20	2012 UN Conference on Sustainable Development (UNCSD)
RTI	Royal Tropical Institute
SC	scheduled castes
SC	steering committee
SD	sustainable development
SDG	sustainable development goal
SEA	strategic environmental assessment

SEEEX	Shanghai Environment and Energy Exchange
SES	social–ecological system
SHG	self-help group
SL	sustainable livelihood
SLA	sustainable rural livelihoods approach
SMART	specific, measurable, attainable (or achievable), relevant and time-sensitive (or time-bound)
SME	small and medium-sized enterprise
SSA	Sub-Saharan Africa
SS-Gate	South-South Global Assets and Technology Exchange
ST	scheduled tribes
START	Strategic Arms Reduction Treaty
SVA	Sahabhagi Vikas Abhiyan
SWOT	strengths, weaknesses, opportunities, and threats
TBI	Tropenbos International
TCX	Tianjin Climate Exchange
TREN	EU Directorate-General of Transport and Energy
UG	user group
UK	United Kingdom
UN	United Nations
UNCBD	United Nations Convention on Biological Diversity
UNCCD	United Nations Convention to Combat Desertification
UNCED	United Nations Conference on Environment and Development
UNCSD	United Nations Conference on Sustainable Development
UNDP	United Nations Development Programme
UNEP	United Nations Environment Programme
UNFCCC	United Nations Framework Convention on Climate Change
UNIDO	United Nations Industrial Development Organization
URBACHINA	Sustainable Urbanisation in China Historical and Comparative Perspectives, Mega-trends towards 2050
URGENCHE	Urban Reduction of GHG Emissions in China and Europe
US(A)	United States (of America)
USAID	United States Agency for International Development
VCA	vulnerability and capacity analysis
WA	watershed association
WB	World Bank
WBCSD	World Business Council on Sustainable Development
WBR	well-being ranking
WC	watershed committee
WDT	watershed development team
WHO	World Health Organization
WORLP	Western Orissa Rural Livelihoods Project
WSSD	World Summit on Sustainable Development

Part I
Introduction

1 Why this book? Why now?

Edith Kürzinger and Astrid Carrapatoso

This publication is primarily based on the revised and, in many cases, substantially enhanced papers originally discussed in the context of the General Conference 2011 of the European Association of Development Research and Training Institutes (EADI). The EADI conference was organised jointly with the Development Studies Association (DSA) on 19–22 September 2011 at the University of York in the United Kingdom on the topic: 'Rethinking Development in an Age of Scarcity and Uncertainty: New Values, Voices, and Alliances for Increased Resilience'.[1]

The main purpose of the four sessions of the EADI Working Group 'Environment, Climate Change and Sustainable Development', subsumed in the present publication, was to organise an exchange between academia and practitioners, with the former bringing in the theoretical discourse and lessons from empirical case studies by researchers around the topics 'climate change, livelihoods, vulnerability and resilience', and the latter offering conceptual reflections on climate-related problems and the deficiencies regarding the design and implementation of international climate policies. The specific objective of the fruitful, even though mostly virtual, dialogue between researchers and practitioners 'on the ground' was to create common ground on the following questions:

- Where and how are climate stressors endangering livelihoods, how are the affected actors responding to them, and what can be learned from a bottom-up perspective for best practice and policy design with respect to climate change management?
- Whether and how are policies and politics at local and national levels effectively supporting these efforts, and which improvements or reforms are needed?
- To what extent and how does the international climate regime provide mechanisms that help (or hinder) local and national adaptation and mitigation efforts, and how could these be improved?
- How can the tardiness, even de facto stagnation, and the limited outcome of the United Nations Framework Convention on Climate Change (UNFCCC) negotiation process be bypassed through bottom-up approaches in the form

of enhanced local, national, and inter-regional action, and (how) could this (re)inject new energy into the global climate management process?

- Finally, what lessons can be drawn for a research agenda on climate-resilient development, and which recommendations can be given for actors at different levels?

Workshop participants critically discussed the challenges, achievements, and shortcomings of the UNFCCC process, and, in the context of the case studies provided, UNFCCC's effect on climate-resilient development. Contributors concurred that there was a need to not only reform the negotiation process (if it was to be kept alive), but also to give more room for bottom-up thinking and initiatives. Activities (and research) 'on the ground' provide best practice examples of climate-resilient development (CRD) for specific local contexts; they also show why implementation of CRD policies is a challenging task as socio-economic, political, and ecological factors must simultaneously be taken into account, considering both development and climate change issues. Participants were of the opinion that paying more attention to the implementation side of global climate policy making and allowing for an enhanced bottom-up process would certainly render societies more resilient to climate change.

Through this book, the contributors want to share their ideas, experiences, and critical thinking on climate policy with a wider audience ranging from academics, policy makers, and diplomats to 'on the ground' practitioners, civil society, and economic actors from both the environment/climate and the development community. This book incorporates discussions of a wide variety of topics raised by actors in both of these policy fields related to climate-resilient development, climate policy and diplomacy, sustainable development, environmental governance, livelihoods approaches, resilience thinking, resource efficiency issues, and development studies.

At the heart of the book are case studies stemming from upwards of 15 countries in Africa, Asia, and Latin America, carried out through empirical research, in some cases through action research (Part II), and the conceptual reflections on various elements of the international climate regime presented by a mix of practitioners and application-oriented scholars (Part III). The contributions by researchers and practitioners in these two parts are guided by the following questions:

- What contribution can the empirical case studies, research, and conceptual reflections make to climate-resilient development in the various countries and/or regions?
- What can be depicted as 'best practice' from a normative *and* problem-solving perspective in the analysed cases, or what has to be improved to transform them into best practice? Who will learn what from which kind of action?
- Which practical lessons can be learned from the analyses for national, regional, and/or international framework conditions regarding climate-resilient development? And what could this mean for the international climate regime?

This book shows that climate policy may have reached an impasse, with the failed climate summits since Copenhagen 2009 proving unable to produce a new global agreement on limiting greenhouse gas emissions that would commit major polluters, including the emerging economies, to reasonable reduction efforts. The contributions to this volume change the reader's perspective from the current top-down approach to global climate policy to a bottom-up perspective: stepping down from the UNFCCC ivory tower, it puts local actors in developing countries and regions and their efforts towards adaptation and mitigation of climate change at the centre of analysis – as a starting point for disseminating lessons learned and good practice. This is an example of the general trend that was visible at the York conference and has also become apparent in other forums. After many decades in which Organisation for Economic Co-operation and Development (OECD) countries claimed to be the model for the developing world, 20 years after Rio's Earth Summit, we may have finally entered into a world that leaves behind the North–South divide and opens the space for global learning from the best examples that can be found in whatever country and region to manage the long and arduous transition towards achieving sustainable, climate-resilient development for all.

The content

Part I: Introduction

In Chapter 2 'Finding a panacea? An introduction into climate-resilient development' by Astrid Carrapatoso and Edith Kürzinger, the authors analyse the theoretical debate on concepts relevant for understanding climate-resilient development and provide the context for the enhanced and modified conference papers. They address the following questions:

- Why is the UNFCCC process, at least at present, a blind alley for the effective management of climate change?
- Why is CRD a value-adding concept that facilitates the integration of ideas and actors from, so far, four separate realms: science, climate diplomacy, policy making, and actors 'on the ground'?
- How is CRD embedded in the wider framework of sustainable development and its implementation problems?
- Why does it make sense to use CRD as a theoretical concept, and how is it defined?
- How is CRD related (or not) to processes, such as Millennium Development Goals (MDGs), Sustainable Development Goals (SDGs), and Green Economy?
- How can CRD contribute towards developing and implementing, bottom up and step by step, a realistic policy model?
- Why and how can CRD trigger a new dialogue between the 'development/ poverty eradication world' and the 'environmental/climate world'?
- What innovative contributions can CRD make to the international climate regime?

Part II: The contribution of local, regional, and national approaches to climate-resilient development or what good practices and lessons learned can be disseminated?

In this part, local, regional, and national approaches to foster climate resilience in Asia, Africa, and Latin America are discussed; the authors especially analyse policies that foster or hamper capacity-building and action at local and national levels and discuss their impact on climate-resilient development, its beneficiaries, and the establishment of best practice. The empirical case studies address the following topics:

- Chapter 3 'Shaping strategies: factors and actors in climate change adaptation' by Ciara Kirrane, Cliona Sharkey and Lars Otto Naess. Through action research on households in four countries in Africa and Latin America, these authors analyse how actors, in this case rural families, are coping with climate stressors and livelihood issues.
- Chapter 4 'Climate change adaptation in southern Benin: a multi-scale perspective on rural communities of Mono and Couffo' by Marie-Ange Baudoin. This author illustrates the felt threat of climate change (CC) to farmers in Benin, their autonomous adaptation and the (lack of) impact of National Action Plans for Adaptation (NAPA) to support local resilience and livelihoods by planned adaptation.
- Chapter 5 'Building community-based institutions in Western Orissa Rural Livelihoods Project for green development' by Gala Bhaskar Reddy and Niranjan Sahu. Based on their work in a community-based rural and 'green' approach to integrated regional development in Orissa, India, these authors present a successful example of institution-building for coping with development and climate stressors to increase the resilience of rural actors.
- Chapter 6 'How good are good practices? Understanding CBDRM in Mozambique' by Luís Artur. This author critically analyses the actual output of what turned out to be an only theoretical bottom-up approach to community-based disaster risk management in Mozambique.
- Chapter 7 'Making a difference through Integrated Natural Resources Management: the role of Kwame Nkrumah University of Science and Technology in Ghana' by Sampson E. Edusah. This author describes the process and results of the university's response to stakeholders' demands to introduce INRM into its teaching, research, and advisory services.

Part III: Climate-resilient development, innovation, and best practice – how to reform and bypass inefficiencies and structural shortcomings of the international climate regime

This part analyses the need and potential to reform the international climate regime, specifically the UNFCCC process with its existing and evolving mechanisms, such as the Clean Development Mechanism (CDM), Reduced Emissions from

Deforestation and Forest Degradation (REDD), carbon trading, and Nationally Appropriate Mitigation Action (NAMA). The authors discuss the pros and cons of these approaches, lessons to be learned, and their implications for effective climate change mitigation and adaptation.

The contributions address the following topics:

- Chapter 8 'Green gold versus black gold: the Yasuní-ITT Initiative as an alternative way forward?' by Amy Woodrow-Arai. This author discusses the results of the REDD process and the innovative Yasuní Ishpingo Tambococha Tiputini (ITT) approach in Ecuador, which aims to trade a national policy of 'not digging out oil' for nature conservation and international financial compensation.
- Chapter 9 'Developing economies in the current climate change regime: new prospects for resilience and sustainability? The case of CDM projects in Asia' by Pauline Lacour and Jean-Christophe Simon. These authors analyse the implementation and impact of the CDM in Southeast Asia and China, and draw lessons for its future application and the effects on the current position of developing countries within the climate regime.
- Chapter 10 'Does the right hand know what the left hand is doing? Similar problem, opposing remedies – a comparison of the Montreal Protocol and Kyoto Protocol's Clean Development Mechanism' by Thomas Grammig. This author describes the reasons for and effects of the overlap between the Montreal and Kyoto Protocols and explores the impact of diverging approaches for phasing out ozone-depleting substances with global warming potential (HFC-R 134a).
- Chapter 11 'Interregional climate cooperation: EU–China relations as a success story?' by Astrid Carrapatoso and Mareike Well. Using the example of the dialogue between the European Union (EU) and China, these authors assess the potential of inter-regional initiatives for stepping up action on concrete climate change management.
- Chapter 12 'How to bypass multilateral gridlocks: resilient climate change management and efficient multi-level climate politics' by Edith Kürzinger.This author analyses the shortcomings of the 'dead horse' UNFCCC and the potential for reform, primarily from a change management perspective. A rest period for stocktaking and evaluation should lead to a redesign of the process based on the subsidiarity principle and a reorientation through new content, perspectives and methods, as well as to 'bypassing mechanisms' bottom up: massive scaling up of successful action experienced at different policy levels, especially the use of the untapped potentials of best practice in resource efficiency, cost-effective change management processes, no regret front-runner approaches, and climate-resilient policy reforms.

Part IV: The way forward to climate-resilient development

The final chapter, 'Conclusions for research and policy agendas' by Astrid Carrapatoso and Edith Kürzinger, brings together the key discussion points and conclusions drawn by the contributors, together with the recommendations resulting from the empirical studies and conceptual reflections. They identify avenues for further research and outline a potential agenda for a way forward. In addition to offering theoretical conclusions, the authors specifically seek to provide practical solutions for policy action.

Note

1 For further information on this conference, see the website by EADI, http://www.eadi.org/gc2011; http://www.eadi.org/index.php?id=1205 (Topic); http://www.eadi.org/index.php?id=1641 and http://eadi.org/gc2011/ (accessed 06.03.2013).

2 Finding a panacea?

An introduction to climate-resilient development

Astrid Carrapatoso and Edith Kürzinger

The UNFCCC process: a blind alley for (effective) management of climate change?

At the heart of the negotiations of the UNFCCC are carbon trading and financing to incentivise global emission reductions. The global carbon trading system as it is designed today is threatened by collapse: in January 2013, the carbon prices of the European Emission Reduction Units (ERUs) reached a record low (Harvey 2012a; Lewis and Chestney 2013); buyers involved in Chinese CDM projects try to step away from their contracts because of falling prices (Reuters 2013a); and discussions on new market mechanisms were postponed to the 2013 Conference of Parties (CoP) in Warsaw because of the uncertain situation of the global carbon market (Reuters 2013b). The fate of this market is shaped, inter alia, by the ongoing economic crisis, an over-allocation of permits that generated huge windfall profits for polluters, and cases of tax fraud (with the probable involvement of banks, such as Deutsche Bank) (Harvey 2012a; Spiegel 2012a).

Further uncertainties exist regarding climate financing. The institutional and financial set-up of the Green Climate Fund (GCF) – the largest source of global financing for mitigation (Harvey 2012b; Green Climate Fund 2012; Germanwatch 2013) – is delayed because of arguments between industrialised[1] and developing countries. These developments not only manifest a profound implementation deficit but also express the inherent structural problems of the UNFCCC process as well as the ongoing power play between industrialised and developing nations. Whether President Obama's reference to CC in his 2013 inaugural speech (Doyle 2013) or the recurrent smog disaster in Beijing improve the chances for injecting energy into the ailing negotiations, for example on a legally binding agreement that would enter into force after 2020, formally endorsed by the last CoP in Qatar (UNFCCC 2012),[2] is dubious. This logjam further illustrates how climate policy making 'is constrained by global economic structures and by the path dependency of prior decisions' (Adger *et al*. 2011: 759). In addition to path dependency that leads to 'more of the same', the most important reasons for the ambiguous and unsatisfactory results, so far, and the de facto stagnation of the negotiation process at the moment, are:

- the consensus principle, leading to outcomes that reflect the lowest common denominator;
- fighting for fixed positions, in particular the 'responsibility trap' in North–South relations, where an unsophisticated perception of 'donors' (as culprits and 'cash cows') and 'recipients' (as victims of CC) prevails;
- ineffective working methods applied by high-level generalist bureaucrats and representatives of the environmental 'silo thinking' in an organisational setting that does not rely on effective mechanisms for output orientation, process reflection, and systematic institutional and personal learning;
- the predominance of 'wishful thinking' recurrently expressed by: scientists, who (rightly) assert that time is running out for keeping CC within a manageable dimension and consequently cannot understand the reasons why politicians are not acting accordingly; by non-governmental organisations (NGOs), who call for a 'fair and just world' (Baer *et al.* 2008), which is difficult to create with over 200 state representatives with opposing interests concerning emission rights involved; and by environmental policy makers, who persistently declare any little progress a success.

All in all, the UNFCCC is, to a large extent, a self-referential or self-related system (Luhmann 1990; Teubner 1992: 191–192); it stabilises itself, becoming ever more resistant and durable, independent of success or failure in performance, and it is 'operationally closed' to the external environment, referring mostly to the other components of the system. The UNFCCC ensures further system formation, for example by adding new bodies and (sub-)processes, it gains identity by using an evolving 'labyrinthine organisational structure' and a vernacular 'UNFCCC-speak', hardly understandable to outsiders, but shaping insiders' minds,[3] it immunises itself against critics by eventually declaring each meeting a success and the UNFCCC process the only alternative to addressing CC. Through this, actors as varied as NGOs, the public (in particular, environment ministries, UN bureaucracy) or private sector, and development co-operation representatives sustain and run the UNFCCC jointly, and also defend their (mostly well-paid) jobs: this demonstrates the characteristics of being a 'closed shop' system (Stewart 1987), which makes critics afraid of stepping too far outside the system and risk being excluded from access to financial resources, new tasks, and bodies (projects, meetings, travel fees, jobs, publicity, reputation, etc.). Some UNFCCC elements hint at a 'closed society' (in contrast to the 'open society' described by Popper [1945] 2002: Chapter 10) in which a 'revolution' or *coup d'état* would be needed to change the leaders (who represent, in many cases, authoritarian 'closed' regimes), where participation in meetings is paid for by the host(s) (UNFCCC finance for developing country delegates, industrialised countries' contributions), where rules are rather fixed and information loops are relatively closed, and no substantive mechanisms for critical self-reflection and impartial evaluation are provided.

The UN response to reform initiatives has always been rather mechanical, and the organisation has been perceived as unwilling 'to address the significant problems that exist within the bureaucracy' and criticised for 'acting in so self-referencing a manner' (Fasulo 2004: 106). The United States (US) UN Ambassador Richard Holbrooke once said in an interview: '... anyone who looks at the UN and sees what a [bureaucratic] mess it is has two choices. You can say to hell with it or let's get rid of the mess or let's not support it. Or you can say it's indispensable, let's reform it' (Cole 2000). The following chapters of this book will show how more holistic thinking in terms of CRD can pave the way towards more effective climate policy making on local, national, regional, and global levels by integrating related topics and actors. It can also offer innovative perspectives on the role that the UNFCCC could and should play in this context.

In this first introductory part, the authors will clarify:

- why it makes sense to use CRD as a theoretical concept, and how it is defined;
- how CRD is embedded in the wider framework of sustainable development and its implementation problems;
- how it is related (or not) to processes such MDGs, SDG, and Green Economy (GE);
- why there are problems with implementing a coherent and realistic policy model;
- why CRD can trigger a new dialogue and integration between the development/poverty eradication world and the environmental/climate world, different sciences, and policy areas and levels;
- why the CRD concept is an innovative contribution to the international climate regime.

Based on these reflections and ideas, the authors of chapters included in this book are guided by the following questions:

- What contribution can empirical case studies, research, and conceptual reflections make to CRD in the various countries and/or regions?
- What can be depicted as 'best practice' from a normative and problem-solving perspective within the analysed cases, or what has to be improved to transform them into best practice? Who will learn what for which kind of action?
- Raising this to a higher level, which practical lessons can be learned from these analyses for national, regional, and/or international framework conditions regarding CRD? And what could this ultimately mean for the international climate regime?

CRD: a new buzz word or a value-adding concept?

In contrast to lingering international negotiation processes, local communities need to act now in order to adapt as quickly as possible to the most severe effects of CC and undertake autonomous efforts to cope with climate stressors that aggravate their already precarious livelihoods (see Part II of this book). Therefore, 'on-the-ground' practitioners look for pragmatic policy solutions and best practice that

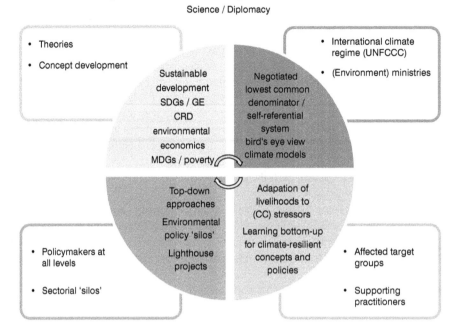

Science / Diplomacy

- Theories

- Concept development

Sustainable
development
SDGs / GE
CRD
environmental
economics
MDGs / poverty

Negotiated
lowest common
denominator /
self-referential
system
bird's eye view
climate models

- International climate
  regime (UNFCCC)

- (Environment) ministries

Top-down
approaches

Environmental
policy 'silos'

Lighthouse
projects

Adapation of
livelihoods to
(CC) stressors

Learning bottom-up
for climate-resilient
concepts and
policies

- Policymakers at
  all levels

- Sectorial 'silos'

- Affected target
  groups

- Supporting
  practitioners

Policy / 'Real World'

Figure 2.1 The four realms influencing climate change policy making

take local sensitivities into account to promote the implementation of sustainable measures, which can foster both a climate-resilient and livelihood-supporting development. When designing such a complex CRD approach the multifaceted nature of the problem and the responses (natural, social, political, etc.) requires the integration of ideas and actors from four realms, whose components usually act independently from each other: science, climate diplomacy, policy making at the regional, national, and local level, and target groups and supporting practitioners 'on-the-ground' (see Figure 2.1).

In our view, the concept of CRD can help to (re-)focus on problem solving and create synergies amongst these four microcosms. CRD is not a static concept but rather, a 'resilience framework [focusing] on understanding processes of change' (Adger *et al.* 2011: 758). It is vital to understand where, why, and how individual, institutional, and policy change happens in response to climate and other stressors, and what can be learned from the respective results – from both successes and failures.

The sustainable development concept: the basis of CRD

Since 1992, the discussion about development in compliance with the natural boundaries of Spaceship Earth has coalesced around the term 'sustainable development' (SD). Notwithstanding the vast overall agreement on the Rio Declaration and Agenda 21, implementation has been modest everywhere and definitional problems have made SD highly accepted verbally but, in practice, a contested concept. Currently, two definitions of SD are widely applied: the 'Brundtland' definition (WCED 1987) and the 'Caring for the Earth' definition (Munro 1991). The former defines SD as 'development which meets the needs of the present without compromising the ability of future generations to meet their own needs', i.e. emphasising the need for global intergenerational distribution; the latter conceives of SD as 'improving the quality of life while living within the carrying capacity of supporting ecosystems', highlighting the ecological limitations to enhanced human activities. As a further elaboration, Haughton (1999) worked out five core principles of SD, which are based on the notion of equity; Jacobs (1999) identified six core ideas. These can be summarised as follows:

1   the integration of environmental protection and economic development;
2   environmental protection and trans-frontier responsibility for environment-related issues (e.g. biodiversity conservation, air and water pollution);
3   inter-species equity, i.e. the importance of biodiversity;
4   futurity and social justice, i.e. inter- and intra-generational equity;
5   a reference to quality of life which implies more than income growth;
6   participation of all societal groups and procedural equity.

These ideas were institutionalised under the Rio framework with the aim of establishing an integrated model of SD principles (Rio Declaration) and providing conceptual guidance for implementation of policies and measures to all major groups (through Agenda 21).[4] The key features of this approach include target- and result-oriented governance, policy integration, co-operative governance, participation, and success monitoring (Jänicke and Jörgens 2007). By adopting Agenda 21, signatory states have at least 'rhetorically accepted that sustainable development does represent a new trajectory for development' (Jacobs 1999: 26).

There are, however, conflicting understandings of what SD should actually mean. Hopwood, Mellor and O'Brien (2005) depict three major groups who interpret SD in different ways:

1   supporters of the status quo, who believe in the power of the market, consumers, and the private sector;
2   reformists, who are in favour of a modest system change;
3   transformationists, who advocate a fundamental restructuring of the social and economic system.

Nowadays, it is difficult to draw a line between the first two categories, and an ongoing dynamic process within the different SD institutions has been observed. Institutions like the World Bank (WB) and the OECD originally promoted a status quo approach to SD but have since moved away from a 'market-only' thinking by integrating a variety of policy tools.[5] Sticking to the tradition of 'liberal environmentalism' (Bernstein 2000, 2002), both supporters of the status quo and reformists believe in the power of the market to achieve SD goals – but in a slightly different way. Supporters of the status quo assert that SD is attainable within the present structures through the power of informed consumers and corporate citizenship without specific government regulations and laws. These days, it is difficult to discern real 'status quo' organisations, and this type of thinking is probably more common in the private sector. Reformists argue in favour of a modest system change: in their view, not only new technologies, good science, and information is needed, but also modification of the market mechanism (internalisation of external costs) and, in particular, reform of government are required to trigger shifts in policy and lifestyles. Government is considered the key driver for incremental change towards SD, but it is expected to involve relevant stakeholders as much as possible. Most environmental and development policy actors share this view in one way or another (Weizsäcker *et al.* 1997), as do many NGOs, like the International Union for the Conservation of Nature (IUCN) and Association pour la taxation des transactions financières et pour l'action citoyenne (ATTAC). This philosophy is also reflected in the UNFCCC process.

Transformationists, such as indigenous or anti-capitalist movements, are much more pessimistic concerning the relationship between society and the environment, and the effectiveness of incremental change. In their view, there is a strong need to fundamentally restructure society and the economic system to avoid a future collapse of the social–ecological system. Required social and political action is driven by a large variety of change agents and groups 'outside the centres of power such as indigenous groups, the poor and working class, and women' (Hopwood *et al.* 2005: 45).

'Radical thinkers' also belong in this group, and demand a new (systemic) view on nature and society and a different development paradigm; for example, complementing 'efficiency' with 'sufficiency', which would imply not only less carbon dioxide (CO_2) content in energy and less energy intensity of prosperity but also, to some extent, less affluence (Bateson 1972; Lovelock 1991 [1979], 2006; Meadows *et al.* 1992, 2004; Meadows 2002; Meadows *et al.* 2004; Weizsäcker *et al.* 2009). Marshall *et al.* (2011) could also be considered as transformationist, given their claim that conceptual thinking locked into an industrial growth society is inadequate to cope with the challenges of sustainability; they frame sustainability as partly a problem of the way we think, related to our mind, perceptions, and values. Consequently, they call for a different perspective to address sustainability issues through a different type of learning: amongst others, by developing an attitude of inquiry, applying action research methods with cycles of action and reflection, and a critical systemic thinking that questions the patterns according to which our (non-sustainable) system is functioning.[6]

What is often left out of SD conceptualisations nowadays is the aspect of 'intra-generational sustainability' (Goodland 1995: 6): 'If the world cannot move towards intra-generational sustainability during this generation, it will be much more difficult to achieve inter-generational sustainability sometime in the future.' If addressed, it is only with respect to North–South distribution, ignoring that (uneven) income distribution and its contribution to SD (or lack thereof) is an important issue in most developing and even industrialised countries, with respect to sustainable consumption patterns of upper (Schiller 2012) and middle classes (Furness *et al.* 2012), on the one hand, and sustainable livelihoods on the other (see Part II, Chapters 3–4).[7]

Since the United Nations Conference on Environment and Development (UNCED, Rio 'Earth Summit') in 1992, global environmental governance structures have also been shaped by the principle of common but differentiated responsibility (CBDR), the polluter pays principle (PPP), and the precautionary principle. Furthermore, core elements of the reformist approach that have been put into practice include the compatibility of the environment and free markets and the predominance of market mechanisms to solve environmental problems.[8] While norms and principles are widely acknowledged and integrated within a variety of international treaties and conventions (e.g. UNFCCC, United Nations Convention on Biological Diversity [UNCBD]), the 2012 UN Conference on Sustainable Development (UNCSD; 'Rio+20') has reconfirmed that there is little progress concerning the widespread implementation of SD practices, and further revealed the lack of consensus on what SD should encompass and how to achieve it.

SD is not an undisputed theory but, rather, the outcome of a major international negotiation effort to agree on the integration of environmental and developmental aspects into a globally feasible development model as a common orientation. In this light, SD combines pieces of scientific evidence with negotiated principles for resource use, and guidelines for co-operation between major actors for various policies and activities. This approach is not accepted as a whole, especially by those forces which, after Rio 1992, intensified their work on poverty and social issues; for example, through the World Summit on Social Development (WSSD) in 2002 and since 1990, the Human Development Report (HDR) published by the United Nations Development Programme (UNDP),[9] which led to the agreement on the MDGs[10] and, to some extent, a parallel line of action under the aegis of development co-operation. The discussion about what to do with the MDGs after 2015 and whether to develop (by two different UN working groups!) a set of revised MDGs and, as the only concrete follow-up to the disappointing 'Rio+20',[11] a set of SDGs shows the continuing discord with respect to SD (Loewe 2012); this needs to be resolved to avoid trade-offs and competition.

Poor implementation of SD: which policy model and management approach is realistic?

Based on the principles of the Rio framework and liberal environmentalist norms, and in view of the limited progress in implementing the decisions of the 1992 Earth Summit and the respective follow-ups, the United Nations Environment Programme (UNEP) launched the 'Green Economy Initiative' in 2008. Its three main objectives are to:

1   provide a conceptual framework for the various initiatives supported or triggered by UNEP to involve the private sector to a larger extent in the implementation of SD;
2   energise the implementation of SD by using language other than SD terminology, which is possibly more acceptable to the major relevant actors;
3   enhance the role of UNEP in the global governance scheme, thus paving the way for justifying the conversion of the United Nations Environment Programme into a fully fledged UN organisation on par with other UN bodies, such as the World Health Organisation (WHO).

The last objective was supported by many national environment ministries and NGOs. The intention was to create one organisation to watch over all existing multilateral environmental agreements (MEAs) in order to ensure more consistency between these agreements, to strengthen the ecological dimension of the SD concept, and consequently to increase the 'environmental' influence at a global level. Thinking one step further, such an approach would, however, sacrifice the mainstreaming potential of SD and possibly deprive it of its normative underpinnings by reducing SD to the idea of a GE.

According to UNEP, 'a green economy ... [is] one that results in improved human well-being and social equity, while significantly reducing environmental risks and ecological scarcities', i.e. an economy 'which is low carbon, resource efficient and socially inclusive'.[12] The GE idea is in line with the reformist interpretation of the SD concept and aims at reconciling 'competing sets of environment and development norms' and legitimating 'economic growth in the context of environmental protection' (Bernstein 2002: 3–4). In view of the content,[13] and UNEP's institutional self-interest as explained above, some doubts arise: is there really such a thing as a (new) 'green economy' paradigm, as it sounds rather like a reformist version of SD practice, reflected in the collection of moderately progressive state-of-the-art know-how throughout the report? Does GE integrate the normative dimensions of SD as outlined above? Or is it a 'diminished' agenda that is more acceptable to SD critics from 'pure market economy' supporters and promoters of the 'development-comes-first' view, which is still found in developing countries and in 'poverty eradication / MDG communities'? GE served another purpose: to keep environmental governance high on the political agenda by differently framing and naming elements, avoiding a more profound frustration with the lack of progress in SD implementation over the past 20 years as recognised at UNCSD 'Rio+20'.

While the core objective for both SD and GE propagators is to integrate environmental and economic policies, GE is a technical approach to get more action on resource efficiency implemented, and, as such, lacks many of the more ambitious and radical SD principles, which would require not more of the same, or doing the same differently, but searching for new thinking about (energy and) resource generation, use, and distribution. Thus, GE has more elements of a management strategy than of a conceptual framework. However, the optimism about growth potential envisaged by GE proponents[14] would surely be challenged by environmental economists (for example, Daly 1974; Goodland 1995; Doppelt 2010) who would highlight the need to achieve sustainable levels at both the production (sources) *and* the consumption (sinks) sides, rather than 'sustainable economic growth', less a 'sustained growth', impossible in view of the finite world ecosystem and population growth (an issue hardly mentioned nowadays in the context of UNFCCC negotiations). Daly (1990: 1) points out that:

> growth is quantitative increase in physical scale, while development is qualitative improvement or unfolding of potentialities. [...] Since the human economy is a subsystem of a finite global ecosystem which does not grow, even though it does develop, it is clear that growth of the economy cannot be sustainable over long periods of time. The term sustainable growth should be rejected as a bad oxymoron.

Yet, discussions regarding GE may have served to finally enhance the more systematic observation of the production factor 'natural resources' in development co-operation programmes (Daly 1990, 1991; GIZ 2012) which aim at private sector promotion. Contrary to what was taught years ago by environmental economists (e.g. Daly 1990, 2007; Goodland 1995; Costanza *et al.* 1997), the reliance on mainstream economics limited attention to three production factors: labour, capital, and soil – treating 'natural resources' either as a 'blind spot', or being comprised by 'soil', supposing that these resources somehow would be available, and neglecting to address its increasing 'material throughput' through production and the economic subsystem with effects also on the sink side. From a more critical look at capitalism, five production factors should actually be taken into account when looking into sustainability issues: natural, human, social, manufactured, and financial (Porritt 2007: 19).

Despite having generally increased attention towards limited resources, GE is controversially discussed because a diverse set of actors, economic sectors, and regions face different challenges when aiming at a fundamental transformation of existing economic structures (Netzer and Althaus 2012: 3). As a consequence, debates range from a simple 'greening' of the economy through 'green development' to more complex perceptions of SD that argue in favour of the CBDR principle, thereby putting a bigger burden on industrialised countries and leaving room for the growth of developing countries and emerging economies, thus focusing on distributional justice and not necessarily challenging existing economic structures. The least radical interpretation of GE basically promotes the status quo and sees technological innovation (with focus on the hardware part) as a panacea. The 'green development' concept shows similarities with the SD perception in that it seeks to take local sensitivities and needs into account in reforming economic structures. Nevertheless, the concept goes one step further by strongly advocating more sustainable consumption and production patterns as well as new thinking about welfare (ibid.: 6). Current debates on GE, however, focus on green growth which often ignores our 'planetary boundaries' (Rockström *et al.* 2009).[15] When 'ecological thresholds', i.e. 'the point at which there is an abrupt change in an ecosystem quality, property or phenomenon' (Groffman *et al.* 2006: 1), and 'tipping points', i.e. 'a critical threshold at which a tiny perturbation can qualitatively alter the state or development of a system' (Lenton *et al.* 2008: 1786), are discussed, the aspect of sufficiency is put at the centre of the discussion: sufficiency would require a 'decoupling of resource consumption from increased productivity' (Netzer and Althaus 2012: 4). With all the different interpretations of GE currently on the table, no clear policy and management model for implementing SD can be identified or is recommended.

To successfully integrate SD principles into policy and management practice, all stakeholders have to develop a coherent management strategy for promoting a low-carbon, resource-efficient, and socially inclusive economy, which, in view of all the inconsistencies of policies, is not an easy task. According to Volkery *et al.* (2006: 213), such management strategies must be based on:

- *leadership*, i.e. developing a vision and overall objectives supported by high-level political commitment;
- *strategic planning,* i.e. governmental agencies have to develop appropriate institutional mechanisms, programmatic structures, and specific policy initiatives;
- *implementation*, i.e. governmental institutions must provide the necessary means to realise policy initiatives;
- *monitoring, review, and adaptation*, i.e. governmental institutions need to develop indicators on how to measure success, with the aim of improving implementation and the economic, social, and environmental state;
- *coordination and participation*, i.e. SD activities must be coordinated with other policy strategies and involve key stakeholders in both the policy making and implementation processes.

If these aspects are not integrated within all types of SD activities and management strategies, the gap between rhetoric and action will persist, and the whole idea of SD will eventually be called into question. This also applies to initiatives like GE, which emphasise the role of the private sector, but also need a conducive political framework (reduction of resource price subsidies, functioning market mechanism instead of oligopolistic structures, etc.) to thrive. When looking at the limited effect of national sustainable development committees' or boards' decisions, of poor realisation of national sustainable development plans, strategies, partnerships, and the result of 'Rio+20',[16] there are doubts about whether the model of a comprehensive, integrated, and thoroughly planned policy approach to SD is realistic and should be kept as an orientation. In view of the large number of successful SD-related projects, a strategy that triggers change towards SD may be more appropriate, for example by turning the government-led, top-down model into a more decentralised, pluralistic, bottom-up, learning-oriented policy process, where things that work on the ground (as experienced by major groups) would be integrated into a structured social learning process and scaled up into an evolving policy framework (sanctioning best practice, front-runner approaches, setting of minimum standards, incentives by internalisation of environmental costs, etc.).

Empirical evidence supports such a political piecemeal engineering approach: already recommended by Popper (Popper [1945] 2002), it is based on using windows of opportunity and builds on incremental action to broaden successes and increase the significance of impact. In reviewing 'Climate Clever: How Governments Can Tackle Climate Change (and Still Win Elections)', Arroyo (2013: 144) asserts that 'the perfect is often the enemy of the good' and that 'at both international and domestic levels ... incremental and non-comprehensive responses appear to be the order of the day' (ibid.: 143), not the exception. Two examples show the successful up-scaling of state initiatives in the US (in the absence of a comprehensive national climate policy) and their impact: Californian greenhouse gas (GHG) emission standards for vehicles were adopted by other states and eventually became the federal standard, influencing the automotive industry which emits one third of US GHG emissions; in the northeast region, the first US GHG emissions trading programme (i.e. the Regional Greenhouse Gas Initiative) limited emissions from electric power generators and raised revenues for investment in renewable energies and energy efficiency. Under the impression that a nuclear catastrophe had occurred in Fukushima in 2011, and not in response to year-long demands from the anti-nuclear movement and the Green Party, the German Chancellor Angela Merkel surprised the public, and without much consultation, by deciding to revoke a recent decision on the prolongation of nuclear power stations' running times, and declaring an immediate withdrawal from the use of nuclear energy in Germany; as she had no clear plan for this 'energy U-turn', its elaboration and negotiation is now the major challenge.[17] Thus, political piecemeal engineering may include the use of windows of opportunity at different levels, and astonishingly strong decisions when 'learning from catastrophes' (Kunreuther and Useem 2010) is imperative.

Incremental scaling up of action which starts with an innovative project, as mentioned above, needs not only the political leader, initiator, or innovator ('first mover') but also followers: the 'first follower' is an under-appreciated form of leadership as this person is the spark who turns the splint (the first mover) into a fire. The 'second follower' represents a turning point by confirming that the first and second have done well and, by becoming three, there is already a group which ideally grows into a crowd, implementing the same project (e.g. GHG emission standards).[18] This learning is also relevant for SD action by interest groups and institutions.

CC+ SD = CRD?

The climate agenda is inherently based on SD principles and norms, which is not surprising as the UNFCCC was opened for signature at the Earth Summit in 1992, but the UNFCCC process has developed its own dynamics and institutional structure. Today, both the prevention of CC (mitigation) and the coping with inevitable climatic changes (adaptation) are equally addressed by UNFCCC member states (parties), although through separate mechanisms. Like SD, CC requires the integration of environmental, economic, and social policies to render societies more resilient to external shocks, as all levels, sectors, policies, and a large variety of actors are affected by CC. When trying to integrate the (sustainable) development agenda and the CC management agenda, CRD can become an important concept.

But what makes CRD different from or similar to SD? And where does GE fit in? SD can be understood as the 'meta idea' behind CRD, with its guiding principles of resource use and the inherent responsibilities of major groups and individual actors for achieving a different type of development. The GE concept could then be seen as one means to foster CRD: when market mechanisms such as the CDM are used to achieve emission reduction goals, 'green' economic incentive structures influence consumer demand for low carbon products and clean technologies to stimulate more energy- and resource-efficient production processes.

In view of the haggling between partisans of MDGs and SDGs and the stagnating UNFCCC process, the CRD concept offers some opportunities for agreeing on a common ground and looking for synergies: CRD takes the negative impact of CC, which is already felt, explicitly into account – something which is not addressed to the same extent, neither by the SD agenda nor the GE concept, which is technology biased and too much focused on energy issues. CRD integrates both preventive and reactive strategies towards CC and turns the aspect of resilience into all kinds of development activities. From a scientific point of view, CRD has to be viewed in the context of research on social–ecological resilience, and as such it seeks to integrate social science and natural science perspectives in defining environmental problem-solving strategies and their relationship to overall (sustainable) development. As Walker *et al.* (2002) point out:

> [t]he goal of resilience management is to prevent an SES [Social-Ecological System] from moving into undesirable configurations. It depends on the system being able to cope with external shocks in the face of irreducible uncertainty. In turn, this requires an understanding where resilience resides in the system, and when and how it can be lost or gained. ... The process of attempting to increase resilience to unforeseeable change is different from attempting to improve system performance during times of stability and growth.

According to Carpenter *et al.* (2001), Walker *et al.* (2002, 2004), and Adger *et al.* (2011: 758–759), resilience requires both the ecological and the social system to adapt to new circumstances by:

- being open to change without losing the overall structure, functions, feedback loops, and identity;
- showing the ability to self-organise;
- enabling adaptation using all available resources such as financial capital, human resources, technology, infrastructure, knowledge, and institutions;
- building up capacities for learning and adaptation.

Smit and Wandel (2006) argue that resilience is not exclusively about being persistent to disruption. It implies the ability to renew a system, to open up new paths, or to recombine already evolved structures. As Folke (2006: 255) contends, resilience is the necessity to learn to manage by change rather than simply to react to it; he points to the key role that individuals and small groups or teams of individuals can play in this context. Resilience implies that uncertainty and surprise are part of the game for which we all need to be prepared and learn to live with. Resilience thinking opens up 'a process that stimulates creative thinking about the future and allows both stakeholders (as an integral component of the Social-Ecological System (SES)) and researchers to compare maps of various pathways of the future' (Walker *et al.* 2004). With its focus on adaptation to climate stressors – while at the same time addressing issues of change management, which also includes mitigating the problem at source – CRD also opens up new ways of thinking about how to actively manage the inevitable effects of CC. Participation of affected social groups and the carrying capacity of ecological systems are core elements of this concept. Resilience analysis and management, and in the same way CRD, offer 'an approach that is better attuned than optimal command-and-control solutions to the conflicting objectives and complexity of a pluralistic modern society' (Walker *et al.* 2004).

Like SD, CRD struggles with definitional problems as it is a concept that is widely used across many disciplines, yielding a variety of definitions and interpretations. The term resilience itself has many characteristics and addresses various levels of analysis as illustrated in Figure 2.2. As a consequence, CRD and SD share many technocratic and political problems. Resilience renders both concepts contestable: on the one hand, they are difficult to operationalise; on the other hand, the definitions are exceptionally vague so that even business as usual (BAU) could be interpreted as being sustainable (Jacobs 1999: 23). Like SD, definitional and interpretative struggles lead to different understandings and usages of CRD in practice, which turns it into an ambiguous concept that can encompass a very holistic and systemic approach (Kunreuther and Useem 2010: 31–32), but can also be reduced to a very simplistic definition as 'human and social security' as a new Goal 7 of revised MDGs (Loewe 2012: 3).

However, as long as the overall principles are acknowledged, this ambiguity is not automatically a problem. On the contrary, CRD argues in favour of context-specific problem-solving strategies 'on the ground', as 'one-size-fits-all' strategies do not necessarily lead to effective solutions. Furthermore, CRD provides a window of opportunity to overcome the 'silos'[19] of the SDG and MDG worlds and the environment/climate processes, and to integrate the concerns of poverty eradication, sustainable livelihoods, and societal change for improved income distribution as a response to the effects of global warming and global governance efforts to mitigate CC. As you will learn from the following chapters, different regions, countries, and communities face a variety of ever-changing problems, and they must develop and prioritise different strategies on their way towards SD and CRD. Because of its focus on the effects of CC on development and the integration of a broadly interpreted resilience perspective for coping with many types of stressors, all in all, CRD is indeed a very attractive concept for policy makers and practitioners alike.

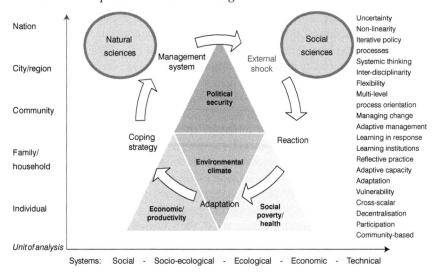

Figure 2.2 Resilience: the many facets of a single concept

The political attractiveness of the CRD concept: serving science, policy, and practice?

Since the 1992 Earth Summit, the UN has been asking member states to develop national sustainable development strategies (NSDSs) for planning and implementing SD policies, projects, and measures. As the translation of SD into concrete action proved to be difficult, scholars developed criteria for good practice of NSDS (see, for example, Meadowcroft 2007); however, these 'clash with core functioning principles of modern government, like the division of sectorial responsibilities, path-dependencies of policy development or the mode of negative co-ordination' (Volkery *et al.* 2006: 211). As a consequence, a step-by-step procedure was introduced which 'initiate[s] learning and continuous adaptation rather than ... challenging the existing institutions and power structures' (ibid.: 212; Arroyo 2013).

The same problems and empirical observations hold true for CC management. Embedded in the logic of SD, climate policy has, so far, followed a step-by-step approach with a strong focus on market-based governance, international negotiations to implement CBDR and avoid free-rider positions, and many climate (especially energy) projects supported either by development co-operation or UNFCCC-sponsored mechanisms (capacity building, pilot projects), which have rarely been scaled up to generalised best practice. But the need to react more expeditiously to CC challenges in a way that contains damage on the ground in the short term, while keeping options open for a more rapid and profound change of unsustainable consumption and production patterns in the mid- and long term, casts doubt on the feasibility and appropriateness of a planned and monitored CC management process of systematic and systemic change controlled from above (as previously described for the SD concept in general): when, for example, affected people are already forced to autonomously adapt (see Part II, Chapters 3 and 4) to locally experienced manifestations of CC, the support through a 'planned adaptation' (Martens and Chang 2010: 2, 8, Chapters 11–15) must be delivered quickly and take account of local needs; otherwise, it would be inappropriate or belated.

The demand on institutional response becomes more complicated by the nature of the CC problem (Martens and Chang 2010: 293, Chapter 14):

- The 'unboundedness' of the climate problem makes it difficult to come to an agreement on what exactly is the issue.
- There is uncertainty and ambiguity about how CC could and should be tackled.
- The problem is unlimited in terms of the time and the resources it risks to absorb in order to be halted.

Thus, the process of effective change management – inquiry, information, reflective action, reaction, adaptation, mitigation, innovation, scaling up, etc. as outlined by Marshall *et al.* (2010) – must be put at the centre of theory, policy, and practice. Resilience thinking may offer new ideas for how to: accept and deal with uncertainties, non-linearity, and imbalances; adapt to changing climate conditions; and manage old (developmental, poverty eradication) and new (climate) stressors through change and using information and advice from a variety of science, policies, and experiences. Resilience opens the door to integrate knowledge from different science and policy 'silos', and especially the perspective of affected stakeholders. While natural sciences and climate models and the International Climate Regime (ICR) work on 'what' should be done – which is useful – more and different information from a social, anthropological, cultural, and economic perspective is needed: the effects of CC on individuals, households, etc. must be better understood by involving them in the process of analysis; effective response strategies need to be designed from the perspective of affected target groups; and the question of 'how' to implement response measures needs to be addressed in ways that increase their resilience and improve their livelihoods.

The case studies in Part II of this book show the usefulness of information collected by field research, especially as resilience issues cannot be addressed easily, if at all, by regression analysis undertaken in offices on the basis of existing quantitative statistics. For example, the study by Trócaire on Kenya, Malawi, Bolivia and Honduras (Part II, Chapter 3) provides first-hand information on the relationship between 'old' stressors on the livelihoods of households and new, climate-related stressors and coping strategies from a CRD perspective. In addition, this study shows the benefits of action research motivated by an investigation of actors' resilience efforts:[20]

- The people 'researched' were involved in identifying the focus of the research in each country, based on the issues they felt were important, i.e. through an inductive exercise.

- The participants actively guided the topics to be discussed in almost all of the focus group discussions that took place.
- Most of the focus groups were conducted using participative techniques, engaging participants in recollection and collective problem solving.
- The research was undertaken to deepen the researcher's (Trócaire) and institutional partners' understanding of vulnerability and adaptation to CC to improve the programme strategies, including targeting and policy recommendations.
- Research and partner staff spent significant periods of time within households and communities in the villages where they were jointly supporting development interventions: this resulted in a deeper level of understanding, joint learning, and reflection, so that the lessons could be 'internalised' and will enrich future planning and decision making.
- Local actors involved included both the households (either small-scale farmers or waged labourers) taking part in the research and the partner organisations in each of the countries (as part of the research team) who work closely with the communities in which the households were located.
- Participants found the process useful in terms of recollecting coping strategies that they would have employed in the past but had possibly forgotten; they also benefitted materially from extra projects (not originally foreseen) as a token of appreciation and in response to observed needs (Kirrane *et al.* 2012: 11–20).

As the editors and the authors of this book, we conceive of CRD as both a complement to and a modification of the SD concept:

- CRD modifies SD in two ways: firstly, climate stressors are explicitly and prominently addressed, giving disaster prevention, risk management, and adaptation to a changing environment a more visible, even key role; secondly, the CC actually being experienced by affected local actors, their coping strategies, and their livelihoods is put at the forefront, demanding concrete, effective, specific support now (not an international legally binding instrument at the Greek calends).
- CRD complements SD as it is about surprising, complex, and even chaotic, 'un-ideal' processes and politics rather than about 'ideal' concepts and top-down implementation of a coherent SD concept, making the politically motivated dysfunctional separation between developing (recipient) countries and industrialised (donor) countries as well as adaptation versus mitigation obsolete; all are in different boats but confronted with similar and diverse challenges for which they need to create their own solutions, including a more equal intra-generational and intra-national income distribution to cope with stressors.

CRD is, on the one hand, even more holistic than the SD concept; on the other hand, it is much more practical and down to earth, possibly providing governments and social and economic actors with guidance on how to achieve SD while at the same time managing incremental change in the social–ecological system in response to CC, and increasing resilience of livelihoods. We also consider CRD as an integrative approach, both horizontally and vertically. The CRD approach and the inherent resilience thinking might stimulate more creativity, having been inspired by a wide range of science and policy fields. It assists in 'generating integrative science and interdisciplinary collaboration on issues of fundamental importance for governing and managing a transition toward more sustainable development paths' (Carpenter *et al.* 2011, as cited in Folke 2006: 260).

Developing a universal roadmap on how to achieve CRD is challenging and hardly possible because local framework conditions must be taken into account and affected groups must be integrated in to the way forward. But, in particular, a more systemic view and systemic thinking can provide the 'out of the box thinking' that is necessary to not 'produce more of the same', but to find innovative solutions to evolving problems. Hence, a multidisciplinary resilience perspective may serve as a 'cognitive playground' to discover and create synergies, and to test new approaches and policy tools in order to develop creative, effective environmental problem-solving strategies.

As resilience is ultimately a result of individual and collective coping with stressors, CRD calls for a bottom-up rather than top-down approach: information on what is happening on the ground and experience with effective local and regional policies need to be translated into globally acknowledged best practice CC management. The challenge is to facilitate the exchange of context-specific best practice in a polycentric CC regime.[21] The case study on Mozambique's disaster prevention strategy (Part II, Chapter 6) sheds light on the shortcomings of an uncritical import of concepts from countries with different conditions and the need to take local populations' socio-economic conditions as much into consideration as the environmental and (technical, social, and political) disaster prevention aspects. The empirical research also shows that a theoretically bottom-up and integrative approach can be turned into a completely top-down exercise by partisan interests, leading to poor results. The analysis of watershed management in Orissa (Part II, Chapter 5) demonstrates how an integrated concept for simultaneously dealing with development and CC issues using a bottom-up approach can lead to better environmental and development results, increasing the resilience of households and communities.

The ICR: can the resilience perspective add value?

Taking a resilience perspective may encourage the development of effective strategies and change structures at local, national, and regional levels as well as stimulate thinking about substantial change within international climate policy arenas, such as the UNFCCC. Ostrom (2010) argues that international institutions are sclerotic and inflexible in dealing with disasters and crises. Current UNFCCC negotiations support this argumentation. As Chapter 12 in Part III demonstrates, it is not only the too narrow climate perspective – stemming from the intellectual ivory tower of climate science, climate diplomacy's bird's eye view, or environmental 'silo' thinking – that leads to ineffective outcomes; but also, and more prominently, structural shortcomings and the institutional set-up of the self-referential UNFCCC process itself, which lacks, amongst other aspects, adequate learning mechanisms, energy for change, and the right focus in view of the subsidiarity principle.

As a result, best practice hardly plays a role in international climate negotiations, even if applied successfully in the diplomats' own countries. Moreover, the 'lighthouse projects' presented as best practice[22] are often relabelled development co-operation projects (which also give development assistance agencies a chance to tap increasing 'climate finance' and expand portfolios); most of them have been implemented, in one way or the other, for years (e.g. energy-saving stoves and solar lighting), but have rarely been scaled up to a generalised best practice. But only scaling up would lead to a 'transformational change', i.e. achieving structural effects that respect the carbon intensity of production and consumption, and increasing the climate resilience of households and systems. The 'what to do' in form of lighthouse projects is easily identified, but it is the large 'space in between them' that has to be filled: for this, the actors of the ICR, of which environment ministers form an essential part, need to understand why scaling up has hardly worked anywhere. Overcoming the obstacles to systematic integration of development co-operation experience and other sector know-how (e.g. agriculture) with CC knowledge would help to avoid the many 'reinventions of the wheel'.

As climate policy is the outcome of a political negotiation process, it is often technically incoherent, unrealistic, and not necessarily compatible with SD criteria. An illustrative example for a one-dimensional policy measure is in the field of energy efficiency. In order to reduce CO_2 emissions from housing, the German programmes[23] which promote investment do not apply a sustainability check of materials or demand their compliance with environmental/social standards during production, transport, and the post-use phase. As a consequence, scarce funds are used to finance the installation of windows or insulation materials made of non-renewable fossil resources (plastic frames, Styrofoam), while alternative products from renewable materials (e.g. wood frames) are available in the market (at a slightly higher price). Even though these programmes certainly give incentives to reduce CO_2 emissions in private housing and corporate buildings, this type of subsidy, at the same time, demonstrates the lack of application of sustainability criteria (e.g. by a simplified carbon footprint or life cycle analysis [LCA]), a narrow climate orientation, and short-term thinking: while reducing CO_2 emissions, the demand for non-renewable resources is involuntarily encouraged, and the future disposal of non-biodegradable materials becomes programmed. This example supports the thesis that often first solutions are still part of the problem and not the answer, if developed without systemic thinking (Marshall *et al.* 2010: 47). Unless basic SD criteria are applied in all sorts of climate-related policies, most action is 'more of the same', repeating the errors already made in other policy fields, instead of moving towards a more climate-resilient and sustainable path.

In the face of institutional deficits and incoherent, often ineffective, policies, the question arises: can CRD and participatory approaches be a panacea to these problems? As Chapter 12 illustrates, the ICR has become a 'dead horse' in some respect, absorbing the energy of politicians and negotiators of all involved countries without having sufficient impact on implementation at sub-global levels to bring about tangible action towards sustainable and CRD. The two major achievements produced by the UNFCCC process over the past 20 years are undisputed: a broad acceptance of anthropogenic CC and the necessity to stay within a two degree scenario of average temperature rise with global GHG emissions. In general, it enabled a 'policy dialogue' amongst its 195 member states and created more 'general awareness'[24] of the CC problem. However, it is questionable whether the set-up of a whole new bureaucracy consisting of an increasing multitude of bodies and the mobilisation of thousands of participants in annual 'climate summits' was really necessary to achieve these outcomes. Other results brought to the fore by supporters of the UNFCCC, such as projects, carbon tax, etc., might also have occurred through the use of existing development co-operation structures or by other mechanisms at lower cost, for example innovative formats such as future conferences or un-conferences.[25]

In view of the lack of energy within the international process (see Chapter 12) and the danger of massive duplication of costly processes and institutions with suboptimal performance, a pause for reflection, assessment, and orientation is needed: Are we still doing the right things, 20 years after beginning the process? No, we aren't. Does more of the same really add value and at reasonable cost? No it doesn't. How can we increase impact, scale up action, and think about structural and transformational change, including new energy for the global level? This will be discussed!

We argue that to gain new momentum, CC management needs to look beyond UNFCCC mechanisms: strong impulses can stem from the application of lessons learned from 'real world experiences' at micro-, meso-, and macro levels, which have so far hardly been scaled up and generalised. The use of innovative and bottom-up approaches, in particular, would tap the unused potential of resource efficiency (Ullrich 2012; Netzer *et al.* 2012), and foster profitable action in all countries and sectors. As Chapter 9 argues, the CDM has at least the potential to do so but, due to existing systemic flaws, it struggles to keep this initial promise.

Why CRD can be the panacea: the contribution of this book

The case studies in Part II specifically focus on the contribution of local, regional, and national approaches to climate-resilient development and what good practices can be disseminated and what lessons can be learned. In this part, the case studies on regions and countries in Asia, Africa, and Latin America analyse, in particular, policies that hamper or foster capacity building at local and national levels and discuss their impact on CRD, its beneficiaries, the establishment of best practice, and offer conclusions for national policy and the ICR, as well as for science.

In their contribution 'Shaping strategies: factors and actors in climate change adaptation' (Chapter 3), Ciara Kirrane, Cliona Sharkey, and Lars Otto Naess seek to deepen understanding of the ways in which climatic changes are interacting with poverty and vulnerability issues in order to improve the way in which Trócaire – as a development agency – and its institutional partners support households in better dealing with livelihood shocks and stressors. These authors summarise their results from a two-year study, embedded within the CRD framework, which differs from many others in its longitudinal approach, high level of familiarity with the studied communities, and the involvement of local actors and partner institutions into its mostly action research-based approach. They draw on rich empirical data as research was carried out in 40 households across seven communities in Bolivia, Honduras, Kenya, and Malawi. Their findings point to the adoption of a variety of adaptation strategies. However, the effectiveness of some of these strategies in improving households' resilience is unclear, either due to barriers in access to these strategies or questions concerning the appropriateness of the embraced strategy, for example searching for additional income from outside while working as waged labour. This shows that CC, resilience, and adaptation need to be tackled by a more holistic and systemic approach, integrating agricultural and rural development with CC issues at local and national levels.

The study on 'Climate change adaptation in Southern Benin: a multi-scale perspective on rural communities of Mono and Couffo' (Chapter 4) by Marie-Ange Baudoin analyses if, why, and in which ways farmers are vulnerable to CC impacts, and how they try to cope with stressors by applying strategies to reducing their vulnerability. The analysis provides valuable insights concerning the room for improvement of the internationally supported NAPA: for example why weak and mistrusted local authorities were unable to effectively support adaptation in agricultural practices; and why central decision makers with an 'environment-only' perspective who are responsible for the NAPA had not involved relevant actors and not addressed the lack of information on weather forecasts, which hampers the autonomous adaptation process of farmers. By providing meteorological data to the different communities, uncertainty could be partly reduced relatively easily when using appropriate means.[26] The author concludes that climate vulnerability is a consequence of the weaknesses in rural development approaches and local institutions. Moreover, she contends that the shortcomings of NAPAs serve as a battleground for ministries and do not address the root causes of vulnerability from a socio-economic perspective.

Gala Bhaskar Reddy and Niranjan Sahu (Chapter 5, 'Building community-based institutions in Western Orissa Rural Livelihoods Project for green development') analyse WORLP as an example of a new approach to watershed development through a sustainable Natural Resources Management (NRM) programme supported by the British Department for International Development (DFID). Their study discusses the benefits of using community-based organisations in a livelihoods-centred approach to the development of a watershed, which is affected by frequent droughts and extreme weather events. The authors positively evaluate the watershed management scheme in the context of a sustainable livelihoods framework as a participatory approach for project management and the sustainable use of natural resources. Bottom-up participatory planning, implementation, and monitoring involve the community at all stages of the project cycle, keeping people at the centre stage of watershed management and promoting environmentally friendly technologies and practices. Grass roots institution-building and community mobilisation are the two sides of the coin that form the programme's building blocks, empowering communities and ensuring ownership.

Luís Artur examines the concepts of hazard and vulnerability, different approaches to disaster relief management and their contribution to climate resilience in his contribution 'How good are good practices? Understanding CBDRM in Mozambique' (Chapter 6). His analytical focus is on the Community-Based Disaster Risk Management (CBDRM) approach, its actual implementation, and the assessment of outcomes in terms of sustainable institution-building and impact on climate-resilient livelihoods. Initially developed in the Asian context, in particular around the Philippines' recurrent natural hazards, CBDRM became a worldwide approach promoted as new, good practice in disaster-prone countries in Africa, Latin America, and the Pacific Islands. Contrary to theory, which claims to adopt a community-based approach when designing and implementing interventions for disaster reduction and adaptation to CC, the reality in Mozambique reveals a top-down approach to CBDRM: the focus on local people's perceptions of disaster, their vulnerability, and means for improving resilience is not put into practice; the abuse of CBDRM for partisan interests and power struggles has led to conflicts, negotiations, and re-appropriation of the approach by the different actors involved; sub-optimal results in terms of (weak) institutions, (poor) means (physical re-equipment and effectiveness of risk management plans), and (less) resilience of local actors were the consequence. The lack of integration of disaster preparedness into the wider context of people's urgent needs to maintain or improve (poor) livelihoods (e.g. by not economically compensating efforts) is another reason for inadequate problem solving. This study shows a decoupling of rhetoric and action 'on the ground' and demonstrates that CBDRM, like other risk management or adaptation strategies, can only increase local resilience if measures also address at least the immediate need to improve livelihoods.

The role of Sub-Saharan universities in providing qualification for climate-resilient, integrated approaches to NRM is discussed by Sampson E. Edusah. In his contribution 'Making a difference through Integrated Natural Resources Management: the role of Kwame Nkrumah University of Science and Technology in Ghana' (Chapter 7), he analyses the initiatives of the College of Agriculture and Natural Resources (CANR) at Kwame Nkrumah University of Science and Technology (KNUST) in Kumasi, Ghana, to integrate INRM into higher education in order to enhance the competencies and capabilities of current and future professionals for managing complex environmental problems from an integrated perspective. CANR interprets INRM as an integrated multi-stakeholder approach to research, development, and education that aims to improve livelihoods, agro-ecosystem resilience, agricultural productivity, and environmental services. The first phase of the project started implementation in 2005 and has, so far, shown a positive effect on attitudes and work ethics, stimulating interdisciplinary team work and the involvement of key stakeholders in the design and implementation of academic programmes. However, the full paradigm shift to INRM and the necessary institutional change, including the incentive structure, has not yet been achieved. The involved stakeholders have questioned whether a large bureaucracy, i.e. KNUST, can be changed through a bottom-up initiative through one college, i.e. CANR. Furthermore, the overall academic objectives of KNUST, and consequently the role of INRM, in this respect, have not been clarified so far. An important component of the INRM project was to build the capacity of CANR staff as well as to collaborate with key stakeholder institutions, such as the Forestry Commission (FC), in undertaking both empirical and action research.

Part III moves beyond the local perspective and investigates the potential to reform the UNFCCC process, critically reflecting on existing and evolving mechanisms, such as the CDM, REDD+, and NAMA. Authors discuss the pros and cons of these approaches, lessons to be learned, alternative solutions, and their implications for CRD.

As a start, an innovative but 'paradoxical approach' in Ecuador is introduced, which intends to trade a national policy of 'not digging out oil' for nature conservation and financial compensation. In 'Green gold versus black gold: the Yasuní-ITT Initiative as an alternative way forward?' (Chapter 8) Amy Woodrow-Arai examines the possibilities for a value shift in economic development and CC policy making through the lens of the Yasuní-ITT initiative. This alternative development model could significantly contribute to CRD by moving away from oil extraction as a source of revenue, to natural resource preservation, thereby valuing the social, environmental, as well as economic benefits of ecosystems services while simultaneously improving local livelihoods and rendering societies more resilient to the impacts of CC. The ITT initiative also shows an alternative approach for supporting an actual climate management project and the respective transfer of financial resources to Ecuadorian policies and stakeholders. The author carefully analyses the advantages of this initiative and its innovative potential as well as the controversies surrounding the project: the ongoing oil extraction in Ecuador and governmental support to finance development programmes, the exclusion of local communities from the decision-making process, and the neglect of indigenous peoples' rights.

The study 'Developing economies in the current climate regime: new prospects for resilience and sustainability? The case of CDM projects in Asia' (Chapter 9) by Jean-Christophe Simon and Pauline Lacour analyses whether the CDM has served as a linchpin in setting off more ambitious and effective national CC policies in Southeast Asia and China and in influencing national interests in UNFCCC negotiations and the effectiveness of the political process. Two issues are addressed in particular: firstly, regional specificity amongst developing areas, and, notably, the pre-eminence of projects located in Asia; secondly, the relevance of CDM projects for both sustainable growth and effective mitigation strategies. The authors come to the conclusion that despite the difficulties of the CDM, it remains an attractive mechanism and helps developing countries to pursue national priorities in climate mitigation. Their study, however, reveals that only countries, such as China, which can afford to build up significant capacities to attract and manage CDM projects, really benefit from this market-based instrument. Furthermore, the CDM is seen as deficient in terms of additionality and calculation methods, which make the need for further reform explicit if the CDM wants to be kept as an efficient and effective tool in climate policy making.

In his contribution 'Does the right hand know what the left hand is doing? Similar problem, opposing remedies – a comparison of the Montreal Protocol and Kyoto Protocol's Clean Development Mechanism (Chapter 10), Thomas Grammig analyses the causes and impact of the regime interplay between the Montreal Protocol (MP) and the CDM of the Kyoto Protocol (KP) of the UNFCCC and outlines potential synergies. After eliminating chlorofluorocarbons (CFCs) across the globe, the scope of the MP has been extended to hydrochlorofluorocarbons (HCFCs). What was meant to be its strength, a multilateral fund (MLF) covering incremental costs, has actually become a weakness, as the incremental cost concept has never been put into practice. For HCFCs and CFCs, funding is made available only in relation to the volume of the chemicals, irrespective of the economic benefits for the users. An example of an HCFC phase-out plan is described to show that the former practice of the MLF is simply continued without checking its actual appropriateness, through bureaucratic inertia in the triangle of MLF/Implementing Agencies/ministries of environment. Interferences between the Montreal and Kyoto Protocols occur particularly because of the division between HCFCs and hydrofluorocarbons (HFCs). The inertia of both regimes contributes to making a solution unlikely, which is defined by a new North–South bargain for HCFC, as the interests of the Group of 77 (G-77) and of OECD members are too diverse. An assessment of the organisational efficiency of both the UNFCCC and the MLF seems unlikely and none has so far been published. The author proposes a different approach of using technical change trajectories to resolve the existing overlap between the two protocols.

Astrid Carrapatoso and Mareike Well assert in their contribution 'Interregional climate cooperation: EU–China relations as a success story?' (Chapter 11) that a concentration on climate-related international problem solving at the UNFCCC level is not promising at the moment, as the recent UNFCCC negotiations in Cancún, Durban, and Doha once again illustrated that member states are neither willing nor prepared to make ambitious commitments regarding binding emission targets and make them now. These authors shift the focus towards other forms of climate co-operation. The analysis of EU–China relations shows that diplomatic talks and concrete collaboration happen at sub-global levels (e.g. the inter-regional level), and prove that inter-regional climate dialogues and co-operation can effectively complement global initiatives by facilitating knowledge sharing and the diffusion of best practice policies. EU–China co-operation has brought about a significant number of joint institutions as 'platforms of diffusion', especially on energy-related issues. This illustrates the importance of the convergence of interests as well as the 'localisation' of policy innovations in diffusion processes, which finally determine the feasibility, adoption, and success of best practice in different national or regional settings.

In 'How to bypass multilateral gridlocks: resilient climate change management and efficient multi-level climate politics' (Chapter 12) Edith Kürzinger critically discusses the possibilities to reform and bypass the 'dead horse' UNFCCC process. She outlines the potential for reorganisation through the use of change management tools, such as 'cycle of change', 'energy for change', and 'interest-based negotiation' – and a recess to profoundly evaluate results and processes. She advocates that such a pause for reflection should be undertaken before entering into a phase of negotiation of new key 'policies and measures' based on a revised approach that follows the subsidiarity principle and incorporates new perspectives on individual emitters, embedded emissions, and general principles for resource use, among others. The recommended 'bypassing' encompasses bottom-up approaches and the scaling up of best practice policies and no regret measures; through this, tangible increases in resource efficiency can be applied widely by actors in all countries without major international transfers of financial resources, while fully tapping their benefits for CRD.

In Part IV 'The way forward to climate-resilient development' and its final chapter, Chapter 13 'Conclusions for research and policy agendas', the editors Astrid Carrapatoso and Edith Kürzinger sum up the book and crystallise the main lessons learned learned by the contributors, the points open for discussion, as well as the recommendations resulting from the empirical studies for policy and research agenda. They offer theoretical conclusions and identify ideas for further research. They also seek to provide practical solutions for future policy action and a stimulating mutual learning process for integrating scientists' and practitioners' views on CRD issues. In sum, this chapter explains why a profound reflection on the process towards CRD by all involved actors is necessary to learn from the past (what works, what doesn't?) and adjust directions, contents, and structures of policy and politics, in particular by using more participatory bottom-up approaches to CRD, which require less financial transfer and yield more effective impact.

Notes

1 As the countries called 'developed' in the United Nations (UN) context and in UN texts do not provide role models for sustainable development due to the lack of replicability of their economic and social systems at a global level, henceforth the inappropriate term 'developed countries' is substituted by 'industrialised' countries.

2 For all decisions of this CoP, see UNFCCC's website, http://unfccc.int/meetings/doha_nov_2012/meeting/6815.php#decisions (accessed 25.02.2013).

3 This makes one think of 'newspeak' in George Orwell's (1949) *1984*, especially the appendix on 'The Principles of Newspeak'; for a linguistic discussion of Orwell's 'newspeak', see, e.g. Dittmann 1984.

4 For the text of the Rio Declaration on Environment and Development, see http://www.unep.org/Documents.Multilingual/Default.asp?documentid=78&articleid=1163; for the text of the Agenda 21, see http://www.unep.org/documents.multilingual/default.asp?documentid=52 (accessed 02.02.2013).

5 The WB, for example, reacted to massive criticism of structural adjustment policies by counting for some years on a team of renowned environmental economists, such as Herman Daly and Robert Goodland; a recent example of 'progressive thinking' of both WB and OECD is a joint publication with bilateral donors on environmental fiscal reform (World Bank 2005); even though speaking about green growth strategy, in 2012, a series of interesting documents on the topic have been published by the WB, e.g. Weber and Johnson 2012.

6 See, for example, a different type of higher education (e.g. MSc in Responsibility and Business Practice) described by Marshall *et al.* (2011).

7 Even in a rich country like Germany, there is a debate about whether people who need to live on state subsidies can afford high energy costs and finance feed-in tariffs that promote renewable energy, where part of the eco-tax is used to reduce labour cost and support employment (Cottrell *et al.* 2011).

8 For an overview of the evolution of environmental norms, see Bernstein (2002), Table 1, pp. 5–6.

9 For an overview of the WSSD, see http://www.un.org/events/wssd/; for more information on the HDR, see http://hdr.undp.org/en/reports/global/hdr2011/download/ (accessed 31.01.2013).

10 For a detailed text on the MDGs, see the UN's official website: http://www.un.org/millenniumgoals/ (accessed 31.01.2013).

11 For further information on UNCSD 2012, see http://www.un.org/en/ecosoc/about/uncsd-rio.shtml and http://www.un.org/ga/search/view_doc.asp?symbol=A/RES/66/288&Lang=E (accessed 31.01.2013).

12 For further information on the GE initiative, see UNEP: About GE, http://www.unep.org/greeneconomy/AboutGEI/WhatisGEI/tabid/29784/Default.aspx; for a list of publications on GE released by UNEP, see http://www.unep.org/search.asp?sa.x=0&sa.y=0&sa=go%21&q=Green+Economy+Report&cx=00705937965475526521 1%3Ajkn gxjgnyii&cof=forid%3A11; and for the General Assembly resolution A/RES/66/288* 'The Future We Want', including the sections on GE and poverty eradication, http://www.un.org/ga/search/view_doc.asp?symbol=A/RES/66/288&Lang=E or http://sustainabledevelopment.un.org/index.php?menu=1225 (accessed 27.11.2012).

13 The discussions within the GE report (UNEP 2011) are somewhat biased towards renewable energy, and overrate the role of technology and investment and 'developed countries' as technological role models (for example: 'Improving the environmental efficiency of production at the global level can occur through technology and knowledge transfer from developed economies or through technology spillovers that occur as a result of international investment and globalised supply chains' (UNEP 2011: 260); in most cases resource efficiency is equal to energy efficiency, as most examples in the section on 'green manufacturing' also refer to energy (see e.g. ibid.: 269); no answers are provided to the key question of why all these good ideas, nicely put together but mostly known for two decades, have not been put into practice on a global scale.

14 See the critique by Victor and Jackson (2012) of the use of global averages in the simulation of the different scenarios chosen for the UNEP GE report and concerning the over-optimistic assumptions for the growth effects to be expected by the GE scenario; the latter also endorses the impression that GE is, in essence, a way to a 'different growth', rather than a strategy towards a different development model, according to SD criteria.

15 For the UN perspective on this topic, see also the UN Secretary-General's High-Level Panel on Global Sustainability Report (2012).

16 For a discussion of 'Rio+20' from different national perspectives, see, for example, Netzer/Althaus (2012) and Netzer *et al.* (2012).

17 Regarding the 'energy U-turn', see, for example, Gross (2012); there is a significant amount of media coverage on Germany's 'energy U-turn'; see, for example, Uken (2012); *Spiegel* (2012); *The Economist* (2012).

18 A short, amateur movie (see http://www.youtube.com/watch?v=hO8MwBZl-Vc) is illustrative of the role of leadership and the process of dissemination; the analysis by Derek Sivers underlines the importance of turning a 'first follower' into a leader, i.e. motivating or persuading someone to follow the same path (as shown by the first mover) is the first vital step to bring about change; see http://sivers.org/ff (accessed 25.02.2013).

19 See, for example, Enterra Insight (2010).

20 Originally conceived by Lewin (1953), 'action research' has evolved into a wide variety of definitions and concepts.

21 For the concept of polycentric institutions, see, for example, Ostrom (2010).

22 For a list and description of UNFCCC's 'lighthouse projects',' see http://unfccc.int/secretariat/momentum_for_change/items/7159.php (accessed 25.02.2013).

23 See, for example, the programmes of the Kreditanstalt für Wiederaufbau (KfW) on energy efficiency in housing, http://www.kfw.de/kfw/en/Domestic_Promotion/Our_offers/Renewable_energy.jsp#KfWRenewableEnergiesProgramme-Standard (accessed 23.02.2013).

24 'Awareness' is a much applied, but terribly vague term, as it can encompass many different concepts: from consciousness, alertness, attentiveness, to knowledge, and even understanding; it is assumed to lead to direct action, as presumed by marketing; but, in practice, it is at most a necessary, but not sufficient condition for modifying behaviour; it is used as pretext for many types of action, especially for activities that lack clear, specific, measurable, attainable, relevant and time-sensitive (SMART) objectives and measurable outcomes; awareness of the CC problem might have been achieved at much lower cost and with less CO_2 emissions, maybe even with a major advertising campaign or telenovelas (Kürzinger and Miller 2009: 118).

25 Based on the Open Space Technology (OST) developed by Harrison Owen (2008), un-conferences facilitate more productive and effective meetings. Instead of having a fixed agenda prepared by conference organisers, participants raise their issues of interest, jointly consolidate topics to be discussed, and finally divide into various discussion groups. This follows the logic that 'the most productive moments often occur in the corridor between meetings; at un-conferences, attendees like to say, it's all corridor'(Craig 2006).

26 For the issue of meteorological data for small-scale farmers, see also Shah *et al.* (2012).

References

Adger, W. N. *et al.* (2011) 'Resilience Implications of Policy Responses to Climate Change', *Wiley Interdisciplinary Reviews: Climate Change*, vol. 2, no. 5, pp. 757–766.

Arroyo, V. (2013) 'Are There Winning Strategies for Enacting Climate Policy?', *Climate Policy*, vol. 13, no. 1, pp. 142–144.

Baer, P. *et al.* (2008) *The Greenhouse Development Rights Framework*, 2nd ed., Berlin: Heinrich Böll Foundation.

Bateson, G. (1972) *Steps to an Ecology of Mind*, New York: Ballantine Books.

Bernstein, S. (2000) 'Ideas, Social Structure and the Compromise of Liberal Environmentalism', *European Journal of International Relations*, vol. 6, no. 4, pp. 464–512.

Bernstein, S. (2002) 'Liberal Environmentalism and Global Environmental Governance', *Global Environmental Politics*, vol. 2, no. 3, pp. 1–16.

Carpenter, S. *et al.* (2011) 'From Metaphor to Measurement: Resilience of What to What?', *Ecosystems*, vol. 4, no. 8, pp. 765–781.

Cole, P. (2000) *On the Record: Richard Holbrooke, United Nations Ambassador, Chicago Tribune*, 23 January 2000, online: http://articles.chicagotribune.com/2000-01-23/news/0001230002_1_security-council-albanians-africa (accessed 06.02.2013).

Costanza, R. *et al.* (1997) *An Introduction into Environmental Economics*, Boca Raton, FL: St. Lucie Press.

Cottrell, J., Schlegelmilch, K., Klarer, J. and Olearius, A. (2011) *Environmental Fiscal Reform: A Practice-Oriented Training for Policy Makers, Administration Officials, Consultants and NGO Representatives*, Training Manual for Participants, Eschborn: Gesellschaft für Internationale Zusammenarbeit (GIZ) and Berlin: Forum Ökologisch-Soziale Marktwirtschaft (FÖS); mimeo; for public information see http:// www.bmu.de/english/ecological_industrial_policy/ecological_finacial_reform/doc/41250.php (accessed 03.03.2013).

Craig, K. (2006) *Why 'Unconferences' Are Fun Conferences*, Business 2.0 Magazine Reports, online: http://money.cnn.com/2006/06/05/technology/business2_unconference0606/index.htm (accessed 26.02.2013).

Daly, H. E. (1974) 'The Economics of the Steady State', *The American Economic Review*, vol. 64, no. 2, pp. 15–21.

Daly, H. E. (1990) 'Toward Some Operational Principles of Sustainable Development', *Ecological Economics*, vol. 2, pp. 1–6.

Daly, H. E. (1991) *Steady-State Economy*, Washington, DC: Island Press.

Daly, H. E. (2007) *Ecological Economics and Sustainable Development*, Cheltenham: Edward Elgar.

Dittmann, J. (1984) 'Sprachlenkung und Denkverbot – George Orwell als Sprachkritiker', *Freiburger Universitätsblätter*, vol. 83, pp. 31–47, online: http://www.freidok. uni-freiburg.de/volltexte/4604/pdf/Dittmann_Sprachlenkung_und_Denkverbot.pdf (accessed 25.02.2013).

Doppelt, B. (2010) *Leading Change Toward Sustainability: A Change-Management Guide for Business, Government and Civil Society*, updated 2nd ed., Sheffield: Greenleaf.

Doyle, A. (2013) *Obama Wins Praise Abroad for Climate Change Goals*, online: http://www.reuters.com/article/2013/01/22/us-climate-obama-reaction-idUSBRE90L0NC20130122 (accessed 16.02.2013).

Enterra Insight (2010) *The Curse of Silo Thinking*, online: http://enterpriseresilienceblog. typepad.com/enterprise_resilience_man/2010/01/siloed-thinking-can-prove-devastating.html (accessed 05.03.2013).

Fasulo, L. (2004) *An Insider's Guide to the UN*. New Haven, CT and London: Yale University Press.

Folke, C. (2006) 'Resilience: The Emergence of a Perspective for Social-Ecological Systems Analyses', *Global Environmental Change*, vol. 16, no. 3, pp. 253–267.

Furness, M., Scholz, I., and Guarín, A. (2012) *History Repeats? The Rise of the New Middle Classes in the Developing World*, Briefing Paper 19/2012, Bonn: GDI, online: http:// www.die-gdi.de/CMS-Homepage/openwebcms3.nsf/(ynDK_contentByKey)/ANES-935EAS?Open&nav=expand:Publikationen;active:Publikationen\ANES-935EAS (accessed 03.02.2013).

Germanwatch (2013) *Songdo wird Sitz des Green Climate Fund*, online: http://www.epo. de/index.php?option=com_content&view=article&id=8865:songdo-wird-sitz-des-green-climate-fund&catid=99:topnews (accessed 31.01.2013).

GIZ (2012) *Green Economy: The Economy of the Future: Approaches to Inclusive, Resource-Efficient and Low-Carbon Development*, Eschborn, online: http://star-www. giz.de/starweb/giz/pub/servlet.starweb?path=giz/pub/pfm.web&r=34052&STAR_AppLanguage=0 (accessed 31.01.2013).

Goodland, R. (1995) 'The Concept of Environmental Sustainability', *Annual Review of Ecology and Systematics*, vol. 26, pp. 1–24, online: http://links.jstor.org/sici?sici=0066-4162%281995%2926%3C1%3ATCOES%3E2.0.CO%3B2-F (accessed 03.03.2013).

Green Climate Fund (2012) *Republic of Korea Selected to Host the Green Climate Fund*, online: http://gcfund.net/fileadmin/00_customer/documents/pdf/GCF_-_Press_20Oct_final.pdf (accessed 06.03.2013).

Groffman, P. M. *et al.* (2006) 'Ecological Thresholds: The Key to Successful Environmental Management or an Important Concept with No Practical Application?', *Ecosystems*, vol. 9, no. 1, pp. 1–13.

Gross, M. (2012) 'Energy U-Turn in Germany', *Current Biology*, vol. 21, no. 10, pp. R379–R381.

Harvey, F. (2012a) *Global Carbon Trading System Has Essentially Collapsed*, online: http://www.guardian.co.uk/environment/2012/sep/10/global-carbon-trading-system (accessed 17.09.2012).

Harvey, F. (2012b) *Green Climate Fund to Discuss $100bn Pledged by Rich Countries*, online: http://www.guardian.co.uk/environment/2012/aug/23/un-green-climate-fund-climate-change (accessed 17.09.2012).

Haughton, G. (1999) 'Environmental Justice and the Sustainable City', *Journal of Planning Education and Research*, March, vol. 18, pp. 233–243.

Hopwood, B., Mellor, M. and O'Brien, G. (2005) 'Sustainable Development: Mapping Different Approaches', *Sustainable Development*, vol. 13, no. 1, pp. 38–52.

Jacobs, M. (1999) 'Sustainable Development as a Contested Concept', in: Dobson, A. (ed.) *Fairness and Futurity: Essays on Environmental Sustainability and Social Justice*, Oxford: Oxford University Press, pp. 21–45.

Jänicke, M. and Jörgens, H. (2007) 'New Approaches to Environmental Governance', in: Jänicke, M. and Jacob, K. (eds.) *Environmental Governance in Global Perspective: New Approaches to Ecological Modernisation*, Berlin: Freie Universität Berlin, pp. 167–209.

Kirrane, C., Sharkey, C. and Naess, L. O. (2012) *Shaping Strategies: Factors and Actors in Climate Change Adaptation: Lessons from Two-Year Case Studies in Africa and Latin America*, Dublin: Trócaire/Institute of Development Studies IDS.

Kunreuther, H. and Useem, M. (2010) *Learning from Catastrophes, Strategies for Reaction and Response*, Upper Saddle River, NJ: Prentice Hall.

Kürzinger, E. and Miller, J. (2009) 'Profitable environmental management', in: Galea, C. (ed.) *Consulting for Business Sustainability*, Sheffield: Greenleaf, pp. 105–127.

Lenton, T. M. *et al.* (2008) 'Tipping Elements in the Earth's Climate System', *PNAS*, vol. 105, no. 6, pp. 1786–1793.

Lewin, K. (1953) *Die Lösung sozialer Konflikte*, Bad Nauheim: TM Christjan.

Lewis, B. and Chestney, N. (2013) *EU Carbon Market Hit Fresh Low After Backloading*, online: http://www.reuters.com/article/2013/01/24/us-eu-ets-idUSBRE90N0EG20130124 (accessed 16.02.2013).

Loewe, M. (2012) *Post 2015: How to Reconcile the Millennium Development Goals (MDGs) and the Sustainable Development Goals (SDGs)?*, Briefing Paper no. 18/2012, German Development Institute, online: http://www.die-gdi.de/CMS-Homepage/openwebcms3.nsf/(ynDK_contentByKey)/ANES-935C9R/$FILE/BP%2018.2012.pdf (accessed 31.01.2013).

Lovelock, J. E. (1991) *Gaia: A New Look at Life on Earth*, Oxford: Oxford University Press [Originally published in 1979].

Lovelock, J. E. (2006) *The Revenge of Gaia*, London: Allen Lane.

Luhmann, N. (1990) 'Über Systemtheoretische Grundlagen der Gesellschaftstheorie', *Deutsche Zeitschrift für Philosophie*, vol. 38, no. 3, pp. 277–284.

Marshall, J., Coleman, G. and Reason, P. (2011) *Leadership for Sustainability: An Action Research Approach*, Sheffield: Greenleaf Publishing.

Martens, P. and Chang, C. T. (eds.) (2010) *The Social and Behavioural Aspects of Climate Change*, Sheffield: Greenleaf

Meadowcroft, J. (2007) 'National Sustainable Development Strategies: Features, Challenges and Reflexivity', *Environmental Policy and Governance*, vol. 17, no. 3, pp. 152–163.

Meadows, D. H. (2002) 'Dancing with Systems', *The Systems Thinker*, vol. 13, no. 2, online: http://www.natcapsolutions.org/Presidio/Articles/WholeSystems/ThinkingInSystems_MEADOWS_TiS%20v13.2_DRAFT.pdf (accessed 31.01.2013).

Meadows, D. H., Meadows, D. L. and Randers, J. (1992) *Beyond the Limits: Global Collapse or a Sustainable Future*, London: Earthscan.

Meadows, D. H., Meadows, D. L. and Randers, J. (2004) *A Synopsis: Limits to Growth: The 30-Year Update,* London: Earthscan.

Munro, D. A. (ed.) (1991) *Caring for the Earth: A Strategy for Sustainable Living*, Gland: World Conservation Union.

Netzer, N. and Althaus, J. (2012) 'Introduction', in: Netzer, N. and Althaus, J. (eds.) *Green Economy: Turning Over a New Leaf towards Sustainable Development?* FES Perspective, online: http://library.fes.de/pdf-files/iez/global/09196.pdf (accessed 08.02.2013).

Netzer, N. *et al.* (eds.) (2012) *Really the Future We Want? Civil Society Voices on Rio+20*, FES Perspective, online: http://library.fes.de/pdf-files/iez/global/09139.pdf (accessed 11.02.2013).

Orwell, G. (1949) *1984*, London: Penguin.

Ostrom, E. (2010) 'Polycentric Systems for Coping with Collective Action and Global Environmental Change', *Global Environmental Change*, vol. 20, no. 4, pp. 550–557.

Owen, H. (2008) *Open Space Technology: A User's Guide*. 3rd ed. San Francisco, CA: Berrett-Koehler Publishers.

Popper, K. (2002) *The Open Society and Its Enemies: Volume 1*, London: Routledge [Originally published in 1945].

Porritt, J. (2007) *Capitalism as if the World Matters,* London: Earthscan.

Reuters (2013a) *Buyers Step Away from Chinese CDM Contracts*, online: http://www.pointcarbon.com/research/promo/research/1.2175053?&ref=searchlist (accessed 18.02.2013).

Reuters (2013b) *New Market Mechanisms After Doha: Proceeding at Snail's Pace*, online: http://www.pointcarbon.com/research/promo/research/1.2132464?&ref=searchlist (accessed 18.02.2013).

Rockström, J. *et al.* (2009) Planetary Boundaries: 'Exploring the Safe Operating Space for Humanity', *Ecology and Society*, vol. 14, no. 2, p. 32, online: http://www.ecologyandsociety.org/vol14/iss2/art32/ (accessed 08.02.2013).

Schiller, A. (2012*) Revenue Structures and the Question of Who Pays Taxes: Understanding the Conditions under which Elites Pay Taxes in Developing Countries*, Discussion Paper 17/2012, Bonn: GDI, online: http://www.die-gdi.de/CMS-Homepage/openwebcms3.nsf/(ynDK_contentByKey)/ANES-943EQV/$FILE/DP%2017.2012.pdf (accessed 03.02.2013).

Shah, P. *et al.* (2012) *Options for Improving the Communication of Seasonal Rainfall Forecasts to Smallholder Farmers: The Case of Kenya*, GDI Briefing Paper 17/2012, online: http://www.die-gdi.de/CMS-Homepage/openwebcms3_e.nsf/%28ynDK_contentByKey%29/ANES-935CGM?Open&nav=expand:Publications;active:Publications\ANES-935CGM (accessed 06.03.2013).

Smit, B. and Wandel, J. (2006) 'Adaptation, Adaptive Capacity and Vulnerability', *Global Environmental Change*, vol. 16, no. 3, pp. 282–292.

Spiegel (2012a) *Head Office Raided in Tax Probe: Deutsche Bank CEO Under Investigation*, online: http://www.spiegel.de/international/business/deutsche-bank-co-ceo-juergen-fitschen-under-investigation-in-tax-probe-a-872563.html (accessed 18.02.2013).

Spiegel (2012b) *Germany 'Must Not Go It Alone': EU Commissioner Attacks Berlin's Energy Plans*, online: http://www.spiegel.de/international/germany/germany-must-not-go-it-alone-eu-commissioner-attacks-berlin-s-energy-plans-a-820767.html (accessed 12.02.2013).

Stewart, M. B. (1987) 'Collective Bargaining Arrangements, Closed Shops and Relative Pay', *The Economic Journal*, vol. 97, no. 385, pp. 140–156.

Teubner, G. (1992) 'Die vielköpfige Hydra: Netzwerke als kollektive Akteure höherer Ordnung', in: Krohn, W. and Küppers, G. (eds.) *Emergenz: Die Entstehung von Ordnung, Organisation und Bedeutung*, 2nd ed., Berlin: Suhrkamp, pp. 189–216, online: http://publikationen.ub.uni-frankfurt.de/frontdoor/index/index/docId/3898 (accessed 04.03.2013).

The Economist (2012) 'Germany's Energy Giants: Don't Mention the Atom', online: http://www.economist.com/node/2157363 (accessed 12.02.2013).

Uken, M. (2012) *Energiewende: Noch fehlt der konsequente U-Turn*, online: blog.zeit.de/gruenegeschaefte/2012/03/06/energiewende-noch-fehlt-der-konsequente-u-turn/ (accessed 12.02.2013).

Ullrich, D. (2012) *Resource Efficiency in Development Cooperation*, Eschborn: GIZ, online: http://www.giz.de/Themen/de/35799.htm (accessed 03.02.2013).

UNEP (2011) *Towards a Green Economy: Pathways to Sustainable Development and Poverty Eradication*, Nairobi, online: www.unep.org/greeneconomy (accessed 01.03.2013).

UNFCCC (2012) *Outcome of the work of the Ad Hoc Working Group on Further Commitments for Annex I Parties under the Kyoto Protocol, FCCC/KP/CMP/2012/L.9*, online: http://unfccc.int/resource/docs/2012/cmp8/eng/l09.pdf (accessed 31.01.2013).

UN Secretary-General's High-Level Panel on Global Sustainability Report (2012) *Resilient People, Resilient Planet: A Future Worth Choosing*, online: http://www.un.org/gsp/sites/default/files/attachments/GSP_Report_web_final.pdf (accessed 23.5.2012).

Victor, P. and Jackson, J. (2012) 'A Commentary on UNEP's Green Economy Scenarios', *Ecological Economics*, vol. 77, pp. 11–15.

Volkery, A. *et al.* (2006) 'Coordinating Sustainable Development: An Evaluation of the State of Play', in Jänicke, M. and Jacob, K. (eds.) *Environmental Governance in Global Perspective: New Approaches to Ecological Modernisation*, Berlin: Freie Universität Berlin, pp. 210–238.

Walker, B. *et al.* (2002) 'Resilience Management in Social-Ecological Systems: A Working Hypothesis for a Participatory Approach', *Conservation Ecology*, vol. 6, no. 1, online: http://www.consecol.org/vol6/iss1/art14 (accessed 16.01.2013).

Walker, B. *et al.* (2004) 'Resilience, Adaptability and Transformability in Social-Ecological Systems', *Ecology and Society*, vol. 9, no. 2, p. 5, online: http://www.ecologyandsociety.org/vol9/iss2/art5 (accessed 25.02.2013).

WCED (1987) *Our Common Future (Brundtland Report)*, Oxford: Oxford University Press.

Weber, E. U. and Johnson, E. J. (2012) *Psychology and Behavioral Economics Lessons for the Design of a Green Growth Strategy*, World Bank Policy Research Working Paper 6240, Washington DC, online: http://elibrary.worldbank.org/docserver/download/6240.pdf?expires=1362153938&id=id&accname=guest&checksum=9B6B576F07DE7F68A7CD6637D5722A05 (accessed 01.03.2013).

Weizsäcker, E. U., Lovins, A. B. and Hunter Lovins, L. (1997) *Factor 4: Doubling Wealth – Halving Resource Use: The New Report to the Club of Rome*, London: Earthscan.

Weizsäcker, E. U. *et al.* (2009) *Factor Five: Transforming the Global Economy through 80% Improvements in Resource Productivity*, London: Earthscan.

World Bank (2005) *Environmental Fiscal Reform: What Should Be Done And How To Achieve It*, Washington DC: World Bank.

Part II
The contribution of local, regional and national approaches to climate-resilient development, or what good practices can be disseminated or mainstreamed?

3 Shaping strategies

Factors and actors in climate change adaptation

Ciara Kirrane, Cliona Sharkey and Lars Otto Naess

Introduction

This chapter details findings of a two-year research project that analysed household vulnerability and resilience in the context of a changing climate. It explores households' livelihood responses to climate and non-climate related shocks and stressors in four case study locations in Bolivia, Honduras, Kenya and Malawi, as well as the factors affecting these responses and, ultimately, resilience. To date, case studies of vulnerability and adaptation have typically examined vulnerabilities in particular localities at particular times. Less attention has been paid to examining findings in different localities and over a time period spanning more than one season. This study provides a more nuanced perspective of vulnerability, adaptation and resilience by contributing to an understanding of (1) how households are experiencing and responding to climate shocks and stressors, (2) what is supporting or undermining their capacity to respond, and (3) whether or not their livelihood responses move them on a path to becoming more resilient in the face of a changing climate.

The research reveals broad trends of adaptation, with households adopting both new strategies (for example, the use of improved drought-tolerant seed varieties in Malawi) as well as traditional methods (e.g. continued reliance on indigenous, more resilient livestock in Kenya) to cope with climate impacts and other challenges. The influence of external factors, such as government policy, on households' ability to manage climate impacts is also clear: in most cases, external support was limited in its scope and coverage, and for many households, innovation and adaptation was impossible without tailored support that addressed the barriers to adaptation. The research clearly highlights the need to address the socio-economic and political marginalisation that makes people vulnerable in the first place if development policy is to move towards a more climate-resilient development model. This chapter deals first with approaches to assess successful adaptation, then outlines the analytical and methodological framework used in the study. The findings from the four case studies are then discussed and six recommendations, grounded in the empirical findings, are outlined for consideration by development actors when designing and implementing climate change adaptation activities.

Measuring and assessing successful adaptation

There is increasing focus on measuring and evaluating successful or 'sustainable' adaptation (Eriksen *et al.* 2011; Silva-Villanueva 2011). This is partly prompted by the need to prioritise scarce funding for adaptation and to address concerns about equity and justice in adaptation outcomes by ensuring that funds are used to support the poorest and most vulnerable. Attention to measuring and evaluating adaptation also relates to the need to build understanding that not all actions aimed at tackling climatic shocks and stressors support longer-term adaptive capacity. Indeed, there is growing literature which shows that climate policies may have negative or maladaptive outcomes for vulnerable populations (Eriksen *et al.* 2011). At the household level, adaptive actions are taken in response to a range of issues, such as resource constraints, market forces, institutional incentives and increased climate variability. Trade-offs may exist between short- and long-term concerns. For the poorest, actions to tackle recurrent drought may lead to assets being run down, thereby reducing longer-term adaptive capacity and entrenching poverty and vulnerability. In order to break these cycles, we need to better understand how they occur and what are the barriers and opportunities for change. This study draws on different approaches for how to assess 'successful adaptation':

- According to Bahadur *et al.* (2010), adaptation outcomes may be viewed against criteria for resilience, which include institutional flexibility, justice, livelihood diversification, an ability to bounce back, withstand shock and self-organise.
- Another approach, by Eriksen *et al.* (2011: 11–15), focuses on four key criteria for moving towards 'sustainable adaptation': first, to recognise the context for vulnerability, including multiple stressors; second, to acknowledge that differing values and interests affect adaptation outcomes; third, to integrate local knowledge into adaptation responses; and fourth, to consider potential feedback between local and global processes.
- Barnett and O'Neill's approach, alternatively, focuses on whether actions taken for adaptation avoid being maladaptive, defined as 'action taken ostensibly to avoid or reduce vulnerability to climate change that impacts adversely on, or increases the vulnerability of other systems, sectors or social groups' (2010: 212). They outline five key factors that would render actions maladaptive: increasing emissions of greenhouse gases, disproportionately burdening the most vulnerable, having high opportunity costs compared to alternatives, reducing incentives to adapt, or locking future actions into particular pathways.

Addressing the drivers of vulnerability: towards a climate-resilient development model

In most cases, reducing vulnerabilities and enabling responses that increase adaptive capacity will require challenging the power structures that are responsible for individuals' and households' vulnerability in the first place. For example, if the problem of food insecurity is caused by the fact that farmers have insecure land tenure and a disincentive to invest in their land, food aid or provision of better climate information will not lead to reduced vulnerability. Such concerns are also central to work in climate change and development, which has been an expanding area of research and policy starting in the late 1990s and early 2000s (AfDB *et al.* 2003), with a more recent focus on terms such as climate-resilient development and climate-compatible development (Bahadur *et al.* 2010; Mitchell and Maxwell 2010). Some of these concepts are largely donor-driven, and it is still unclear what they mean in practice and whether they involve synergies or trade-offs between development and adaptation outcomes.

Poverty reduction and adaptation differ in important respects. Development interventions may increase people's incomes but leave societies more vulnerable to climate change. An example is shrimp farming that involves the clearing of coastal mangroves, which, in turn, makes people more susceptible to the effects of coastal erosion or storm surges. Likewise, tourism may increase incomes but the incomes may be sensitive to changes in climatic patterns or changes in consumer behaviour. It is clear that in many areas, society is not fully adapted to the current climate: we have an 'adaptation deficit' (Burton and May 2004: 31). For example, a household may be unable to recover and rebuild assets after a period of flooding or drought, due to their existing levels of poverty. In some cases, this adaptation deficit is increasing as the climate changes, with more settlements in exposed areas, or through loss of knowledge, skills and resources that help manage climate risks; for example, the loss of plant materials used in the past for alternative income-generating activities during periods of drought. If development policy is to move towards a more climate-resilient development model, it is imperative to address the socio-economic and political marginalisation that makes people vulnerable in the first place.

Analytical framework: a modified sustainable livelihoods approach

The sustainable livelihoods (SL) framework (Scoones 1998) formed a starting point for the analysis in this study. The SL framework has been used widely in development research and has, more recently, been applied to climate change adaptation. Key strengths of the framework include the focus on assets as a basis for livelihoods, the emphasis on context-specific analysis, and the role of institutions in adaptation. For the purposes of this study, the SL framework has been modified to highlight the linkages across scales, as a common critique of the SL framework is that it fails to show these linkages. The modified framework (Figure 3.1) recognises that a variety of actors and factors exist at various scales (local, national, international) which are simultaneously impacted by climate variability and change, and which impact on household livelihood strategies. Livelihood strategies are seen as an outcome of the assets or capital at household level, the shocks and stressors affecting these, as well as the policy and institutional environment.

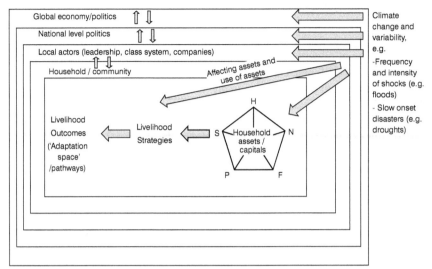

H=human capital; N=natural capital; F=financial capital; P=physical capital; S=social capital

Figure 3.1 Analytical framework

Throughout the study, there was no prior assumption that climate variability and change was the most important or defining factor in people's decision making. What was of interest was to see how changes made to livelihood strategies – in response to climate variability but also to other factors such as market forces, national policy and NGO intervention – were affecting people's vulnerability and their resilience to a changing climate. Therefore, during fieldwork, 'climate change' as a subject, was not used as the starting point of questioning or as the single focus of any activity, thus avoiding the influence that the use of this term could have on responses.

Methodology: a mixed methods approach

The findings are based on data collected during fieldwork carried out during September 2009 to November 2011 in a number of communities in Bolivia, Honduras, Kenya and Malawi. These four countries were selected to achieve sufficient diversity and geographical spread in the results. Within the four countries, seven villages were selected as case studies of how people are experiencing and responding to climate variability. The study focused predominantly on the resilience of agriculture and agriculture-based livelihoods systems. Data was collected on livelihood responses taken by households to tackle climate and non-climate related shocks and stressors, the constraints and opportunities faced in doing so, and on the impact of external support and regulations. In total, six visits were conducted at intervals of four to six months across the four locations over a two-year period of study. Both qualitative and quantitative methods were employed during the fieldwork, through a survey, semi-structured interviews, and focus group discussions using participatory rural appraisal (PRA) techniques.

A 'wealth ranking' exercise was conducted at the beginning of the fieldwork. Based on this, 40 households were selected to participate in the study, proportionately representing the main wealth groups found in the overall population and identified in the ranking exercise. Another layer of stratification was added by incorporating an approximately representative number of male- and female-headed households within the sample. The head of household was the primary respondent throughout the research, except in cases where this was not possible; for example, due to migration. The sample of 40 households per research location took part in the survey and interviews, and a wider group (of up to 60 people) took part in the focus group discussions.

A baseline survey was conducted at the beginning of the fieldwork to establish a general reference point on the following key areas: (1) household data, (2) household resources, (3) social networks, and (4) livelihood challenges and responses. Follow-up surveys were composed of the same core areas and questions; these captured information only on changes that had occurred in these areas since the previous visit. Qualitative activities were conducted in conjunction with the survey during each visit. PRA activities such as 'village hazard mapping', 'seasonal calendars', 'trend lines/historical timelines' and 'social institutions mapping' formed the basis of early focus group discussions. More tailored focus group discussions were conducted in the case study locations as the issues developed and diverged over time. Finally, semi-structured interviews were used to complement and in some cases replace the survey in the final stages of the research as the questions became more focused and as the need for 'filling the gaps' became greater. Interview questions were semi-structured and were designed for each individual case study. Table 3.1 outlines the different tools used for data collection over the course of the study. All activities were conducted in the local language, in collaboration with local partner organisations.[1]

While common research questions guided the overall direction of the study, space was given to allow a particular focus to emerge within each case study so that the investigation could be both relevant and manageable. Table 3.2 outlines the focus area for each case study.

Summary of the findings

The framework used to analyse the data collected for this research considered the impact of climate shocks and stressors, the policy context, and socio-economic and environmental changes on household assets and livelihood strategies. Resilience was viewed as the outcome of this process, taking into account the various factors that impact on household livelihood strategies while simultaneously being impacted by climate variability and change. The following section summarises the findings from each of the case studies before moving on to draw out some overall findings for this study.

Table 3.1 Topics and tools used for data collection

	1st fieldwork	2nd fieldwork	3rd fieldwork	4th fieldwork	5th fieldwork	Final fieldwork
Bolivia	• Survey • Wealth ranking • Village profile • Venn diagram	• Survey • Risk mapping • Trend lines • Natural resource mapping	• Survey • Daily activity clocks • Diversification focus group discussion (FGD)	• Survey • Sources of weather information FGD	• Agricultural system trends FGD	• Interviews on irrigation practices
Honduras	• Survey • Wealth ranking • Village profile	• Survey • Daily activity clocks • Land and agriculture FGD	• Survey	• Economic, social and environmental trend lines • Livelihood options FGD	• Interviews • Wage labour and livelihoods FGD	• Interviews • Trend lines • Livelihoods FGD
Kenya	• Survey • Wealth ranking • Village profile • Seasonal calendars • Trend lines • Venn diagram	• Survey • Daily activity clocks • Trends in agriculture and diversification FGD	• Survey • Changes in livestock and crops FGD	• Survey • Challenges with changing livelihoods FGD	• Survey • Interviews • Resources and drivers of changes FGD	• Interviews • Institutional support FGD
Malawi	• Survey • Wealth ranking • Village profile	• Survey • Risk mapping • Seasonal calendars • Trend lines • Venn diagram	• Survey • Farm Input Subsidy Programme FGD	• Survey • Crop and livelihood diversification FGD	• Survey • Interviews • Drivers of diversification FGD	• Interviews • Barriers to diversification FGD

Table 3.2 Case study focus areas

Bolivia	Irrigation and adaptation in the Bolivian Highlands Water scarcity is a key limiting factor to households achieving adequate and reliable agricultural production in the communities where this research was conducted. Irrigation is emphasised as an important strategy to address this problem by community members, the government and other institutional actors working in these communities. The case study therefore explored what is supporting or undermining households' capacity to take up or enhance their use of irrigation, and whether or not irrigation is seen as supporting them to become more resilient in the face of a changing climate.
Honduras	Small-scale agriculture and waged labour in northern Honduras In the Aguán valley in northern Honduras, tropical storms, hurricanes and flooding are increasing in frequency and intensity. Most households in the research community have shifted from small-scale farming to a reliance on waged employment in local palm plantations and cattle ranches, and the issue of the livelihoods mix in the community was identified as a key issue. A focus on the factors supporting or undermining livelihood strategies and how different livelihood options affect resilience to climate shocks formed the basis of this case study.
Kenya	Changing farming systems in semi-arid Kenya The research took place during a period of drought in the region, offering the opportunity in this case study to investigate livelihood strategies in the context of extreme conditions. Changes in farming systems, in particular the shifting emphasis between crop production and livestock keeping, and the incorporation of improved seed varieties and livestock breeds, were considered the most significant changes being made in livelihood practices. These areas were explored to understand the factors affecting the adoption of these strategies and whether they are supporting increased resilience in the face of increasing climate variability.
Malawi	Drought and diversification in southern Malawi Food security remains a key challenge in Malawi. Given its dependence on rain-fed agriculture and its vulnerability to climate variability and change, the integration of adaptation measures into food security strategies is of critical importance if this challenge is to be tackled over the long term. This study looked at how farmers are adapting their agricultural practices in the face of these challenges, for example adopting improved seeds and diversifying their crops, the factors that are supporting or hindering them to do so, and whether strategies being adopted are contributing to increasing household resilience.

Case study findings

Table 3.3 contains the overall findings from the case studies.

Key overall findings

Climate variability and change are experienced by households as
additional stressors on already vulnerable livelihood systems

Households in the case study communities face multiple livelihood stressors. High poverty levels, socio-economic and political marginalisation, rapid population growth, increased pressure on natural resources (especially land and water), limited livelihood opportunities and illness are just some of the key factors contributing to vulnerability. Climate variability and change are experienced by households as additional stressors on already vulnerable livelihood systems. Research participants cited changes in rainfall patterns, increased drought and more frequent extreme weather events as factors that undermine agricultural production, food security and on- and off-farm incomes. Climate variability and change are directly affecting people and their livelihoods, as well as interacting with and exacerbating other drivers of vulnerability, such as natural resource pressure.

Household responses to observed climate changes are shaped by
multiple factors and stressors

Changes in livelihood strategies, in general, and agricultural strategies, in particular, were identified across the four case studies. Households have been changing the balance between crops and livestock, diversifying their crop production and livestock assets, increasing their use of improved varieties and breeds, adopting technology such as irrigation, or moving out of small-scale agriculture entirely in response to resource constraints, market forces such as consumer demand for different crops and vegetables, institutional incentives such as crop and fertiliser subsidies, and increased climate variability. Responses are driven by multiple stressors and not any single factor. In the Kenya case study, for example, improved seed varieties have been adopted for their greater drought tolerance and potential to produce more on less land but also as a result of external support from government and development organisations. Similarly, in the Honduras case study, increasing risks associated with agriculture as well as limited access to land, reinforced by government policy that promotes large scale agro-industrial production, has driven a shift in livelihood strategies away from small-scale farming.

In addition to their main livelihood strategies, most, if not all, households are also engaging in activities to supplement their income and reduce risk, such as casual labour, petty trade/services or nature-based enterprises. Migration is a strategy employed by households, particularly in Honduras, and increasingly in Kenya, as a result of the recent food crisis of 2011. Whilst diversifying livelihoods

Table 3.3 Case study findings

	Bolivia case study	Honduras case study	Kenya case study	Malawi case study
Observed climate changes and impact	Households are experiencing a variety of changes in climate patterns, for example rising temperatures and changes in precipitation, including increasingly unpredictable and intense rain. These changes are affecting their ability to produce food for consumption and sale. There are also indications of social strains as a result of increasing competition for water.	Households are experiencing extremes in weather on a regular basis and are vulnerable, in particular, to flooding. Excessive levels of rainfall during tropical storms or hurricanes often lead to local rivers bursting their banks and flooding surrounding areas. Access to and availability of work for wage labourers is hampered during these periods, while farmers suffer losses to crops and livestock. Drought is also increasingly affecting these livelihood activities.	Households are experiencing changes in rainfall patterns, in particular a decrease in rainfall volume and reliability. This is impacting upon agricultural production and food and income availability.	Households are experiencing declining rainfall levels and more erratic patterns of rainfall, as well as regular incidences of drought and flooding, affecting crop production and food security.
Livelihood responses	Changes in climate patterns, external institutional support and market signals are combining to encourage many households in the communities to take up or increase their use of irrigation. Evidence was found of positive impacts as a result of the adoption or increase in the use of irrigation, including increased food security, rising incomes and household investment.	There has been a shift in the overall livelihoods mix from small-scale agriculture to a reliance on waged labour on African palm plantations and cattle ranches. This is in response to a variety of factors including climate shocks and land, agriculture and rural development policies. As a result people are more dependent on external options for their livelihoods.	Households have been adapting their farming systems, shifting the balance between crop production and livestock keeping. They have also been increasing the use of improved seed varieties and livestock breeds. Changes are being made in response to a variety of factors including changing rainfall patterns, changes in the land tenure system, and as a result of support from government and non-governmental external actors.	Changes in rainfall patterns and challenges in meeting food security needs are prompting many farmers to both grow a wider range of crops and to use improved seeds as well as other external inputs.

continued...

Table 3.3 continued

	Bolivia case study	Honduras case study	Kenya case study	Malawi case study
Constraints	There are a variety of constraints and challenges to taking up or increasing the use of irrigation, including access to water, the cost of equipment, and time and labour demands that inhibit or prevent certain households in the community from practising irrigation and/or benefitting from the institutional support offered.	Failure to redistribute land, inappropriate rural development and agricultural policy, and the lack of investment in rural livelihoods has undermined people's ability to access land, perpetuating fragile livelihoods which are unreliable and highly sensitive to global economic trends, such as employment in palm plantations and a reliance on remittances from migrants.	Households face various constraints and barriers in adopting improved seed and breed varieties such as lack of financial resources, limited availability of inputs, lack of appropriate training and information, and the limitations of the strategies. Land is a key limiting factor affecting the viability of livestock and crop production strategies, as well as access to natural resources, which in turn is inhibiting people's ability to practise diversified livelihoods.	Lack of access to resources, including labour availability, financial resources to access inputs, technical training and adequate land, or to external institutional support which could enable access to them (e.g. through NGOs or the Farm Input Subsidy Programme) limit the extent to which certain groups, especially the elderly and poor farmers who are not included in support, can take up strategies of crop diversification and the use of improved seed varieties.
Tensions/ trade-offs	This case study reveals tensions in certain strategies being promoted, such as support for crop or seed varieties that fetch a better market price but which are irrigation dependent in an area where water availability is a key challenge. The impacts of some forms of irrigation on soil erosion were also highlighted as a concern.	Wage labourers have the advantage of earning an income, albeit insecure, without the risks of individual investment but are dependent on external opportunities and thus particularly vulnerable to external shocks. Small-scale farmers have more autonomy over the means of production and consumption, but there are higher personal risks in terms of losses of investment.	Although the use of improved seed varieties and livestock breeds have benefits, e.g. attaining high market prices, they are more susceptible to disease and require additional inputs and household investment.	While improved seeds offer higher yields and drought-tolerant properties, the need for chemical inputs requires additional financial outlay and may foster dependency on external inputs while having negative environmental consequences.

	Bolivia case study	Honduras case study	Kenya case study	Malawi case study
External institutional support	While coverage remains limited, external NGO and government support is seeking to enhance access to water by repairing, reinforcing or building water and irrigation infrastructure. In the face of uncertain climate scenarios, however, the importance of explicit consideration of both short-term and long-term water availability emerged clearly as a crucial factor in building long-term resilience.	Inadequate and inappropriate support for rural livelihoods is failing to build robust livelihoods. People are ill-equipped to cope with livelihood shocks and stressors, resulting in a deficit in their ability to cope with and adapt to the added challenge of current and future climate impacts.	External support from government and NGOs remains focused on the use of improved livestock breeds and seed varieties, despite the fact that these strategies – designed and adopted to guard against drought – are in more extreme conditions still not sufficiently well adapted.	Weaknesses in the design and implementation of the Farm Input Subsidy Programme to promote crop diversification undermine its potential effectiveness as a food security and adaptation measure.

is seen as key to spreading risk in the face of increasing climate variability, in most cases, these supplementary income-generating activities (e.g. casual agricultural labour) are as vulnerable to climatic factors as the main livelihood strategies.

Access to natural resources such as land and water emerged as key limiting factors in households' options and abilities to adapt their livelihoods to the changes they are experiencing. Population pressures coupled with more unreliable productivity linked to climatic changes are increasing pressure on resources and aggravating vulnerability. In Kenya and Malawi, these processes are limiting the options for alternative livelihood strategies. In Bolivia, competition for water resources is creating heightened tensions. Furthermore, government policy plays a key role in determining access to resources. In Honduras, for example, government policy reinforces an inequitable distribution of land, thereby limiting livelihood options and making people more dependent on external options for their livelihoods.

Governmental and non-governmental support, and governmental policy are key in influencing livelihood strategies and adaptation options

A variety of strategies are being promoted by a range of actors, with evidence of tensions (e.g. between the models of agriculture supported), trade-offs and limitations in livelihoods outcomes and resilience. The evidence shows that some of these strategies contributed to increased food and income security. Households in the case study communities are aware of both the benefits and trade-offs of strategies being promoted with regard to their future resilience. For example, the trade-off between increasing productivity from using external inputs (e.g. seeds, chemical fertilisers) against their affordability and environmental impact over the longer term in Malawi and Kenya; and the promotion of crops in Bolivia that fetch a good market price but which are irrigation-dependent in a context of increasing water scarcity.

Responses also indicated that certain strategies, which are promoted and adopted in agricultural production or waged agricultural labour, are ultimately limited in their potential to offer resilient livelihoods. In the Kenyan case study, even drought tolerant crops failed during periods of severe drought. In Honduras, waged labour on African palm plantations and cattle ranches appears as risky as farming with respect to climatic and other shocks, despite the fact that climatic risk associated with farming is a key factor in why some households move out of farming. Across all four case studies, whatever changes households are making, it remains the diversity and flexibility in households' livelihoods strategies that determines resilience.

Inadequate and incoherent external support, and inappropriate government policies, limit the livelihoods outcomes and resilience of vulnerable households

Many options for increasing resilience exist, and there is significant scope for building on those strategies where households are seeing positive outcomes from crop diversification in Malawi or small-scale irrigation in Bolivia. However, it was also clear in these case studies that support (whether governmental or non-governmental) does not reach all households, and households face constraints in adopting the supported strategies. External support was often limited in its scope and coverage, poorly targeted and inappropriate for particular households. In the Malawi case study, only a small percentage of households reported receiving the governmental subsidy for farm inputs. In Honduras, external support for diversified livelihoods, farming or other rural livelihoods is extremely limited. Across each of the case studies, community members highlighted financial costs, time and lack of skills and appropriate training as affecting their ability to take up new strategies or to implement them effectively.

There is also a lack of coherence in support. While in many cases policy rhetoric supports diversified low-input approaches to sustainable agriculture, in practice, governmental support often emphasises systems that involve costly inputs, such as improved seeds, chemical fertilisers and pesticides. At the same time, the progress made by various actors in promoting low-input models of agriculture is being hindered by the lack of consistency between policy and practice. In Honduras, government policy is focused on large-scale agro-industry and has played a part in many households' decision to move out of small-scale agriculture and to become more dependent on agricultural wage labour. Lack of access to land limits households' livelihood options and promotes a dependence on wage labour, which is vulnerable to both climatic and economic shocks.

Conclusion and six recommendations

Although the synergies between sustainable development and climate change adaptation appear self-evident, the disconnect that continues between the conceptual and practical elements in both fields highlights the need for a re-evaluation. Findings from this research reaffirm the need for conceptual frameworks to be broadened: resilience must become a core consideration in sustainable development while climate change adaptation must take account of multiple drivers of vulnerability beyond those linked to climate shocks and stressors alone. Local peoples' knowledge and experience offer strong signposts for how external support to adaptation and development can be improved. In this research, households were adapting and innovating by themselves, but faced barriers to accessing and using external support and in scaling up those strategies that worked. Hence, strategies aimed at building resilience for rural communities in developing countries should take into consideration the following recommendations.

1 Broad-based rural development strategies are required to increase resilience

The overall livelihoods mix determines the resilience of households. Increasing agricultural resilience, while necessary, is not sufficient to increase overall resilience. More broad-based rural development strategies that reduce dependency on a narrow range of climate dependent livelihood options are required, especially those that support the creation of non-farm livelihood strategies.

2 The design and implementation of effective support to adaptation should be embedded within agricultural and rural development programmes

Development actors must recognise climate variability and change as an important additional stressor on already-vulnerable livelihood systems, which directly affect households and their livelihoods, as well as interacting with and exacerbating other drivers of vulnerability. This research highlights the need to go beyond a snapshot view of household strategies, and to take account of the multiple livelihood stressors households are responding to when designing adaptation interventions. While vertical programmes that address climate change can support the scaling up of resources, care must be taken to ensure adequate recognition of the context within which climate vulnerability is occurring. The barriers and constraints that some households face in accessing or benefitting from support highlights the need for institutional actors to improve their strategies for targeting and tailoring support. Institutional support must be adequate, appropriate and adaptable. In other words, support should be sufficient in its scope and coverage to meet the needs of the target group; due consideration should be given to the different needs of beneficiaries, especially the most vulnerable; and support should be flexible enough to allow for uncertainty and change.

3 Investment in agriculture, particularly low-input, agro-ecological approaches and rural development, needs to be scaled up

This study has found that institutional support is inadequate and results in limited impacts and unreached potential. This highlights the need for increased investment in agriculture and rural development, placing the rights and resilience of the most vulnerable communities at the centre. This should include increased investment in agricultural research, particularly in low-input, agro-ecological approaches, as well as pilot projects and extension services, which should be as close as possible to the community level, incorporating and building on existing knowledge, practices and institutions. Assistance for the creation of non-farm income sources is also critical for diversified livelihoods and increased resilience to multiple livelihoods shocks and stressors.

4 Governments, NGOs and other institutions with greater access to information and technology should assess and address the implications of tensions and trade-offs in strategies being promoted

The findings in this study acknowledge and reflect the fact that there is no silver bullet that will solve and serve adaptation, and that strategies must be both context specific and dynamic to enhance resilience in managing uncertainty. In situations where existing poverty levels render people ill-equipped to deal with current climate events, short-term needs may be met without addressing long-term vulnerability, or at the risk of undermining long-term resilience. The promotion of intensive agriculture has implications for soil fertility and productivity, which needs to be acknowledged and addressed, as do the risks of locking households into pathways that are dependent on high-cost external inputs. Where tensions or trade-offs are unavoidable in the short term, these must be managed and a strategy for transition to approaches that are more socially, economically and ecologically sustainable incorporated. For example, given the predictions for increasing water scarcity, external institutions promoting irrigation-dependent crops to improve households' current production and income levels should ensure that soil and water conservation strategies are strengthened in order to reduce water demand in the future.

5 Socio-economic integration, political participation and the realisation of rights of vulnerable households is critical to securing resilient livelihoods outcomes

The four case studies show that a variety of government policies related to agriculture, land and water influence households' ability to adapt to stressors: while some have been developed partly in response to climate change adaptation imperatives, others have not. A holistic and horizontal approach to development at national level is needed to ensure a new type of policy coherence which makes all policies and sectors, whether rural/agricultural or otherwise, more resilient by taking into account climate change adaptation. A critical question, however, is what or whose interests are at the centre of these policies, and who stands to lose or gain in their implementation. This study has reaffirmed that those who are vulnerable to the additional stressors resulting from increased climate variability are the same households whose ability to cope with existing livelihoods shocks and stressors is already in deficit. A rights-based approach, guided by the principles of human rights and social justice, is needed to ensure policies and support for adaptation focus on the most vulnerable and empower them to secure their rights, while enhancing the government's ability to promote, protect and fulfil them.

6 Inequitable access to resources, such as land and water, must be addressed to improve climate resilience

The studies have confirmed that declining access to natural resources is a key limiting factor in households' options and abilities to adapt their livelihoods to additional stressors. Policies and frameworks that promote more equitable access to resources are needed at both the national and local level to address current and future challenges around increasing competition for resources, such as access to land and water, for small-scale producers and vulnerable groups.

Note

1   A partner organisation is another civil society organisation that Trócaire supports in some form to achieve mutually agreed objectives, with the ultimate aim of serving the basic needs and supporting the rights of poor and marginalised people in the developing world.

References

AfDB *et al.* (2003). *Poverty and Climate Change: Reducing the Vulnerability of the Poor through Adaptation.* Nairobi: UNEP.
Bahadur, A.V., Ibrahim, M., and Tanner, T. (2010). *The Resilience Renaissance? Unpacking of Resilience for Tackling Climate Change and Disasters.* Strengthening Climate Resilience Discussion Paper 1, IDS, Brighton, online: http://community.eldis. org/.59e0d267/resilience-renaissance.pdf (accessed 04.03.2013).
Barnett, J. and O'Neill, S. (2010). 'Maladaptation', *Global Environmental Change*, vol. 20, pp. 211–213.
Burton, I. and May, E. (2004). 'The Adaptation Deficit in Water Resources Management', *IDS Bulletin*, vol. 35, no. 3, pp. 31–37.
Eriksen, S. *et al.* (2011). 'When Not Every Response to Climate Change is a Good One: Identifying Principles for Sustainable Adaptation', *Climate and Development*, vol. 3, no. 1, pp. 7–20.
Mitchell, T. and Maxwell, S. (2010). *Defining Climate Compatible Development*, Climate & Development Knowledge Network (CDKN), London, online: http://www.cdkn. org/wp-content/uploads/2011/02/CDKN-CCD-DIGI-MASTER-19NOV.pdf (accessed 04.03.2013).
Scoones, I. (1998). *Sustainable Rural Livelihoods: A Framework for Analysis*, IDS Working Paper 72, Brighton: Institute of Development Studies.
Silva-Villanueva, P. (2011). *Learning to ADAPT: Monitoring and Evaluation Approaches in Climate Change Adaptation and Disaster Risk Reduction – Challenges, Gaps and Ways Forward*, Strengthening Climate Resilience Discussion Paper 9, Brighton: Institute of Development Studies, online: www.csdrm.org (accessed 04.03.2013).

4 Climate change adaptation in southern Benin

A multi-scale perspective on rural communities of Mono and Couffo

Marie-Ange Baudoin

Climate change and the challenge for adaptation in Benin

According to the Intergovernmental Panel on Climate Change (IPCC) reports on climate change, Sub-Saharan Africa (SSA) is highly vulnerable (IPCC 2001; 2007; 2012). Adverse climate effects in this region include hydrologic stresses, temperature increase and sea level rise. The changes are expected during this century, and some of them, for example increased temperature, have already been observed (IPCC 2007: 444–451). However, major gaps remain in the study of CC in Africa: this recent field of research suffers from a lack of qualitative and quantitative data, for example SSA only has one eighth of the number of meteorological stations recommended by the World Meteorological Organisation and many established installations are not functional (Hellmuth *et al.* 2007: 10). As a consequence, current and future CC impacts have not been precisely assessed yet; the distinction between CC – referring to long-term trends in temperature or rainfall – and climate variability – referring to trends in the shorter term (ibid.: 4–5) – sometimes remains unclear.

Southern Benin is already facing, or is very likely to face, CC impacts. Despite a lack of accuracy of current climate predictions, studies (Ago *et al.* 2005; Ahomadegbe *et al.* in review; Hountondji & Ozer 2010) have suggested more variable rain patterns, including increased droughts, floods and excessive rainfall (with high variation at the local level); higher average temperature has already been observed. These climate stresses, whether linked to CC or variability, have negative impacts on rain-fed agriculture, which remains the main source of income and food for the majority of Benin's rural population (Dovenon 2010), thus endangering food security and farmers' incomes.

The present case study analyses the causes for South Beninese farmers' vulnerability to CC from a local-to-national perspective, and with a focus on institutional capacities to reduce CC vulnerabilities. It analyses farmers' current responses to observed climate stresses and the efficiency of national and international support to climate change adaptation (CCA). The research is based on data collected in southern Benin[1] through interviews and group discussions with farmers, representatives from public institutions and NGOs, as well as relevant literature and reports, which were used to define research approaches and concepts and to support the findings.

Acknowledging that the scientific validity of current CC impacts in southern Benin cannot be precisely assessed due to the lack of data and recent field study, the focus of this study is on what climate perturbations, or increased climate variability, are felt by farmers at the local level; these are referred to as 'observed climate perturbations/stresses'. Farmers' responses to these observations will be assessed through field surveys. Many studies (Hesse *et al.* 2006; Macchi 2008; Pouliotte *et al.* 2009; Cuni-Sanchez *et al.* 2012) have underlined local 'indigenous' practices to deal with climate variability by adjusting agricultural techniques. This local knowledge in Africa is also being promoted as 'good practice' for CCA, for example within the UNFCCC's NAPAs.

NAPAs are promoted in order to help countries with low human development, such as Benin, to face CC impacts more successfully (PNUD 2008); they are supported through the Least Developed Country Fund (LDCF) managed by the Global Environment Facility (GEF). These programmes aim at meeting the urgent adaptation needs of the sectors considered very vulnerable to CC, such as water management, food security or health, and they must strengthen local institutional capacities necessary to deal with future CC. Adaptation projects within NAPAs are supposed to be prepared in a bottom-up approach, rely on local knowledge on climate adaptation and, after a successful implementation of local initiatives in pilot areas, be scaled up. In 2008, a NAPA was launched in Benin, and the funding to implement its first adaptation project has been released.[2]

This chapter analyses both national and international capacities to reduce Beninese farmers' climate vulnerabilities through the NAPA approach. The research method adopted uses the concept of vulnerability as defined in the IPCC's 2007 report on climate change as a function of exposure, sensibility and the adaptive capacity of a system to face CC. While exposure and sensibility refer to the nature of the experienced stress, and the degree to which it affects a system (due to its nature), adaptive capacity – also defined as capacity to deal with a stress – are linked to, or built in, a specific societal context characterised by distinctive socio-economic, institutional, cultural, etc. factors (IPCC 2007: 720). A growing number of studies have underlined the contribution of these societal factors to CC vulnerability; for instance, Kelly & Adger (2000), Adger *et al.* (2001), Leary *et al.* (2008), Magnan (2009) and Schipper (2009).

Based on the above-mentioned research, this chapter focuses on societal factors with the aim of understanding farmers' climate vulnerability in southern Benin. The assumption is that vulnerability does not rely mainly on CC impacts, but rather is built through societal processes. The research provides insights into climate vulnerabilities with a multi-scale perspective, linking local data collected in the field with analysis of national socio-economic and institutional factors in Benin, and the findings are used to assess local adaptation needs and capacity in Benin, as well as to identify weaknesses in national and international support for adaptation. Due to limits of the present research, the details provided mainly refer to institutions, their contribution to local climate vulnerability, and their impacts regarding national and international capacity to support adaptation. In essence, international adaptation support is studied through the NAPA framework.

Although some results may be specific to the southern Benin case, more general suggestions to strengthen local adaptation capacities and to reconsider adaptation within international policies are provided as conclusions.

Benin as a case study: methodological reflections

Case selection: departments of Mono and Couffo in southern Benin

The southern part of Benin, itself a small country within western Africa, is characterised by a high density of the majoritarian rural population (60 per cent).[3] Since over one third of the population lives on less than a dollar per day, poverty is an important issue, reflected by the country's categorisation as 'Low Human Development' (PNUD 2008). The research was carried out in Mono and Couffo (Figure 4.1), both situated in southern Benin. These departments were chosen as cases due to their similar socio-economic, institutional, religious and cultural contexts, as well as their seasonal patterns. These similarities are expected to help in highlighting the societal factors which contribute to climate vulnerabilities in southern Benin. However, choosing very different case study sites would allow for comparison between regions and could be an extension of the current research.

Benin's gross domestic product (GDP) relies mainly on agriculture (with a share of over 30 per cent), and on the export of agricultural products, such as cotton. Subsistence farming is the main activity of the rural population (Dovenon 2010). In southern Benin, maize is the main food crop; beans and peanuts are the

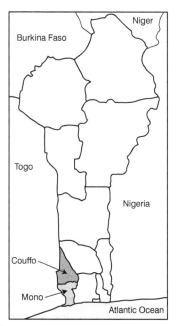

Figure 4.1 The selected departments for household discussions in southern Benin, with regard to climatic zone and socio-political context

main vegetables (Van den Akker 2000). Rice production tends to increase because of the presence of suitable fertile soil in the riverbeds, and because of support from state and foreign development projects to respond to increased internal consumption, mostly from the urban population (Van den Akker 2000). Aside from a few large government-supported projects, farmers' food-crop production remains small scale and does not always cover food needs. Ineffective agricultural policies and the lack of support for family-run production, overexploited soils, small field size (linked to the high population density),[4] use of manual tools and some climate hazards contribute to this sometimes precarious situation in rural areas (INSAE 2004: 5).

In order to pay for food, schooling, transportation, health care or religious ceremonies, farmers have to complement food-crop production with other activities (e.g. selling wood, crafts or transformed products[5] along the roads; animal husbandry; fishing; temporary work in town). Another consequence of poor livelihood conditions in rural areas is the migration of many young, job-seeking people to cities or neighbouring countries (Albert 1993).

Since the beginning of the 1990s, Benin has been a multi-party democracy. Following a decentralisation process that started in 2003, municipalities and mayors received new responsibilities for managing the villages, but with insufficient financial or human means for execution (Banégas 2003). With respect to agriculture, the Centre Régional de Promotion de l'Agriculture (CeRPA), a decentralised institution of the Ministry of Agriculture, is in charge of training and technical advisory services for farmers at the local level. However, their means and knowledge to help farmers are limited, and due to unfulfilled promises or unsuccessful advice, farmers tend to mistrust this institution (Hountondji in Amin *et al.* 2000). Finally, state institutions and their representatives at the local level are often criticised for corruption, which is confirmed by the UNDP corruption index (PNUD 2008) and Transparency International's corruption rate which classified Benin in 2009[6] as 106th out of 180 states surveyed. Hence, the rural population remains close to traditional authorities such as animist chiefs (Voodoo), although their power is symbolic (Banégas 2003).

During the democratisation process, numerous NGOs have been created and become active in Benin as registered entities recognised by the government. Their characterisation as 'non-governmental' has been questioned by Pirotte and Poncelet (2003) and Poncelet *et al.* (2006) in this context, as they can implement both state development policies and international development projects. NGO members are often young educated people, who are unable to find a job due to the economic context in Benin, and take advantage of the work opportunities offered by NGOs.[7]

Other civil society organisations at the local level are comprised of farmers' groups and farmers' unions. Unlike NGOs, these organisations are currently not formally supported by the public sector, although historically they have been set up by the state with the aim of improving cotton production; farmers' groups were unpopular and tended to decrease with the decline of this export crop. Today, however, it seems that farmers' groups and unions are slowly (re-)emerging to sustain food crops, but their current means and level of organisation are still very weak, while farmers have turned to food-crop production on an individual basis. Members of groups and unions are illiterate farmers or with little education. Financial capacity is weak, as farmers' groups and unions do not receive public subsidies and rely only on members' contributions. A certain lack of willingness to work in groups in the field was also pointed out by Hountondji (in Amin *et al.* 2000) as to partly explain the weak organisational structure of food-crop production in southern Benin.

Benin is a tropical country, which comprises three different agro-climatic areas. The villages studied in the departments of Mono and Couffo are located in a humid area characterised by average annual rainfall between 800 and 1100 mm (INSAE 2004: 3) and a bimodal rainfall regime: the main rainy season from mid-March to July, and the shorter one from September to November; two dry periods separate the rain seasons during which farmers grow maize. The Couffo and the Mono Rivers cross both departments and some of the villages studied, usually swelling around September or October and causing important floods in some areas.

Qualitative case study analysis: data acquisition and evaluation

This study is of an exploratory, inductive nature. The research process was therefore open and based on document analysis, qualitative interviews and focus group discussions. The interviews were conducted during three field trips to Benin[8] during which time was divided between stays in villages to observe and have discussions with farmers and representatives from local institutions, and stays in Cotonou to interview state officials and representatives of international development co-operation.

Individual and focus group interviews were carried out within 46 households from seven villages in the departments of Mono and Couffo. Farmers were selected on the basis of two main criteria: (1) having grown up in the village, and (2) subsistence agriculture being their main economic activity essentially for personal consumption. Research samples therefore included people with a similar socio-economic background, who were able to witness climatic changes from their childhood (referred to during discussions as *au temps des parents* – at the parents' time) until now. Some farmers interviewed were involved in agricultural development projects supported through international co-operation policies. Protos is a Belgian development agency whose projects are implemented by local Beninese NGOs under the supervision of Protos' representatives in Benin. Protos-supported projects typically aimed at improving water management and increasing food security through the promotion of rice cultivation during both rainy and dry seasons through support for irrigation.[9] Some participants in the research were also part of the first preparation phase of Benin's NAPA. These particularities were used to compare responses from farmers involved in international-supported activities and independent ones. Focus groups comprised either members of the same gender or of similar age; these were used to cross-check information from individual households. Interviews were undertaken in the local language, since few local farmers know French. Beninese interpreters translated questions and responses. Due to the variety of local languages in southern Benin it was not possible to keep the same interpreter for all interviews, but they were always persons known and trusted by the local community, often involved in a local NGO active in the neighbourhood.

After having spent two to three days within a village – for observation of habits and for them to get to know us – volunteer participants were chosen with the help of the interpreter and asked questions regarding their observation of climatic changes in the area and how they influenced their agricultural activities. They were asked to:

*   compare the personally perceived seasons and weather patterns as they are now with those at the time when they were younger (à *l'époque des parents – at the parents' time*);
*   outline their agricultural (or other) activities during observed climate stresses;
*   describe what support they received from local institutions or organisations while their economic activities were challenged by climate stresses.

Interviews were not exempt of risks, misunderstandings or biases as most of the participants were unfamiliar with the concept of CC and the interpreters unaware of the research goals. To avoid misinterpretation, data collected on observed climate changes was cross-checked with literature on CC in southern Benin and with similar research involving interviews of farmers: see for example Ago *et al.* (2005), Ernest *et al.* (2008), and Hountondji & Ozer (2010). Cross-checking results on agricultural activities with relevant literature also confirmed the use of similar agricultural practices (to those described by the farmers) in SSA to face CC and variability: for instance in Breusers *et al.* (1997), Raynaut (1997), Thebaud (2002), and Aho (2007), as well as in Benin's NAPA (MEPN 2008: 49). Most interviews with farmers were held without appointment, which sometimes resulted in an abrupt end to the discussions before all questions were asked, depending on the farmers' working schedule. Looking at all interviews together was useful to compare and complete missing data.

At the institutional level, interviews were led in municipalities, with mayors and their deputies, with agents from the CeRPA, state officials involved in the NAPA process, the person from the Ministry of Environment in charge of that programme, and with international development co-operation agents posted in Cotonou, for example Belgian 'Cooperation Technique Belge', and the Danish international development agency DANIDA. These discussions were held in French and were by prior appointment.

Through field research and discussions with institutional and civil actors at local to national levels in Benin, this research contributes insights regarding the causes of farmers' vulnerability to CC. Based on previous work led by Adger *et al.* (2001), Leary *et al.* (2008) and O'Brien *et al.* (2010), these causes were expected to be mainly linked to socio-economic weaknesses, cultural and religious characteristics, or institutional deficits; due to the multiplicity of these factors, the current study focused on the last category, which is often poorly addressed as part of CCA activities. Findings on vulnerability analysis were compared with the preparation and content of the NAPA to check whether it was likely to contribute to reducing farmers' vulnerability to CC.

Empirical results

As mentioned above, participants were asked to describe any changes in climate patterns observed since their childhood, including the occurrence of new, more intense or more frequent climate stresses/variability – such as extreme rainfalls or strong winds. These were referred to as 'climate perturbations' or 'climate stresses'. Personal losses or damage resulting from these perturbations were underlined. Participants were also asked to describe the practices or activities currently used during climate stresses, whether they were related to agriculture or not, and the person from whom they had acquired the practice – parents or outsiders such as technical trainers from CeRPA or other organisations.

The impact of climatic modification on agricultural activities and farmers

Observed climate perturbations are indicated in Figure 4.2. Changes in rain patterns reflected in the delay of the main rainfall period was strongly felt by most participants and described as new compared to other climate perturbations, such as drought pockets or heavy rainfalls: although these last stresses were felt during childhood, participants claimed that they had recently become more severe or frequent. Some observations were felt everywhere, while others were rather local, for example phenomena such as greater winds, heat or more insects.

Figure 4.2 shows that most farmers have noticed:

- a delay of the main rainfall season by at least one month;
- severe floods for those living near the Mono River or caused by heavy rain during the beginning of the primary (April or May) and the small rainfall season (August or September);
- that rain is also more erratic than before during the main rainfall period, multiplying the drought pockets or period of excessive rain.

Notwithstanding the aforementioned gaps in climate predictions in Africa and lack of data to scientifically assess all forms of CC in Benin, combining individual interviews in several villages with focus groups, and cross-checking field results with other research on CC within Benin, such as Ago *et al*. (2005), Ernest *et al*. (2008), Ahomadegbe *et al*. (2010), Hountondji & Ozer (2010) and Cuni-Sanchez *et al*. (2012), as well as the IPCC's 2007 report on Africa, allows the following assessment of CC in southern Benin:

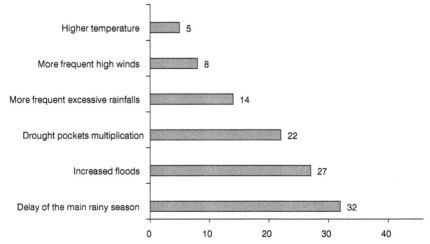

Figure 4.2 Climate perturbations observed by local farmers, and number of households that observed each phenomenon from a total of 46 (based on discussions with farmers)

- temperature has increased during the last decades, as scientific evidence from IPCC's 2007 report supports; however, this increase was not felt by many participants;
- delayed rainy seasons have been suggested from precipitation analysis in Ahomadegbe *et al.* (2010) and in Baudoin (2012); they were greatly felt by participants, although more scientific evidence would be needed to confirm this;
- changes in rainfall patterns within rainy seasons (more heterogeneity) had not been scientifically assessed due to the lack of data and the high variability of rain at the local level; however, they were observed by participants in the form of more frequent drought pockets and heavier rainfalls;
- more frequent strong winds were also underlined in farmers' statements in this research, as well as in Ahomadegbe *et al.* (2010), although this cannot be scientifically assessed due to lack of data.

Local variation of these perturbations could be observed in the field as not all participants experienced all climate perturbations to the same extent.

Farmers' cultivation activities are consequently affected by observed perturbations. Moreover, heavy rains felt during July, August and September cause floods and destroy maize crops. Increased floods in some areas of southern Benin have been confirmed by the literature (see Ago *et al.* 2005: 5–10), but, so far, there have not been any conclusive results on their exact causes. The reasons for aggravated floods are manifold:

- changes in rainfall patterns;
- demographic pressure in the south with more people living along the riverside;
- intensive land use;

- riverbank development;
- deforestation;
- construction of a dam on the Mono River.

The villagers confirmed that the observed CC stressors tended to increase pressure on local livelihoods. They identified the following main consequences as a result of the above-outlined climatic modifications:

- Maize cannot be grown during the small rainfall season as before because the soil is flooded by excessive rainfalls or swelled rivers.
- Yields are affected during the main rainfall period because of erratic rainfall and a delayed start of the rainfall season, which renders farmers completely uncertain about the appropriate time for sowing.

The resulting weak yields are also associated with other socio-economic conditions, such as lack of access to appropriate equipment (tractor or machine for husking rice), sufficient labour force, expensive inputs for improvement of yields (fertiliser, pesticides), agricultural training and additional income sources from complementary activities.

Adaptation of agricultural activities

Figure 4.3 sums up the agricultural activities and practices used by participants when confronted with observed climate perturbations. It appears that not all are aimed at adapting food-crop production to climate perturbations, and not all contribute to reduce related agricultural vulnerabilities. Many activities (e.g. fishing and animal husbandry) were not directly induced by observed climate

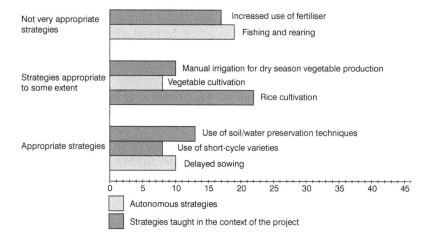

Figure 4.3 Agricultural strategies used by households, number of households using each strategy, and adequacy with climate change adaptation

perturbations, as farmers would resort to them whether their agricultural activities were challenged by CC or not (see earlier in this chapter); however, farmers tend to resort to them more frequently now that their yields are affected by new climate stresses. It also appeared that some practices, such as rice production, are already challenged under the current climate stresses.

In Figure 4.3, observed agricultural activities were classified according to three categories regarding the way they are related or respond to observed climate perturbations:

- the 'not very appropriate strategies' illustrate activities that are not addressing CC impacts on agriculture under current climate conditions;
- the 'strategies appropriate to some extent' were not implemented in order to respond to climate changes but contribute to improve food-crop production under current climatic conditions;
- the 'appropriate strategies' were specifically implemented to respond to observed climate perturbations.

The horizontal axis of Figure 4.3 shows the number of farmers that mentioned the activity and illustrate how frequently activities linked to climate adaptation are used amongst the rural population of southern Benin, and whether farmers were trained in them by outsiders or acted on their own. This information is analysed below.

The practice of delayed sowing is applied in a context where the beginning of the main rainfall season is late. It directly responds to recent changes in climate patterns, as farmers observe a delay in the start of the main rainy season. In this context, they tend to wait for the first raindrop before sowing, delaying the 'usual' date sometimes by a full month compared to the normal start of the season (at the beginning of March).

The use of different seed varieties, which need a shorter growth period, is an adaptive response to the erratic rainfalls during the main rainfall season and, due to current observations of increased frequency of drought pockets and a shorter duration of the rainfall period, it contributes to food-crop production adaptation. This reaction was quoted during the survey of farmers involved in Protos development projects. These projects were not aimed at, or labelled as, CCA, but promoted food security, for example by training and access to agricultural inputs; in Mono and Couffo, farmers learned to use short cycle varieties with a growth period of 2.5 months.

Two other techniques for the preservation of soil fertility and water, classified as responding to climate perturbations, were reported by farmers involved in the same Protos development projects who provided respective training: *zaï* and mulch protect soil against direct solar irradiation, preventing evaporation and seeds from burning, and the construction of small dams and embankments safeguard fields against floods or keep the water on the field during a dry period.

The shift to rice cultivation was also promoted through Protos' projects. This shift could be related to climate adaptation as in most cases rice was developed on unused land with the appropriate characteristics: since flooding is increasing, probably at least to some extent due to CC, more areas are becoming suitable for rice instead of maize farming. As the main reason for the support of rice production is the goal of satisfying Benin's internal rice consumption, this was classified as 'related to some extent' to climate perturbations. Rice production is already challenged by extended floods in some research areas, a fact discussed in the next section.

Gardening and cultivation of different crops during both the rainfall and the dry periods (using irrigation) were reported by farmers as to mainly provide alternative sources of income; however, it contributes to the diversification of varieties, thus reducing the risk of losing all food crops as a result of high rainfall variability. Irrigated gardening decreases rain dependency, and, grown during both rainy and dry periods, vegetables can provide a source of income the whole year round. Protos' projects made water available through the construction of wells or ponds. In other areas outside Protos' projects, farmers would produce vegetables in smaller quantities during the rainy seasons as additional source of income (see above).

Fishing and animal husbandry have been developed for decades to complement the economic results from crops. In the context of CC, relying on non-weather-related activities may reduce climate vulnerability, although food crops remain the key economic activity in rural areas. Finally, participants reported an increased use of fertiliser. Whereas this practice may improve yields in the short term, chemicals can have long-term negative impacts on soil and water and are expensive, which is why mainly participants involved in development projects obtained access to expensive fertilisers. Fishing, animal husbandry and the use of fertiliser are not aimed at adapting food-crop production to climate or to observed climate perturbations.

Adaptation by non-agricultural activities

In addition to the agricultural activities mentioned in Figure 4.3, other non-agricultural practices, which do not involve agricultural work nor improve yields, were used by participants to meet their socio-economic needs or to face losses in food-crop production. These are presented in Figure 4.4, with the horizontal axis showing the number of participants who mentioned the practice.

Except for reforestation, which was only mentioned by two participants as reducing the impact of stronger winds and taught in the context of a development project, the non-agricultural activities were applied autonomously; they mainly rely on experience (taught by parents, according to farmers) and are not new or specific to CCA, being applied whether climate perturbations are felt or not. In recent times, however, farmers have resorted to them more frequently, when facing yield losses due to increased climate perturbations. Some activities can even enhance vulnerability, for example increased work in town intensifies the rural exodus and brain drain, which in turn reduces the number of young people available for agricultural work (Johnson *et al.* 2006). Several participants complained about a lack of available labour for fieldwork.

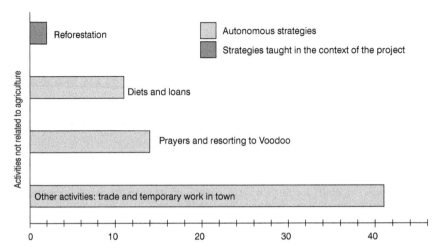

Figure 4.4 Other strategies used by households, and number of households using each strategy

Religious activities, such as prayers (asking the gods for more rain or better yields) and small sacrifices of animals, are frequent in some regions of southern Benin. Loans and diets were described as necessary when none of the above-mentioned practices could produce sufficient food or income to meet the needs of the family, and consequently this renders the local population even more vulnerable.

Discussion of results

Adaptation efforts

Farmers mentioned many activities that are not really specific to CCA. Some of these do not even contribute to reducing the increased vulnerability of farmers by sustaining or improving crop production in the context of a climate disruptive event. In fact, most of them have been used for decades to meet socio-economic needs (school, health, etc.) by complementing food-crop production with income from the production of other varieties (such as vegetables through gardening) or fishing. Observed activities were either taught by parents, relied on experience (autonomous activities are represented in gray bars in Figures 4.2 and 4.3), or were learned through development projects, which involved local NGOs (regarding Protos' agricultural projects, they are represented in black bars in Figures 4.2 and 4.3). None of them was seen as a 'CCA strategy' by the participants; most of them ignored the concept of CC and its implications for food-crop production, although a few activities were guided by changes in climate patterns (for instance, delayed sowing in response to delayed rainfall periods). None involved a long-term perspective, which anticipates future CC. However, some appear more resilient to current climate stresses than others, which is why this section uses the following classification for summarising observed activities and agricultural practices, and to assess their relevance as CCA strategies: autonomous activities, development co-operation-induced activities and climate-induced activities.

Autonomous activities

This category includes:
- fishing and animal husbandry;
- gardening during rainy season;
- trade and temporary work in town;
- loans and diets;
- prayers and resorting to Voodoo.

Farmers have always relied on temporary work in town, fishing (when situated near a river) or selling handcraft or vegetables in village markets to improve income; such practices were widespread among participants, whether they were involved in a development project or not, and are also described in studies on farmers' practices in Africa, for example in Breussers *et al.* (1997) and in Raynaut (1997). Trade and temporary work in towns are well-established strategies in Africa, carried out mainly for economic reasons (Rain 1999). They provide a source of income, which is not influenced by CC, and complement food-crop production whether climate changes are felt or not; but they do not contribute to adapting agriculture, which remains the main activity in rural areas and main income source within the studied communities, to CC.

Our results show that farmers actually turn to these activities more often – when food-crop production is threatened or undermined by new climate stresses – and when fishing or trading is not sufficient to compensate for crop losses. Some households cannot avoid resorting to loans and diets. The need to find new sources of income can lead farmers to leave their village in search of temporary work in town, eventually resulting in a labour shortage in rural areas and increasing vulnerability in villages. Finally, religious beliefs also guide investment, as some farmers rely on Voodoo sorcery to improve yields or call for rain, or, as during past decades, to face other types of stresses, such as social and chronic family problems (Thebaud 2002).

Development co-operation-induced activities

This category includes:
- increased use of fertiliser;
- gardening all year long through irrigation;
- rice cultivation;
- use of soil preservation techniques;
- use of short cycle varieties;
- reforestation.

The use of varieties with short growth periods and training on easy and cheap agricultural techniques, such as *zaï* or embankment, were used to face CC perturbations. However, in the cases studied, these techniques were only available to farmers trained through Protos' development projects by authorised local NGOs. Access to new varieties is often limited by their cost, market availability, or knowledge of how to use these or related agricultural practices. The same conclusions apply for the diversification of varieties, for example through vegetable cultivation during dry seasons using irrigation, or rice cultivation: it reduces climate vulnerability but is only available to farmers with permanent access to water and training on how to grow new crops or varieties.

The replacement of maize farming by rice cultivation has had varied results according to where it has been implemented. Although the shift has been a success in terms of adapting food-crop production to appropriate land, some areas suffer extended floods, a factor not addressed as part of the projects' promotion of rice production; consequently, in some areas, the newly introduced rice crop is already challenged by the high intensity of floods, and farmers who live close to a river risk losing the entire harvest, as well as their houses.

Fertiliser promoted through some development projects often is chemical not organic fertiliser (as observed in the Protos' projects). Training to use organic fertiliser, which is cheaper and less noxious to soil and water resources, is an alternative to chemical fertiliser, but also needs external provision of training. However, this was not observed in the studied areas and is not yet a priority within Benin's agricultural sector.[10]

Climate-induced strategies

This category includes:
• delayed sowing.

Delayed sowing is used as a direct response to the late arrival of the main rainy season. The same practice was reported from farmers in the north of Benin in the study by Cuni-Sanchez *et al*. (2012). However, this autonomous adaptation strategy, applied without knowledge of the weather forecast (reflecting daily or weekly atmospheric conditions), seemed unable to respond to the delay of the rainfall season: farmers admitted waiting for the first raindrop to arrive before sowing, which can be a full month after the 'normal' start of the rainfall period, and which implies the risk of losing all crops if the rain stops again a few days later. In this case, resorting to the above-mentioned autonomous activities remained their main response to feeding their families.

Study results indicate that without external assistance – in most cases provided in the field by local NGOs – farmers are becoming more vulnerable, and face yield losses as a result of observed climate stresses or increased climate variability, such as erratic rainfalls. Risks of food insecurity or economic breakdown are indeed present, while autonomous activities remain unable to compensate for decreased yields. If poverty and the widespread reliance on rain-fed agriculture can partly explain farmers' current climate vulnerability, results also show that the use of low-cost soil and water preservation techniques or diversification of varieties can reduce this vulnerability. These techniques, however, require external support, facilitating access to new inputs (e.g. improved seeds), appropriate training, the promotion of rice culture, use of new seeds and dry season agriculture. The case studies also show that development projects aiming at improved food-crop production are already challenged by increased climate variability; in flood-prone areas, rice culture promotion has led some participants to lose their seasonal yield (the same observation can be drawn regarding the long-term impacts of chemical instead of organic fertiliser). In this case, the term 'maladaptation' can be used, referring to a situation where current (and future) climate trends are not integrated into the promoted agricultural activities, causing present or future damage to food-crop production.

The role of local actors: institutions, farmers' unions and NGOs

Exposure to climate stressors alone cannot explain why farmers are vulnerable (Pouliotte *et al.* 2009), as the presence of climate-resilient activities afield illustrates. The lack of support and training and a limited knowledge of CC at the local level, including no access to climate forecasts, are responsible for increased food insecurity in some of the studied areas. It appears that the weaknesses of local institutions in southern Benin can partly explain current farmers' climate vulnerability; and while local institutions, such as municipalities and CeRPAs, at present lack the capacity to effectively help farmers, the farmers in return revealed a lack of trust in state representatives during discussions and highlighted the role of local NGOs in providing missing training and assistance.

Farmers were asked about the role of local authorities in helping them to face climate hazards' impacts, such as yield losses; results showed that farmers remain largely isolated within villages and receive little assistance from municipalities or the CeRPA, whose role is to train farmers and disseminate improved production techniques. The discussions with farmers' households showed mistrust at the local level towards these state representatives as a main feature: CeRPA agents, municipalities and mayors were seen as distant and not concerned with the farmers' worries, and as lacking capacity to help.

CeRPAs were criticised for their absence in the field, or, when present, for their inability to answer farmers' needs or the inaccuracy of the advice provided, a usual problem of agricultural extension. Participants pointed to the missing specialisation in any crop variety and the lack of valid specific advice on how to grow a particular crop in the current circumstances. Municipalities have received many new responsibilities since the decentralisation process (launched in Benin in 2003); literature (Auracher and Ulricht 2010) and interviews with mayors and their representatives showed that the central government's financial support is weak and does not allow the implementation of the rural district's annual development plan and the new responsibilities. These weak capacities also undermine their ability to manage climate-related risks, or to respond to CC impacts. Neither the

CeRPAs nor the municipalities are informed on CC issues as these are not taken into consideration by the annual development plan. Consequently, the institutions are unable to respond to farmers' concerns regarding food-crop production, and, in the case of a specific crisis such as severe floods, the mayor typically has to turn to the central government for supplies or tents to help the population to cope with the threats.

Up till now, associations of farmers, farmers' groups at the village level and farmers' unions at regional level have made little impact in southern Benin; in the field, the observed general preference amongst farmers for family work (rather than work in groups) is confirmed in studies by Hountondji (in Amin *et al.* 2000). Field observation and discussions with farmers showed that although unions are more appreciated than state institutions (as their members are part of the local community), they remain unable to implement specific activities or to advise farmers, due either to missing skills or financial and technical means.

In contrast to all other institutions and organisations, interviews showed an appreciation of local NGOs as having more capacity to implement specific actions. Some participants involved with local NGOs in the context of development projects underlined all the benefits brought by their training or easier access to some agricultural inputs or tools; other participants not involved in development projects claimed their need to be trained and helped by local NGOs. The members of local NGOs often belong to the community or live nearby, and are trusted. But their activities depend on foreign aid, and their scope of action is limited to certain farmers and areas. Finally, some NGO activities are also challenged by CC impacts, such as severe floods, which threaten rice production in some of the studied areas; this reflects the fact that CC is not well known in Benin and not explicitly taken into account within international development co-operation activities, agricultural sector policy or projects.

The role of local traditional authorities cannot be neglected in southern Benin; interviews with farmers showed the relevance of religious answers to climate hazards and the trust of rural people towards their Voodoo sorcerers (*note*: the relevance of religion varies highly from one village to another). Adaptation 'responses' such as prayers and calls of Voodoo priests were quoted. The mystical perception of climate and the attribution of new phenomena to unnatural causes is stronger in some areas (shown by the variability of 'resorting to Voodoo' as a response to climate perturbations) and led some participants to reject scientific explanations for CC.

Three main observations can be drawn from the study of local actors and their role in reducing climate vulnerability. Firstly, the study of local institutions suggests that they may not be able to reduce CC vulnerability in their current situation. However, they remain closer to farmers than central government institutions and, in contrast to NGOs, their scope of action should enable them to reach a large number of villages. At present, their weak capacities do not allow them to fulfil current responsibilities and provide appropriate training to local actors; the latter could be part of the adaptation process based on the identified causes of vulnerability. The lack of dialogue between farmers and state representatives contributes to the feeling of being decoupled from local concerns and needs, which in turn increases the lack of trust that characterises the present relationship between farmers and local state representatives.

Secondly, local development activities, when implemented through local NGOs, seem to have a positive impact on reducing farmers' climate vulnerabilities; the more climate-resilient activities were implemented through development co-operation projects, in which local NGOs provided training and technical assistance to farmers. In the context of international co-operation, these structures tend to compensate for weak municipalities. They strengthen local development processes – and poor CeRPA agents – and provide training and technical assistance to farmers.

Thirdly, findings show that all local actors, including farmers, lack information on CC and have limited access to weather forecasts. This lack of knowledge has led to inappropriate projects or activities within development co-operation, as shown by the development of rice cultivation in flood-prone areas. The lack of sensitivity to CC and projected changes and trends in rain patterns or seasons prevent municipalities and CeRPAs in guiding appropriate agricultural investment or training. The case studies confirm that local institutions do not provide farmers with relevant agro-meteorological information; seasonal forecasts would provide predictions on current and short-term weather, which could be very useful in planning agricultural activities or early responses to anticipated climate-related risks (Hellmuth *et al*. 2007: 5).

Finally, the question of the role of traditional authorities in reducing farmers' climate vulnerability can be raised, as these actors have a strong influence in some areas of southern Benin.

International support to climate adaptation in Benin: the case of the NAPA

Benin's NAPA process

The NAPA process – its preparation and implementation – was launched in Benin in 2008 when the programme was submitted to, and approved by, the GEF. Funding to support the implementation of its first project was released in 2010 from the UNFCCC's LDCF. Access to UNFCCC funds is restricted to central government institutions; in Benin, a team named *Point Focal* (Focal Point) within the Ministry of Environment is in charge of the NAPA and followed the guidelines for its preparation; the process was supervised by the UNFCCC Least Developed Country Expert Group.[11]

Focal Point conducted field research to prepare five adaptation projects included in the NAPA,[12] to be implemented in five different sectors, and described in this document as very vulnerable to CC: agriculture and food security; renewable energy; water management; health; and coastal zone management. These sectors are frequently present within African NAPAs, as similar adaptation projects in NAPAs from Senegal and Burkina Faso confirm. Following the guideline for preparation, each project must reflect local needs, which were identified during surveys carried out in Benin amongst farmers, farmers' organisations, traditional and religious authorities, and decentralised institutions in pilot areas.

The first project to be implemented in agriculture aims to ensure food security by setting up climate forecasts and early warning systems in selected rural areas. Its global goal is to provide meteorological information to farmers so that they can react on time, using appropriate agricultural techniques. To reach this main objective, three steps have been planned:

1   improving climate data collection and analysis to provide better predictions;
2   informing farmers about potential climate stresses that could affect agriculture;
3   promoting more climate-resilient agricultural techniques and informing farmers about CC.

Discussion of NAPA efficiency to reduce climate vulnerability

From field interviews and observation, three main gaps within the NAPA preparation process and content were identified; relevant literature supports these observations:

1   Weak involvement of decentralised institutions and communities in the NAPA preparation process was pinpointed. Interviewees reported that local representatives from Bopa (a village in a NAPA pilot area), the municipality and CeRPA, as well as farmers, were not informed on CC or possible adaptation strategies.[13] It is unclear how farmers contributed to the first project's elaboration, as the participants from pilot areas remain unaware of CC; the NAPA content does not reflect local agricultural practices but, rather, promotes technical adaptation measures – such as the use of early warning systems to inform farmers of future potential climate stresses. The weak investment of local communities is a recurrent criticism against NAPAs, which has been supported by the IPCC report on climate change (IPPC 2007: 732; Klein and Persson 2008; Huq and Hugé 2010). Discussions in Bopa also showed that local NGOs and traditional authorities, on which the rural population relies, were not involved, which, together with the weak involvement of local institutions, puts in question the sustainability of NAPA projects and their ability to strengthen the capacities of local institutions, one of the actual goals of the NAPA.
2   The lack of collaboration between the Ministry of Environment and other ministries is another weakness. The Ministry of Agriculture was not involved in the first project on agriculture. Conflicts regarding access to UNFCCC financial resources are considered a possible reason for weak institutional collaboration.[14] The Ministry of Environment, in charge of the NAPA and seemingly the only institution aware of the first project's content, received millions of US dollars for the preparation of the NAPA as well as for the

implementation of the first project. In their research, McGray *et al.* (2007), Mace (2008) and Huq and Hugé (2010) supported this criticism of NAPAs regarding weak collaboration between ministries and the lack of links between the NAPA and other national development plans. Existing links between climate vulnerabilities and development issues have, however, been clearly underlined through field studies.

3   Regarding content, NAPA projects were elaborated using a top-down approach and focused on CC impacts. It started with the study of a climate scenario when elaborating adaptation projects aimed at reducing the sector's vulnerability to specific CC impacts, and seems to rely on very limited exploration of the socio-economic or institutional causes for climate vulnerability. It is quite unclear whether results from this poor societal study, briefly mentioned in the NAPA itself, served in the project's elaboration; likely, they were not incorporated. The first agriculture-related project of Benin's NAPA focuses on technical measures, such as an early warning system that essentially relies on improved forecasts to reduce vulnerabilities, while other social needs, such as raising risk awareness among the communities, promoting diversification of varieties or the strengthening and training of local institutions and communities, have, so far, been poorly implemented. But according to field observations, local institutions' weak capacities and ignorance of CC clearly restrain their capacity to effectively assist the population in adaptation efforts. The same observations for Africa were underlined by Huq and Hugé (2010), who highlighted the NAPA's focus on technical adaptation aspects, while local communities were poorly trained. Studies have also shown that early warning remains useless if risk awareness – in this case, CC-related risk awareness – has not been supported first (Vermaak and van Niekerk 2004: 562; Hellmuth *et al.* 2007:11).

Execution seems to be delayed as the NAPA's activities in Benin should have been launched in March 2010, as the person in charge of the NAPA at Focal Point confirmed. Possible explanations discussed with Focal Point representatives and research partners in the field include conflicts of interest within and between Beninese ministries regarding the programme management (and its financial resources), the complex access to UNFCCC's funds, and weakness of available resources for adaptation. Research from Mace (2005) and Tubiana *et al.* (2010) made the same observations regarding the complex access to financial resources for adaptation.

Although not yet implemented, the NAPA fails, in its content, to address the causes of farmers' vulnerability by not involving local actors in the process and not addressing socio-economic or institutional factors, which contribute largely to CC vulnerability. Factors, such as weak diversification of activities and high reliance on rain-fed agriculture and their contribution to climate vulnerability, were detailed in multiple studies in Leary *et al.* (2008), as well as in the present research. But these are not addressed as part of the adaptation process within NAPA. On the contrary, technical adaptation activities proposed on the basis of aggregated CC impact studies tend to prevail. Moreover, the NAPA projects are to be implemented by national actors who are often unaware of local needs; all this reflects a top-down rather than the demanded bottom-up approach to adaptation. But institutions in their current states may not be suitable actors for implementing adaptation strategies as, at the local level, communities mistrust state representatives. This is not improved by the weak integration of local NGOs and traditional authorities (both actors trusted by farmers) into the NAPA.

Finally, the NAPAs in their actual form are more an aggregation of sectorial activities than global adaptation programmes; they fail to address important aspects of farmers' vulnerability by focusing on one sector and on technical adaptation strategies to respond to specific CC impacts. Their activities are aimed at decreasing climate exposure at the local level without addressing other societal issues, at multiple levels, that can explain farmers' vulnerabilities – for instance the lack of financial support from the central government to local institutions, such as municipalities and CeRPAs, or general weaknesses in rural development.

Lessons learned and recommendations

The present case study analyses, from a local perspective, the causes for farmers' vulnerability to CC in southern Benin, and uses field results and literature to evaluate the national institutional capacities and the NAPA's efficiency to decrease this vulnerability. General recommendations to improve communities' resilience at the local level, and the efficiency of national and international support to adaptation, are suggested in the light of the results described above.

The empirical study shows that the weaknesses of rural development contribute to farmers' CC vulnerabilities, which are enhanced by the weak capacities of local institutions to implement their responsibilities. In this particular context, the NAPA does not address the multiple causes of vulnerability. Three main findings are described below.

Farmers' own response strategies to CC are effective but limited

From field study, we expected to link climate vulnerability to societal factors, rather than climate drivers, as in Adger *et al.* (2001) and Leary *et al.* (2008). Results point to multiple aspects of climate vulnerabilities and multiple scales at which vulnerability factors must be addressed. As our research and field studies show that without receiving external assistance for training or to facilitate access to inputs, farmers are quite alone within villages, facing risks of economic breakdown and food insecurity; these risks are increased by current trends in climate patterns. This situation is not directly linked to climate stresses, such as more frequent droughts, but rather to societal factors, including high poverty in rural areas in Benin, reliance on rain-fed agriculture, little variety diversification, limited access to climate forecasts, and limited knowledge of CC. These factors tend to reduce the scope for autonomous adaptation strategies, such as investing in new inputs to improve yields and diversification. Most vulnerability factors can be related to development issues, although some are more specific to CC. The lack of awareness regarding this issue at the local level does not allow farmers to make climate-resilient decisions regarding food-crop production.

Local institutional structures are currently not able to reduce farmers' climate vulnerabilities

The study shows that local actors have a role to play in reducing climate vulnerabilities by providing training and technical support to farmers. This role is mainly carried out by local NGOs acting in the context of international development co-operation, while local institutions – in charge of rural development and farmers' training – are unable to increase farmers' resilience. Their weak financial and technical means to implement local development plans, the lack of skills to provide farmers with appropriate technical support and training under current climate conditions, and scarce knowledge of these actors regarding CC were pointed out. These findings can be related to problems at the national level in Benin, where the transfer of responsibilities to lower levels during the decentralisation process was not combined with the allocation of sufficient financial resources. It also reveals a weak investment in rural development. Limited knowledge on CC at the local level and amongst institutional actors reflects a situation where CC remains an issue enclosed within the Ministry of Environment, which rarely collaborates with other institutions/ministries. As observed above, discussions with international co-operation representatives suggested a lack of knowledge (or interest) regarding CC within the agricultural sector and of addressing environmental issues within agricultural activities, which may explain the use of chemical instead of organic fertilisers. Finally, corruption problems were raised regarding Benin's institutions and contribute to farmers' mistrust. In this respect, our findings seem to provide a different conclusion from studies supported by Adger *et al.* (2005), Pittock (2009) and Kashaigili *et al.* (2009), which stress the need to provide implementation and ownership of adaptation projects to local institutions in order to increase the chance of success and sustainability of adaptation measures. In their current state, however, local institutions in Benin do not seem to be appropriate actors to implement CCA.

The international approach to CCA fails to address the actual causes of vulnerability

The international approach to CCA by means of the NAPA Benin was assessed in the light of previous findings on vulnerability and institutional capacities, which highlighted its failure to address vulnerability factors. The weak involvement of local actors, including farmers' communities, was observed during field research and when studying the NAPA projects. The focus remains on climate drivers that contribute to risks, while socially driven sources of vulnerability remain unaddressed. As a consequence, activities promoted through adaptation projects provide technical responses to CC – such as setting up early warning systems – and little societal improvement; the necessary but not sufficient technical measures are presented in the form of sectorial projects, not linked to other issues, such as development policies. These findings are not limited to Benin's NAPA, but generally observed in the top-down approach of CCA generally adopted within the UNFCCC. Regarding NAPA efficiency, questions were also raised about the crucial role played by a national institution in preparing and implementing the programme. Actors at this level have little knowledge of local vulnerabilities and needs. The mistrust of local communities towards state representatives in Benin suggests that institutional actors may not be suited at all, at the moment, to implement effective adaptation activities.

Among the societal factors contributing to climate vulnerability, institutional weaknesses cannot be neglected; however, institutional strengthening is poorly implemented within adaptation projects such as those contained in the NAPA, as they tend to only focus on climate drivers of vulnerability. Field results also underline the necessity to link local vulnerabilities to the broader national or even supranational context to address all responsible factors: CC-related, economic, institutional and societal. Based on the research findings in southern Benin, the following general suggestions to facilitate local adaptation initiatives and improve international adaptation policies are proposed:

- CCA must combine socio-economic measures which decrease vulnerabilities at all levels with climate-specific actions. As illustrated through the case studies from development projects, support of agriculture and rural development is an insufficient answer to CC. Its impact is already challenging current and new practices (e.g. rice cultivation); climate-oriented agricultural research is needed to provide technical answers to CC, but may be efficient only if combined with activities that deal with the socio-economic causes of vulnerability, mostly linked to development issues related to livelihood.
- Weather and season forecasts should be made available, even in the most isolated areas, to help farmers make climate-resilient decisions regarding their production. Forecasts can be transmitted by radio.[15]
- Training and technical assistance in agriculture must be provided at the local level as part of the adaptation process, promoting diversification of varieties or water and soil preservation techniques.
- Increasing local governmental AND especially non-governmental institutions and associations' capacities through appropriate financial transfers, capacity building with respect to climate topics, and training may enhance their current competencies and enable them to support rural development, and may, furthermore, contribute to CCA. However, risks of corruption remain at institutional levels, which underline the need to integrate other actors, such as NGOs and traditional local authorities, and to strengthen the role of the farmers themselves when implementing adaptation strategies.
- As corruption and self-interest may prevail within institutional structures, the currently foreseen role of central government within the adaptation process and international negotiations should be questioned. Local actors need to be

systematically included within the adaptation process; although not always appreciated, even local public actors remain closer to local needs than central government institutions. Mistrust of them also points to the need to include other local actors and their representatives, such as communities or religious authorities, in any adaptation process.

• Dialogue between farmers and institutional representatives, including those involved in internationally-supported adaptation processes such as NAPA, is necessary to assess local needs, design appropriate measures and restore trust. The current top-down approach prevailing in UNFCCC adaptation support must be challenged and farmers included in projects providing adaptation options: they themselves need to implement them, receive the benefits and bear the consequences in case of failure. Discussion of risks and available options to improve food-crop production under current climate conditions would contribute to empowering farmers and reducing their current insecurity.

More widely, tackling the causes of CC vulnerabilities goes beyond the way adaptation is defined at present by the UNFCCC and addressed through the NAPA. It involves the need to rethink the links between vulnerability, adaptation and development issues in a way that prevents mal-adaptation, and to promote 'climate-resilient development' – defined as promoting livelihood improvements while taking into account current and future climate changes. Research into innovative approaches to strengthen local people's capacities to deal with present and future stresses, including CC, must continue, regarding the remaining and unavoidable uncertainties that prevail in climate predictions in Africa.

The case study shows that resilient development in the context of CC implies both societal and technical responses; the first is often neglected in the context of current CCA policies/projects. It also underlines the role of local actors – institutions or organisations – for potentially improving farmers' and local communities' resilience through training or technical assistance; local actors are more appropriately able to assess target groups' concerns and needs than national or international structures. Finally, the case studies show the link between local causes of vulnerability and national features: therefore, local causes must be addressed through action at a subsequent level; for example, increasing state investment in rural development or strengthening financial transfers towards local institutions.

The key to improve resilience in the context of CC is operating through local actors, who provide general development support and policies which are developed in the light of current knowledge on climate trends/changes. Improving rural development through the inclusion of climate data will support resilient decision making for farmers and communities; this integration of climate data within development activities is currently missing in Benin. In sum, societal drivers of vulnerability must be studied and addressed, as well as climate drivers; the involvement of local actors, including communities, organisations and institutions (once trust issues have been addressed, if they can be addressed at all) is necessary to make them part of the adaptation process. This will contribute to sustainable actions, improving long-term resilience in a context of CC and uncertainties.

Acknowledgements

We thank Edwin Zaccaï, the ULB-CEDD and our Mini-Arc fund for making this research possible.

We thank Ago Expedit and the Beninese NGO A2D for organising our field surveys in several villages in southern Benin and for setting up interviews with ministries and local authorities. We also thank the participants for their willingness and time.

Notes

1 I collected data in Benin during my PhD from November to December 2008, September to November 2009 and December 2010 to January 2011.
2 For further information on NAPAs, see: http://unfccc.int/national_reports/napa/items/2719.php (last accessed 19 November 2012).
3 For further information on the socio-economic and demographic characteristics of Benin, see http://www.indexmundi.com (last accessed 13 July 2012).
4 Field size can often be less than 1 ha in southern Benin, due to demographic pressure (Hountondji in Amin *et al.* 2000).
5 Such as gari, which is made out of manioc.
6 For further information on corruption rate in Benin, see PNUD 2007–2008, and http://www.transparency.org/ (last accessed 19 November 2012).
7 This information was confirmed during discussions with a person working at the Direction for Promotion of Associations, at the Civil Society Ministry, in Cotonou, December 2010.
8 November to December 2008, September to November 2009, December 2010 to January 2011.
9 Programmes d'Aménagements Hydro-Agricoles et Renforcement des Organisations des Producteurs par l'Aménagement Hydro-Agricole – Départements des Mono/Couffo et Atacora/Donga. For further information on Protos' PAHA-ROPAHA project in Benin, see http://www.protos.be (last accessed 11 March 2012).
10 Discussions with international development co-operation representatives in Cotonou, during December 2010, led to the conclusion that environmental preocupation is not high within the agricultural sector in Benin, which leads to its under-consideration within development projects on this field.
11 For further information on UNFCCC's process, see http://www.unfccc.org (last accessed 16 November 2012).
12 Information on Benin's NAPA was collected through literature (MEPN 2008) and through interviews during stays in Benin in 2008, 2009 and 2010. Interviews were conducted with the chief of project in Focal Point, as well as with people and policy representatives in one of its experimental areas (Bopa in the department of Mono).
13 This observation comes from discussions led in September 2009 with farmers and local authorities in Bopa, one of the experimental areas for the NAPA project, where surveys were carried out in 2008 to elicit information in preparation for the first project.
14 This conflict of interest between the two ministries was suggested by a field research partner working with the NGO Initiative pour un Developpement Integre et Durable (IDID) during discussions in Porto-Novo, Benin, 5 January 2011.
15 In some villages in Mali, information on climate is spread to farmers via radio. For more information on this project, see http://www.unmultimedia.org/radio/french/detail/102620.html (last accessed 16 November 2012).

References

Adger, N., Kelly, P. and Huu Ninh, N. (2001) *Living with Environmental Change: Social Vulnerability, Adaptation and Resilience in Vietnam*, London: Routledge.

Adger, W.N., Arnell, W. and Tompkins L. (2005) 'Successful Adaptation to Climate Change across Scales', *Global Environmental Change Part A*, vol. 15, no. 2, pp. 77–86.

Ago, E., Petit, F. and Ozer, P. (2005) *Analyse des Inondations en Aval du Barrage de Nangbeto sur le Fleuve Mono (Togo et Bénin)*, online: http://orbi.ulg.ac.be/handle/2268/17768 (accessed 10 July 2012).

Aho, N. (2007) *Les Mesures Endogènes ou Locales d'Adaptation aux Changements Climatiques en République du Bénin. Conférence Régionale sur les Changements Climatiques et les Phénomènes Extrêmes en Afrique Subsaharienne*, Cotonou, Benin: MEPN-IRD.

Ahomadegbe, M., Ozer, P. and Dogot T. (in review) *Etude des Stratégies Endogènes d'Adaptation des Communautés du Plateau d'Abomey Face aux Risques Climatiques*, GEO-ECO-TROP.

Albert, I. (1993) *Des Femmes une Terre: une Nouvelle Dynamique Sociale au Bénin*, Paris: L'Harmattan.

Amin, S. *et al.* (2000) *Economie et Société: Le Bénin, d'Hier à Demain*, Paris: L'Harmattan.

Auracher, T. and Ulrich, N. (2010) 'The Right Balance', *Development & Cooperation*, vol. 37, no. 9, pp. 336–337.

Banégas, R. (2003) *La Démocratie à Pas de Caméléon, Transition et Imaginaires Politiques au Bénin*, Paris: Ed. Karthala.

Baudoin, M.A. (2012) *Etude de l'Adaptation aux Changements Climatiques des Populations Rurales Africaines: le Cas de Communautés Rurales Agricoles au Sud du Bénin*, Bruxelles: Thèse de doctorat en Science de l'Environnement, Université Libre de Bruxelles.

Breusers, M. and Daane, J. (1997) 'Introduction', in Daane, J., Breusers, M. and Frederiks, E. (eds), *Dynamique paysanne sur le plateau Adja du Bénin*. Paris: Karthala, pp. 9–28.

Cuni-Sanchez, A., Fandohan, B., Assogbadjo, A. and Sinsin, B. (2012) 'Local farmers' perception of climate change in Benin (West Africa)', *Climate and Development*, vol. 4, no. 2, pp. 114–128.

Daane, J., Breussers, M. and Frederiks, E. (1997) *Dynamique paysanne sur le plateau Adja du Bénin*, Paris: Karthala.

Dovenon, N. (2010) *Le Bénin: Quelles Solutions pour un Développement Durable?* Paris: L'Harmattan.

Ernest, A., Camberlin, P. and Perard J. (2008) *Instabilité Spatio-Temporelle des Régimes Pluviométriques dans le Bassin versant du Mono-Couffo (Afrique de l'Ouest) de 1961 à 2000*, France: CRC, Université de Bourgogne.

Hellmuth, M., Moorhead, A., Thomson, M. and Williams, J. (eds.) (2007) *Climate Risk Management in Africa: Learning from Practice*, New York: International Research Institute for Climate and Society (IRI), Columbia University.

Hountondji, Y.C. and Ozer, P. (2010) *Trends in Extreme Rainfall Events in West Africa: A Case Study in Benin (1960-2000)*, Annales des Sciences Agronomiques du Bénin, Cotonou.

Huq, N. and Hugé, J. (2010) 'National Adaptation Program of Action (NAPA): An assessment of workers' rights', 'Climate Change, Impacts on Employment and the Labour Market – Responses to the Challenges' Seminar, Bruxelles: International Trade Union Centre/Global Research Network/International Labour Office.

INSAE (2004) *Cahiers des Villages et Quartiers des Villes, Département du Mono – Couffo*, Cotonou: Direction des Etudes Démographiques.

IPCC (2001) *IPCC Third Assessment Report Climate Change 2001 Working Group II: Impacts, Adaptation and Vulnerability*, Cambridge, UK: Cambridge University Press.

IPCC (2007) *Climate Change 2007: The IPCC Fourth Assessment Report*, IPCC reports, Cambridge, UK: Cambridge University Press.

IPCC (2012) *Managing the Risks of Extreme Events and Disasters to Advance Climate Change Adaptation (SREX)*, Cambridge, UK: Cambridge University Press.

Johnson, P.M. *et al.* (2006) *Governing Global Desertification: Linking Environmental Degradation, Poverty and Participation*, London, UK: Ashgate.

Kashaigili, J., Rajabu, K. and Masolwa, P. (2009) 'Freshwater Management and Climate Change Adaptation: Experience from the Great Ruaha River Catchment in Tanzania', *Climate and Development*, vol. 3, no. 1, pp. 220–228.

Kelly, P. and Adger, W.N. (2000) 'Theory and Practice in Assessing Vulnerability to Climate Change and Facilitating Adaptation', *Climatic Change*, vol. 47, no. 4, pp. 325–352.

Klein, R. and Persson, A. (2008) *Financing Climate Change Policy in Developing Countries: Compilation of Briefing Papers*, Brussels: Policy Department Economic and Scientific policy, European Parliament.

Leary, N. *et al.* (2008) *Climate Change and Vulnerability*, London: Earthscan.

Macchi M. (2008) *Indigenous and Traditional People and Climate Change: Issues Paper*, Geneva, Switzerland: Union Internationale pour la Conservation de la Nature.

Mace, M.J. (2005) 'Funding for Adaptation to Climate Change: UNFCCC and GEF Developments since COP-7', *Review of European Community and International Environmental Law*, vol. 1, no. 3, pp. 225–246.

Magnan, A. (2009) 'Proposition d'une Trame de Recherche pour Appréhender la Capacité d'Adaptation au Changement Climatique', *VertigO: la Revue Electronique en Sciences de l'Environnement*, vol. 3, no. 9, online: http://vertigo.revues.org/9189 (accessed 19 November 2012).

McGray, H., Hammill, A., Schipper, L. and Parry, J.E. (2007) *Weathering the Storm: Option for Framing Adaptation and Development*, Washington, DC: WRI Report.

MEPN (2008) *Plan d'Action National pour l'Adaptation aux Changements Climatiques: PANA*, Cotonou: Ministère de l'Environnement et de la protection de la Nature.

O'Brien, K. L. and Wolf, F. (2010) 'A Values-based Approach to Vulnerability and Adaptation to Climate Change', *Wiley Interdisciplinary Reviews: Climate Change*, vol. 1, no 2, pp. 232–242.

Pirotte, G. and Poncelet, M. (2003) *Société Civile et Nouvelle Gouvernance au Bénin: Quelques Réflexions Illustrées à Aartir de l'Analyse du Nouveau Secteur ONG à Cotonou*, France: Bulletin de L.A.P.A.D., 26.

Pittock, J. (2009) 'Lessons for Climate Change Adaptation from Better Management of Rivers', *Climate and Development*, vol. 3, no. 1, pp. 194–211.

PNUD (2008) *Responsabilité Sociale, Corruption et Développement Humain Durable au Bénin*, Bénin: PNUD Rapport National 2007–2008.

Poncelet, M. *et al.* (2006) *Les Organisations Non Gouvernementales en Villes Africaines: Etudes de Cas à Cotonou (Bénin) et à Lubumbashi (RDC)*, Louvain-La-Neuve, Belgium: Bruylant-Academia.

Pouliotte, J., Smit, B. and Westerhoff, L. (2009) 'Adaptation and Development: Livelihoods and Climate Change in Subarnabad, Bangladesh', *Climate and Development*, vol. 1, no. 1, pp. 31–46.

Rain, D. (1999) *Eaters of the Dry Season*, Boulder,CO: Westview Press.

Raynaut, C. (1997) *Sahels: Diversité et Dynamiques des Relations Sociétés-Nature*, Paris: Ed. Karthala.

Schipper, L. (2009) 'Meeting at the Crossroads? Exploring the Linkages between Climate Change Adaptation and Disaster Risk Reduction', *Climate and Development*, vol. 1, no. 1, pp. 16–30.

Thebaud, B. (2002) *Foncier Pastoral et Gestion de l'Espace au Sahel: Peuls du Niger Oriental et du Yagha Burkinabé*, Paris: Ed. Karthala.

Tubiana, L., Gemenne, F. and Magnan, A. (2010) *Anticiper pour s'Adapter: le Nouvel Enjeu du Changement Climatique*, Paris: Pearson France.

Van den Akker, E. (2000) 'Major Crops and their Regional Distribution in Benin. Atlas of Natural and Agronomic Resources of Niger and Benin', in Herrmann, L. *et al.* (eds) Germany University of Hohenheim, online: https://www.uni-hohenheim.de/atlas308/startpages/page2/english/content/title_en.htm (accessed 16 November 2012).

Vermaak, J. and van Niekerk, D. (2004) 'Disaster Risk Reduction Initiatives in South Africa', *Development Southern Africa*, vol. 21, no. 3, pp. 555–574.

5 Building community-based institutions in Western Orissa Rural Livelihoods Project for green development

Gala Bhaskar Reddy and Niranjan Sahu

Introduction: the project context

Orissa is primarily based on an agrarian economy with agriculture and animal husbandry contributing 21.11 per cent to the net state domestic product (NSDP) and providing employment to about 70 per cent of the total workforce as per the 2001 census (Government of Odisha 2010). Over the past two to three decades, agriculture in Orissa has stagnated, the triannual compound growth being well below the national average and showing wide disparities: districts like Kalahandi and Koraput rank much lower in agricultural growth than other districts.

Some of the Western Orissa districts rank amongst the poorest in India with 70 per cent of their four million people below the poverty line. The population is highly vulnerable to climate change: partly as poverty limits their capacity to deal with shocks and stresses, and partly as a result of living in an area of high environmental risk. Orissa is a region where the mean temperatures are rising, and where the vulnerability profile qualifies the state as one of the highest risk areas in the country (OWDM 2008b).

The Western Orissa Rural Livelihoods Project (WORLP) operates in the four Western Orissa districts of Bolangir, Nuapada, Kalahandia, and Bargarh, covering 1,180 villages and an area of 150,000 ha, which is around 7 per cent of the country's geographical coverage. WORLP is implemented on a watershed platform and has adopted the participatory sustainable rural livelihoods approach (SLA) (Scoones 1998; OWDM 1999). NRM, capacity building, and livelihoods improvement are the three major components of the project. Some of the key interventions are afforestation, rehabilitation of degraded forests, soil and moisture conservation, improved cropping systems, generation of alternative livelihood opportunities, organization of communities, and development of social capital.

The analysis of 50 years of meteorological data has helped to identify a number of climate risks in the project area (OWDM 2008b):

- high variability of rainfall in the region, leaving people with two peak periods of food shortage;
- drought and dry spells at a two-year interval, with a major drought every 5–6 years; and
- flash floods during the rainfall season.

Recent thinking on climate change has suggested that people living in this region are very likely to witness deteriorating climatic conditions, with increased risks from disease and pests, with the respective implications for human and livestock health. Thus, the capacity of people living in these areas – in particular, the poor – to adapt to a changing climate, and their potentially increased vulnerability to higher levels of stress, becomes a strategically important issue. Building social capital by organizing communities into various community-based organizations helps these communities to become more resilient towards these climate-induced changes (OWDM 2008b).

WORLP: the methodological approach

The Orissa state authorities have implemented around 10 different watershed programmes and projects through the Orissa Watershed Development Mission (OWDM); this autonomous state agency (constituted under the Department for Agriculture) plans, implements, and monitors watershed development programmes. WORLP is one of these programmes. It was implemented over a 10-year period from 2000–2010 through a partnership between the Government of Orissa and the UK's DFID (OWDM 1999).

The aim of WORLP is to alleviate poverty and reduce vulnerability in four of the most disadvantaged districts in the state where human development indicators are very low: it was designed to cover 1,180 villages in 677 watersheds in Bargarh, Bolangir, Kalahandi, and Nuapada districts. The project initiated a new approach to watershed management, termed 'Watershed Plus' during its design, which put the focus on the poor, their ways of making a living, and the provision of a range of livelihood support services.

The goal, purpose, and outputs of the project, as described in the logical framework, are as follows (OWDM 1999):

- Super goal: reduction of poverty in rain-fed areas of India.
- Goal: more effective approaches to SLA adopted by government agencies and other stakeholders in Kalahandi, Bolangir, and Koraput (KBK) districts and elsewhere.
- Purpose: sustainable livelihoods, particularly for the poorest, promoted in four districts (Bolangir-14 blocks, Nuapara-5 blocks, Bargarh-4 blocks and Kalahandi-6 blocks) in replicable ways by 2010.
- Outputs: the five project outputs of WORLP with their potential bearing on climate change are shown in Figure. 5.1.

WORLP : unique institutional arrangements

The delivery mechanisms for watershed programmes in Orissa are unique within the country. In 2000, the state government undertook a major institutional restructuring, which resulted in the creation of a 'single window' system for watershed management: a single agency, the OWDM, was made responsible for

Five outputs	Potential bearing on CC
The poorest are organized and are able to plan and implement participatory livelihood-focused development effectively.	Where social capital is raised, communities are more resilient and better equipped to handle climate shocks effectively.
The livelihood asset base for the poorest is enhanced and diversified in 290 micro-watersheds.	An enhanced and diversified asset base, especially for natural and financial assets, should permit increased adaptability and reduced vulnerability.
Government, Panchayati Raj Institutions, and NGOs work together to implement participatory, livelihood-focused development effectively.	Better convergence and pooling of ideas and resources will strengthen the capacity of stakeholders to deal with climate stresses and encourage building on each other's strengths.
Policy and practice constraints to livelihoods are reduced in the areas of non-timber forest produce, migration, land rights, disaster preparedness, and gender issues.	Policy issues, which all have a direct bearing on reducing climate stress.
The project approaches are replicable elsewhere in the KBK region and Orissa.	Approaches proven helpful in reducing climate stress can be identified and scaled up.

Figure 5.1 Project outputs and potential bearing on climate change

managing and delivering all watershed projects, irrespective of the scheme or the sponsoring agency. This 'single window' system enabled:

- stronger oversight of the watershed programmes;
- better consolidation of learning;
- convergence of vision and action;
- more flexibility and responsiveness to changes and demands at the ground level through the new institutional arrangements;
- innovation in the institutional and delivery processes at every step down to the household level.

These institutions have been established at state, district, block, and watershed level for the implementation of the watershed programme in the state. Based on Reddy (2009) and the OWDM (1999) *Project Memorandum*, the institutional arrangement at each level is presented below (Figure 5.2).

State level

At the state level, management consultants engaged by DFID provide technical and consultancy support to the project. A team of subject matter specialists are positioned as a project support unit (PSU) under OWDM to provide, exclusively for the project, technical support in the field of NRM, livelihoods and micro-enterprise promotion, capacity building and communication, monitoring and evaluation, social development and gender issues, etc. Managers and assistant

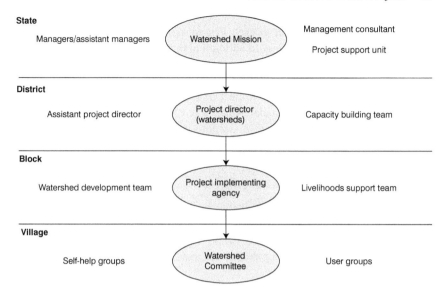

Figure 5.2 Institutional structure of the WORLP

managers provide managerial support for the smooth implementation of watershed programmes in the state.

District level

As a result of WORLP, the institutional structure of watershed project management at district level has been transformed. As recognized early in the design phase of WORLP, the project director (the District Rural Development Agency, or PD-DRDA), who was originally responsible for all watershed projects, was overburdened and unable to devote sufficient resources to effectively manage watershed projects. At the outset, it was therefore agreed that at district level, dedicated project director – watersheds (PD-WS) offices would be created in the four western districts where WORLP was working (Bolangir, Nuapada, Kalahandi, and Bargarh). These offices work under the guidance of OWDM and were further strengthened by WORLP through the provision of capacity-building teams (CBTs), consisting of four locally recruited staff members. These brought complementary skills to those of the PD-WS staff. The assistant project directors (APDs) provide managerial support to the PD-WS.

Block level

At block level, full-time Project-Implementing Agencies (PIAs) have been engaged for the implementation of 10 to 15 micro watersheds (each micro watershed covering approximately 500 ha). This has prevented PIAs from being overstretched and has dramatically improved performance. Three to four full-time teams (watershed development teams, or WDTs) have been recruited from the open market and attached to each PIA to assist in the watershed planning, implementation, and monitoring. In addition to these WDTs, a livelihood support team (LST) of three to four members (contracted full-time) has been attached to each PIA to support various livelihood interventions in the watersheds. Some of the PIAs have been recruited from the leading NGOs, namely Gram Vikas, the Council of Professional and Social Workers (CPSW), Sahabhagi Vikas Abhiyan (SVA), and the Agriculture Finance Corporation (AFC), thereby utilizing their expertise in community mobilization and social development.

Watershed level institutional arrangements

The 2001 census counted 51,349 villages in 6,234 *Gram Panchayat* (local self-government) in Orissa, which comprise on average eight villages (i.e. the 21,000 micro watersheds in the state each cover an area of about 500 ha and two to three villages). Thus, each micro watershed covers part of a *Gram Panchayat* (OWDM 2010).

Each micro watershed can be divided into upper, middle, and lower reaches in the valley portion. Generally, the upper and middle reaches are rain-fed agriculture and are populated by very poor and poor families who mostly belong to the Scheduled Castes and Scheduled Tribes (SC and ST, respectively, both marginalized communities). These areas have been categorized as 'Priority One' areas for project activities.

All adult members of each household in the watershed are members of the Watershed Association (WA) registered under the Societies Registration Act, 1860. The WAs are community-based and community-owned institutions with a formal legal standing. Being closest to the community, the responsibility of implementation has been entrusted to these watershed associations. The Watershed Committee (WC) is the executive body of the WA, which itself is composed of landless, women, small and marginal farmers, SC and ST who are representing various groups, such as self-help groups (SHGs), user groups (UGs), common interest groups (CIGs), etc.[1] Forty-four per cent of WC members are women, and 67 per cent of the WCs are working effectively. Of the SHGs, 80 per cent are for women, with 79 per cent of the poorest households being part of a SHG or CIG (OWDM 2008a).

The WCs implement the project at community level. This ensures strong participation by the community and has resulted in better community ownership of projects. The *Sarpanch* (chairperson) of the *Gram Panchayat* and ward members[2] of the watershed villages are co-opted as members in the WC. At the grass roots level, smaller groups such as landless SHGs, CIGs, UGs, farmer interest groups, and others are constituted. The watershed level institutional arrangement is shown in Figure 5.3.

Other important institutions at this level include: village information centres, grain banks (which address food security), and markets. Landless people who have constituted SHGs are federated to take up income-generation activities in the non-farming sector, and these federations are being linked to consumer markets.

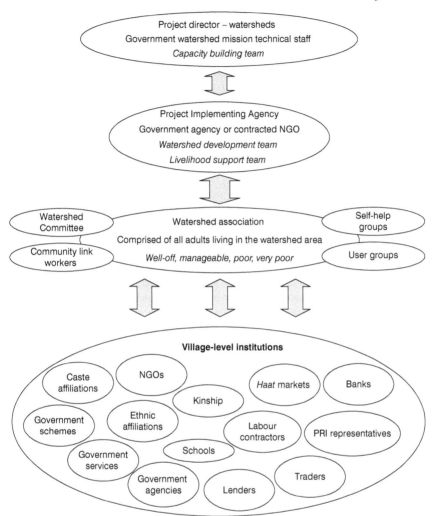

Figure 5.3 WORLP institutions at watershed level

The establishment of WAs, the WC, SHGs, UGs and the promotion of community link workers has created an environment of decentralized governance and effective service delivery mechanisms. Community link workers are service providers at the community level. They act as a link between the project and the community. This has enabled communities to get access to financial credits, technologies, and services related to agriculture and allied sectors and are of relevance to livelihoods as well as micro-enterprise promotion.

All this has led to the creation of green jobs in agriculture, soil and water conservation, livelihoods promotion, and a contribution towards eco-restoration and conserving biodiversity (OWDM 2008a).

Institutionalized capacity building: behavioral change, green jobs, and environmentally sustainable practice

Capacity building of primary stakeholders is important, as watershed project delivery depends on the capacity of individuals and groups to increase available social and human capital. Significant levels of external expertise were sourced, supplemented by capacity-building processes for primary stakeholders, and for the preparation of training modules. To streamline the process of capacity building, the OWDM has established cluster-level resource centres (CLRC) through NGOs that were already working in the project area. Based on the capacity-building need analysis of the community, standardized training modules on different topics were developed by expert resource organizations. These included modules on community health, right to information, agriculture, horticulture, livestock management, and soil and water conservation. The training modules are designed to suit the needs and profile of the primary stakeholders and make extensive use of pictures and audiovisuals. A pool of resource persons was trained to deliver the training modules through the CLRCs. This has catalyzed observable behavioural changes, and communities have started selecting, adopting, and scaling up improved practices in their own homes and on their land, which are environmentally sustainable and create green jobs.

Community-based organizations and development interventions: a successful strategy

The development interventions that create green jobs primarily consist of *in situ* soil and water conservation, tree plantation, water harvesting, organic farming, composting, low cost micro-irrigation techniques, etc. Most of the NRM activities have been implemented by UGs on common land and by individuals on private land. Alternative livelihood activities, which reduce pressure on natural resources, are promoted through SHGs and CIGs. These interventions provide ecosystem services, such as availability of water, food, and clean air, and they also mitigate the effect of GHG emissions. The creation of green jobs and the ecosystem services have had a positive impact on lives, livelihoods, and the environment.

Food security has improved by establishing grain banks at SHGs and at community level and through the promotion of kitchen gardens and tuber crops; the latter have provided additional food and nutritional supplements and the number of households that suffer the 'lean season' food deficit days has decreased from 25 per cent before the project to 5 per cent in 2009. The enhanced food security results from an enhanced coping capacity and higher income through increased agricultural production and diversified livelihood activities (OWDM 2009).

WORLP has strategically identified the poor and most vulnerable households through a participatory well-being ranking.[3] The organization of these poor households via SHGs has led to effective institution building in watershed villages. More than 4,254 SHGs with around 65,000 members established and strengthened during the project continue to function well. The number and strength of SHGs has increased social cohesion, reduced people's vulnerability, and improved the opportunity for collective action in case of climate-related shocks. Groups are better able to manage common property resources, and provide quicker, better informed, and more appropriate responses to stress situations. SHG activities were particularly beneficial for the status and entitlement of women.

In Western Orissa, the capacity to adapt to changes in climate depends, to a large extent, on secured access to natural resources, particularly to water. The control over resources assures that effective strategies are available to people when dealing with climatic change: for example soil and water conservation, investment in resilient agriculture, based on pest- or drought-resistant seeds and improved farming practices, as well as on the ability to draw on alternative sources of food and income when the main supply fails. The implementation of watershed activities by UGs and WCs has enhanced the entitlement processes in the community. The communities are able to access the common property resources, such as water bodies and plantations. Female SHGs are taking up pisciculture in water bodies.

The independent impact assessment of WORLP (OWDM 2008a carried out in 2008) confirmed the key results evidenced in the projects; they are synthesized with respect to the five constituent assets (capitals) of the SLs framework in Table 5.1.

Lessons learned

Building on people's strengths, WORLP has supported an increase in capital assets upon which people draw their livelihoods. Further, community-based institutions and collectives have made the community resilient to climate change. The impacts and learning of WORLP are summarized hereunder:

- WORLP was one of the first DFID projects to function and be housed fully within government. This decision was controversial: opinions were divided between those who felt that WORLP would be stifled within a government environment and unable to innovate, and those who felt that this might be an acceptable price to pay in order to ensure replication and scaling up. In fact, the project was able to innovate and generate new knowledge, and these lessons have been passed on and scaled up throughout the national (Indian) watershed programme, now enshrined within the new *Common Guidelines for Watershed Development Projects* (NRAA 2008). Currently, 2,332 micro watersheds have adopted 'watershed plus' approaches in the state of Orissa.
- WORLP has succeeded in reducing poverty: 30 per cent of the people have moved out of poverty, i.e. from below the poverty line; it seems (likely) that this is a prerequisite for any efforts to develop greater adaptability to climate change. In the absence of alternative sources of livelihoods, poor people rely, to a large extent, on those natural resources to which they have access, as they have nothing else to fall back on, and a destructive cycle of depletion leads into a downward spiral. Reducing poverty through increasingly diversified livelihoods seems to offer a relatively foolproof and proven platform from which to launch a climate change agenda.

Table 5.1 Adaptation strategies and results in WORLP

Assets	Adaptation strategies	Results in WORLP
Natural	Enhanced agricultural production	Productivity of paddy has increased by almost 47 per cent in project watersheds (in comparison to 28 per cent in control watersheds), with the crop being grown on almost 75 per cent of the cultivated area. Cropping intensity status shows an increase of 20 per cent in project watersheds, from 1.06 to 1.26.
	Improvement in the coping capacity with respect to drought	Almost three fifths of the marginal farmers in the project area reported improvement in disaster coping capacity, i.e. with respect to drought. Almost 44 per cent of the marginal farmers attributed the improved capacity to the increase in agricultural production.
Physical	Physical infrastructure for soil and water conservation	Fifty-four per cent of the households have undertaken soil and moisture conservation activities, namely field bunding, construction of contour ditches, check of dams in their field.
Financial	Access to financial services	More than 70 per cent of the sampled households in project villages have access to financial services.
	Household income	More than 85 per cent of households indicate an increase in agricultural and non-agricultural income. Approximately 26 per cent of households in project villages (24 per cent of the poor) exhibit an increase in agricultural income of more than 50 per cent.
	Enterprise development	Two fifths of the SHGs have started off-farm and on-farm micro enterprises.
Social	Inclusion in groups	Almost 79 per cent of the poorest households are part of SHGs or CIGs formed in the project areas, and are involved in specific activities mandated for the groups.
Human	Access to information	The project population shows significantly better access to information with respect to the three assessed parameters: agriculture, non-agriculture, and government schemes. More than 50 per cent of households report access to agricultural and non-agricultural information.
	Access to livelihood-related services	Community link workers and community livelihood resource centres are the new institutional models which enhance the access to livelihood-related services.
	Decrease in morbidity caused by malaria and other water-borne diseases	In the project villages, almost 73 per cent of the respondents considered sick days caused by malaria were reduced. Approximately 53 per cent of the households reported the decrease in days of illness following acute watery diarrhoea.
	Access to safe drinking water	More than three fourths of the households have access to safe drinking water within 100 metres of the house, compared with 66 per cent of households before the project.

Source: Adapted from OWDM 2009.

- WORLP has implemented both NRM-based 'watershed' interventions' and 'watershed plus' work focused on livelihoods and reducing vulnerability. The increased capacity of the community to adapt to climate-induced shocks has been achieved through implementation of both components working in tandem. It would be very hard to attach values to these contributions or to attempt to separately measure the contribution of their effects. Both components are indispensable, and neither would work without the other. Some kind of synergy appears to be in play, but again, this would be very hard to quantify.
- It is evident that project activities have enhanced resilience to current climate variability. However, it may well be that future climate change might be of a different order; many scientists subscribe to this view. Therefore, the adequacy of current strategies for long-term solutions on climate change projections may be reassessed to counter anticipated future impacts.
- The plurality of institutions at the watershed level has enabled the implementation of pro-poor strategies, and has helped to reduce the vulnerabilities of the poor. Dedicated support structures which start from the state level and reach to the cluster level have paid dividends in terms of achieving project outputs and objectives.
- Watershed development, which focuses on area development and livelihoods promotion for the poor and marginalized community through community participation, can be scaled up to make the community climate resilient.
- Decentralized governance of natural resources by community-based institutions can be adopted as a best practice in NRM and watershed development.

Notes

1 SHGs are groups of 10 to 20 members, usually women, who engage in savings and credit activities, whereby credit may be extended to smooth consumption as well as income-generating activities. UGs are generally formed by users who use a common asset such as a water harvesting structure or plantation. CIGs are formed to achieve a common task or objective. They may be members from different SHGs or UGs (Reddy 2009).

2 Ward members are the elected representative of a ward. A few wards constitute a village and a few villages constitute a *Gram Panchayat*.

3 Participatory well-being ranking (WBR) is a PRA tool to rank households into different groups depending on their wealth status and living conditions. In WORLP, households are categorized into very poor, poor, manageable, and well-off categories as per WBR. For further study, see Chambers 2007.

References

Chambers, R. (2007) *Who Counts? The Quiet Revolution of Participation and Numbers*, IDS Working Paper 296, online: http://www.ids.ac.uk/files/Wp296.pdf (accessed 05.02.2013).

Government of Odisha, Directorate of Agriculture & Food Production (2010) *Odisha Agriculture Statistics 2009–2010*, Odisha, Bhubaneswar.

NRAA (2008) *Common Guidelines for Watershed Development Projects*, online: http:// dolr.nic.in/dolr/downloads/pdfs/Common%20Guidelines_2011[1].pdf   (accessed 04.03.2013).

OWDM (1999) *WORLP Project Memorandum*, online: http://www.worlp.com/images/ publication/PROJECT%20MEMORANDUM.pdf (accessed 21.01.2013).

OWDM (2008a) *WORLP Impact Assessment*, online: http://www.worlp.com/images/ publication/IMPACT%20ASSESSMENT%20FINAL%20EVALUATION%20 REPORT%20OF%20WORLP%202009.pdf (accessed 21.01.2013).

OWDM (2008b) *Synthesis Report: Effects of Climate Change in WORLP*, online: http:// www.worlp.com/images/publication/SYNTHESIS%20REPORT%20EFFECTS%20 OF%20CLIMATE%20CHANGE%20IN%20WORLP.pdf (accessed 21.01.2013).

OWDM (2009) *Climate Change Adaptation in Western Orissa: A Policy Brief*, online: http://www.worlp.com/images/publication/CLIMATE%20CHANGE%20 ADAPTATION%20IN%20ORISSA.pdf (accessed: 21.01.2013).

OWDM (2010*) Perspective and Strategic Plan for Watershed Development Projects Orissa*, online: http://www.orissawatershed.org/admin/UploadGuide/Guide_119.pdf (accessed 04.03.2013).

Reddy, G. B. (2009) 'Institutional Delivery for Watershed Management in Orissa', in: Premchander, N., Sudin, K. and Reid, P. (eds) *Finding Pathways: Social Inclusion in Rural Development*, 1st edition, Bangalore: Books for Change, pp. 203–211.

Scoones, I. (1998) *Sustainable Rural Livelihoods: A Framework for Analysis*, IDS Working Paper 72, Brighton, UK: Institute of Development Studies.

6 How good are good practices?

Understanding CBDRM in Mozambique

Luís Artur

Putting CBDRM into context: increased hazards and disasters

The world is facing hazards and disasters[1] of an unprecedented nature. The sheer number of 'natural' disasters has more than quadrupled over the past 30 years. While in the 1970s an average of 90 disasters per year were recorded, the planet has witnessed nearly 450 disasters per year throughout the 1990s and early 21st century (Webster *et al.* 2009: 5). The number of people affected has more than tripled in the same period from about 55 million per year to 262 million per year (UNDP 2009: 30). If urgent and concerted actions are delayed, a greater death toll is likely, and economic losses from disasters might surpass US$300 billion per year (NEF and BCAS 2002: 2). This recent trend is, to a large extent, related to climate change. Climate change is estimated to produce annual losses corresponding to over 5 per cent of world GDP (Stern 2006: 1) and has put 20–30 per cent of fauna and flora species at risk of extinction, with accompanying implications for biodiversity and livelihoods (Ypersele 2008: 4).

Different approaches have been called upon to reduce the occurrence of disasters and the negative impacts of climate-related disasters, including the recent *Hyogo Framework of Action 2005–2015* (ISDR 2006). Amongst the identified measures, community-based disaster risk management (CBDRM) has emerged as the most effective and efficient approach. Critics have suggested that the lack of local participation in disaster management has resulted in ineffective disaster management measures and increased losses. It is argued by different scholars that local people are better suited than anyone else to understand local opportunities and constraints; hence, their involvement in disaster management is vital and allows disaster reduction measures to be more effective and efficient compared to classical top-down disaster management approaches (Luna 2001: 219; Pearce 2003: 213; Heijmans 2004: 118; Thomalla and Schmuck 2004: 375; ISDR 2006: 7; ADPC 2006: 4).

This chapter explores CBDRM in Mozambique and aims to contribute to the academic debate on good practices on disaster risk reduction (DRR) and climate-resilient development (CRD). The following questions are addressed:

- How did CBDRM evolve in Mozambique and in what respect does the history of CBDRM impact on the implementation?
- How has CBDRM been implemented in Mozambique and which factors have hampered or supported effective implementation?
- Which lessons could be learned in terms of establishing best practice in CBDRM?

The chapter comes to the conclusion that despite the conceptual strengths of CBDRM, the approach should be measured by the quality of its practical implementation and impact on local population. The experience in Mozambique shows that CBDRM is influenced by power struggles, conflicts and negotiations by the different actors involved, and it was largely a top-down approach. This contradicts the very nature of CBDRM as a participatory approach and hinders the integration of local knowledge as an important source for context-based CRD.

This contribution is based on empirical data collected over 18 months (from January 2007 to July 2008) in the districts of Mutarara, Caia, Mopeia, Marromeu, and Chinde along the Zambezi River in Mozambique. It is also informed by recent fieldwork (January 2011 and July 2012) in the districts of Caia, Govuro, and Jangamo. The research methods included secondary data collection and document analysis, participant observation along the delta of the Zambezi River, semi-structured interviews with key actors, group discussions, and a survey. In total, the author spent about one year living in communities along the Zambezi River, where he interviewed 128 people using semi-structured interviews and 198 people using a survey. He attended 16 church services, two funerals, three weddings, and had 28 group discussions (with about 15 persons in each group).

An introduction into the Mozambican context serves to clarify the development context, the effects of climate change as well as disaster response and the emergence of CBDRM. Then the different applications and limitations of CBDRM in the country are discussed. Finally, conclusions on an improved use of CBDRM in Mozambique are drawn, and key lessons for CBDRM as an approach for adaptation to climate change are described.

Development and climate change in Mozambique

Mozambique is one of the poorest countries in the world. Although its economic growth has been impressive over the past years, with a reduction of the absolute poverty by 15 per cent over the period 1997–2003 (MPF *et al.* 2004), by 2008 more than half of the population still lived on less than one US dollar per day as poverty reduction has stagnated (MPF 2008). The Human Development Index (HDI) ranks Mozambique in the bottom four (just above Burundi, Niger, and Democratic Republic of Congo; UNDP 2011a: 130). In 2008, nearly half of the children under the age of two were chronically malnourished and more than half of the population had no access to potable water and hospital care (UNDP and GoM 2008: 12). Due to its prevailing poverty, Mozambique has been depending on external aid for more than 25 years, getting about US$50 of aid per person per year, nearly three times the

Table 6.1 Key socio-economic indicators, 2008

GDP, current prices (US$ billions)	9.9
Real GDP growth (%)	6.7
GDP per capita, current prices (US$)	478
Inflation (% annual average)	10.3
Poverty (% population below national poverty line)	54
Life expectancy at birth (years)	50
Infant mortality (per 1,000 live births)	92
Literacy (% of population aged 15+)	55
Access to an improved water source (% of population)	47

Source: Adapted from UNDP 2011b.

average aid to other African countries (Consdier DFID 2005: 9). Table 6.1 presents some of Mozambique's key 2008 socio-economic indicators.

Poverty in Mozambique emerges from a complex array of factors which includes colonization policies from Portugal, unsustainable socialism development policies and practices following independence from Portugal in 1975, civil war from 1976 to 1992, and natural hazards and disasters. It is in this context (of poverty) that Mozambique addresses climate change and attempts to develop in a sustainable and climate-resilient way.

Responses to climate change in Mozambique can be traced as far back as 1992, when the civil war ended. That year also marked the beginning of the new international agenda on sustainable development through the United Nations Conference on Environment and Development (UNCED), which raised global awareness on climate change. Following the 1992 Rio Summit, Mozambique ratified the three conventions on climate change, biodiversity, and, later on, desertification. In Mozambique, climate change has become one of the major factors that hamper the international and national development efforts as the majority of the population live in rural areas, making their livelihoods mainly from agriculture and natural resources which are highly influenced by increased climate variability and changes. Droughts, floods, and cyclones have been increasing in frequency and intensity. Furthermore, there has been a shift in rain patterns with a noticeable reduction in rainfall and changes in the start and end of the rainy season all over the country (Van Logchem and Brito 2009: 2). Impacts of climate change in the national economy have already been observed. The great floods in the year 2000, linked to climate change, claimed about 800 lives, affected about 25 per cent of the national population, i.e. some five million people, and produced economic losses estimated at US$600 million (GoM 2000: 17). Recent economic analysis of the impacts of climate change in Mozambique suggest that if no adaptation measures are taken, the national GDP could fall between 4 and 14 per cent by 2040–50 and the country could experience annual losses estimated at about US$400 million (World Bank 2010: xix). Therefore, tackling climate change and addressing CRD are urgent matters for the government as well as for donors who want to strengthen

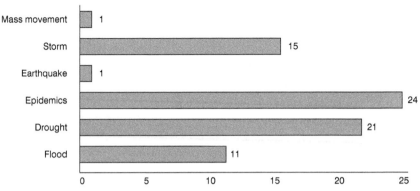

Figure 6.1 Major natural hazards (number of each event) in Mozambique, 1980–2010

disaster management policies in Mozambique. The following section outlines the national response to disasters, climate change, and the emergence of CBDRM.

The emergence of CBDRM: a response to increased hazards

Mozambique has a long history of disaster response linked to the recurrence of hazards and disasters, which is partly related to its geographical context. Geographically, Mozambique is a disaster-prone country, being situated along the Indian Ocean where, every year, cyclones of different intensities are formed and make landfall in the country. Mozambique is also the lower riparian country of nine international rivers that drain their waters into the Indian Ocean: excessive rainfall together with the mismanagement and environmental degradation of rivers and dams has produced flooding of various magnitudes in the country over the years. Furthermore, some regions have a semi-arid climate, making drought historically part of people's everyday life. Hence, droughts, flooding, and cyclones are three major natural hazards that produce disasters in Mozambique. During the past 50 years, the country has been hit by 68 natural disasters which have killed more than 100,000 people and affected up to 28 million people. As much as 25 per cent of the population is at risk from natural hazards (World Bank 2010: 8). By 2011, Mozambique ranked as the world's eighth most vulnerable country (Bündnis Entwicklung Hilft and UNU-EHS 2011: 28). Figure 6.1 provides an overview of the major hazards in Mozambique.

Historically, the first formal public commitment and planned attempt of disaster management was established after independence in 1978. Due to heavy floods in the Limpopo Basin in 1977 and the Zambezi Delta in 1978, the new Mozambican government created a commission in 1978 for relief mobilization and coordination called the *Commissão Inter-Provincial das Calamidades Naturais e Aldeias Comunais* (Inter-Provincial Commission for Natural Disasters and Communal Villages). As the name suggests, this commission was not only involved in relief mobilization, but also had a political mandate to mobilize and organize people, especially flood victims, to live in communal villages. Aid was distributed selectively to people willing to move to communal villages, in order to pursue the political objective of rural socialization, which was decided in 1977 at the third FRELIMO[2] congress held in Maputo. According to Coelho (2001: 7), the first 26 communal villages were established in Gaza province because of the flooding in 1977, while in 1978, many other communal villages were settled after the flooding of the Zambezi Delta. On the Zambezi Delta, people still recall the 1978 flooding as the communal village flooding *madzi a maldeia*. So disaster management was (ab)used for the political objective of the socialist government. This top-down and politicization of disaster response is still ongoing in the use of CBDRM in Mozambique, as discussed later in this chapter.

Critical reflection of CBDRM in Mozambique

Interventions related to disaster reduction and adaptation to climate change worldwide favour a community-based approach, either in practice or by endorsing it in their policy statements. Initially developed in the Asian context, especially around the Philippines' recurrent natural hazards, CBDRM became a worldwide approach that has been promoted in disaster-prone countries in Africa, Latin America, and the Pacific Islands. The approach involves the engagement of communities exposed to risk in the identification, analysis, treatment, monitoring, and evaluation of disaster risks in order to reduce their vulnerability and enhance their capacities (ADPC 2006: 17). Essentially, the CBDRM concept is valued for its focus on local people's perceptions of disaster, their vulnerability, and resilience. By engaging local people, the approach is considered to promote ownership of the process and outcomes by the local communities, which lead to empowerment and sustainability (Pearce 2003: 214).

Despite the published positive outcomes from local participation and bottom-up approaches, little knowledge has so far been generated regarding the challenges that the CBDRM approach faces at local level. There is little critical knowledge reflecting the process, achievements, and lessons from CBDRM interventions. Several authors (cf. Mosse 2001: 28; Twigg 2005: 64–65) have argued that much of the research hitherto published contains superficial descriptions with too much attention on the strengths of community-based approaches and a lack of analysis of its limitations in practice. CBDRM does not occur in a vacuum; it takes place in arenas of power struggles, with different and sometimes conflicting interests which are, indeed, ill-researched or overlooked.

CBDRM in Mozambique consists mainly of creating local committees for disaster risk management composed of 18 people, and the provision of a preparedness kit whose content is described in Table 6.2. The committees have the mandate to guide communities to develop disaster prevention, preparedness, and mitigation activities (INGC 2010: 8). The committee members are supposed to work on a voluntary basis but receive equipment such as boots, rain jackets, and gloves. The 18 members of the local committees are subdivided into small teams to carry out the following activities:

- follow news from the media;
- make early warnings based on media reports;

Table 6.2 Preparedness kit content

Items	Quantity
Bicycles	2
Inner tube	4
Bicycle tyres	4
Bike reparation kit	2
Cutlass	5
First-aid kit	2
Megaphones	2
Shovel	5
Batteries (boxes)	5
Flags (green, orange, and red)	3
Oil lamp	2
Pairs of boots	18
Rain jackets (trousers and jacket)	18
Gloves (pairs)	18
Rope (50 metres)	1
Rescue kit	1
Plastic roll for house cover (10 metres)	2
Handsaw	2
Radios	1
Solar lamp	2
Whistle	5
Life-saving jackets	5
Stretcher	2
Canoe	1
Pickaxe	2

- help with evacuations;
- support rescue operations;
- help with shelter;
- develop damage assessment and information management.

The positive impacts of these committees on disaster reduction in terms of early warning dissemination, risk monitoring, mobilization of at-risk communities to evacuate, rescue, and accommodate disaster victims have been overwhelmingly acknowledged by the government, donors, and NGOs (cf. Matsimbe 2003: 11; Fergunson 2005: 22; INGC 2009: 17). This chapter focuses on some of the challenges which tend to be overlooked.

Theory versus practice of CBDRM

Notwithstanding the participative element of the theory and the positive impact on disaster management, there are problems with the practical implementation of CBDRM and its sustainability as well as impact on the target group. As these influence the efficiency of disaster risk reduction (DRR), its contribution to the adaptation of local actors to climate change and CRD has brought mixed results. The following aspects related to CBDRM will be analysed in the next section:

- the top-down nature of CBDRM;
- the issue of ownership of CBDRM;
- the politicization of CBDRM;
- the reactive nature of CBDRM;
- the issue of leadership, participation, and turnover;
- the quality and impact of training provided to the committees;
- the simplification of CBDRM interventions into 'one size fits all' approach.

The top-down nature of CBDRM

By definition, CBDRM is a process by which local people apply locally available resources, including local knowledge, to reduce their exposure to and management of disaster risks. External resources are welcomed and incorporated into local everyday practices of disaster reduction to enhance them. External actors help to improve local knowledge and practices in a mutual learning process without subordinating indigenous knowledge or attempting to impose their views and approaches. Usually, external interventions start from a Vulnerability and Capacity Analysis (VCA), which helps to identify strong and weak points for disaster reduction within communities; this is done by using participatory methodologies (IFRC 2006: 28; CARE 2009: 2).

Many people interviewed during the research were annoyed by the fact that interventions were based on a set of predefined objectives, methodologies, and activities. In many communities, no assessments were carried out and the composition and responsibilities of the committees were virtually imposed from the outside. During interviews with project managers and officers from governmental and non-governmental organizations (NGOs), it was common to hear: 'We are teaching local people how to respond to disasters; we are setting local committees in order to teach people about disaster management'.[3] Such expressions indicate that local knowledge was hardly perceived as relevant for attempts to reduce disasters and as a basis for being complemented by additional external knowledge.

Many of the proposed actions were also unrealistic and inappropriate in certain contexts. In many cases, committees and communities were provided with radios to receive early warnings and megaphones to disseminate the messages; but no money was available to buy batteries nor were there markets to eventually repair this equipment. It was assumed, without confirmation, that the communities themselves would provide this. Communities, however, were not asked whether they wanted these devices and did not necessarily appreciate their relevance. Along the Zambezi River, people questioned the relevance of megaphones as their radius for outreach was very limited and the sound did not have any meaning for the local people; they preferred to apply the historically used local warning mechanisms, such as bells made from pieces of railways, which are attached to the chief's house or the school and also have a larger range; or to use horns or drums with a larger range whose sounds are known to convey danger and caution. In Govuro, Inhambane province, along the Save River, the radios that communities received were of such low quality that they could not tune in their community radio (their major source of information), and some broke within just a few days. They also found no need to provide radios because many people already had better and more powerful radios; it was just a matter of having more effective local involvement to use these existing means. Along both the Zambezi and Save Rivers, some communities were also provided with canoes for evacuation, but in interviews people laughed at their small sizes. When asked if they would use them for evacuation, many refused. They claimed that they were too risky compared to the canoes already in use within the community. Another innovation was the definition of evacuation routes to facilitate rescue operations. This was generally described as unnecessary because there is no such thing as 'a route' in the bush. In some communities, people live in scattered houses and use different paths and shortcuts to reach different places. Some of these are seasonal and disappear during the rainy season and others are gender-sensitive, i.e. women or men may not use them, according to local norms. What ought to be done, which is relevant to the local population, is to indicate the assembly point, not one exact route to reach it.

These empirical findings show the lack of local participation in the planning of CBDRM interventions, which is against the participatory orientation of the concept. This lack makes many actions unnecessarily costly and ineffective. However, innovations in disaster management as well as for CRD, in general, need to be context-based and start from existing capabilities and needs. In fact, the need for local participation was pointed out by Robert Chambers in the 1980s (Chambers 1983) and by further studies (i.e. DFID 1999; IFRC 2006; CARE 2009). Despite this knowledge, processes turn out to be quite different in the field, and in-depth local participation is still an unrealized vision. Among the different endogenous and exogenous reasons, the present study found the limited skills of the professionals to engage in participatory approaches as well as the rush and speed to intervene of particular relevance. Finally, the research found that some project thinking and logframes do not foster genuine local participation. They tend to reward (quantitative) outcomes (i.e. number of committees created and material handled) but hardly reflect on the processes and lacked orientation towards (sustainable) impact on the beneficiaries. So, the theoretically 'well-equipped and functional' committees might not be able to face climate change induced and other disasters any more effectively than before.

The issue of ownership of the CBDRM

The establishment of local committees in the ways described above has produced some dubious responsibilities. Committee members present themselves as part of INGC[4] staff and tend to ask for payment and other incentives from the government. On 7 February 2008, the author attended a meeting between INGC staff and a local committee in the Caia district. Committee members complained that their colleagues were leaving the committee and claimed that the CBDRM was disintegrating because they failed to produce incentives; they requested payments to fulfil their duties because these absorbed much of their time, which could instead be used for income-generating activities. Similar complaints were heard in Govuro and Caia during field visits on 23 January and 18 August 2012.

INGC has insisted that the work of committee members remain on a voluntary basis. In interviews, INGC staff claimed that when establishing local committees, they stressed the voluntary nature of the committee members' work; that they should not expect any payments; and should accept working for the well-being of their communities.

But, as local people perceive the committees as being part of INGC,[5] the commitment to and support for local committees has been quite low in many communities.[6] The committee members and local people expect the government to support local committees through INGC, while the government expects local communities to give their full support and incentives to local voluntary committee members. As the message of voluntarism communicated by INGC did not reach the target groups or has had limited local support due to livelihood demands by the committee members, there is a gap of ownership with respect to the committees, including unclear responsibilities between INGC and the local communities.

The politicization of CBDRM

Theoretically, CBDRM is supposed to be a neutral process of engaging at-risk populations in a process of risk reduction, without any discrimination and political influence. In practice, however, CBDRM is very much a political process: high-ranked government officers are present at inaugurations of new committees or during the distribution of risk prevention kits, making it clear that the committees are part of FRELIMO's programme and have to respond to FRELIMO's demands. District administrators are requested to supervise the work of the committees and they are institutionally the heads of the committees. Messages and songs of 'Viva FRELIMO' are an integral part of these meetings.

In Cocorico, for one of the communities along the Zambezi River in Mopeia district, which the researcher followed closely for more than six months, CBDRM became a source of internal power conflicts and contributed to the disintegration of the community itself. Through CBDRM, the committee members received bikes and other personal benefits. Those not involved asked for interventions that could benefit the entire community, such as a hospital or water pumps. They claimed that the chiefs involved were selecting people from their network, benefiting their family members and close friends. These complaints produced three small subgroups within the community. One group was composed of those who were directly involved with the CBDRM and their supporters; another group comprised those who felt excluded from the CBDRM intervention and their supporters; and, in between, was a third group of the 'undecided'. The first group started to coin the critics as opposition members, i.e. belonging to RENAMO[7] – the opposition – not to FRELIMO – those in power – and claimed to be the true FRELIMO members because they were receiving orders from FRELIMO and acting accordingly.

The political struggles extended to the internal work of the committees themselves. When committees faced difficulties in carrying out their duties or members had personal quarrels, they accused each other of belonging to different parties and of sabotaging the operation. In the Caia district, one committee received a canoe but certain members argued that the committee leader belonged to the RENAMO party and used the canoe against FRELIMO's mandate and committee duties. The leader told the researcher this was just an excuse from other members who intended to become leaders. In some cases, the committee leaders were not the same individuals as the local leaders, which tended to produce power clashes and (for some local leaders) a sense of parallel command lines within the communities.[8]

This politicization of CBDRM brings along unintended consequences. Some community members who were interviewed told the researcher that they did not support the local committee because they did not agree with the fact that FRELIMO wanted to appropriate it. They argued that it should be clear that in the communities there were supporters of different parties, but that politics should be left outside CBDRM and that the objective of tangible risk prevention should be at the centre of the work.

The reactive nature of CBDRM

The current debate on disaster management stresses the need to foster proactive strategies, which reduce vulnerability and increase local resilience to climate change and threats to livelihoods. CBDRM was conceived, partly, within this framework; local committees should be responsible for promoting disaster risk-reducing activities. However, this is not reflected by the actual institutional set-up and the day-to-day activities. The kits provided by INGC and other stakeholders include material related to emergency preparedness and response. The set-up of the committee is aligned with this, designating members responsible for issuing warnings in the vicinity of floods, for rescue, and for resettlement. In practice, the activities of the committee, where they are active at all, cease when the rainy season is over: there are no tasks outside emergencies and most of the committee members are not even aware of aspects concerning vulnerability reduction. In every committee visited, the members complained that INGC and other stakeholders only approached them when flooding was forecasted.

The international NGO *World Vision* attempted a different set-up for the committees through a programme called GERANDO (Gestão de Risco à Nivel da Comunidade – Community-Based Disaster Risk Management), which links emergency-related activities with long-term activities that address risk reduction. In addition to emergency response, dissemination of DRR information and the creation of local committees, it funds mitigation/risk reduction plans, which are designed by the communities to address their major hazards, including those induced by climate change. This is one case to learn from when addressing DRR and CRD.

The issue of leadership, participation, and turnover

The performance of the committees depends on the leadership, member participation, and the continuity of efforts. Good leadership means, amongst other aspects, that the leaders are accountable to members, are proactive, inspire the committee with ideas that are transformed into plans collectively, and are active in advocacy and activities within their communities. From group discussions and observations in the field, it appeared that many committee leaders lacked these qualities and many of them just expected INGC and other partners to lead the process. The research found also that the legitimacy of the leaders (how he/she was selected and how people perceived the leader), their levels of (formal) education, their access to information, and their ages (young or not) mattered for committee performance. It was also suggested that good leaders should avoid the partisan politics (discussed above) and try to bring everybody on board.

The issue of participation and commitment by the committee members emerged in every meeting as *the* major handicap for an effective committee and good leadership. As the activities are supposed to be done by volunteers, it was very difficult to systematically mobilize members to be part of the process, as this was perceived to conflict with the need to secure their own livelihoods. This is not easy to solve and tended, in itself, to perpetuate the practice of limiting committees' engagement to only emergency preparedness, rather than also tackling risk reduction through more continuous work. The issue of turnover of personnel was also related to incentives. Due to limited incentives in every committee, members withdrew and many lacked replacement: in some local committees, half of the initial people left for different reasons.

As discussed earlier, some have proposed the provision of incentives but the kind of incentive was a matter of hot debate. Some proposed a system similar to Red Cross volunteers (based on training and food basket distribution when funds are available); others would be happy if committees were funded with income-generating projects.

Participation was also affected by local norms and values. The research recorded different participation between males and females. In a number of regions, husbands refused to let their wives be part of the committees. Furthermore, nationwide, women are the main food producers in rural areas and are generally overloaded with work, which limits their participation in training, meetings, and enrolment in planned activities.

The quality and impact of the training provided to committees

In every committee, people claimed to have gone through training. Overall, those who were in the committees from the beginning mentioned having attended at least one training session, being glad to have attended, and receiving a lot of information. However, the quality of the training and the issues tackled during the training deserves discussion. An effective training requires a set of materials that include: (1) manuals, notes, or guides for trainers to use to run the training; (2) visual aids for the training session itself; (3) handouts and exercise sheets for the trainees to use in the training session; (4) posters or booklets for the trainees to take away; and (5) media support or take-home visual aids to help people implement what they have learned. Depending on the target group, different training methodologies and approaches need to be devised, for example, training sessions for the illiterate or people with lower levels of formal education must be based on visual aids and group discussions instead of conventional training or the lecture method. Therefore, effective material needs to be appropriate in terms of language and culture, as well as in relation to the subject matter.

During the field research, people reported that training sessions mostly used the conventional lecturing method and provided limited practical training material. In general, only one trainer's manual was available, which eventually was copied for the participants. People suggested that visual aids for application at home would have made their sensitization campaigns in the communities more effective.

Training content included a wide range of issues. It started with a conceptual discussion of disaster, vulnerability, hazards, resilience, and hazard mapping, and evolved into measures to address major hazards, followed by discussion of the constitution and functioning of the local committees. In some communities, drill exercises were carried out to practice CBDRM.

People interviewed considered that training had been very useful in providing theoretical information on DRR and for exchange of experiences and discussion of activities. When asked the question; 'What have you really learned in the training?', people used to stammer when pronouncing 'technical terms' such as vulnerability, hazards, DRR, and so on – an indicator for an eventual lack of clarity of learning objectives and success indicators of the training. But many were enthusiastic and praised the drill exercises much more than they appreciated the theoretical material. Thus, more practical application-oriented content and exercises would make the training more effective.

The simplification of CBDRM interventions into a 'one size fits all' approach

As outlined above, the CBDRM format and mandates include information collection, early warning, rescue, and resettlement when necessary. Whenever possible, the committees are equipped with a preparedness kit with material appropriate for flood response. But committees with the same composition, responsibilities, and kit content are promoted nationwide, i.e. also in areas prone to drought and cyclones.

The committees in areas with imminent drought doubt that they actually need members responsible for search and rescue, accommodation, or devices such as canoes, megaphones, and life jackets. This takes us back to the already analysed arguments that stress the top-down character of the CBDRM. If the community itself had defined its own priorities or had been fully engaged in the process of risk management as spearheads rather than as beneficiaries/recipients of top-down 'orders', these costly and ineffective oddities would have been avoided right from the start.

Key lessons and recommendations

This contribution explored CBDRM in Mozambique and contributes to the academic debate on good practices on DRR and CRD. Globally, CBDRM is being praised as good practice for disaster reduction and offers good prospects for CRD. But, to fulfil its promises, we need to have a closer look at its implementation in order to see what makes it a good practice and what might limit its application. Based on the empirical findings, this case study from Mozambique provides key lessons and recommendations, which can help to design and implement CBDRM in a more efficient and effective way.

General lessons regarding CBDRM

First, this case study shows that the CBDRM concept can be an important element of effective risk management in a climate-change-determined environment (e.g. the *World Vision* experience of linking DRR to development). This is possible if:

- the intervention starts from context-specific strengths, weaknesses, opportunities, and threats (SWOT) analysis;
- integrates the local beneficiaries right from the start; and
- follows a flexible approach based on action research, process learning, and flexible interventions.

Second, the practical implementation of CBDRM as a bottom-up approach requires a difficult but necessary change in:

- thinking about policy-making and implementation processes;
- training of personnel (in participatory methods); and
- institutional set-up of national political actors (external support to locally owned processes, integration of development and environment/climate policies), donors, and the appropriate elements of the ICR.

Third, the ICR institutions and actors would have to apply a different logic when deciding on commitments, policies, and measures, i.e.:

- putting local people and their realities, know-how and needs at the centre;
- reconsidering the role of risk management within broader approaches to support adaptation; and
- abandoning the narrow focus on climate change measures supported by the international climate regime's (ICR) financial mechanism.

Fourth, in order to put the principles of sustainable and climate-resilient development into practice, risk prevention has to:

- be analysed from a less sectorial, much broader scope;
- integrate long-term aspects, for example by combining CBDRM with more long-term adaptation measures to climate change;
- provide economic and other incentives to trigger income-generating activities and projects to improve the short-term livelihood of local people; and
- open up CRD options for the future.

Specific lessons for the Mozambican context

First, the concrete implementation of CBDRM in Mozambique is, contrary to the theoretical concept, far from being a bottom-up approach because:

- objectives, methodologies, and activities are set beforehand by intervening actors at the national level, and 'handed down' by hierarchical and partisan political structures to the local communities;
- local existing knowledge and means are not taken into account, which leads to unsatisfactory outcomes in terms of a very limited participation and a lack of ownership by local communities.

Second, CBDRM is promoted in a single format regardless of the many ecological, technical, and social particularities of each context (e.g. nature of risk, existing means, values, institutions, leaders, livelihoods situation). This results in:

- a lack of cost-effectiveness and sustainability of risk management;
- a limitation of activities to periodic risk prevention; and
- untapped potential for a more comprehensive and long-term adaptation approach to risk and climate change.

Third, risk management is restricted by the poor livelihoods of the changing voluntary committee members and the whole community as a result of a limited learning process. Two reasons can be identified:

1   There is hardly any reflection on the limits of the interventions and the adjustment of the approach, which would be necessary to meet the increased challenges of natural and climate-induced risks.
2   The long-term livelihood needs of each community are very limited.

Fourth, the research shows that CBDRM has been highly influenced by:

- partisan politics; and
- a neglect of local norms.

Both aspects prevent the participation of different political and social groups and women, thereby limiting the support required for a truly locally owned process.

Key recommendations for CBDRM from the case study

In general, the integration of local actors and the adequacy of CBDRM to the specific local conditions have to be strengthened. Based on the lessons learned, recommendations refer to the institutional set-up, the learning process, politics, and policy integration, as follows:

- *Institutional set-up.* The institutional development process should always start with an assessment of local strengths and weaknesses as well as opportunities and threats for DRR, adaptation to climate-induced risks, and livelihood requirements for CRD. This will require:
  - Time and flexibility for (1) a better understanding of the context (including what knowledge and means are available, what works and what does not), (2) full involvement and buy-in of the intended beneficiaries and the local leadership, and (3) the necessary training of external actors in participatory methods and action research.
  - Flexible interventions which respond to changing contexts and needs and aim at achieving agreed tangible objectives measured by indicators that show the impact on the beneficiaries (target groups).
- *Learning process.* Organize a learning process that enables different knowledge and methodologies to cross-fertilize and strengthen CBDRM as a continuous improvement process. The 'one size fits all' approach has clearly shown itself to be unrealistic in diverse, changing, and ever more complex environments. A pool of approaches and particular tools should be available for use, depending on the assessment carried out at the beginning of the interventions.
- *Politics.* Depoliticize (national) interventions to prevent the generation of conflicts, division of people, and the weakening of the representation of communal interests. Politics should only be brought in when there is a need to guarantee a minimum of equality of actors and the involvement of disadvantaged groups.
- *Policy integration.* Integrate disaster reduction with interventions that strengthen livelihoods and CRD as there is a clear link between increasing (and climate-induced) disasters and development. As this contribution has illustrated, local people need knowledge on disaster response as well as the resources to make their lives and livelihoods more resilient to stressors, including climate change. Focusing solely on hazards, per se, will prove to

be ineffective for resilient development and sustainable disaster reduction if not accompanied by interventions aimed at strengthening livelihoods and long-term adaptation to climate change.

Notes

1 Hazard represents the potential occurrence of a natural- or human-induced physical event that may cause loss of life, injury, or other health impacts as well as loss of property, infrastructure, livelihoods, service provision and environmental resources (IPCC 2012: 560). Disaster is defined as a serious disruption of the functioning of a community or a society involving widespread human, material, economic or environmental losses and impacts, which exceeds the ability of the affected community or society to cope using its own resources (UNISDR 2009: 9). Disasters are often described as a result of the combination of the exposure to a hazard; the conditions of vulnerability that are present; and insufficient capacity or measures to reduce or cope with the potential negative consequences.
2 FRELIMO stands for Frente de Libertação de Moçambique.
3 Interview with the Minister of State Administration, Head of INGC, with the media on 16 January 2008.
4 INGC stands for Instituto Nacional de Gestão de Calamidades.
5 This is also reinforced by the working material that the committee members receive in the setting. Each member gets a pair of boots, a rain jacket with the INGC logo, gloves, and some other equipment.
6 Interviews with committee members in Mopeia, Caia, and Mutarara, 2008, in Govuro and Jangamo in February 2012, and Caia in August 2012.
7 RENAMO stands for Resistência Nacional Moçambicana.
8 Interview with the local chief in Caia, 6 May 2008; interview with committee leader and local chief in Govuro, 9 February 2012.

References

ADPC (2006) *Community-Based Disaster Risk Management for Local Authorities*, Bangkok, Thailand.

Artur, L. (forthcoming) 'The Political History of Disaster Management in Mozambique', in Hilhorst, D. (ed.) *Disaster, Conflicts and Societies in Crisis: Everyday Politics of Crisis Response*, London: Routledge.

Artur, L. and Hilhorst, D. (2010) 'Climate Change Adaptation in Mozambique', in Martens, P and Chang, C. (eds.) *The Social and Behavioural Aspects of Climate Change: Linking Vulnerability, Adaptation and Mitigation*, Sheffield, UK: Greenleaf Publishing Limited, pp. 114–129.

Bündnis Entwicklung Hilft and UNU-EHS (2011) *World Risk Report*, Bonn: Bündnis Entwicklung Hilft.

CARE (2009) *Climate Change Vulnerability and Capacity Analysis*, UK. Available online at www.careclimatechange.org.

Chambers, R. (1983) *Rural Development: Putting the Last First*, London: Longman.

Coelho, J. (2001) *State, Community and Natural Calamities in Rural Mozambique*, Maputo: Centro dos Estudos Africanos.

Consider DFID (2005) *Developments Magazine*, Issue 29, London: Department for International Development.

DFID (1999) *Sustainable Livelihoods Guidance Sheets*, London: Department for International Development.

Fergunson, J. (2005) *Mozambique: Disaster Risk Management Along the Rio Buzi: Case Study on the Background, Concept and Implementation of Disaster Risk Management in the Context of GTZ Program for Rural Development (PRODER)*, Germany: GTZ.

GoM (2000) *Post-Emergency Reconstruction Program,* International Reconstruction Conference, Rome, Italy.

Heijmans, A. (2004) '*From Vulnerability to Empowerment'*, in Bankoff, G., Frerks, G. and Hilhorst, D. (eds.) *Mapping Vulnerability: Disaster, Development and People,* London, UK: Earthscan, pp. 115–127.

IFRC (2006) *What Is VCA? An Introduction to Vulnerability and Capacity Assessment,* Geneva: IFRC.

INGC (2009) *Mozambique: National Progress Report on the Implementation of the Hyogo Framework of Action,* Maputo, Mozambique: INGC.

INGC (2010) 'Comité Local de Gestão de Risco de Calamidades (CLGC)'. Paper presented at workshop held in Pemba, August 2010. INGC, Maputo Mozambique.

IPCC (2012) *Managing the Risks of Extreme Events and Disasters to Advance Climate Change Adaptation: Special Report of the Intergovernmental Panel on Climate Change,* New York, USA: Cambridge University Press.

ISDR (2006) *Hyogo Framework for Action 2005–2015: Building the Resilience of Nations and Communities for Disasters,* Geneva: UNISDR.

Luna, E. (2001) 'Disaster Mitigation and Preparedness: The Case of NGOs in the Philippines', *Disasters,* vol. 25, no. 3, pp. 216–226.

Matsimbe, Z. (2003) *The Role of Local Institutions in Reducing Vulnerability to Recurrent Natural Disasters and in Sustainable Livelihoods Development: Case Study in Buzi, Central Mozambique,* Maputo, Mozambique: FAO and GTZ.

Mosse, D. (2001) 'People's Knowledge, Participation and Patronage: Representation in Rural Development', in Cooke, B. and Khotari, U. (eds.) *Participation: The New Tyranny?,* London and New York: Zed Books, pp. 16–35.

MPF (2008) *Pobreza e Bem-Estar em Moçambique: Terceira Avaliação Nacional,* Maputo, Mozambique: MPF.

MPF, IFPRI and UP (2004) *Pobreza e Bem-Estar em Moçambique: Segunda Avaliação Nacional,* Maputo, Mozambique: MPF.

NEF and BCAS (2002) *The End of Development? Global Warming, Disasters and the Great Reverse of Human Progress,* UK: New Economics Foundation.

Pearce, L. (2003) 'Disaster Management and Community Planning, and Public Participation: How to Achieve Sustainable Hazard Mitigation', *Natural Hazards,* vol. 28, pp. 211–228.

Stern (2006) *The Stern Review: The Economics of Climate Change – Summary of Conclusions,* London: HM Treasury.

Thomalla, F. and Schmuck, H. (2004) '"We All Knew That a Cyclone Was Coming": Disaster Preparedness and the Cyclone of 1999 in Orissa, India', *Disasters,* vol. 28, no. 4, pp. 373–387.

Twigg, J. (2005) *Community Participation-Time for Reality Check?,* in ISDR (ed.) *Know Risk,* Geneva: UNISDR.

UNDP (2009) *Overcoming Barriers: Human Mobility and Development,* Human Development Report. Oxford: Oxford University Press.

UNDP (2011a) *Sustainability and Equity: A Better Future for All: Human Development Report 2011,* New York: Palgrave Macmillan.

UNDP (2011b) *Mozambique Quick Facts: Economic and Policy Analysis Unit*, Maputo, Mozambique: UNDP.

UNDP and GoM (2008) *Report on the Millennium Development Goals*, Maputo, Mozambique: UNDP.

UNISDR (2009) *UNISDR Terminology on Disaster Risk Reduction*, Geneva: UNISDR.

Van Logchem, B. and Brito, R. (eds.) (2009) *Synthesis Report: INGC Climate Change Report: Study on the Impacts of Climate Change on Disaster Risk in Mozambique*, Maputo, Mozambique: INGC.

Webster, M. *et al.* (2009) *The Humanitarian Costs of Climate Change*, Medford, MA: Feinstein International Center, Tufts University.

World Bank (2010) *Economics of Adaptation to Climate Change: Mozambique Country Study*, Maputo, Mozambique: World Bank.

Ypersele, J. (2008) *Climate Change: What Do We Know According to IPCC WG II?* Warsaw, Poland: Pre-COP IPCC Workshop.

7 Making a difference through Integrated Natural Resources Management

The role of Kwame Nkrumah University of Science and Technology in Ghana

Sampson E. Edusah

Introduction

This chapter explores the Integrated Natural Resource Management (INRM) principles and approaches, and assesses the implications of these concepts for institutions of higher learning in Sub-Saharan Africa. The chapter reviews the experiences, achievements, and challenges of implementing the INRM project at the College of Agriculture and Natural Resources (CANR) of Kwame Nkrumah University of Science and Technology (KNUST) in Kumasi, Ghana. The first phase of the INRM project was implemented from July 2005 to June 2008; it was immediately followed by the second phase from July 2008 to June 2012. In the execution of the project, the college partnered with a consortium of four Dutch institutions: Tropenbos International (TBI), Centre for Development Innovation (CDI), International Centre for development-oriented Research in Agriculture (ICRA), and the Dutch Network for Sustainable Higher Education (DHO) at the University of Amsterdam. The project emerged in response to CANR's desire to use the INRM principles and approaches to contribute to sustainable and climate-resilient development and environmental and NRM in Ghana. Specifically, the project aimed at strengthening the capacity of CANR to offer INRM-based programmes from an integrated perspective to enhance competencies amongst current and future professionals for the management of complex natural resource problems and climate-resilient development.

The use of INRM concepts as an innovative system is gaining wider use by natural resource organisations and institutions because the concept is perceived as a more cognitive approach; that is, a conscious process of incorporating multiple aspects of natural resources use into a system of sustainable management. There is no doubt that issues of NRM have engaged worldwide attention and may continue to engender debate for years to come because of the effects on the survival of humanity. There is no doubt that a considerable number of the rural poor across the globe, particularly in Sub-Saharan Africa, are largely dependent on natural resources for their very existence and survival in terms of food, building materials, clothes, and medicine. Indeed, these constitute a key element of rural livelihoods; their unsustainable use by poor people themselves or by more powerful stakeholders, such as timber companies and large-scale farmers, can result in water and land degradation, loss of habitat and biodiversity, and environmental pollution (Campbell *et al.* 2006). This renders rural livelihoods vulnerable and less resilient to external shocks. Hence, serious concerns have been raised over the years about the unsustainable use of natural resources in developing countries, like Ghana, where most of the world's poor live (see Kaimowitz 2003: 199). Endowed with huge natural resources, large deposits of extractive minerals (gold, diamond, bauxite, salt), and the prospect of soon producing about one million barrels of crude oil per day, the sustainable management of natural resources is of utmost importance for the country's future.

Presenting the case: KNUST

KNUST[1] is the second largest public university in Ghana after the University of Ghana at Legon in Accra. Situated in the commercial city of Kumasi in the middle of Ghana, it was established in 1952 and has a student population of nearly 38,000. The vision of KNUST is to be globally recognised as the premier centre of excellence in Africa for teaching in science and technology for development, producing high-calibre graduates with knowledge and expertise to support the industrial and socio-economic development of Ghana and Africa. The mission of KNUST is to provide an environment for teaching, research, and entrepreneurship training in science and technology for the development of Ghana and Africa. Since January 2005, KNUST has been transformed from its previous centralised system of administration into a significantly decentralised collegiate system. Under this system, the various faculties have been condensed into six colleges, of which CANR is the smallest with a student population of about 3,000.

Over the years of its existence, KNUST has, through its programmes (teaching, research, and service to the community) strived to play a leading role in sustainable natural resource utilisation in Ghana. This is because countless studies have documented the deficiencies of efforts to conserve natural resources and to improve livelihoods particularly in the developing countries. McShane and Wells (2003), for example, argue that because of generally disappointing experiences, the World Bank, the UNCBD, the GEF, and the United Nations Convention to Combat Desertification (UNCCD) have recently adopted policies that strongly commit the organisations to new approaches for tackling environmental problems. Much thought, however, is needed to avoid the failures experienced by previous projects initiated by the World Bank and other institutions.

The approaches and principles of INRM overlap considerably with other innovation system concepts, such as the Integrated Agriculture Research for Development (IAR4D) and Agriculture Research for Development (ARD) as used by ICRA and its partner institutions and organisations in countries like South Africa, Kenya, and Uganda. IAR4D and ARD are two innovative system concepts used by the European Initiative for Agriculture Research for Development and Enabling Rural Innovation practised by the Consultative Group on International Agricultural Research (CGIAR), and their partners in Africa and elsewhere (Hawkins *et al*. 2009: 9).

INRM: a definition

Different authors and institutions have put forward varied definitions of the term INRM. There are two key references that underpin the philosophy of the INRM project and both use different terminology: IAR4D and research and development (R&D). The first is well elaborated in Hawkins *et al*. (2009); the second, by Campbell *et al*. (2006). Other terms that have principles similar to INRM are referred to as 'interdisciplinary approach', 'ecosystem approach', and 'multiple stakeholder approach' (for example, see Campbell *et al*. 2006). In general, INRM is an approach to managing resources sustainably by helping resource users, managers, and other stakeholders accomplish their different goals by consciously taking into account and aiming to reconcile and synergise their various interests, attitudes, and actions (Frost *et al*. 2006: 1; Thomas 2002: 53). INRM is interdisciplinary and multi-scaled, encompassing different but linked levels of social and biophysical organisation. INRM has been defined as 'an approach that integrates research on different types of natural resources into stakeholder-driven processes of adaptive management and innovation to improve livelihoods, agro-ecosystem resilience, agricultural productivity and environmental services at community, eco-regional, and global scales of intervention and impact' (Hawkins *et al*. 2009: 22). These authors argue that the INRM approach seeks to empower relevant stakeholders and help in resolving their conflicting interests, foster adaptive management capacity, deal with complexity by focusing on key causal elements, integrate levels of analysis, merge disciplinary perspectives, make use of a wide range of available technologies, guide research on component technologies, and generate policy and technological and institutional alternatives (Hawkins *et al*. 2009). According to CGIAR (2002), INRM research is fundamentally about the need to balance competing individual and societal interests in multiple uses for any natural resource, including both the physical elements (soil, water, etc.) and the genetic element. In that sense, INRM could be described as an approach to research that aims at improving livelihoods, agro-ecosystem resilience, agricultural productivity, and environmental services. Above all INRM aims to augment social, physical, human, natural, and financial capital by helping solve complex real-world problems that affect natural resources in agro-ecosystems. Its efficiency in dealing with these problems comes from its ability to:

*   empower relevant stakeholders;
*   resolve conflicting interests of stakeholders;
*   foster adaptive management capacity;

- focus on key causal elements (and thereby deal with complexity);
- integrate levels of analysis;
- merge disciplinary perspectives;
- make use of a wide range of available technologies;
- guide research on component technologies;
- generate policy and technological and institutional alternatives.

'Natural resource' is understood to include the geographical resources of water, soil and its productive qualities, intermediate and long-term carbon stocks, biodiversity of the managed landscapes, and the stability and resilience of the ecosystem of which agriculture forms part (Harwood and Kassam 2003). It is therefore recognised that NRM is complex and multifaceted, as it encompasses policy, institutional, social, economic, and technical dimensions, and as there can be many different reactions to dynamic change within NRM:

- existing management practices and technologies, policies, and institutional arrangements may no longer be sufficient;
- power relations, benefit distribution, and interests may no longer be in balance;
- ecological functions may be disrupted;
- risks may exceed management capacity;
- economic forces may outstrip conservation forces;
- sanctions and cultural heritage associated with management practices, as well as ownership patterns, may no longer be operating.

NRM needs to deal with these issues and circumstances as they arise. Consequently, a paradigm shift is needed if NRM is to be responsive to the emerging environmental issues and aggravating climate change problems, a shift from 'business as usual' to 'business unusual', and a shift from a linear and sectorial approach to an interdisciplinary and integrated approach. It is crucial for the paradigm shift to start with institutions of higher education. Universities are particularly well placed to initiate appropriate actions and the necessary curriculum changes that will, in future, turn out professionals that have the skills and knowledge to develop and implement an 'interdisciplinary approach to problem solving', which means that professionals of different backgrounds work together in teams to solve a complex NRM problem.

The integration of INRM principles at CANR

Responding to this need for a paradigm shift and the growing concern about natural resource use, in 2004 CANR elaborated a proposal for the project 'Institutionalisation of Integrated Natural Resource Management (INRM) principles and approaches in the strategy and academic programmes of the College of Agriculture and Natural Resources (CANR) of Kwame Nkrumah University of Science and Technology (KNUST)'; the Royal Dutch Government supported it through The Netherlands

Programme for the Institutional Strengthening of Post-Secondary Education and Training Capacity (NPT); funding was administered by The Netherlands Organisation for International Cooperation in Higher Education (NUFFIC).

CANR understands the defining principles of INRM in the same way as elicited for IRA4D by Hawkins *et al.* (2009: 10) and applied by institutions such as ICRA and the Royal Tropical Institute (RTI). The principles were modified to suit CANR's purpose, as follows:

- INRM integrates the perspectives, knowledge, and actions of different stakeholders around a common theme. The theme or 'entry point' represents a research and development 'challenge', identified by one or more stakeholders who recognise that a broader working alliance is needed to achieve the desired development impact. The interests and actions of the different stakeholders go beyond information and technology, and include business, politics, finance, organisation, management, etc., and the links between these aspects.
- INRM integrates the learning that stakeholders achieve through co-operation. More than a simple concerted *action* process, INRM is a social *learning* process, with stakeholders learning from the experience of working together. This learning focuses primarily on the processes of stakeholder interaction, rather than on the specific solutions to the R&D 'challenge'. This learning takes place at individual, organisational, and institutional levels.
- INRM integrates analysis, action, and change across the different (environmental, social, and economic) 'dimensions' of development. The general and current concepts of 'sustainable development' and 'multi-functional agriculture' emphasise the interlinked 'dimensions' of such development. These include economic growth (linking farmers to markets), conservation of natural resources (soil fertility, biodiversity, limited carbon-dioxide production to prevent climate change, etc.), social inclusion, equity ('pro-poor development'), as well as food security.
- INRM integrates analysis, action, and change at different levels of spatial, economic, and social organisation. INRM innovation is an emergent property of the broader 'innovation system'. To effectively promote innovation, INRM needs to promote change and enhance learning throughout the broad innovation system at all levels of organisation. These include 'spatial' levels (field, farm, watershed, etc.), economic levels (product, firm, value chain, business cluster, etc.), and social levels (individual, group, community, organisation, innovation system, etc.).

INRM was introduced at CANR to modify the role of universities in NRM, responding to a perceived need for NRM in Ghana. Solving the complex problems of agricultural communities requires strategies that enhance both natural *and* social resources in order to capitalise the benefits to be gained from improved crop varieties and animal breeds. INRM-based professional training and research play a vital role in developing and implementing these strategies. INRM, as a holistic approach, fits into CANR's mandate of teaching, research, and community service, reflecting the offer of the college with regard to academic programmes in agriculture and natural resources.

Objectives of the INRM project at CANR

The overall objective of the project is to enhance the capacity of CANR to offer programmes based on the approaches and principles of INRM in order to strengthen the INRM capabilities amongst institutions and organisations in the natural resource sector, such as the Forestry Commission and the Ministry of Lands and Natural Resources. Based on the overall objective of the NPT project, the following specific objectives were formulated:

- to consolidate building of capacity within CANR in INRM principles and approaches;
- to institutionalise and incorporate the INRM approaches and principles into the learning (undergraduate and graduate) programmes of CANR;
- to engage stakeholders as partners in the institutionalisation, and incorporate INRM approaches and principles into the academic programmes of CANR to train professionals who will apply the INRM approaches and principles within their institutions and organisations.

The rationale for introducing INRM

Over the past six years, KNUST has been restructured into six colleges in order to effectively respond to the need for training highly skilled professionals who are able to respond to the rapidly changing socio-economic situation of Ghana. As a middle income and oil-exporting country, there are considerable opportunities for the country's socio-economic transformation. However, the changing fortunes of the country have implications for natural resource use and sustainable development. This is a challenge which institutions of higher education in Ghana, particularly universities, have to address within their teaching programmes and research. CANR therefore took up the challenge to implement the INRM project in order to become 'a centre of excellence for the advancement of knowledge and technology in sustainable agriculture, renewable natural resources management and rural development in Africa' (CANR Strategic Plan 2005: 6). In its strategic plan, CANR points out the following challenges:

- the increasing world population and changing consumption patterns and their combined impact on natural resources;
- the concern of global warming and water scarcity that increases production risks;
- increasing globalisation and commercialisation which exert stress on the environment, as well as on societal structures in terms of competition, growing inequality between social groups;
- other related collateral damage of liberalised market economies.

At the interface of environmental conservation and development, a whole range of national, regional, and global governance mechanisms have been developed over the years: the Rio conventions in the early 1990s, for example the UNCBD and the UNFCCC, the UNCCD, Integrated Conservation and Development Projects (ICDPs), as well as integrated trans-boundary projects and more local community-based NRM approaches. Two examples of ICDP are the Annapurna Conservation Area Project in Nepal, and Bwindi Impenetrable Forest in Uganda. These approaches add yet another complicating 'environmental governance' dimension to NRM, apart from 'conservation' and 'development'. However, the questions of 'how to' manage natural resources, with whom, for whose benefit, and at whose cost are not clearly specified. Hughes and Flintan, for instance, have asserted that the conceptual basis proposed by ICDP practitioners – i.e. the use of development tools to achieve conservation objectives – was neither understood by implementing counterparts in national and provincial governments nor sufficiently integral to ICDP design and practice (Hughes and Flintan 2001: 8).

Since the 1990s, initiatives to improve the conservation and sustainable use of natural resources in developing countries – particularly in countries in Africa – have illuminated the problem of weak institutions and inadequate institutional arrangements (Buck *et al.* 2003). Efforts to strengthen the capacity and performance of institutions and institutional arrangements to govern and manage the land, minerals, forest, wildlife, and water resources which are central to the livelihoods of a large majority of the population reveal the need for pluralism in institutional design – because the rural people who live close to and depend on natural resources were thought to be central to any meaningful planning for sustainable NRM. Furthermore, there has been a global trend over the past decade to adopt a participatory approach to natural resources, particularly to forest management, integrating rural communities to secure their commitment and achieve sustainability of natural resources (Azeez *et al.* 2011: 164). Kio (2002) suggests that radical change in forest policy is necessary for mobilising the rural population in the interest of sustainable management of forest resources, which would stop further deforestation and land degradation. It is therefore obvious that the 'business as usual' mode of university research and teaching could not offer effective responses to current global environmental conservation and development problems. There is widespread recognition that university research and teaching will have to give more emphasis to the management of risks and complexity, power dynamics amongst stakeholders, avoidance of long-term depletion of productive potential, and more careful control of environmental externalities. It is argued that research needs to reinvent itself, hence the need for an NRM approach that embraces multiple scales of interaction and response, systems rather than linear thinking, uncertainty and ambiguity, and involving multiple stakeholders with often contrasting objectives and activities. It is said that multiple scale of interaction (collaboration) does not happen as easily or as often as might be expected. The barriers can be considerable: differences in timescale, mindsets, and daily realities. The approach needs to have an impact

Table 7.1 A paradigm shift at CANR

From	To
Seeing knowledge generation as a final objective	Seeing it as a means to achieve change
Research	Action research
A focus on technology	A focus on people
Mainly reductionist analysis (understanding of the parts)	Systems analysis (understanding the relationships between the parts)
Mainly 'hard systems analysis' (improving the mechanics of the system)	Also 'soft systems analysis' (determining what the system should achieve)
Seeing participation as a matter of consulting beneficiaries	An interactive learning between stakeholders
Working individually	Working with others
Teaching	Learning
Being taught	Learning how to learn
Individual learning	Social learning
An exclusive focus on individual merit and competition	Collaboration and teamwork within and between organisations

Source: Edusah and Rozemejier (2011: 5).

on real-world problems. Complex issues and the multiple factors that have, so far, limited the solution of major problems need to be tackled by an approach that is better able to address issues in their social and institutional context (Campbell *et al.* 2006).

This paradigm shift in NRM increasingly prompts universities to change their way of carrying out teaching and research activities, and requires that KNUST and CANR deliver effectively upon their mandates in teaching, research, and outreach (KNUST statutes), thus transforming CANR into a regional centre of excellence by recognising this paradigm shift and positioning itself accordingly (see Table 7.1).

For the purpose of the NPT project, CANR adopted a working definition of INRM as a holistic and collective approach to resolving complex environmental problems (NPT/GHA/278 Project Proposal 2008: 3). This definition is based on new thinking in development and NRM, and addresses the concerns of actors in the natural resource sector. Table 7.2 presents the INRM approach in line with the thinking of CANR as a set of principles for innovation.

INRM as an innovative approach to learning

How different is INRM from conventional approaches to learning? The INRM approach, as conceptualised and presented in Figure 7.1, is markedly different from the linear or conventional approach to teaching and learning which has characterised the work of Ghanaian universities over the years, in that:

Table 7.2 Integrated Natural Resources Management (INRM) principles

Integrated NRM	I *Natural Resources* M	INR *Management*
• Integrating the perspectives, knowledge, and actions of different stakeholders around a common theme (inter-institutional, inter-disciplinary, trans-disciplinary) • Integrating learning by stakeholders from working together (interactive, flexible) • Integrating analysis, action, and change across the different dimensions (economic, social, environmental) of sustainable development (system thinking, process-oriented) • Integrating analysis, action, and change between different levels of spatial, economic, and social organisation	• Deals with agriculture, NRM, and development • Holistic approaches such as integrated river basin/coastal zone management, collaborative management approaches, ecosystem management, and landscape planning approaches • Local, context specific	• Broader working alliance, stakeholder engagement (more than participation) • Social learning process, generating knowledge, continuous reflection, and adaptation • Interlinked dimensions • Broad innovation system • Ownership, relevance to society • Problem/opportunity focused

Source: Edusah and Rozemeijer (2011: 7).

- NRM or, better still, environmental issues are complex and call for an interdisciplinary approach;
- the learning processes of INRM are alternative generic training programmes; it is a new way of teaching, particularly at the graduate level where learning is organised around interdisciplinary teams;
- the interdisciplinary approach relies on the competence of team members to train present and future professionals to be able to solve complex problems;
- the approach makes use of stakeholder engagement as a key ingredient in curriculum development;
- INRM is an ideal teaching method for running programmes meant to upgrade the skills of professionals;
- INRM relies on the strength of teamwork, institutional collaboration, and stakeholder engagement.

Implication of the INRM project for CANR

The introduction of INRM principles to CANR has implications for each of its three core mandates of teaching, research, and service to community (Table 7.3).

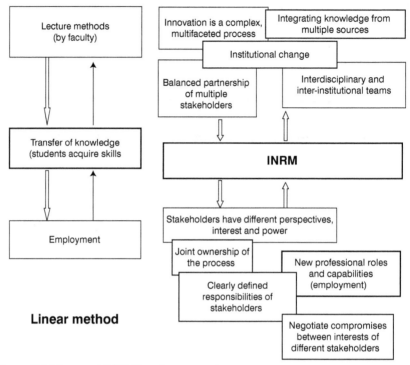

Figure 7.1 Linear and INRM learning approaches

To institutionalise these principles and integrate them into the academic programmes and strategies of CANR, the pragmatic steps described below had to be made.

Institutional arrangement for project implementation

It is important to recall that the INRM project was approved during CANR's formative years when the central administration was very much in control of the management of the university. For this reason, CANR and its consortium partners decided to put in place a flexible implementation mechanism to ensure a smooth take-off of the project and to circumvent the bureaucratic university administrative system. It was, for instance, recognised that statutory bodies of the college, such as the academic board, have the potential to slow down activities. A major decision was taken to put in place a project implementation committee (PIC) to facilitate the implementation of the first phase of the project and, more importantly, to allow for the participation of stakeholders in the activities of the college. In accordance with INRM principles, members of the PIC were drawn from various departments of the college and from key stakeholder institutions. At the beginning of the second phase of the project, the management structure used for first phase was modified to make the implementation of the project more effective. A nine-

Table 7.3 Implementation of the INRM principles by CANR

Education	Research	Service to the community
• External stakeholders engaged in curricula development/design and teaching • Room for experiential learning by doing (rather than being taught) • Focusing on problem-solving capacities (rather than on just acquiring knowledge) • Room to apply real world issues in a professional context (rather than on classroom case studies or artificial/academic field work situations) • Room for inter-disciplinary curriculum development and teaching within and between faculties • Collective learning (rather than individual)	• Joint research with stakeholders • Room for inter-disciplinary research within and between faculties • Problem-oriented research co-identified/ co-researched and (partly) paid for by external stakeholders • Research more linked to policy processes with long-term strategic engagement • Research linked to teaching around real life cases • More consistency and complementarities in research programmes • Experimentation with other research models such as action research	• Clear strategic orientation on intended impact and service delivery (whose problem will be solved?) • Consistency in programme to translate new knowledge (research result) in societal impact • Long-term R&D assignments in support of change processes in society • Quality checks in place by engagement of independent bodies

Source: Edusah and Rozemeijer (2011: 8).

member steering committee (SC) with the provost as chairman and including three key stakeholders replaced the PIC. The SC gave the project policy direction and met quarterly. Below the SC was the change implementation committee (CIC) made up of five members and also chaired by the provost with stakeholder representation. This committee was responsible for the overall management of the project and worked through three working groups: (1) Strategic Planning Working Group; (2) Embedding and Strategy Group, in charge of embedding the INRM principles in the strategy and academic programmes of the college, and (3) Programme Design and Delivery Group, in charge of developing and delivering new programmes based on the INRM principles (Figure 7.2).

Capacity building

As it became clear at the start of the project that the staff of the college lacked sufficient skills and knowledge in INRM principles, considerable effort and resources were committed to building the capacities of the college's academic staff through workshops, training programmes, and special courses delivered both in Ghana and The Netherlands. Examples of courses in which staff participated

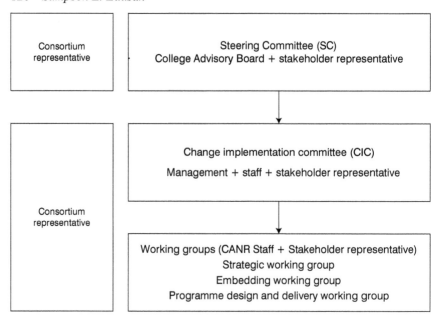

Figure 7.2 Project organisation chart

included: principles in team building and teamwork, general principles in INRM, stakeholder engagement, and monitoring and evaluation (M&E) for INRM. Presently, two staff members are working on their PhD programme at the University of Wageningen in The Netherlands on INRM topics as part of the strategy to integrate INRM into the college. The completion of these two programmes will considerably strengthen the college's INRM capacity. The college organised a series of workshops for stakeholders on the principles and approaches of INRM to build a common understanding of INRM principles and ensure that stakeholders would be able to fully participate in the activities of the college for mutual benefit.

Stakeholder engagement

The INRM approaches and principles stress active stakeholder engagement at all levels. This challenge was taken up by the college and a number of natural resource sector institutions, such as the Ministry of Lands and Natural Resources (MLNR), Ministry of Food and Agriculture (MoFA), the FC, and NGOs like Forest Watch and Friends of Water Bodies. The partnership approach and collaborative arrangements between CANR and these stakeholders built on trust, ownership, and a joint commitment to project objectives, which has been beneficial to both the college and stakeholders. Opportunities were offered to stakeholders to regularly interact with the college and participate in its activities. The removal of communication barriers between the college and stakeholders has enabled stakeholders to make direct and substantial inputs into the design and delivery of academic and professional programmes of the college such as the newly designed MSc programmes and short courses. It is refreshing to note that the college can now count on continuous quality stakeholder contributions: inter alia, they bring in practical experience to the design and delivery of learning programmes and they provide scholarships for their staff on training programmes. A key lesson learned in pursuing a multi-stakeholder approach is that due to different and often conflicting interests, active stakeholder engagement is expensive and time-consuming. But experience has also shown that the benefit justifies the effort and investment.

Teamwork

It was realised from the onset of project implementation that there was the need for the formation of interdisciplinary teams that were capable of working effectively across disciplines, and had good team management. This was necessary because of the fact that the various faculties and centres that now constitute the college were independent of each other, competed against each other, and rarely worked together.

The most outstanding experience gained during project implementation was that the individualistic attitude amongst the staff of the college has given way to teamwork, and competition has given way to collaboration. The staff and management of the college now appreciate that teamwork yields better results and can be rewarding. Several factors, however, led to difficulties for team working, including:

- lack of commitment on the part of some team members;
- lack of time to enable full participation of all team members;
- slow decision-making processes amongst team members;
- tendency of outspoken members to hijack the process and try to force their views on the team;
- tendency of some team members to retard (pull back) the processes;
- persistent demand for reward for team members.

Challenges for the INRM project

Institutionalising INRM principles at CANR called for changes to its strategy, management, and human and financial resources. Unfortunately, the process of change took place at a slow pace, partly because the newly established college was struggling to find its place and identity. An evaluation of the project commissioned by the college and carried out by MDF, a Dutch institutional expert organisation,[2] concluded that awareness of INRM principles and the rationale of embedding them into the college is still low amongst staff. It concludes that:

> CANR should clearly convey the message that its future success is linked to its ability to institutionalise INRM principles and approaches into the

work culture of all staff. The focus should be on communicating intensely the College's vision and mission which integrates INRM principles. This would require an urgent addendum to the Strategic Plan which currently has no mention of INRM and has no performance indicators promoting INRM.

(MDF 2010: 5)

The slow pace of institutionalisation of the INRM principles at CANR can also partly be attributed to the culture of the university. There is still a contradiction between participatory theory and practice. While the cultural practices of the INRM project within CANR envisage that work should be for the good of the university, have a business-like orientation, focus on teamwork and multidisciplinary teams, show intensive collaboration and a high level of accountability, be open and transparent, promote communication, and motivate staff, the predominant present culture is quite the opposite: individuals are primarily concerned with themselves, following an ethos of 'what I can get' rather than 'what I can contribute to the university', and show resistance to new ideas and reluctance to change, although there are clear signs that the college desires change.

A major challenge was that the staff of the college grappled with the set of tools (teamwork, stakeholder engagement, etc.) and methodologies needed to effectively integrate INRM approaches and principles. This was to be expected since most of the staff members have a background of linear training and were somehow oblivious to the opportunities offered by INRM principles. The MDF report examined 12 categories of organisational life within the college and concluded that although the college had embraced the concept of INRM, staff were treading cautiously and thus retarding the process of change. For instance, teaching remains predominantly traditional, research is largely individual, and community engagement is low, as is stakeholder engagement. There are reasons for this: the extra workload brought in by the project was not factored into the job descriptions of the project teams, a weak appraisal system, and very little reward or motivation strategies for the project team. The young college initially found it difficult to extricate itself from the university system and to establish its own identity. As a result, by the end of the project's first phase, limited changes had occurred at CANR with respect to the traditional university system. This was understandable since the college was not an island unto itself but had to operate within the confines of the university's structures:

- The academic staff involved in the project continued to maintain their full teaching loads with the college's various departments. This was a great disincentive and, as a result, they tended to adopt lukewarm attitudes towards some activities of the INRM project.
- The large number of staff members, institutions, and other stakeholders involved in the project made coordination difficult and it took considerable time to implement some activities. The design of the MSc programmes, for instance, suffered considerable delays due to the extensive engagement

of stakeholders and institutions. Furthermore, the university bureaucracy's requirements tended to slow down some activities of the project, particularly the development and approval of new programmes.

- The challenges to the change were accentuated by the bureaucratic inertia of the university. It became clear to CANR and the consortium partners that change at CANR, being only a subsystem of KNUST, was going to be slow and difficult. As the university is governed by its statutes, any major change must be approved by the academic board and the university council, which is a very lengthy process.

Lessons learned

In spite of the challenges and constraints encountered during a critical evaluation of achievements, the implementation of the INRM project indicated that CANR has nevertheless experienced visible change, and that INRM principles have begun to take root within the college, although the process has been slow. Looking into the future, CANR needs to build on its success and direct its energies to strengthening teamwork; therefore, the college must see itself as working together, learning together, and changing together.

Working together

- Working together as a college demands that the management of the college must take the lead to hasten the process of change by ensuring that the ownership of INRM principles shifts from the project context to the college. The change coordinating committee, which was the apex body instituted for project implementation, has to be maintained to lead the process.
- The management of the college led by its provost should make a conscious effort to get the buy-in of the central university administration through the office of the vice chancellor to push the boundaries of INRM within the university, especially to reach human resource management (HRM) systems and procedures, in order to embed a new way of working into the work culture of CANR: reward/remuneration policies need to be developed and implemented which foster INRM behaviour, revised responsibilities need to be clearly outlined and captured in job descriptions, performance management systems need to be developed, and a competency framework needs to be developed which integrates HRM processes and planning according to the INRM approach.
- The management must make it a priority to invest in long-term, mutually beneficial partnerships, create platforms to foster INRM practices, and build networks around R&D themes to feed into the development of academic programmes at the college.
- CANR should continue to engage stakeholders in a business-oriented approach in cost and benefit sharing in order to address research challenges presented by stakeholder institutions, by feeding the outcomes into the design

of academic programmes and enriching outreach activities of the college, thus jointly designing, implementing, documenting, and reviewing (preferably interlinked) the research activities, educational programmes, and outreach activities of the college.

Learning together

Infrastructure and facilities to promote INRM principles and practices have been provided through the project and were intended to encourage staff and stakeholders to learn together. For this to be effective, the college must:

- Recognise the importance of communication in a change process and develop a communication strategy that views all communication strategically and which uses advanced techniques to communicate CANR's vision and mission to relevant internal and external stakeholders, especially raising the visibility of INRM principles.
- Recognise the link between learning and change in the working culture of the college. The current culture within the college is focused on project activities, but systems need to be considered for the promotion of learning. Learning outcomes could be integrated into CANR's strategy; learning should be at the heart of the performance review and M&E systems, as well as building learning opportunities into the working environment.
- Make time and space available for staff to reflect on and exchange experience, both formally (learning-oriented M&E, publications, and seminars), and through informal gatherings, such as coffee breaks and regular meetings with stakeholders. This is down to the CANR management.
- Design incentive structures and working processes that encourage working, experimenting, and learning in teams and partnerships. This has to be reflected in the HRM system (described above).
- Document and capitalise on learning; encourage documentation of lessons learned and have knowledge sharing and management procedures in place.

Changing together

- An important step for enhanced INRM implementation would be for CANR to update or revise its strategic plan, which was prepared before the introduction of the project, to incorporate INRM principles. This would ensure that the INRM principles are reflected in CANR's vision, mission, goals, and strategic objectives as well as in its annual budgets. Similarly, faculty strategic plans would also need updating to reflect the revised college strategy plan.

Table 7.4 summarises and clarifies how the INRM approach and principles can be translated into required staff competencies, organisational norms, and culture and institutional change.

Table 7.4 Summary of INRM approaches and principles

Strengthening INRM capacities		
At individual staff level (competencies)	*At CANR/KNUST organisational level (norms and culture)*	*At institutional level (conditions and mechanisms for inter-institutional linkages)*
• Apart from knowledge in the individual academic discipline also in meta-disciplines: systems thinking, knowledge management, strategic planning, knowing how to learn, effective writing, use of ICT, etc. • In social skills: communication, teamwork, networking, facilitation, etc. • In mindsets and attitudes: empathy, self-awareness, self-regulation, self-motivation, social awareness	• In structures and processes needed to provide performance and incentives that encourage interdisciplinary teamwork • In partnerships with other stakeholders • With emphasis on mutual learning • Improved communication • With effective knowledge management that promotes learning and change	• That allow different stakeholders – individuals and organisations, from public and private sectors – to come together on a 'level playing field' • Finding appropriates ways to manage and finance inter-institutional space • Linking education and research to policy development, remaining relevant and problem-oriented

Source: Edusah and Rozemeijer (2011: 10)

Recommendations

CANR has come a long way in the implementation of the INRM project, which is in line with current thinking and development in environment and NRM. CANR recognises that issues related to NRM are complex and encompass different disciplines, that the conventional approach to teaching and learning is outdated, and that stakeholder institutions and organisations, particularly those that employ graduates from the university, are asking for graduates with the ability and skills to function in teams which, in turn, are able to meet new challenges easily. The INRM approach offers the alternative to traditional teaching and linear, sectorial thinking. It is a platform for teaching and learning that will turn out professionals who will deal with INRM issues in a holistic manner, in interdisciplinary, flexible teams, which can address complex climate change issues, sustainable environmental management, and climate-resilient development in general in Ghana.

However, it has also become clear that:

• putting theory into practice is far more complicated and takes far more time than initially assumed;
• the involvement of new stakeholders in a participatory approach renders decision making slower, but is eventually more sustainable;

- without changing incentive structures for involved actors, the change process remains scant and unsatisfactory;
- the challenge to change a traditional institution such as KNUST, through one institute, i.e. CANR, does have its pros and cons: on the one hand, application of INRM principles is easier when starting in one area; on the other hand, the university can limit the success of the project even at CANR through its overall structure, rules, incentives, etc.

The experience of CANR with the implementation of the project shows that INRM principles and approaches, if adopted by institutions of higher learning, would have the potential to address the many challenges the world is facing as a result of climate change and to ensure climate-resilient development, and especially address the complex nature of climate change by inter- and multidisciplinary approaches. The INRM principles and approaches create the platform for universities to meaningfully engage stakeholders in the design of appropriate learning programmes to deal with climate resilience issues. Over the last seven years, for instance, together with stakeholders, CANR has developed programmes that seek to promote climate-resilient development and ensure sustainability. Courses developed by CANR and stakeholders include Governance in Natural Resources, and Adaptive Management of Natural Resources Management. These courses have become very attractive to students because of their interactive and interdisciplinary nature.

As compared to the post-project period, the culture of the college and the work ethic of its lecturers have changed considerably over the last few years, particularly during the second phase of the project. Lecturers have come to the conclusion that they are no longer individuals and experts in their areas of specialisations, but are increasingly seeing themselves as members of an inter- and trans-disciplinary team (academics, students, and stakeholders) working towards fulfilling the college's mandates in teaching, research, and extension, and towards the college's vision to become the centre of excellence in INRM in the sub-region. Over the years, stakeholders have built confidence in their relationship with the college and feel encouraged by its genuine desire to engage and involve them in its programmes. The INRM project has also created a platform for intensified networking amongst its members.

The implementation of the INRM project has brought to the fore key lessons for national, regional, and international actors concerned with climate-resilient development:

- First, it has become clear that climate change and environmental problems are complex, multifaceted, and transcend regional and disciplinary boundaries and require an interdisciplinary approach, collaborative effort of all stakeholders, and teamwork to solve them.
- Second, the project has shown that it is possible for universities and stakeholders to collaborate in an effort to develop academic programmes that aim to produce graduates who will be capable of contributing to climate-resilient programmes in a holistic manner.

- Third, stakeholder institutions are convinced that, with their input, the universities will be producing the right type of graduates (individuals who are team players and capable of thinking out of the box) to take up challenging positions in various organisations, handling climate-resilient development programmes.
- Finally, it is widely recognised that climate-resilient development in developing countries demands a different kind of research that is based on the views of multiple stakeholders with often contrasting objectives. The College of Agriculture and Natural Resources at the University of Science and Technology in Kumasi, Ghana, has chosen to apply the principles and approaches of INRM and is encouraged by institutions such as CGIAR, the Center for International Forestry Research (CIFOR), the International Center for Tropical Agriculture (CIAT), the International Center for Agricultural Research in the Dry Areas (ICARDA),[3] etc., that have a pioneering role in promoting INRM in order to address climate-resilient development issues.

Notes

1 For more information about KNUST, see http://www.knust.edu.gh (accessed 14.01.2013).
2 For further information on MDF, see http://www.mdf.nl (accessed 25.01.2013).
3 For information on CGIAR, CIFOR, CIAT, and ICARDA visit their websites as follows: http://www.cgiar.org; www.cifor.org; http://ciat.cigar.org/; www.icrada.org (accessed 30.01.2013).

References

Azeez, I. O., Ikponmwonba, O. S., Labode, P., and Amusa, T. O. (2011) 'Land Use Activities among Forest Environments' Dwellers in Edo State, Nigeria: Implications for Livelihood and Sustainable Forest Management', *International Journal of Social Forest*, vol. 3, no. 2, pp. 164–187.

Campbell, B. M. *et al.* (2006) *Navigating Amidst Complexity: Guide to Implementing Effective Research and Development to Improve Livelihoods and the Environment*, Bogor, Indonesia: Center for International Forestry Research.

CANR Strategic Plan (2005) *A Strategic Plan Prepared by College of Agriculture and Natural Resources, Kwame Nkrumah University of Science and Technology*, Kumasi, Ghana.

CGIAR (2002) *Pre-Proposal for a CGIAR Challenge Programme: Improving Livelihoods and Natural Resource Management in Sub-Saharan Africa*, online: http://library.cgiar. org/bitstream/handle/10947/627/3.a1ssa.pdf?sequence=1 (accessed 04.02.2013).

Edusah, S. E. and Rozemeijer, N. (2011) 'A Concept Paper on Integrated Natural Resource Management, Project (NPT/GHA/278)', Kumasi, Ghana: Kwame Nkrumah University of Science and Technology (KNUST).

Frost, P., Campbell, B., and Usongo, L. (2006) 'Landscape-Scale Approaches for Integrated Natural Resources Management in Tropical Forest Landscapes', *Ecology and Society*, vol. 11, no. 2, p. 30.

Harwood, R. R. and Kassam, A. H. (eds.) (2003) *Examples of Research Problems, Approaches and Partnerships in Action in the CGIAR: Research towards Integrated*

Natural Resources Management, FAO, Rome: Interim Science Council, Centre Directors Committee on Integrated Natural Resources Management.

Hawkins, R. *et al.* (2009) *Integrated Agricultural Research for Development (IAR4D), A Concept Paper for the Forum for Agricultural Research in Africa (FARA) Sub-Saharan Africa Challenge Programme (SSA CP)*, Accra, Ghana: FARA.

Hughes, R. and Flintan, F. (2001) *Integrating Conservation and Development Experience: A Review and Bibliography of the ICDP Literature*, London: International Institute for Environment and Development.

Kaimowitz, D. (2003) 'Forest Law Enforcement and Rural Livelihoods', *International Forestry Review*, vol. 5, no. 3, p. 199.

Kio, P. R. O. (2002) 'Community Forest for Sustainable Forest Development', in Popoola, L. (ed.), *Forests, People and the Environment: Proceedings of a Workshop organized by FAN Consult and Edo State Forestry Department 5–6 September 2002.*

McShane, T. and Wells, M. P. (2003) *Getting Biodiversity Projects to Work: Towards More Effective Conservation and Development*, New York: Columbia University Press.

MDF Report (2010) Organisational analysis in the context of the project 'Institutionalisation of Integrated Natural Resource Management' Report of findings & recommendations NPT-GHA 278 (2008-2012), Kwame Nkrumah University of Science and Technology, Kumasi, Ghana.

NPT/GHA/278 Project Document (2008), prepared by BIRD and Dutch Consortium Partners, Kumasi.

Thomas, R. J. (2002) 'Revisiting the Conceptual Framework for INRM Developed in Penang and Cali'. in Turkelboom, F. *et al.* (eds), *Putting INRM into Action*, 4th INRM Workshop held at CARDA, Aleppo, Syria, 16–19 September 2002, pp. 53–57.

Part III
Climate-resilient development, innovation, and best practice

How to reform and bypass inefficiencies in the international climate regime

8 Green gold versus black gold

The Yasuní-ITT Initiative as an alternative way forward?

Amy Woodrow-Arai

The Yasuní-ITT Initiative: towards an innovative CRD model?

With the triple crises of economic turmoil, peak oil, and bleak predictions of the impacts of climate change, a basic concern for international development is the reduction of carbon emissions and the respective rearrangement of international cooperation and action. Furthermore, regions, countries, and communities have to prepare themselves for the inevitable effects of climate change. Adaptation has therefore moved to the top of the international negotiating agenda. However, as the various climate summits reveal, reaching consensus on what should be done, how much, and by whom, is a complex and multifaceted process.

Initiatives to integrate mitigation and adaptation can be subsumed under the term 'climate-resilient development' (CRD), which is the climate sensitive strategy on sustainable development. There is, as yet, no agreed definition for sustainable nor CRD; however, institutions such as the World Bank and the World Resources Institute use the term 'resilience' to describe preparation and protection against climatic threats in a business-as-usual scenario (Brown 2011). This approach is limited in its ability to achieve a transition towards more sustainable development as it does not challenge the basics of the system that has caused, and is accelerating, climate change and insecurity. As discussed in the introduction of this volume, CRD can be a complementing strategy as well as a modification of the dominant market-based concepts of 'sustainable development', thus seen as

> a bottom-up rather than top-down approach: information on what is happening on the ground and experience with effective local and regional policies need to be translated into globally acknowledged best practice of climate change management (see Chapter 2: 25)

and thus requires a substantial change of socio-economic structures. This is an increasing imperative as we hurtle toward dangerous transgressions of our planet's boundaries (see Rockström *et al.* 2009). The ability of multilateral negotiations under the auspices of the United Nations Framework Convention on Climate Change (UNFCCC) to reduce global greenhouse gas (GHG) emissions will be inadequate unless a concerted effort is made to address a systemic dependence on fossil fuels, which, on the current trajectory, seems unlikely or, at least, extremely slow.

This chapter looks at the possibilities for CRD through the lens of Ecuador's Yasuní-ITT Initiative. The Yasuní-ITT Initiative is a proposal to leave oil reserves untapped, to prevent the production of carbon emissions. Ecuador will forgo the revenue that extraction would create for the country and, in exchange, receive compensation from the international community as a bilateral climate change mitigation strategy. The Ishpingo-Tambococha-Tiputini (ITT) oil fields within the Yasuní National Park, located in the Amazon region of Ecuador, hold an estimated 846 million barrels of crude oil – approximately 20 per cent of Ecuador's total oil reserves. The Yasuní-ITT Initiative proposes to leave the oil untapped in exchange for receiving 50 per cent of the projected revenue from the international community. Over half of the Yasuní National Park is inhabited by indigenous communities including two non-contacted groups: the Tagaeri and Taromenane. It is also one of the most biodiverse places on Earth, with one hectare holding more tree species than the US and Canada put together (Bass *et al.* 2009).

Ecuador is substantially dependent on its petroleum resources, which make up over half of the country's export earnings and about one third of all tax revenues (EIA 2012). In addition to finding innovative approaches to environmental protection, disclaiming 50 per cent of future revenues from the ITT oil fields can thus be understood as substantial ecological commitment by Ecuador. There are, however, controversies. Firstly, oil expansion continues across Ecuador and at the borders of the Yasuní National Park (Garcia 2012); secondly, the international community has seemed somewhat unsure of the efficacy of such a test case (Bernier 2012).

Contributions to the Yasuní-ITT Initiative will accrue in a Social Capital Fund (i.e. the Ecuador Yasuní-ITT Trust Fund), administered by the United Nations Development Programme (UNDP). Interest earned from this fund will be reinvested into renewable energy projects, social development programmes, and conservation preservation, research, and forest management. According to its authors, the initiative is a move to 'put social and environmental values first, [while] exploring other ways to benefit the country economically' (Larrea 2010: 2).

The question is whether the Yasuní-ITT Initiative will be able to meet the challenge of effectively preventing GHG emissions at source, to reduce energy consumption and to invest in alternative energies throughout the country. The focus of this chapter is therefore on the following questions: will the Yasuní-ITT Initiative be more effective regarding CRD compared to other mechanisms such as the Clean Development Mechanism (CDM) or Reducing Emissions from Deforestation and Forest Degradation (REDD)? What are some of the issues and the contradictions related to this initiative? Which lessons can be learned to turn it into a progressive and alternative development model?

This chapter illustrates that the Yasuní-ITT Initiative has the potential to serve as a best practice model for CRD and to go beyond the currently predominant market-based model in climate policy. The analysis of the Ecuadorian development model does, however, reveal many contradictions: saving a highly biodiverse carbon sink[1] by leaving oil reserves untapped while at the same time increasing oil extraction throughout the country and not adequately consulting, for example, indigenous people being affected by these activities does not signify a carefully designed and ecologically focused development model. The Yasuní-ITT Initiative thus raises many normative questions regarding sustainability, resilience, equity, and justice and should not only be viewed as a pragmatic problem-solving strategy.

In the first section, the Yasuní-ITT Initiative is explained, including differences to the UNFCCC mechanisms: CDM and REDD+. The aim is to show the Initiative's potential to serve, as an alternative, more CRD-oriented strategy. The discussion continues by reviewing some of the controversies surrounding this project. The following section then illustrates that the Ecuadorian government is pursuing a highly contradictory policy which brings forward the question of whether Ecuador is really moving in the direction of a low carbon society and economy.

Deficiencies of the UNFCCC process

The ineffectiveness of the climate regime's economic rationale

Central to the Kyoto Protocol mechanisms is the financialisation of nature in order to institutionalise collective international action on carbon emission reductions. The attribution of economic value to natural processes is the core rationale for climate change negotiations. This has required the translation of the wealth of nature's processes into tradable units of natural capital. Communicating the urgency of climate change in a language that adheres to the international market is at the core of climate change agreements. Pivotal influencing works reflect this. *The Stern Review* (2007), for example, frames climate change as history's greatest market failure; equally prominent, *The Economics of Ecosystems and Biodiversity* (TEEB 2010) makes the 'invisibility' of the value of biodiversity to the global economy tangible, predicting the cost of biodiversity and ecosystem damage at 18 per cent of global economic output by 2050.

While engaging business and the biggest polluters in climate change action is an imperative, the respective focus of action might divert the objective of GHG reduction to the financial opportunities of this new, lucrative market. The 'Green Economy'[2] threatens to concentrate the attention of polluting agents on profit-making opportunities via the commercialisation of nature's processes (water, biodiversity, land, air) and, in doing so, achieves very little in terms of emission reductions (GRAIN 2012).

Carbon trading as a false solution to GHG reductions

One major element of this approach is carbon trading. According to the International Energy Agency (IEA 2011), global CO_2 emissions from fossil fuel combustion reached a record high of 31.6 gigatonnes (Gt) in 2011. This represents an increase of 1.0 Gt compared to 2010 figures. With an estimated increase in energy demand by one third between 2010 and 2035 – considered necessary to meet the needs of a global population increase of 1.7 billion people – offsets, carbon credits, and the carbon market are not going to be enough to stabilise climate change.

We can see an example of the ineffectual logic of carbon markets if we look at the involvement of Ecuador and the United Kingdom (UK) in the CDM. The CDM has two main objectives: to assist developing countries in achieving sustainable development (SD), and to help industrialised countries meet their emission reduction targets. This is through emission reduction projects that earn developing countries Certified Emission Reduction (CER) credits. They are equivalent to one tonne of CO_2, and can be purchased by industrialised countries and traded to offset their carbon emissions to remain within their allocated GHG targets. There are currently 18 registered CDM projects in Ecuador, of which 11 are in the renewable energy sector: seven hydroelectric, two wind power, and two cogeneration projects. The remaining six projects are in the waste-handling and disposal sector, with one project distributing energy-efficient light bulbs to households (UNFCCC 2012a).

The UK is the Annex I country partner[3] in 4 out of the current 18 CDM projects in Ecuador, generating an estimated 555,270 metric tonnes worth of CO_2 of annual emission reductions[4] (UNFCCC 2012a). In relation to the global carbon market, UK companies account for 31.02 per cent of all CERs earned through the CDM. Involvement in 1,651 projects worldwide means that they are at the centre of the global carbon market (UNFCCC 2012b). The skewed logic of 'offsetting' is exemplified by the UK's proposed expansion of Heathrow airport. Heathrow's third terminal, should it go ahead, is expected to produce an extra 180 million tonnes of CO_2 per year, equal to 3.1 per cent of the UK's overall carbon emissions (Bullock *et al.* 2009: 19). However, the UK's transport minister (Geoff Hoon), at the time of announcing the expansion, summed up this reasoning as 'any growth in aviation emissions from expansion at Heathrow would be fully offset by a reduction in emissions elsewhere' (ibid.).

Carbon trading avoids the most effective and obvious solution: to consume less and leave fossil fuels in the ground, i.e. 'effective action on climate change involves demanding, adopting, and supporting policies that reduce emissions at source as opposed to offsetting or trading' (Smith 2006). 'End-of-pipe' solutions to pollution result in a net increase in GHG emissions. Each project in developing countries that is offset against industry in industrialised 'developed' countries allows the latter to continue to pollute and consume over and above reduction limits. What actually occurs is that companies gain doubly: to contaminate and to sell false solutions (in the form of) funding comparatively cheap projects in developing countries.

REDD+: a false promise?

The recognition of the intrinsic value of forests in climate change mitigation is the motivation for the development of the UN-REDD Programme. The

Intergovernmental Panel on Climate Change (IPCC) states that reducing and/ or preventing deforestation, thereby avoiding the release of carbon into the atmosphere, is the mitigation option with the largest and most immediate impact for action against climate change (IPCC 2007). Forests are natural carbon sinks, absorbing CO_2 as part of their biological processes, as well as storing carbon in soil and trees. Deforestation accounts for nearly 20 per cent of global GHG emissions, more than the entire global transportation sector (Parker *et al.* 2009; UN-REDD Programme 2010).

Acknowledging the scope of the impacts of forest protection, REDD+ goes beyond deforestation and forest degradation, and includes the role of conservation, sustainable management of forests, and the enhancement of forest carbon stocks:

> It is predicted that financial flows for greenhouse gas emission reductions from REDD+ could reach up to US$30 billion a year. This significant North–South flow of funds could reward a meaningful reduction of carbon emissions and could also support new, pro-poor development, help conserve biodiversity and secure vital ecosystem services.
>
> (UN-REDD Programme 2010)

REDD+ is relevant to the Yasuní-ITT Initiative because the Amazon accounts for one tenth of the total carbon stored in land ecosystems (Kozloff 2010: 50), and because it is a mechanism under consideration for a post-Kyoto Protocol climate regime that addresses the *prevention* of potential carbon emissions as well as the protection of biodiversity, with major implications for forest-dwelling people.

Ecuador has one of the highest proportions of forest cover in the world, with an estimated total land cover of approximately 55 per cent (UN-REDD Programme 2012). It also has the highest deforestation rate in South America at 1.8 per cent compared to a regional average of 0.5 per cent (FAO 2011: 118). Studies show that, if protected, the total avoided deforestation within the borders of the ITT oil fields over a 30-year period would reach 1.35 million hectares, with avoided emissions of 791 million tonnes of CO_2 (Silvestrum 2009, cited in UNFCCC 2011: 8).

Criticisms of REDD+: corruption and monoculture plantations

A main challenge for REDD+ is to simultaneously deal with the complexities of forest ecosystems, the sensitivities of local and national governance structures, forest protection, and the financial incentives of leasing or selling land for agricultural use, all the while maintaining a focus on overall GHG reductions.

A major problem with trading the carbon stored in forests is that GHG emissions need to be reduced and *as well* deforestation needs to be stopped. Global GHG emissions will not decrease if one type of emission is traded off against another. A focus on deforestation in developing countries lessens the incentive for high emitter (industrialised) countries to make real reductions in their own emissions.

Brown (2010) addresses REDD+'s vulnerability to corruption, outlining three principal areas where this is likely to occur. Firstly, in setting baseline levels, there are built-in incentives to increase deforestation rates before the start date of the programme's commitment period: the higher the level of baseline deforestation, the greater the potential for REDD+ credit accumulation. Secondly, corrupt government officials could claim REDD+ credits and 'double count' for areas that are already being protected under national initiatives. Thirdly, there are strong financial motives for corruption for those in charge of protecting forests and those monitoring forest stocks with the effect of reporting false monitoring data.

REDD+ also fails to address the main drivers of deforestation. An increase in meat consumption due to rising populations, rising incomes, and demand for meat and dairy resulting from Western-style diets (Hertwich *et al.* 2010) has contributed to deforestation for cattle ranching, which accounts for nearly 80 per cent of the deforestation in the Brazilian Amazon (Greenpeace 2009: 3). Additionally, timber companies eager to protect their interests have become increasingly active in REDD+ negotiations. The International Tropical Timber Organisation (ITTO)[5] calls for 'sustainable forest management', which includes logging and 'production forests' or monoculture plantations (Hall 2010: 15). Monoculture plantations are a contentious element of the REDD+ programme as they provide a cheap option for carbon sequestration. However, monoculture plantations are not biologically diverse, may have a negative impact on soil and water cycles, and capture considerably less carbon than traditional forests, especially when non-native plants are introduced. Various studies show that non-indigenous plantations (especially eucalyptus) have had devastating impacts on land and communities. They are hugely water intensive, depleting soil and groundwater, and they cause long-term environmental degradation and the disruption of ecosystems (Petermann and Langelle 2006; Acosta 2011; Overbeek *et al.* 2012). Traditional forests, on the other hand, are highly biodiverse and provide a rich habitat for regionally specific forest life. They are complex self-regenerating systems, consisting of soil, water, and micro-climates and a wide variety of plants, animals, and humans cohabiting in a mutually enhancing way. Inclusion of monoculture plantations in REDD+ would provide enormous subsidies to the timber industry, without contributing to the reduction of GHG emissions (Lang 2009; Kanowski and Catterall 2010). Thus, reforestation through monocrop plantations and the introduction of non-native plant species fails to recognise that forests support interconnected ecosystems and host a diversity of species and humans that have been able to manage forests and livelihoods in a sustainable way for millennia.

REDD+: a centralised, government-dominated process

Perhaps of most relevance to the Yasuní-ITT Initiative is the impact of REDD+ on the livelihoods of forest-dwelling people and their representation in the mechanism. Okereke and Dooley (2009) maintain that REDD+ fails to bring about equitable and just outcomes for indigenous people, despite its attempts to incorporate forest communities, due to different ways of viewing the world and value ranking. The commitment to neo-liberal concepts of equity and justice, and market-based solutions that focus on technical and methodological issues, fails to recognise that forests are central to numerous human and biological processes and cannot be reduced to tradable units of carbon. The market-based approaches envisaged by REDD+ produce unequal power relations between actors, as they are founded in a system of governance that does not give a pronounced voice to non-state actors.

REDD+ also creates pressures to centralise forest governance, undermining the social, ecological, and carbon benefits of traditional forest management and the traditional livelihoods of forest-dwelling peoples (Phelps *et al.* 2010; Clark 2010). The use of market-based mechanisms, in this way, means that the odds are stacked against forest-dwelling peoples as they are in a weaker negotiating position, particularly those with no legal tenure, communities without the requisite governance or organisational structures, and groups unable to afford expensive environmental impact assessments to fulfil a range of quantifiable qualification criteria. This set-up of REDD+ undermines local autonomy and inevitably leads to increased corporate governance of forests (Global Forest Coalition 2008; Lohmann 2008). This is especially the case in Ecuador where indigenous opposition to REDD+ presents a considerable challenge (Reed 2011).

Within the UNFCCC, however, much has been done to address these issues regarding the implementation of REDD+ – not least in response to objections from forest-dwelling communities and indigenous groups from around the world (see IPCCA 2011; AIPP 2011; IEN 2012). In spite of this, the critical issue remains that REDD+ infers the onus of responsibility for forest preservation and carbon sequestration on communities who have traditionally cared for forests, but, at the same time, compromises their autonomy by incorporating nature's common goods and their land and land tenure into REDD+ projects as part of national development plans.

The Yasuní-ITT Initiative as an alternative CRD model

Considering the problems of the current climate change regime and its mechanisms, any alternative approach would have to address the following challenges:

- Trading carbon credits is failing to decrease overall GHG emissions. A cessation of oil extraction and fossil fuel production needs to occur as well as tackling the national and international dependence on energy produced by fossil fuels.
- A new, more CRD-oriented model is needed, which assigns value to nature and invests in the development of alternative energy production, thus incorporating a transition to a post-oil dependent economy.

In this respect, the Yasuní-ITT Initiative is groundbreaking for two reasons. Firstly, it is a proposal from the South as opposed to the North-centric climate negotiations of the Kyoto Protocol. Secondly, it synthesises local and global needs, as it is, on the one hand, geographically specific, impacting local people, the local environment, biodiversity, and the economic sustainability of Ecuador, and, on the other hand, it will reduce carbon emissions and address global climate change. In achieving its aims, it will serve as an example of an alternative development model that embodies a fundamental value shift: recognising the wealth of natural resources maintained *in situ* as well as the need for socially equitable development and investments in renewable energy production. Its implementation would signify Ecuador's transition from the current oil-dependent development model to a new strategy, based on sustainability and equality. Globally, the project would provide an example of a successful alternative development model, which could be replicated in comparable regions of the world.[6] It could also be extended to other extractive operations such as coal mining and hydraulic fracturing (fracking).

The Yasuní-ITT Initiative proposes:

- an innovative option for combating global warming, by avoiding the production of fossil fuels;
- protecting the biodiversity of Ecuador and supporting the voluntary isolation of indigenous cultures living in the Yasuní National Park;
- a move away from an oil-dependent economy and towards the use of renewable energy sources, as part of a strategy aimed at consolidating a new model of development in the country.

On 3 August 2010, Ecuador signed an agreement with UNDP, to set up a trust fund to manage the funds of the Yasuní-ITT Initiative. It is overseen by a steering committee that consists of six members (each with one vote): three representatives from the Ecuadorian government, two from contributing governments, and one Ecuadorian civil society representative (UNDP 2010a: 3).

The Multi-Donor Trust Fund Office is administrated by UNDP, and contributors to the Yasuní Fund include governments, private and public entities, NGOs, intergovernmental organisations (IGOs), and individuals. The Yasuní-ITT Trust Fund has two windows: a Capital Fund Window and a Revenue Fund Window. The Capital Fund Window is financed directly by contributions to the Yasuní Fund Account and funds will be used to invest in renewable energy projects (hydro, geothermal, solar, wind, and biomass). The Revenue Fund window will be replenished by investment revenue and interest from the Capital Fund Window and will fund activities in conservation, reforestation, energy efficiency, agro-forest management, social programmes, and research efforts – particularly in the generation of goods and services based on bio-knowledge (UNDP 2010a).

The minimum capital compensation needs to be equal to half the sum Ecuador would otherwise receive through the extraction of oil in the ITT block, equivalent to the value of potential CO_2 emissions stored underground according to the value of credits on the carbon market. Ecuador is inviting the global community to contribute 50 per cent of the income it is forgoing, amounting to US$3.6 billion (over a 13-year period) (UNDP 2012a). In the initial stages of the Initiative, numerous deadlines were set by President Rafael Correa to raise the required funds.

The eventual decision was that the Yasuní Fund must reach a minimum threshold of US$100 million by the end of 2011. In the case that the Yasuní fund did not meet this target, the government would refund contributors. In December 2011, Correa confirmed the government's commitment to extend the Initiative based on the positive response from national governments, NGOs, corporations, and individuals. The Yasuní 2011 annual financial report (UNDP 2012b) announced that 2011 contributions – consisting of firm pledges, commitments, and deposits – reached over US$116 million, including Germany's pledge to contribute US$47 million in bilateral cooperation that will be used for sustainable activities in the Yasuní National Park. Italy has contributed the largest donation in the form of nearly US$50 million in debt cancellation. The next largest sums are from the regional government of Wallonia, Belgium (US$1,903,695) and US$1,400,400 from Spain (UNDP 2012c).

The innovative potential of the Yasuní-ITT Initiative: opportunities and challenges

The expected benefits

The Yasuní-ITT Initiative *prevents* the production of carbon emissions. Estimates show 846 million barrels of untapped crude oil. By committing to not extract the full amount, the Yasuní-ITT Initiative will prevent the emission of 407 million tonnes of CO_2. The real value of the emissions avoided is far greater when taking into account the direct and indirect deforestation that occurs through oil exploration, the emissions generated through the construction of infrastructure, and the extraction process itself. This is a globally significant amount, surpassing the annual emissions of France (373 million tonnes) or Brazil (332 million tonnes) (Larrea 2010: 4). With regard to tackling climate change, this guarantee of not emitting is clearly preferable to the trading of emission reductions, as it is not an offset or a reduction in emissions, but an abatement of future emissions. In addition, the Initiative works towards steering the economy away from fossil fuel dependency through the reinvestment of the generated funds in alternative energy production and forest protection. Therefore, the total reduction of GHG emissions achieved by the Initiative must also include a decrease in emissions from future renewable energy production and the preservation of carbon stocks.

Integrating the Yasuní-ITT Initiative into carbon trading: a false logic?

Monetising the value of nature within the Yasuní-ITT oil block does not compromise the principles of the Initiative. However, including the avoided GHG emissions in the existing carbon market does. In exchange for financial contributions, the Ecuadorian Government will issue Yasuní Guarantee Certificates (CGY is the Spanish acronym) which will correspond to the nominal amount of metric tonnes of CO_2 avoided and be priced equivalent to emission allowances (EU allowances; EUAs) under the EU Emissions Trading Scheme (ETS) at the date of purchase.

The decision to hitch CGYs to the European carbon market has been a contentious one and caused considerable disagreement amongst the actors involved in formulating the original Initiative. The initial conception of the Yasuní-ITT Initiative was based on compensatory global donations to keep the oil underground. The Initiative was first conceived in 2006 by two NGOs, OilWatch (International) and Acción Ecológica (Ecuador), while contracts were being written up to grant drilling concessions in the Yasuní-ITT Block (Martin 2010: 20–23). It was an opportune moment to push for a radical alternative to oil extraction, with the incoming president's 'Citizen's Revolution of 21st Century Socialism' and the signing of the 'Rights of Nature' into the constitution.

There were considerable disagreements among NGOs and international non-governmental organisations (INGOs) in the design of the financing mechanism, which was exacerbated by President Correa's threats to grant drilling concessions by the setting of arbitrary deadlines to raise the funds. The smaller INGOs, such as Amazon Watch, Finding Species, and Pachamama pushed for the Initiative to remain outside any Kyoto Protocol mechanisms, while other larger INGOs, such as The Nature Conservatory and Conservation International, were concerned that it needed to apply to the Kyoto Protocol regime in order to be effective (Martin 2010: 22–35).

The final decision, as stated in the *Yasuní Trust Fund: Terms of Reference* (UNDP 2010b), is that CGYs are not included in the European carbon market and cannot be traded. They currently represent straight contributions to carbon sequestration. This does not mean that they will not be included in the future. On the contrary, as a pilot project, CGYs are linked to EUAs with the possibility for carbon markets to accept them as equivalents to emission permits in a post-Kyoto Protocol climate regime. There are also proposals for bilateral agreements with the US and Canada, should they adopt binding GHG limits. In this case, CGYs would be accepted as equivalent to emission permits within a cap and trade system (Larrea 2010: 22). This compromises the Initiative, as it would alter CGYs to have the same function as carbon credits and allow GHG emissions to be offset elsewhere.

The problem arising here is the issue of incentives: if CGYs are not part of a trading scheme, the uptake from governments and business may be limited. Donations have not been overwhelming. The budgetary austerity adopted by governments, post-2008 in the context of the global financial crisis, has not been helpful in this respect. The fund has now been opened up to individual donations. The disproportionately high level of individual donations from the UK is likely due to *The Guardian*[7] newspaper, which has been following the progress of the Initiative. The latter suggests that there is a potential for the Initiative to be kept afloat if a far-reaching publicity campaign is embraced by civil society or picked up by prominent NGOs. To date, the international coverage and commentary on the Initiative has been poor considering that it is an innovative solution to tackle climate change, especially as it plans to invest in an alternative energy matrix and social development projects. It has not been backed by environmental NGOs as supportively as one might expect. This has been due, in part, to an uneasiness expressed by some critics that the Yasuní-ITT proposal amounts to 'environmental extortion' or 'ecological blackmail' (Pirard 2011; Bernier 2012).

Towards a post-oil dependent economy: why Ecuador needs a new development model

Funds for a new CRD model?

The capital funds generated by the sale of CGYs will be invested into renewable energy projects to steer the Ecuadorian economy away from oil dependency, and redirect national consumption of electricity toward non-GHG emitting energy production. Ecuador has great hydroelectric, geothermal, wind, and solar power potential (Larrea 2010: 24). These projects will provide the state with fixed interest payments, independent of any company profits. Administered by the UNDP Trust Fund, these sources will fund Ecuador's National Development Plan. The plan includes (Larrea 2010: 13; Warnars 2010: 65–66):

- preserving and preventing deforestation in 44 protected areas, constituting 4.8 million hectares, 19 per cent of Ecuador's territory;
- reforestation, forestation, natural regeneration, and the management of one million hectares of forest;
- research in science and technology for programmes that enhance bio-knowledge, sustainable and integrated river basin management, and investment in a change in Ecuador's energy matrix;
- investment in social development programmes in education, health, and the creation of jobs in sustainable activities, such as ecotourism, agriculture, and agro-forestry.

The Yasuní-ITT Initiative is clearly a preferable development model over Ecuador's previous oil-dependent economic model (see below). It incorporates the objectives of REDD+ projects, through avoided deforestation and the protection of forested areas, and pre-emptively writes clear objectives for social outcomes into the Initiative's administrative architecture: the protection of indigenous groups and investments in health, education, and training programmes, as well as job creation in sustainable activities, such as ecotourism, agriculture, and agro-forestry. The Yasuní-ITT Initiative avoids the devastating consequences of oil pollution within a programme sensitive to environmental and social concerns. With clearly directed reinvestment of the profits of keeping oil underground, it manages to reverse the trend of oil as a 'resource curse'. In this way, the Yasuní-ITT Initiative embraces CRD as it embodies a different relationship with natural resources, by unlocking the equity of fossil fuels retained *in situ* and reinvesting this money into renewable energies to bring about a non-oil dependent economy. According to President Correa, it is a new development model that embodies a value shift: '[The project] would not only reduce global warming, which benefits the whole planet, but also introduce a new economic logic for the 21st century, which assigns value to things other than merchandise' (Correa 2007).

However, the devil lies in the details. For the investments to be considered a contribution to CRD, the projects must not simply be replications of REDD+ frameworks. A concerted effort must be made not to invest in projects that exacerbate environmental damage or are 'false solutions' to environmental protection or climate change. The 'reforestation' must not include monocrops, the 'ecotourism' must be properly monitored for environmental and social impacts, and any renewable energy projects must not interfere with or disrupt ecosystems and subsistence livelihoods.[8]

Ecuador and the oil industry: a negative balance

Various studies have explored the extent of the oil reserves in the Yasuní region and have produced projections (Isch 2007; Boedt and Martinez 2007). Estimates show that the 846 million barrels (20 per cent of Ecuador's reserves) under the Yasuní National Park would generate US$7.25 billion dollars for Ecuador in oil revenue (Larrea 2010: 4), much needed revenues for a developing country like Ecuador.

Ecuador's economic history and relationship with oil mirrors that of many oil-dependent developing countries. Oil was first discovered in the Ecuadorian Amazon in 1967. The wealth generated transformed the country, but the economic impact was fast and uneven. Political fragmentation and corruption were exacerbated, and an over-dependency on oil as the main export product heightened Ecuador's vulnerability to fluctuations in international oil prices. Environmental degradation and disruption of indigenous livelihoods characterised the oil business in the region (Gerlach 2003; Sawyer 2005). Ecuador has experienced the much-analysed 'resource curse' (Sachs and Warner 2001; Humphreys *et al.* 2007; Collier 2007), which refers to the tendency of states with large reserves of natural resources (specifically oil) to be less developed than similar states which lack such resources. Oil wealth has not filtered down to the majority of the Ecuadorian population. Up until 2005, 85 per cent of oil profits left the country, absorbed by foreign oil companies (Warnars 2010: 44). Prior to Correa's election, urban unemployment remained high, and between 2002 and 2008, over one million people emigrated (Baird 2008). Calculations showed a stagnant growth of only 0.5 per cent, and 38.3 per cent of the population living on less than US$1.00 per day (World Bank 2010).

In addition to the lack of positive development outcomes from the oil business in Ecuador, the environmental and social costs have been devastating. The activities of Texaco (now Chevron) in the Amazon region demonstrate this: between 1964 and 1990, more than 18 billion gallons of toxic wastewater were dumped, over 17 million gallons of crude oil spilled, and hazardous waste was left in hundreds of open pits dug out of the forest floor in the Amazon basin region. Contamination of soil and water courses caused health problems in local residents in the form of mouth, stomach, and uterine cancer; birth defects; and miscarriages (Dematteis and Szymczak 2008). State-owned Petroecuador's record has been equally appalling: in 2001, the company was responsible for 75 oil spills. A 2003 survey found that everyone living near Petroecuador installations presented some form of poisoning; Petroecuador was also directly implicated in the assassination of an environmental activist opposing their operations (Ransom 2008: 15).

Extractive industries in Ecuador: Correa as 'the people's capitalist'

Today, the oil industry remains a vital organ of the Ecuadorian economy; retaining profits from the vast oil reserves continues to be a major concern for the government regardless of environmental issues. Foreign oil companies manage about 40 per cent of Ecuador's total daily oil production, with the rest accounted for by state entities: Petroecuador, Petroamazonas, and Rio Napo. Petroecuador produces between a third and half of the country's oil and, since 2006, holds the block 15 concession (near the ITT block), which is the most productive block in the country. Petroecuador is also pushing ahead with developments for oil extraction in block 31, which is adjacent to the ITT block (Watts 2012). Oil expansion is central to the country's development plan. Ecuador was producing 486,000 barrels of oil per day in 2010 and aspires to increase this to 600,000 barrels per day by 2013 (EIA 2012). The Yasuní-ITT Initiative appears tokenistic when positioned against the wider extractive policies of Correa's government.

Ecuador's 2009–2013 National Development Plan emphasises poverty reduction and promotion of social inclusion, equality, and justice. Public spending rose from 24 per cent of GDP in 2005 to 57.6 per cent in 2011. The poverty rate declined from 37.6 per cent in 2006 to 28.6 per cent in 2011, whereas extreme poverty fell from 16.9 per cent in 2006 to 11.6 per cent in 2011 (World Bank 2012). Funding President Correa's ambitious initiatives and programmes as part of Ecuador's 'citizen's revolution of 21st century socialism' relies on wealth generation from Ecuador's oil, gold, silver, and copper mining reserves. His policies regarding mining oil and gas expansion hugely contradict not only his own statements on indigenous rights and the environment but also his vociferous backing of the Yasuní-ITT Initiative.

Correa's pre-election campaign garnered huge indigenous and popular support. Central to his election promises were an anti-imperialist fight against the US and previous Ecuadorian administrations' neo-liberalist policies, and a stand against indigenous marginalisation and environmental destruction. He continues with the same socialist and environmental rhetoric, but his presidency has largely contradicted this. Instead of working toward renewable alternatives to oil, Correa has sought to expand the oil and mining sectors, and aggressively represses indigenous dissent (Denvir 2009; Dangl 2010a).

In January 2009, the government passed a mining law that granted Canadian corporations no limits on the number of concessions that can be held by a company, and mining concessions of renewable 25-year terms (Kinross 2009). Burbach (2009) claims this law is written in the neo-liberal model, favouring foreign investment over social and environmental concerns, placing the extraction of minerals over the rights of communities and, additionally, criminalising protest. Specific sections of this law grant the State access to indigenous people's land and exclude them from any mining negotiations. Article 2 mandates the participation of private and public actors in discussions over mining concerns, but does not include community members affected by mining. Articles 15, 16, and 28 assert 'state dominion over mines and oil fields', declaring them a 'public utility' which can be 'freely prospected' for the common good. This serves to protect mining corporations under corporate law and rescinds indigenous rights (Dosh 2009; Dangl 2010b: 51–55). These provisions contradict the declared objective of integrating local communities into the decision processes and the benefits of the use of natural resources.

The expansion of the extractive industries has further widened the gap between Correa's administration and Ecuador's indigenous population. In March 2012, this culminated in a two-week march across the country for 'Life, Water, and Dignity of the Peoples' by thousands of indigenous people over government investment in large-scale mining (Koenig 2012). This growing mistrust of the government is also making indigenous participation in any government-led forest protection schemes, such as REDD+, more strained (Reed 2011). Part of the reason for the conflict between indigenous groups and the government is due to a difference in worldview. While Correa asserts that the Yasuní-ITT Initiative is written within the constitutionally sanctioned 'Rights of Nature', many indigenous groups are experiencing the contradiction. Humberto Cholango, president of CONAIE,[9] claims that there has been no consultation between the state and the indigenous groups affected by the Yasuní-ITT Initiative. CONAIE's position is that the government has a constitutional duty to leave oil in the ground regardless of any economic objectives, and that compensation from the international community amounts to blackmail (EJOLT 2012). Resistance to oil developments in the Amazon has increased after the government's most recent round of oil block auctioning in the region. In November 2012, the government invited energy companies to bid for the oil development of 13 oil blocks, covering nearly 10 million acres of south-eastern Amazon (Johnson 2012). Objections were raised at the UNFCCC COP18 in Doha in December 2012 by indigenous leaders, claiming that agreements for prospecting were illegitimate because deals were made between government institutions and select groups of individuals within the affected communities, and not in adherence with the larger decision-making structures of the communities. Government institutions have not respected local decision-making norms and have lacked proper procedure in the native language (Peterson 2012). This imbalance is a familiar occurrence elsewhere in the Amazon when deals are struck with selected individuals without the consent of the wider community (Watts 2013).

Leifsen (2009) outlines what he sees as Correa's dilemma: in order to free the country from the economic dependence of natural resources and channel revenue to the poor and needy sectors of society, he must exploit oil and mining reserves and take advantage of the surplus. A precondition of this is the implementation of laws and state apparatus to manage and administer these revenues (Leifsen 2009: 4). Correa's actions represent a conflict between a drive for national social and economic imperatives and the protection of indigenous and environmental rights.

Correa sees no contradiction in his policies. He believes that markets are an economic reality and that they can be harnessed for social and environmental gains (Correa 2010). It is evident that the government's main concerns for Ecuador are about continued economic development at the expense of the environment. What is left out of the equation is that natural resources are finite. Ecuador may develop economically, and even invest in renewable energy production, but, again, we see an example of using the same economic models that caused the problem in the first place. Reapplying neo-liberal practices nationally to the oil business undermines the Yasuní-ITT Initiative, both ideologically and practically. It is a twisted logic that sees conflicting economic and environmental models of development existing side by side, literally, in the Yasuní National Park. This compromises the project as it puts into question its ability to protect the region indefinitely. As an international precedent, however, the Yasuní-ITT Initiative is immeasurably significant, not only because it is an innovative and practicable option for CRD and a transition towards a post-oil economy, but it will protect and preserve the ITT block from oil development, regardless of the wider contradictions. It outlines a different relationship with natural resources. It underscores that the most effective CO_2 reduction policies are not emissions mitigation through preventing deforestation and trading carbon credits, but preventing emissions in the first place and protecting the ecosystems (in this case, the Amazon) which naturally regulate climatic change. For international action on climate change, this ideological and symbolic shift cannot be underestimated.

Lessons learned and recommendations

The current climate change regime's ability to affect GHG reduction is markedly limited. The myopic vision of the possible options for climate change mitigation reflects the international system that continues to reapply the same models and logic of the market to combat climate change. The Yasuní-ITT Initiative is a development model – in theory, at least – that offers a solution for more sustainable resource use and is a big step towards CRD within the possibilities of the current global system. It manages to address the problems highlighted regarding REDD+ and carbon trading, as it is a multifaceted programme with specific objectives. These objectives cover indigenous, biodiversity, and environmental protection, alternative energy production, as well as the retention of oil and avoidance of potential carbon emissions. It is a holistic answer to a multifaceted problem. It is also an example of an initiative led by civil society that incorporates local, national, and international concerns.

The Yasuní-ITT Initiative will not only avoid the production of CO_2 emissions in the first instance, but it also maintains carbon stored underground and in protected forests. By addressing the problem at source, it circumvents the potential for oil spills, pollution, and the devastating impacts on indigenous livelihoods that characterise oil activities in such critically biodiverse and sensitive areas. It is an innovative option for a transition from an oil-dependent economy to a post-fossil fuel economy by unlocking the value of natural resources retained *in situ* and reinvesting in an alternative energy matrix, while also benefiting Ecuadorian citizens through increased public spending on social projects. It also serves as an example of concerted private/public, national/international effort to wean a national economy off oil and a move towards an energy-secure, more climate-resilient, and sustainable future. As a pilot CRD model, it could be replicated in other parts of the world. Its successful implementation in Ecuador and other similar critically biodiverse, carbon-rich forested regions would have a vast global impact on GHG emission stabilisation.

The Initiative is, however, compromised by the continued expansion of politically influential and lucrative extractive industries within Ecuador. The need for revenue to fund progressive social reform in Ecuador is a main concern for President Correa. The urgency of his drive for revenue accumulation is reflected in his numerous deadlines set to raise compensation (as an element of international bargaining) and the further opening up of the Amazon to oil extraction and the development of mining projects across the country. This brings into question the viability of the Yasuní-ITT Initiative, as it might not have the necessary governmental support needed for its final success. For the Initiative to work, it will need continual reinforcement of the motivations and objectives, and must not be promoted solely for economic gain. The Initiative could benefit from a concerted publicity push, internationally, that would garner greater support from INGOs, governments, and civil society, thus inviting more investment in the project and also highlighting Ecuador's responsibility to refrain from drilling indefinitely.

The Initiative is still in its relative infancy and, hence, it is difficult to draw conclusions about its effectiveness. This chapter has shown, however, that there are concerns that need to be fully addressed if it is to be a viable alternative to the current climate management mechanisms. These are:

- CGYs need to remain outside the carbon market – as it is an ineffective mechanism for carbon emissions reduction.
- Indigenous and local actors need to be continually consulted in a participatory process developed and agreed by all parties (communities, state, and business entities).
- Projects financed by the Revenue Fund need to be socially and environmentally sound and inclusive.
- In addition, national and transnational civil society groups, NGOs, and INGOs need to maintain pressure on the government to uphold its obligation to refrain from oil extraction in the Yasuní-ITT block indefinitely.

The development and success of the Initiative can have a considerable contribution internationally, as it is an example of an innovative local and national solution to CO_2 reduction and CRD that goes beyond the limits of conventional 'development' thinking.

Countries that are currently pursuing carbon-intensive development and have substantive carbon reserves can consider an alternative development path as they tap, for a certain time, income from this sector to move to a less carbon-dependent and CRD path. As discussed, these countries can make an important contribution to global CO_2 reduction by avoiding GHG emissions at source. Due to the higher proportion of indigenous and land-based communities whose livelihoods depend on forests, the development of regionally and culturally specific frameworks for negotiations will need to be built into any similar models. This will require a rigorous and thorough consultation process, and in some cases where land tenure is not clearly established or where indigenous custodianship of the land is at odds with the country's environmental law, due process and agreement amongst all parties needs to be established.

A final point to make is that the failure to conserve non-renewable oil in the subsoil and failure to protect non-contacted tribes is a development outcome that would be irreversible. Therefore, protecting the area from *any* oil development is an optimum solution. In this sense, the administrative, structural, and international co-operation in this project will be supporting one of the most effective ways of stabilising the climate – that is, to protect these highly biodiverse areas indefinitely, allowing for the most effective GHG mitigation strategy: keeping the oil in the soil and leaving these ecosystems untouched to naturally store and process CO_2.

Notes

1 Carbon sink: natural and potentially man-made features on the Earth's surface where carbon dioxide (CO_2) is removed from the atmosphere. The major natural sinks are forests and oceans, which have processes that absorb CO_2. Carbon sinks are vital to fighting global warming because they counteract sources of carbon emissions, such as industry and transport. Carbon Positive: http://www.carbonpositive.net/viewarticle. aspx?articleID=44 (accessed 30 January 2013).

2 The 'Green Economy' is the incorporation of natural capital and ecological services into the economy. As stated by the United Nations Environment Programme (UNEP), rather than a drain, or an alternative to the growth economy: 'the greening of economies has the potential to be a new engine of growth, a net generator of decent jobs and a vital strategy to eliminate persistent poverty' (UNEP 2011: 16).

3 Annex I countries are the 41 industrialised countries and countries in transition, including the EU, which have ratified the Kyoto Protocol, committing to reduce their emission levels of GHGs to targets that are mainly set below their 1990 levels. For further information, see the text of the Kyoto Protocol, http://unfccc.int/resource/ docs/convkp/kpeng.pdf (accessed 30 January 2013).

4 Figures were calculated by the author using data supplied by project participants.

5 The ITTO is an intergovernmental organisation comprised of the major producers and consumers of tropical timber. For further information, see http://www.itto.int/ (accessed 28 January 2013).

6 Developing countries where tropical forests are concentrated with significant fossil fuel reserves in highly biologically and culturally sensitive areas include: Brazil, Colombia, Costa Rica, Democratic Republic of Congo, Ecuador, India, Indonesia, Madagascar, Malaysia, Papua New Guinea, Peru, Bolivia, the Philippines and Venezuela (Larrea 2010: 4–5).

7 For *The Guardian* newspaper coverage of the Yasuní-ITT Initiative: http://www. guardian.co.uk/search?q=yasuni&section=environment (accessed 30 January 2013).

8 For critiques of 'sustainable' development options and their impact on ecosystems, communities, and indigenous livelihoods, see, for example, Isaacs (2000) on ecotourism, Ernsting (2012) on biofuels, or coverage by the magazine *Intercontinental*

Cry on hydroelectricity, http://intercontinentalcry.org/topics/hydro-dams (accessed 30 January 2013).
9 CONAIE (Confederación de Nacionalides Indígenas del Ecuador) is the largest Ecuadorian indigenous organisation, officially representing 14 indigenous peoples. It comprises three regional federations, which span the Amazon, central mountain region, and the coast. For further information see http://www.conaie.org (accessed 30 January 2013).

References

Acosta, I. (2011) '"Green desert" monoculture forests spreading in Africa and South America', *The Guardian*, 26 September, online: http://www.guardian.co.uk/environment/2011/sep/26/monoculture-forests-africa-south-america (accessed 18 October 2012).

AIPP (2011) *Statement of Concern on REDD+ in Centray Kalimantan, Indonesia: Indigenous Peoples Alliance of Archipelago – Central Kalimantan Chapter. 17 June 2011. Wisma Soverdi, Palangkaraya, Central Kalimantan*, online: http://ccmin.aippnet.org/index.php?option=com_content&view=article&id=386:statement-of-concern-on-redd-in-central-kalimantan-indonesia-indigenous-peoples-alliance-of-archipelago-central-kalimantan-chapter-&catid=17:national-statements&Itemid=29 (accessed 12 December 2012).

Baird, V. (2008) 'Endgame in the Amazon', *New Internationalist*, no. 413, July, pp. 5–10.

Bass, M. *et al.* (2009) 'Global conservation significance of Ecuador's Yasuní National Park', *PLoS ONE*, vol. 5, no. 1, online: http://www.plosone.org/article/info:doi/10.1371/journal.pone.0008767 (accessed 13 December 2009).

Bernier, A. (2012) 'Ecuador's plan falters: leaving oil in the soil may cost too much', *Le Monde Diplomatique*, online: http://mondediplo.com/2012/07/12ecuador (accessed 12 December 2012).

Boedt, P. and Martinez, E. (eds.) (2007) *Keep Oil Underground: The Only Way to Fight Climate Change*, Oil Watch publication, online: http://www.oilwatch.org/doc/documentos/Keep_oil_underground.pdf (accessed 9 July 2009).

Brown, K. (2011) *Rethinking Progress in a Warming World: Integrating Climate Resilient Development*. Development Studies Association and European Association of Development Research and Training Institutes General Conference 2011: Rethinking Development in an Age of Scarcity and Uncertainty – New Values, Voices and Alliances for Increased Resilience. 19–22 September 2011. York, UK.

Brown, M. (2010) 'Limiting corrupt incentives in a global REDD regime', *Ecology Law Quarterly*, vol. 37, no. 1, pp. 237–267.

Bullock, S., Childs, M. and Picken, T. (2009) *A Dangerous Distraction: Why Offsetting is Failing the Climate and People: The Evidence*. London: Friends of the Earth.

Burbach, R. (2009) *Ecuador's Neo-Liberal Model: Indigenous Groups Confront Rafael Correa*, North American Congress on Latin America (NACLA), online: https://nacla.org/node/6378 (accessed 2 November 2010).

Clark, R. (2010) 'Moving the REDD debate from theory to practice: lessons learned from the Ulu Masen Project Law', *Environment and Development Journal*, vol. 6, no. 1, pp. 36–60.

Collier, P. (2007) *The Bottom Billion*. Oxford: Oxford University Press.

Correa, R. (2007) Speech Given to the UN Forum on Climate Change, New York, 22 September 2007, online: www.un.org/webcast/climatechange/2007/pdfs/ecuador-eng.pdf (accessed 2 May 2010).

Correa, R. (2010) *Ecuadoran President Rafael Correa on WikiLeaks, the September Coup, U.S. Denial of Climate Funding, and Controversial Forest Scheme REDD*, Democracy Now!, online: http://www.democracynow.org/2010/12/9/ecuadoran_president_rafael_correa_on_the (accessed 10 December 2010).

Dangl, B. (2010a) *Ecuador's Challenge: Rafael Correa and the Indigenous Movements*, Thursday, 21 October 2010, Upside Down World, online: http://upsidedownworld.org/main/ecuador-archives-49/2743-ecuadors-challenge-rafael-correa-and-the-indigenous-movements- (accessed 2 February 2011).

Dangl, B. (2010b) *Dancing With Dynamite: Social Movements and States in Latin America*. Edinburgh: A K Press.

Dematteis, L. and Szymczak, K. (2008) *Crude Reflections: Oil, Ruin and Resistance in the Amazon Rainforest*. San Francisco, CA: City Lights Publishers.

Denvir, D. (2009) 'Resource wars in Ecuador: Indigenous people accuse President Rafael Correa of selling out to mining interests', *In These Times*, 28 February, online: http://www.inthesetimes.com/article/4252/resource_wars_in_ecuador/ (accessed 12 December 2009).

Dosh, P. (2009) *Correa Vs. Social Movements: Showdown in Ecuador*, NACLA Report on the Americas, online: https://nacla.org/node/6094 (accessed 20 July 2010).

EIA (2012) *Country Analysis Brief: Ecuador*, online: http://www.eia.gov/EMEU/cabs/Ecuador/pdf.pdf (accessed 14 September 2012).

EJOLT (2012) *Yasuní, Good Living*. An Arturo Hortas Film for EJOLT, online: http://vimeo.com/43112933 (accessed 10 January 2013).

Ernsting, A. (2012) *Sustainable Biomass: A Modern Myth*. Biofuel Watch Publication. Available online at: http://www.biofuelwatch.org.uk/2012/biomass_myth_report/ (accessed: 15 January 2013).

FAO (2011) *State of the World's Forests 2011*, Food and Agriculture Organization of the United Nations, online: http://www.fao.org/docrep/013/i2000e/i2000e.pdf (accessed 18 November 2012).

Garcia, E. (2012) *Ecuador to Launch Oil Block Auction amid Protests*, Reuters, online: http://www.reuters.com/article/2012/11/28/ecuador-oil-auction-idUSL1E8MR3I120121128 (accessed 1 December 2012).

Gerlach, A. (2003) *Indians, Oil and Politics: A Recent History of Ecuador*. Wilmington, DE: Scholarly Resources Books.

Global Forest Coalition (2008) *Life as Commerce: The Impact of Market-Based Conservation on Indigenous Peoples, Local Communities and Women*, online: http://vhgfc.dpi.nl/img/userpics/File/publications/LIFE-AS-COMMERCE2008.pdf (accessed 12 November 2010).

GRAIN (2012) *Behind the 'Green Economy': Profiting from Environmental and Climate Crisis*. Joint Publication by GRAIN, The Biodiversity Alliance, World Rainforest Movement (WRM), Friends of the Earth Latin America and the Caribbean. Availalble online at: http://www.grain.org/article/entries/4571-behind-the-green-economy-profiting-from-environmental-and-climate-crisis (accessed 10 January 2012).

Greenpeace (2009) *Amazon Cattle Footprint: Mato Grosso: State of Destruction*. Sao Paulo: Greenpeace Brazil.

Hall, R. (2010) *REDD: The Realities in Black and White*. The Netherlands: Friends of the Earth International Publication.

Hertwich, E. *et al.* (2010) *Assessing the Environmental Impacts of Consumption and Production: Priority Products and Materials*, online: http://www.unep.org/resourcepanel/documents/pdf/PriorityProductsAndMaterials_Report_Full.pdf (accessed 12 November 2010).

Humphreys, M., Sachs, J. and Stiglitz, J. (2007) *Escaping the Resource Curse.* New York: Columbia University Press.

IEA (2011) *Global Carbon-Dioxide Emissions Increase by 1.0 Gt in 2011 to Record High,* Environmental Intelligence Agency, online: http://www.iea.org/newsroomandevents/news/2012/may/name,27216,en.html (accessed 14 September 2012).

IEN (2012) *Kari-Oca 2 Declaration, Indigenous Peoples Global Conference on Rio+20 and Mother Earth,* Kari-Oka Village, Sacred Kari-Oka Púku, Rio de Janeiro, Brazil, 17 June 2012, online: http://indigenous4motherearthrioplus20.org/kari-oca-2-declaration/ (accessed 12 December 2012).

IPCC (2007) *Climate Change 2007: Synthesis Report: Contribution of Working Groups I, II and III to the Fourth Assessment Report of the Intergovernmental Panel on Climate Change.* Geneva, Switzerland: IPCC.

IPCCA (2011) *Press Release: Indigenous Leaders Alert the UNFCCC and the World to the Imminent Threat that REDD Poses to their Territories and Livelihoods.* Indigenous Peoples' Biocultural Climate Change Assessment Initiative. Durban, UNFCCC COP 17, 29 November 2011, online: http://ipcca.info/blog/2011/11/29/indigenous-leaders-alert-the-unfccc-and-the-world-to-the-imminent-threat-that-redd-poses-to-their-territories-and-livelihoods/ (accessed 12 December 2012).

Isaacs, J. (2000) 'The limited potential of ecotourism to contribute to wildlife conservation', *Wildlife Society Bulletin,* vol. 28, no. 1, pp. 61–69.

Isch, E. (2007) *Yasuní-ITT Project: Conserving Crude Oil in the Subsoil.* Concept Document Prepared for the Oil Watch Technical Team, online: http://www.sosYasuní.org/en/files/ow_itt_proposal_v8-ingles.pdf (accessed 20 November 2009).

Johnson, L. (2012) 'Ecuador's indigenous leaders oppose new oil exploration plans in Amazon region', *Earth Island Journal,* 13 November, online: http://www.earthisland.org/journal/index.php/elist/eListRead/ecuadors_indigenous_leaders_oppose_new_oil_exploration/ (accessed 12 December 2012).

Kanowski, J. and Catterall, C. (2010) 'Carbon stocks in above-ground biomass of monoculture plantations', *Ecological Management and Restoration,* vol. 11, no. 2, pp. 119–126.

Kinross (2009) *Kinross Provides Update on New Ecuadorian Mining Law.* Kinross Gold Corporation, Press Release 9 January, online: http://www.kinross.com/news-articles/2009/kinross-provides-update-on-new-ecuadorian-mining-law.aspx (accessed 2 November 2010).

Koenig, K. (2012) *Ecuador's Indigenous Peoples Reach Quito After 600-km March for Water, Life, and Dignity,* Amazon Watch, online: http://amazonwatch.org/news/2012/0323-ecuadors-indigenous-peoples-march-for-water-life-and-dignity (accessed 20 January 2013).

Kozloff, N. (2010) *No Rain in the Amazon: How South America's Climate Change Affects the Whole World.* Basingstoke: Palgrave Macmillan.

Lang, C. (2009) 'Forests, carbon markets and hot air: why the carbon stored in forests should not be traded', in Böhm, S. and Dabhi, S. (eds.) *Upsetting the Offset: The Political Economy of Carbon Markets.* London: Mayfly, pp. 214–229.

Larrea, C. (2010) *Yasuní-ITT: An Initiative to Change History: Yasuní-ITT Initiative Document.* Concept Document Commissioned by the Government of Ecuador, the UNDP and the Millennium Development Goal Achievement Fund, online: Yasuní-itt.gob.ec/wp-content/uploads/initiative_change_history_sep.pdf (accessed 12 November 2010).

Leifsen, E. (2009) *Conflicting Interests in the Andean Region: The New Extraction and the Prior Consultation Principle.* Masters thesis. University of Oslo.

Lohmann, L. (2008) 'Carbon trading, climate justice and the production of ignorance: ten examples', *Development*, vol. 51, no. 8, pp. 359–365.

Martin, P. (2010) *Global Governance from the Amazon: Leaving Oil Underground in Yasuní National Park, Ecuador*. Paper presented at the 51st Convention of the International Studies Association, New Orleans, Louisiana, 16–21 February 2010, online: http://indigenouspeoplesissues.com/attachments/4662_Global_Governance2010.pdf (accessed 20 May 2010).

Okereke, C. and Dooley, K. (2009) 'Principles of justice in proposals and policy approaches to avoided deforestation: towards a Post-Kyoto Climate Agreement', *Global Environmental Change*, vol. 20, no. 3, pp. 82–95.

Overbeek, W., Kröger, M. and Gerber. J. (2012) *An Overview of Industrial Tree Plantations in the Global South: Conflicts, Trends and Resistance Struggles*. EJOLT Report No. 03. EJOLT publication. Available online at: http://www.ejolt.org/wordpress/wp-content/uploads/2012/06/EJOLT-Report-3-low1.pdf (accessed 30 July 2012),

Parker, C. *et al.* (2009) *The Little REDD+ Book: An Updated Guide to Governmental and Non-Governmental Proposals for Reducing Emissions from Deforestation and Degradation.* Oxford: Global Canopy Programme.

Petermann, A. and Langelle, O. (2006) *Plantations, GM Trees and Indigenous Rights,* Seedling. GRAIN publication, July 2006. Available online at: http://www.grain.org/article/entries/565-plantations-gm-trees-and-indigenous-rights (accessed 12 July 2012).

Peterson, R. (2012) *Ecuador Launches Oil Auction amid Indigenous Protests,* Intercontinental Cry, online: http://intercontinentalcry.org/ecuador-launches-oil-auction-amid-indigenous-protests/ (accessed 20 January 2013).

Phelps, J., Webb, E. and Agrawal, A. (2010) 'Does REDD+ threaten to recentralize forest governance?'. *Science*, vol. 328, no. 5976, pp. 312–313.

Pirard, R. (2011) *Yasuní-ITT: The Virtues and Vices of Environmental Innovation,* 7 December, Mongabay, online: http://news.mongabay.com/2011/1207-pirard_yasuni_commentary.html (accessed 12 December 2012).

Ransom, D. (2008) 'Toxic blocks', *New Internationalist,* July, no. 413, pp. 14–16.

Reed, P. (2011) 'REDD+ and the indigenous question: a case study from Ecuador', *Forests,* vol. 2, no. 2, pp. 252–549.

Rockström, J. *et al.* (2009) 'Planetary boundaries: exploring the safe operating space for humanity', *Ecology and Society*, vol. 14, no. 2.

Sachs, J. and Warner, A. (2001) 'The curse of natural resources in fractionalized countries', *European Economic Review*, vol. 50, no. 6, pp. 1367–1386.

Sawyer, S. (2005*) Crude Chronicles: Indigenous Politics, Multinational Oil and Neoliberalism in Ecuador*, Durham, NC: Duke University Press.

Smith, K. (2006) *Obscenity of Carbon Trading,* BBC Science News The Green Room, no. 9, 9 November, online: http://news.bbc.co.uk/1/hi/sci/tech/6132826.stm (accessed 12 November 2010).

Stern, N. (2007) *The Economics of Climate Change: The Stern Review.* Cambridge: Cambridge University Press.

TEEB (2010) *The Economics of Ecosystems and Biodiversity: Mainstreaming the Economics of Nature: A Synthesis of the Approach, Conclusions and Recommendations of TEEB*, released on 20 October 2010 at the COP10 in Nagoya, online: http://www.teebweb.org/InformationMaterial/TEEBReports/tabid/1278/Default.aspx (accessed 02 November 2010).

UNDP (2010a) *Memorandum of Agreement between the Government of Ecuador and the United Nations Development Programme for Management and Other Support Services*

Related to the Ecuador Yasuní-ITT Trust Fund, signed 3 August 2010, online: http:// mdtf.undp.org/Yasuní (accessed 2 December 2010).

UNDP (2010b) *Ecuador Yasuní-ITT Trust Fund: Terms of Reference 28 July 2010*, online: mdtf.undp.org/document/download/4492 (accessed 12 December 2012).

UNDP (2012a) *United Nations Development Programme Ecuador Yasuní-ITT Trust Fund*, online: http://mptf.undp.org/yasuni (accessed 14 September 2012).

UNDP (2012b) *2011 Annual Report of the Ecuador Yasuní ITT Trust Fund: Report of the Administrative Agent of the Ecuador Yasuní ITT Trust Fund for the period 1 January–31 December 2011*, online: www.mdtf.undp.org/document/download/9360 (accessed 14 September 2012).

UNDP (2012c) *Capital Fund Contributions*, online: http://mptf.undp.org/factsheet/ fund/3EYC0 (accessed 12 January 2013).

UNEP (2011) *Towards a Green Economy: Pathways to Sustainable Development and Poverty Eradication*, p. 16. Roskilde: Danish Technical University.

UNFCCC (2011) *The Yasuní-ITT Initiative: Enhancing Cost-Effectiveness of, and Promoting Mitigation Actions*. Presented at Ad Hoc Working Group on Long-term Cooperative Action under the Convention Fourteenth session. Bangkok, 5–8 April 2011, and Bonn, 6–17 June 2011.

UNFCCC (2012a) *Clean Development Mechanism by Project: Ecuador*, online: http:// cdm.unfccc.int/Projects/projsearch.html (accessed 12 October 2012).

UNFCCC (2012b) *Clean Development Mechanism: Projects by Inverso Parties*, online: http://cdm.unfccc.int/Statistics/Registration/RegisteredProjAnnex1PartiesPieChart. html (accessed 12 October 2012).

UN-REDD Programme (2010) *About REDD*, online: http://www.un-redd.org/AboutREDD/ tabid/582/Default.aspx (accessed 2 November 2010).

UN-REDD Programme (2012) *Ecuador*, online: http://www.un-redd.org/ AboutUNREDDProgramme/NationalProgrammes/Ecuador/tabid/7073/Default.aspx (accessed 20 October 2012).

Warnars, L. (2010) *The Yasuní-ITT Initiative: An International Environmental Equity Mechanism?* Masters thesis. Radbound University.

Watts, J. (2012) 'World's conservation hopes rest on Ecuador's revolutionary Yasuni model', *The Guardian*, 3 September, online: http://www.guardian.co.uk/environment/2012/ sep/03/ecuador-yasuni-conservation?newsfeed=true (accessed 4 September 2012).

Watts, J. (2013) 'Petition to halt oil exploration in Ecuadorean Amazon gets 1m signatures', *The Guardian*, 6 February, online: http://www.guardian.co.uk/world/2013/feb/06/ petition-oil-ecuadorean-amazon-signatures?INTCMP=SRCH (accessed 7 February 2013).

World Bank (2010) *World Bank Country Data: Ecuador*, online: http://data.worldbank. org/country/ecuador (accessed 11 November 2010).

World Bank (2012) *Ecuador: Country Overview*, online: http://www.worldbank.org/en/ country/ecuador/overview (accessed 14 September 2012).

9 Developing economies in the current climate regime

New prospects for resilience and sustainability? The case of CDM projects in Asia

Pauline Lacour and Jean-Christophe Simon

Integrating developing countries into the international climate regime through the Clean Development Mechanism: the rationale

Recent trends in world negotiations on climate change (CC) have made the new positions of developing countries more apparent. Emerging economies, and particularly Brazil, Russia, India, China and South Africa (the BRICS countries) have shown a strong common standing, and other developing and less developed countries have created their debate arena during the successive CC negotiations (Conference of Parties, CoP) of the United Nations Framework Convention on Climate Change (UNFCCC).

The question to be addressed is whether the Clean Development Mechanism (CDM) as a market-based instrument has triggered more ambitious CC policies in developing countries and whether this influences national interests in UNFCCC negotiations and consequently the effectiveness of the whole process as such. This paper reviews the impact of the CDM over the past decade on developing countries' integration into the international climate regime (ICR). It illustrates shared positions attained by developing economies in UNFCCC negotiations, focusing on some key elements such as climate mitigation and the CDM. Furthermore, this paper suggests that climate policy can indeed be integrated into coherent development strategies, which aim at both sustainability and climate resilience. The geographical focus is on the Southeast Asian region and China.

The global CC challenge has generated a new governance or 'global climate regime'[1] – despite multiple obstacles which range from scientific controversies, vested interests and economic lobbying to social and political debates. The foundations of the climate regime consider that 'developed' or industrialised countries have been the first and main historical contributors to emissions of greenhouse gases (GHG), particularly throughout the 20th century, and are therefore obliged to be at the forefront of strategies to combat CC. This is backed by several international agreements under the UNFCCC, particularly the Kyoto Protocol (1997). Therefore, 'developed' countries are expected to make decisive efforts to reduce their GHG emissions – which is reflected in their pledges within the Kyoto Protocol[2] – while mustering resources to back up efforts undertaken by developing economies lacking both finance and technologies.

The CDM was designed to address these challenges and is one of the flexible instruments implemented by the Kyoto Protocol. The CDM enables developing countries to implement climate friendly projects that will reduce actual GHG emissions, with decisive external financial support. The contributing industrialised (or 'developed') countries will, in turn, benefit from tradable carbon credits granted by a CDM international body allocating emission reduction certificates.

As there is much at stake for developing countries concerning CC, they have adopted a strong position within international negotiations regarding industrialised countries' commitments, but also with respect to funds required for mitigation projects in their countries. In addition to the instruments under the Kyoto Protocol, the Bali Conference (2007) and its roadmap have placed emphasis on climate strategies that combine mitigation and adaptation measures. Two major challenges have to be faced: on the one hand, developing economies claim a 'right to develop', and thus climate policy should not be an additional obstacle to the reduction of poverty, satisfaction of basic development needs and increased welfare. On the other hand, they also face increased vulnerability and thus adaptation and mitigation objectives are also to be seen as components of development policies, taking into account specific local conditions. In this respect, climate policies will contribute to resilience to the extent that they actually integrate more diverse actors (from civil society, public and private organisations) and mobilise multiple resources (know-how, technology, finance).

This paper is structured as follows: first, it provides an overview of conceptual aspects of CDM as a tool for climate policies in developing countries with contributions from the developed world, and it presents major features from CDM projects approved over the past decade. It then places special emphasis on the Asian region as the world's major host of CDM projects, in spite of wide disparities in national levels of development and energy consumption. The analysis shows how several countries have been successful in building the framework of national policies and accommodating CDM projects. The Asian region reveals differentiated experiences and the strategic appropriation of the CDM mechanism, in particular by China – this is in spite of strong sectoral concentration bias and limited additionality of funds.

The Kyoto Protocol and the CDM: exploring the challenge of the ICR for developing countries

The CDM, established within the Kyoto Protocol, is admittedly quite an original and innovative instrument, due to its flexibility and its ambition to integrate developing countries into the ICR. The basic principles and conceptual issues behind the design and implementation of the CDM will be analysed: the core concept of additionality, as well as the economic efficiency and climatic effectiveness. Then, the review of empirical data concerning the mechanism's past period of implementation, or the take-off stage with several thousand of projects approved, facilitates a characterisation of the actual focus of the mechanisms, which reveals the geographic and sectoral concentration of projects, and questions the pertinence of including all developing countries into the climate regime. Subsequently, the Asian context is further explored to better understand the magnitude of the climate mitigation challenge being faced by this part of the world.

CDM: fundamental principles and governance

The differentiation between industrialised and developing countries and their respective contributions to global warming explains the bipolar dimension of the struggle against CC (Demaze 2009). The CDM relaxes the commitments of industrialised countries to reduce GHG emissions and has the objective to actively integrate developing countries into the ICR by providing financial support to projects. As defined by the 12th article of the Kyoto Protocol, the CDM allows a private actor, for example a company or investment fund, from a country listed in Annex I (i.e. industrialised countries) to finance projects that aim at emission reductions in non-Annex I countries (i.e. developing countries). By this, the private actor can acquire certified emission reductions (CERs), which can be used or traded on the carbon market.

CDM implementation can lead to positive externalities in the three spheres of sustainable development (Nygard *et al.* 2004):

1   *Environmental benefits.* This mechanism integrates developing countries into the struggle against CC due to the implementation of climate mitigation projects (e.g. GHG emission reductions, improvement of energy efficiency, reduction of pollutants and waste treatment, use of renewable energy).
2   *Economic externalities.* The CDM generates emission reductions at lowest cost in the most economically profitable area (Vieillefosse 2006). Further benefits include additional earnings through the implementation of taxes on CERs, which have an impact on development and social issues.
3   *Development and social dimension.* The CDM favours technology transfer to developing countries and strengthens their sustainable development strategies (UNEP 2000; Joumni 2003; Borde and Joumi 2007). To be effective, CDM projects need to be consistent with domestic climate strategies and development objectives. Furthermore, the CDM creates social benefits, like job creation, as well as general welfare externalities through increased income. It also supports a cognitive shift towards more environmental awareness.

Before a project becomes operational under the CDM, it must fulfil specific criteria in the validation process. The additionality issue is probably the most important one in this respect. The concept of additionality has three dimensions:

1 *Environmental additionality.* The project must prove that anticipated GHG emissions in the CDM project are below the baseline, i.e. the business-as-usual (BAU) scenario. This counting of GHG emissions is central to the acceptance of the project and to the issuance of CERs (Boulanger *et al.* 2004). However, the definition of the baseline and, consequently, the assessment of the environmental additionality raises many difficulties (Wanko and Smida 2001; Boulanger *et al.* 2005). Assessing the actual reduction in emissions compared to the baseline is challenging. So far, there is no universally accepted assessment methodology. This lack of technical support is often cited by investors to justify their reluctance to finance CDM projects. If the baseline is not appropriately defined, i.e. overestimating the emission levels of production technologies actually available in developing countries, it would lead to fictitious, and credited, emission reductions (Godard and Henry 1998). This overestimation of emissions in the baseline could lead to the realisation of 'non-ambitious' projects with few environmental gains and could strengthen the so-called 'hot air phenomena'. This problem would cause a sharp decline in the international value of emission permits, which would then discourage investment in future research and development activities.

2 *Investment additionality.* This means that a CDM project must lead to a new investment to actually reduce GHG emissions. The investment should be additional to the baseline scenario – thus again proving the environmental additionality of the project (Boulanger *et al.* 2004). Moreover, this principle implies that economic flows in the CDM should not be a substitute for any other financial flow to developing countries, and particularly to official development assistance (ODA) flows (Organisation Internationale de la Francophonie 2005).

3 *Technological additionality.* Projects that receive carbon credits must finance the implementation of a technology that would not have been implemented without the use of the CDM (Meunié 2004; Meunié and Quenault 2007). The CDM should favour the deployment of environmentally friendly technologies or 'clean' technologies that are still rare in developing countries. Developing countries stress that so-called green technologies benefit from expensive protection by patents and licences (intellectual property rights). These countries also suffer from the relative scarcity of domestic capital resources. Therefore, the carbon credits or CERs contribute with respect to balancing the investment budgeting of the project. Domestic firms should have positive externalities because of the implementation of these technologies and acquire new competences in their field. These technological dimensions and the capabilities of domestic firms are considered in the approbation process of CDM.

In addition to the difficulties in defining additionality, there are also challenges regarding the governance of the CDM. The framework conditions for the CDM were agreed at the UNFCCC level. National governments are responsible for the implementation. The success or failure of the CDM thus largely depends on the institutional capacity within a developing country to govern this mechanism. National governments are responsible for elaborating their climate policy and setting up a designated national authority (DNA) to supervise national CDM projects. They are consequently in charge of defining priority objectives and evaluating and registering the projects before these are processed at the international registration level. The DNAs are also free to impose specific supplementary criteria or even stringent sustainability conditions for CDM projects. In addition to the level of additionality, environmental impacts of the projects (protection of the local environment), its social externalities (impacts on employment, low-income groups, and/or the industrial and regional integration of the project), its economic outcome (balance of payments, cost-effectiveness of the project), and its technological repercussions (contribution to the technological upgrading, local innovation, and transfer of imported technologies) must be taken into account. Moreover, the CDM is designed to operate as a monitoring, reporting, verification[3] (MRV) scheme. Consequently, the effectiveness of the mechanism depends on the availability of domestic and foreign expertise and on the intervention of a reliable public sector framework for which developing countries display a wide spectrum of disparity related to each country's experience, resources, and level of development. Consequently, weak governments, deficient (local) administrative capacities, and lack of expertise typically hamper the successful implementation of the CDM. Due to the above-mentioned factors, it is therefore less surprising that there is a geographical as well as sectoral bias in the distribution of CDM projects, which will be discussed in the following section.

CDM implementation: positive effects but geographical inequality?

The implementation of the CDM is characterised by strong disparities between regions and countries as well as across sectors. According to official statistics (UNFCCC 2012), most projects, i.e. 70 per cent of all registered projects, relate to the energy sector (renewable sources), waste handling and disposal (13 per cent), and manufacturing industries (5 per cent). Within the category of renewable energy, 29 per cent are hydropower projects, 27 per cent wind energy, 10 per cent biomass energy, and only 2 per cent of projects use a solar energy source.[4] These four subsectors of renewable energy are also those which generate most of the CERs, representing 41 per cent of annual CERs and 28 per cent of credits to be issued by 2012 (Table 9.1).

Since the start of its implementation in 2005, the advantage of the CDM in terms of flexibility for GHG emission reduction commitments for Annex I countries explains the substantial growth of projects which reached more than 4,463 registered projects in May 2012.[5] This take-off reveals two linked phenomena. On the one hand, the implementation of the mechanism is supported by DNAs, which needed time to be established and become operational. On the other hand, the growth in the number of projects proposed since 2009 might also be due to more relaxed selection criteria and windfall profits for some investors in countries with low screening capacity (e.g. Lao People's Democratic Republic, Cambodia).

Table 9.1 CDM registered by types of projects (1 September 2012)

Type	CDM registered					
			CERs/year		2012 CERs	
	(No)	*(%)*	*(000)*	*(%)*	*(000)*	*(%)*
Hydro	1317	28.97	140638	21.44	341559	15.55
Wind	1247	27.43	123883	18.89	269138	12.25
Methane avoidance	462	10.16	17644	2.69	73101	3.33
Biomass energy	440	9.68	28302	4.32	115864	5.27
Landfill gas	248	5.46	59728	9.11	171913	7.82
Energy efficiency own generation	226	4.97	35320	5.39	132504	6.03
Solar	100	2.20	2863	0.44	3589	0.16
N_2O	74	1.63	51004	7.78	249300	11.35
Fossil fuel switch	72	1.58	35194	5.37	129236	5.88
Energy efficiency industry	66	1.45	1740	0.27	9163	0.42
Coal bed/mine methane	59	1.30	26696	4.07	86462	3.94
Energy efficiency supply side	34	0.75	13911	2.12	14990	0.68
Energy efficiency households	33	0.73	1282	0.20	2799	0.13
Reforestation	32	0.70	1304	0.20	10592	0.48
Fugitive	25	0.55	15801	2.41	53784	2.45
Hydrofluorocarbons	22	0.48	81319	12.40	473629	21.56
Cement	20	0.44	3313	0.51	21510	0.98
Transport	15	0.33	2161	0.33	4421	0.20
Perfluorocarbons (PDFs) and sifur hexaflouride (SF6)	14	0.31	4939	0.75	11569	0.53
Geothermal	13	0.29	3249	0.50	12955	0.59
Energy distribution	12	0.26	4934	0.75	5944	0.27
Afforestation	7	0.15	197	0.03	1576	0.07
EE service	5	0.11	59	0.01	330	0.02
CO_2 usage	2	0.04	24	0.00	139	0.01
Tidal	1	0.02	315	0.05	1104	0.05
Total	4546	100.00	655820	100.00	2197170	100.00

Source: Adapted from UNEP (2012).

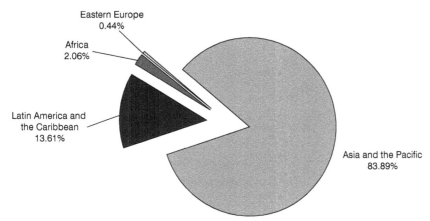

Figure 9.1 Registered CDM projects by region (percentage of total world CDM projects, September 2012)

However, the geographical focus of the CDM on emerging countries – particularly on Asian countries – limits the scope of the mechanism to integrate a large variety of developing countries into the ICR and assist them in more climate-resilient development. When analysing the geographical distribution of CDM projects, it appears that areas with a strong economic development attract the greatest number of projects: Asia hosts 84 per cent of registered projects (up to September 2012). In comparison, 14 per cent of the projects are located in Latin America and the Caribbean. Only 2 per cent of registered projects have been implemented in Africa (Figure 9.1). CDM projects have focused on emerging countries due to the coupling of environmental and economic logics, which is inherent in the mechanism. Furthermore, a diversity of GHG emission sources offers a wider scope for mitigation investment opportunities.

Although the financial flows mobilised are not quantitatively important compared to the bulk of foreign direct investment (FDI), it is essential to highlight the inequalities between developing countries as this has been observed in the case of FDI flows over the past two decades (UNCTAD 2008). The attractiveness of some countries relates to their economic environment and the robustness of their infrastructure; this is valid for CDM projects as well. However, the unequal distribution of CDM projects can be mostly explained by national differences in the quality and efficiency of the DNA. In some developing countries, these authorities cannot provide sufficient technical and methodological support for the elaboration of project design documents nor for the registration of GHG emissions in the baseline. Moreover, differences in project size explain the differentiation in countries' attractiveness; large projects experience lower transaction costs due to the CER accounting (ENTTRANS 2007).

China and India are the major beneficiaries of CDM projects, with 50 per cent and 20 per cent, respectively, of worldwide registered projects. Their share is predominant in Asia-Pacific: 61 per cent of projects (in this region) are located in China and 24 per cent in India (Figure 9.2). The leadership of China in global

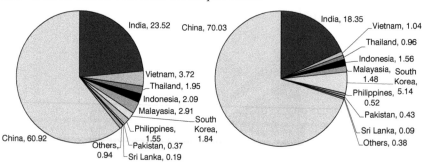

Figure 9.2 CDM registered projects by Asian countries/CERs issued up to 2012 by Asian countries (percentage of total in Asia)

CDM projects can mostly be explained by its strong institutional framework for regulating CDM, the numerous opportunities for emission reductions in its territory, and the extended domestic market for energy-related equipment. For example, CDM projects that increase the production efficiency of a particular good, such as electricity, are also directed by market opportunities (Winkelman and Moore 2011). Moreover, the Chinese government has implemented incentive policies that favour the energy sector and technology transfer (Szymanski 2002) – which also encourages projects with low additionality or are easier and more profitable to implement – the so-called 'low hanging fruits'.

Although they look less attractive based on sheer numbers, countries such as Vietnam (139 representing 4 per cent of projects in Asia), Malaysia (109; 3 per cent), Thailand (73; 2 per cent), and Indonesia (78; 2 per cent) have also been able to take advantage of the mechanism. This also demonstrates domestic efforts to establish efficient DNAs and attract international investors. The fact that most of the CDM projects are based in Asia could also be explained by the active participation of Japan, which comes third in the ranking of global investors. Japan finances 10 per cent of all registered projects, behind Switzerland (21 per cent) and the United Kingdom (31 per cent).[6]

The CDM showed right from the beginning that it has the potential to benefit all parties. It was consequently labelled a 'win–win mechanism' at the Kyoto Conference. But after more than six years of implementation, it appears that its overall relevance for integrating developing countries into the ICR has been limited to those countries which have also successfully integrated their economies into the world economy. The above outlined figures show that some countries and regions have benefited more than others. The definitions of the environmental additionality and the baseline constitute a set of difficulties that weaken the efficiency of the mechanism, explaining why least developed countries have, in fact, been under-represented since the implementation of the mechanism.

Concerning the relevance of the CDM for climate strategies, technology transfer becomes a genuine issue. Some areas have been ignored in domestic criteria and project selection (e.g. transport, sea wave power, and geothermal energy). Many reports point out the lack of technology upgrading in many projects and the potential for substantial improvement (Dechezlepretre *et al*. 2008; Flamos 2010; UNFCCC 2010). Many analysts also criticise the multiple small-scale projects, with limited investment in too few sectors: this would make them irrelevant to initiate genuine national climate mitigation commensurate with the magnitude of emissions.

The Southeast Asian Region and China: facing the challenge of proactive climate policies

Asia, as a whole, is known to be particularly vulnerable to CC as many countries and their populations depend on activities such as agriculture, fisheries, or tourism, which are sensitive to changes and hazards produced by climatic events (ADB 2009; Reddy and Assenza 2009). Southeast Asian countries[7] display notable differences in their GHG emission levels as well as in their energy intensity (gross domestic energy consumption per GDP) and the energy consumption per capita; this can be explained by their vigorous growth over four decades (Table 9.2). It is both understandable and remarkable that many Southeast Asian countries are in favour of international climate negotiations while, at the same time, they are steadily building up policy instruments to address national issues (Krechowicz and Fernando 2009). This facilitates the anticipation of problems and mobilisation of both international and domestic resources to adapt to CC and to promote mitigation.

It is relevant to consider China for comparative reasons. It is now the world's largest GHG emitter, with 24 per cent of the world total in 2010 versus less than 6 per cent for India (IEA 2012) although its carbon intensity is on a downward trend (carbon emissions per GDP). Considering the continued growth of activities and population, this tremendous level of emissions is going to last well into the middle of the twenty-first century. Due to increasing energy needs, it may be difficult to 'decarbonise' economic growth in China at a sustained rate in the coming decades. At present, the manufacturing industry and the electricity sector are the major CO_2 emitters – electricity making up 49 per cent of total and industry 32 per cent (IEA 2012). The electricity sector will remain a major source of emissions due to a large share of coal-fired plants. In contrast to what is observed in more developed countries, like Japan and Korea, transport and residential sectors represent an insignificant share of total emissions (about 5 per cent each in 2010 (IEA 2012)). The CDM strategy towards China has, to a large extent, been influenced by these developments (see above).

Members of the Association of Southeast Asian Nations (ASEAN) show a diverse picture regarding their emissions and carbon intensity (carbon emissions per GDP in purchasing power parity (PPP)). In total, the ASEAN average is below the global average of carbon intensity (0.37 versus 0.44 in 2010 (IEA 2012)). Carbon intensity has declined over the past decade. But the quantity of total carbon emissions is clearly on an upward trend. Newly industrialised countries (NICs) in ASEAN display the highest carbon intensity, but have shown a slowing down or even decreasing trend over the past 15 years. This trend remains to be confirmed but could be a sign that their growth will become less carbon intensive and that

Table 9.2 Indicators for countries and regions, 2010

Country/region	Population (millions)	GDP PPP (billion 2000 USD)	CO_2 emissions[1] (Mt of CO_2)	Share in world emissions	TPES (Mtoe)	CO_2/GDP PPP (kg CO_2/2000 USD)	CO_2/population (t CO_2/capita)
Cambodia	14.1	27.8	3.8	0.01%	5.0	0.14	0.27
China	1345.4	9417.1	7258.5	23.97%	2469.5	0.77	5.40
South Korea	24.3	103.5	63.0	0.21%	18.5	0.61	2.59
Indonesia	239.9	930.7	410.9	1.36%	207.8	0.44	1.71
Japan	127.4	3895.3	1143.1	3.78%	496.8	0.29	8.97
Malaysia	28.4	375.3	185.0	0.61%	72.6	0.49	6.51
Philippines	93.3	332.1	76.4	0.25%	40.5	0.23	0.82
Singapore	5.1	263.8	62.9	0.21%	32.8	0.24	12.39
Thailand	69.1	530.4	248.5	0.82%	117.4	0.47	3.59
Vietnam	89.9	249.9	130.5	0.43%	59.2	0.52	1.50
USA	310.1	13017.0	5368.6	17.73%	2216.3	0.41	17.31
India	1170.9	3762.9	1625.8	5.37%	692.7	0.43	1.39
OECD	1232.0	37113.0	12440.0	41.09%	5406.0	0.34	10.10
Asia[2]	2228.6	9072.1	3330.6	11.00%	1524.1	0.37	1.49
World[3]	6825.0	68431.0	30276.0	100.00%	12765.0	0.44	4.44

Source: Data extracted from IEA (2012).
Notes:
1 CO_2 emissions from fuel combustion only. Emissions are calculated using the IEA's energy balances and the Revised 1996 IPCC Guidelines.
2 Data for China excluded.
3 CO_2 emissions include emissions from international aviation and international marine bunkers.

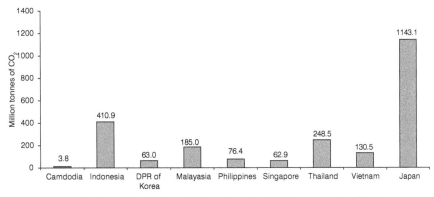

Figure 9.3 Estimation of total CO_2 emissions in selected Asian countries, 2010

economic growth rates decrease and changes in sector proportions occur. ASEAN NICs are already substantial GHG emitters whereas the three less developed countries – Burma/Myanmar, Lao, and Cambodia remain very small emitters (which is also reflected in the small numbers of implemented CDM projects). Recent estimates, using comparable bases, suggest that the five more advanced economies emit between 76 million tonnes (MT) of CO_2 (Philippines) and 410 MT (Indonesia) (see Figure 9.3). In 2010, Singapore stood at 63 MT, Myanmar at 8 MT, and Cambodia had less than 4 MT CO_2.

On a sectorial basis, excluding the energy sector, emissions in ASEAN NICs originate mainly from industry and transport, whereas residential and agriculture remain less significant contributors (see Figure 9.4).

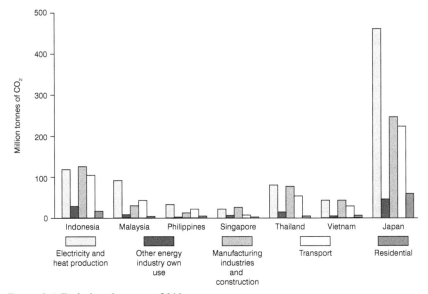

Figure 9.4 Emissions by sector, 2010

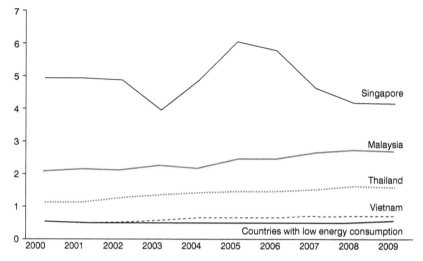

Figure 9.5 Energy consumption per capita in ASEAN countries, 2000–2009

It is worth noting that industries that are energy and GHG emission intensive have already been subject to targeted policies (part of the national energy strategies) and promotional measures to steer them towards lower emission activities. Energy policies have been actively implemented since the early 1980s when the emerging 'Tigers' started to bear the brunt of higher energy intensity and significant price shocks on the global energy market. Lately, the challenge of sustainability emerged: securing energy for development of production and final consumption on the one hand, and tackling CC on the other. This challenge was perceived by both individual countries and regional bodies. It requires both national policies and regional cooperation (ESCAP 2007), which has led to a stabilisation or even a reduction of energy consumption (see Figure 9.5). Several NICs of Southeast Asia have designed and implemented national climate action plans over the past decade (ADB 2009).

For Southeast Asia as a whole, the challenge of emissions originating from agriculture and forestry is to be considered separately: they are determined by transformation of agricultural and forestry systems, and current trends in socio-economic dynamics. In these areas, GHG emission control and reduction – also because of their magnitude and some socio-political controversial aspects – are beyond the scope of the CDM itself.

CDM in action in Asia: from CDM to broader CC policies?

The Asian region merits special attention as their climate policies are based on a double dynamic: on the one hand, emissions growth in this region explains the concerns of the international community regarding voluntary commitments to reduce GHG emissions; on the other hand, climate policies also correspond to a growing concern for sustainable development policies that place a special emphasis on the environmental/energy/climate package. National climate policies in emerging Asian economies are influenced by three forces that bear on the design of national development strategies (Lacour and Simon 2012):

- high energy costs leading to a higher risk of market instability and an increase in costs for importing energy;
- climate-related environmental problems, such as soil degradation or resource depletion;
- equity problems leading to social conflicts.

The next section investigates how CDM projects are integrated in the global development trends in East and Southeast Asia. It highlights national climate strategies, which offer food for thought about the scope for public intervention where project implementation can be a first step towards wider climate policies. It considers first the contrasting characteristics of CDM project initiation in various countries in Asia. Then, the focus is placed on the Chinese experience and the domestic appropriation of the mechanism, which is characterised by the establishment of a DNA and the orientation of CDM projects according to national energy priorities.

CDM projects in national contexts in Southeast Asia and China: contrasting approaches

Southeast Asia and China are indeed facing a major challenge to curb emissions – and, as seen above, energy intensity also has to be kept under control. This situation sets the framework for CDM project selection and development in a region which has attracted the major part of CDM projects. Governments within many countries have adopted a proactive attitude towards the establishment and operation of DNAs. In several cases, domestic policy on CDM project targeting has been tailored to fit national ambitions for climate-resilient and sustainable development.

A major feature of the overall stock of CDM projects throughout the Southeast Asian region and China is their focus on the energy sector. This sector accounts for 75 per cent of all projects, a figure slightly above the world average presented in Table 9.1 (70 per cent of all world projects are energy-oriented). In fact, there is a large diversity of project formats and sizes and sub-activities represented within the 25 areas or economic activities covered which emit GHGs. As presented in Table 9.1, CDM projects are conspicuously absent or marginal in the transport and residential sectors; this can be due to a lack of motivation from the private sector and also because of a lack of financial sources provided, for instance, by the World Bank's Climate Technology Fund for national and local government initiatives. The situation also indirectly concerns agriculture in terms of biomass or biofuels (see Table 9.1).

The focus on the energy sector is indeed telling: sustained growth and industrialisation have triggered a demand for energy which, in turn, makes this

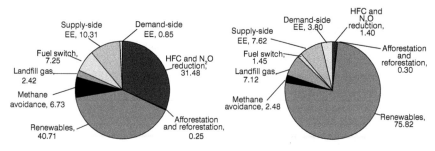

Figure 9.6 Categories of projects in Asia

sector a primary target for mitigation actions. Moreover, one may consider that developing countries in Asia are seeking a double windfall by promoting CDM actions concerning energy (Figure 9.6): they promote energy efficiency and they seek net financial gain on emission reduction (thus co-financing profitable projects in exchange for emission reduction certificates).

Concerning energy-generating activities, hydropower and wind power take the lead; obviously hydropower can capitalise on hitherto untapped small-scale projects as well as the historical tradition to master large watershed areas. Electricity from wind power has benefited from commercial promotion of new technologies of generators, which allow for use at large scale. This is particularly true for India and China, which host over 80 per cent of all projects in Asia (UNEP 2012).

In addition to the production of renewable energy, some less glamorous activities are testimony of the many untapped opportunities for reducing CO_2 emissions and of a burgeoning drive towards a low carbon economy: projects promoting energy efficiency and use of waste and biomass, which represent about 20 per cent of all projects presented at DNAs (UNEP 2012).

In the energy sector, a large majority of projects (about 60 per cent (UNFCCC website)) have been selected because of easy investment and financial returns; therefore, the effective additionality of these CDM projects can be questioned. This is confirmed by the fact that really innovative projects based on sea power or geothermal sources seem to be very few because the potential of reduction emissions from conventional fossil energy is still very important.

The five large ASEAN member countries, the NICs or so-called 'Tiger Cubs', have made inroads to host between 50–90 projects of various magnitudes and sectors (UNEP 2012). Public policy in Indonesia has shown a dual attitude. On the one hand, emissions related to agriculture and deforestation are still a politically sensitive issue and thus difficult to deal with, due to the argument of basic needs in an economy based on the agricultural sector. On the other hand, state agencies have taken a proactive attitude to promote CDM projects as part of a new wave of development initiatives. This has resulted in a selection of the largest diversity of project types among ASEAN countries. Thailand, for its part, has experienced a slow start, with ambiguous positions at first. Over the past years, it has made up for lost time and promoted CDM projects as a complement to its energy policy.[8]

The DNA of Thailand has followed the Ministry of Energy and approved 60 per cent of energy-related projects (mostly biogas and methane with very few based on hydro and wind power).[9]

Vietnam may be a special case; either because of political conservatism or on an opportunistic basis, it has given hydroelectricity top priority. Hydropower constitutes 70 per cent of all projects, with most hydro turbines imported from China (Nguyen *et al.* 2010).

Less developed Asian countries (namely Lao, Cambodia and Myanmar) have managed to promote more than 10 projects each, having been selected to complement traditional development projects as they do not yet have major domestic emissions constraints. In addition, these countries do not face substantial energy problems due to still low energy intensity, and availability of large renewable energy resources for Lao, and oil/gas deposits for Myanmar and Cambodia (ADB 2009; see Table 9.2).

The Chinese experience: matching CDM projects with policy orientation and technology transfer

China is the first global recipient of a CDM project and has since become the major market for this mechanism. This development can be explained by China's economic environment and the potential for GHG reduction at low cost (mainly reduction and recuperation of pollutants: oxide nitrous emissions, hydrofluorocarbons (HFCs)) (Jung 2006; Lacour 2012)). Although the environmental additionality of CDM projects in China still remains limited (409 thousand tonnes of annual reduction of emissions in September 2012), the sectorial repartition of CDM projects and China's energy and climate objectives are identical, because of financial incentives for CDM investments (Guérivière 2008; Wang 2010). The attractiveness of China can also be explained by the regulations and institutions that supervise the mechanism and the legal framework securing the investment environment for foreign firms (Teng and Zhang 2010).

China – at both central and local government level – has taken special measures to establish bodies and promote an institutional network to foster projects throughout the country in line with the targets of the 11th National Plan (NDRC 2006). In 2004, the Chinese government published *Measures for Operation and Management of Clean Development Mechanism Project*,[10] which relates to the climate and energy targets of the country. China's priorities for CDM projects, which are defined by the fourth article of this official publication, concentrate on the amelioration of energy efficiency, the development and utilisation of renewable energy sources, and the recovery of methane (ENTTRANS 2007; Maoshang and Haites 2006; Shuang 2005). The correspondence between the CDM and domestic climate targets is also guided by the instauration of a tax system on CERs. Projects using renewable energy sources, forestation, or methane recovery projects are taxed at 2 per cent; these sectors correspond to the climate and energy priorities of the country. Conversely, CERs from projects that reduce nitrous oxides are taxed at 30 per cent. This tax rate reaches 65 per cent for projects that reduce

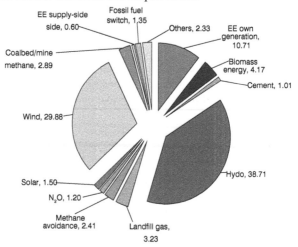

Figure 9.7 CDM in China by activity (September 2011)

HFCs and perfluorocarbons (PFCs) reduction (NCCCC 2005, Article 24). These tax benefits are transferred to a special fund which supports the development and utilisation of renewable energy sources in China (Guérivière 2008). This tax system counterbalances the benefits of projects that reduce pollutants at low cost (HFC, PFC, and oxide nitrous) and directs investors towards long-term projects. In the same way, innovative environmental equipment, which does not have local substitutes, is exempted of duties and value added tax, encouraging environmentally friendly technology imports (Wang 2010).

The matching of the major energy priorities of China with the sectorial repartition of CDM projects is presented in Figure 9.7. It can be observed that 50 per cent of carbon emissions in China were generated by the energy sector in 2010, becoming the first emitter of carbon behind the industry sector since mid-1990 (IEA 2012). Therefore, priority has been given to the development of renewable energy: these projects concern 74.3 per cent of CDM projects implemented in China before 1 September 2011. The major part of CDM projects are related to hydropower – 39 per cent of CDM in China – and wind energy projects – 30 per cent of total projects – because of the availability of water resources. It is important to highlight that energy efficiency projects represent 10 per cent of CDM in China (UNEP 2011): the government is fully aware of the obsolescence of the technologies of production and utilisation of energy in China (Meunié 2004; 2009).

Through this approach, the CDM should foster technology diffusion, in particular, sustainable technologies and clean-up technologies (Schroeder 2009; Wang 2010). This channel for disseminating technology should facilitate the technological upgrading of China, in terms of energy exploitation, supply, transformation, transmission, and distribution. Indeed, the energy efficiency in China is 10 per cent lower than the average of industrialised countries; its energy consumption by unit of energy intensive products is 40 per cent higher (NDRC 2007).

Lastly, the attractiveness of China could also be explained by the existence of national technological capabilities, which facilitate the absorption of innovative technologies. Technologies used in small hydropower and small- and large-scale wind farms are at a stage of commercialisation in China, explaining the attractiveness of these kinds of projects for CDM investors. By contrast, biomass and waste technologies are still at the prototype stage, so the number of CDM projects in this area is comparatively small (OECD 2009). As CDM projects using these technologies for energy generation cannot be supported by the existing technological bases in these categories of projects, investors should transfer technologies and implement learning programmes for local employees in China.

To sum up, China is the first global recipient of CDM projects. In addition to benefiting from emission reduction financed by foreign firms, it appears that the CDM is also a channel for the transfer of environmentally friendly technology, which could contribute to the energy transition in this country. At the same time, the additional resources devoted to finance emission reduction projects foster the absorption of innovative technologies and the implementation of training programmes. Although the environmental additionality of the CDM projects is still limited, its national appropriation by China explains the correspondence between the sectorial repartition of these projects and the country's energy and climate priorities and policy.

Conclusions

Does the CDM foster national climate policy making and thus contribute to more climate-resilient development? Despite the fact that confidence in the problem-solving capacity of the UNFCCC process is shrinking, the number of CDM projects is not decreasing. This shows that governments and investors still believe in the effectiveness and profitability of the mechanism. Four salient facts have emerged from this analysis:

1 High emitters and attractive economies with high growth rates attract more CDM investments, a repartition that reflects the polarisation of FDI on emerging areas. The CDM is supported by the private sector, and determinants of the location of CDM are similar to the determinants of the direction of FDI flows.
2 The CDM can contribute to climate resilience by making countries less dependent on fossil fuels. As the analysis has shown, especially for China, the question of climate resilience for rapidly developing countries has been related to the implementation of CDM projects if the localisation of the mechanism serves national climate objectives. In this respect, the Chinese national institutional framework allows for the orientation of projects towards domestic climate priorities; namely, the development of renewable energy and energy efficiency. For Asian countries, CDM projects have boosted domestic efforts in the field of energy diversification, but the potential of manufacturing sectors has not been exploited, attracting less than 5 per cent of CDM projects.

3   Beyond the environmental additionality of CDM projects, this flexibility mechanism of the Kyoto Protocol can also contribute to the dissemination of clean technology and to the transmission of 'good practices' for the management of CC.

4   The analysis has shown that national institutional capacities impact on the efficiency and effectiveness of the CDM. This means that national institutions, such as the DNAs, must be strengthened. In addition, some general technical aspects regarding the definition of additionality and calculation methods have to be improved to make the mechanism more efficient. The determination of the environmental additionality and the definition of the baseline should be better supervised by the UNFCCC and the Intergovernmental Panel on Climate Change (IPCC). As mentioned above, many energy generation projects are well in line with earlier trends, and technologies used in CDM projects do not differ from other national programmes. Therefore, additionality can be a counterproductive and highly ambiguous criterion (Aldy *et al.* 2010). Moreover, the scope of CDM must be discussed. There are few projects in the manufacturing and agricultural sectors, although these sectors show a large potential for GHG reduction, specifically in ASEAN countries. New economic incentives must be implemented to increase the return on investment on these kinds of projects. In spite of these shortcomings, Asia shows a diversity of experiences and lessons for future development: China has benefited from the mechanism thanks to the institution-building which makes CDM projects compatible with national climate priorities. Larger ASEAN countries welcomed projects focused on the energy sector, which are now a basis on which to build more ambitious climate mitigation policies and to make these countries more resilient regarding energy supply and the provision of income-generating jobs. Based on this study of CDM projects in Southeast Asian countries and China, negotiations on a future climate convention should focus on the reform of the CDM, i.e. improving the above-mentioned deficiencies and encouraging a greater diversity of projects and sectors in order to generate and enable more congruence between the international framework and national CC priorities.

Notes

1   International regime, i.e. 'sets of implicit or explicit principles, norms, rules, and decision-making procedures around which actors' expectations converge in a given area of international relations' (Krasner 1983: 2).

2   Some major actors such as the USA are not part of it! And many countries, such as Russia and Japan, are now pressing against its renewal.

3   The MRV approach was set up in the Bali Action Plan and confirmed at the Cancun Conference. It aims at a coherent, robust, transparent approach to emissions-tracking and climate policy measures implementation.

4   These data are extracted from the CDM Pipeline 2012, http://cdmpipeline.org/ (accessed 1 September 2012).

5 From the UNFCCC website, http://cdm.unfccc.int/ (accessed 2012/09/01).
6 These data are extracted from the UNFCCC website, http://cdm.unfccc.int/ (accessed 1 September 2012).
7 See Annex I which illustrates the differences in the level of development, population, carbon emissions, and energy consumption in Asian countries.
8 See The Energy Policy and Planning Office of Thailand, online: http://www.eppo. go.th/ (accessed 1 September 2012).
9 Thailand Greenhouse Gas Management Organization, http://www.tgo.or.th/ (accessed 2012/09/01).
10 Available on the website of Clean Development Mechanism in China, http://cdm. ccchina.gov.cn/english/ (accessed 1 September 2012).

References

ADB (2009) *Understanding and Responding to Climate Change in Developing Asia*, Manila, Philippines: Asian Development Bank Publishing.

Aldy, J.E. *et al.* (2010) 'Designing Climate Mitigation Policy', *Journal of Economic Literature*, vol. 48, no. 4, pp. 903–934.

Borde, A. and Joumni, H. (2007) 'Le Recours au Marché dans les Politiques de Lutte contre le Changement Climatique', *Revue International et Stratégique*, vol. 3, no. 67, pp. 53–66.

Boulanger, P.M. *et al.* (2004) *Le Mécanisme pour un Développement Propre: Conception d'Outils et Mise en Oeuvre*, Plan d'Appui Scientifique à une Politique de Développement Durable (PADD II), Politique Scientifique Fédérale, January.

Boulanger, P.M., Brechet, T. and Lussis B. (2005) 'Le Mécanisme pour un Développement Propre Tiendra-t-il ses Promesses, Reflets et Perspectives', *Tome LIV*, no. 3, pp. 5–27.

Dechezlepretre, A., Glachant, M. and Meniére, Y. (2008) 'The CDM and the International Diffusion of Technologies: An Empirical Study', *Energy Policy*, vol. 36, no. 4, pp. 1273–1283.

Demaze, M.T. (2009) 'Le Protocole de Kyoto, le Clivage Nord-Sud et le Défi du Développement Durable', *Espace Géographique*, vol. 2, no. 38, pp. 139–156.

ENTTRANS (2007) *Promoting Sustainable Energy Technology Transfers through the CDM: Converting from a Theoretical Concept to Practical Action*, European Union Sixth Framework Programme, Project: The Potential of Transferring and Implementing Sustainable Energy Technology through the Clean Development Mechanism, January 2006–December 2007.

ESCAP (2007) *Ten as One: Challenges and Opportunities for ASEAN Integration*, Bangkok: United Nations Economic and Social Commission for Asia and the Pacific.

Flamos, A. (2010) 'The Clean Development Mechanism – Catalyst for Widespread Deployment of Renewable Energy Technologies? Or Misnomer?', *Environment Development and Sustainability*, vol. 12, no. 1, pp. 89–102.

Godard, O. and Henry, C. (1998) 'Les Instruments des Politiques Internationales de l'Environnement: la Prévention du Risque Climatique et les Mécanismes de Permis Négociables', in Bureau, D. *et al.* (eds.), *Fiscalité de l'Environnement*, Paris : Rapport au Conseil d'Analyse Economique, La Documentation Française, Collection des Rapports du CAE, pp. 83–174.

Guérivière, D.P. (2008) *Les Mécanismes pour un Développement Propre*, Chambre de Commerce et d'Industrie Française en Chine, April–May, online: http://fce.ccifc. org/2008-05/doc/Proparco_MDP.pdf (accessed 5 March 2013.)

IEA (2012) *CO₂ Emissions from Fuel Combustion: Highlights*, Paris: International Energy Agency.

Joumni, H. (2003) 'Les Perspectives de Mise en Oeuvre du Mécanisme de Développement Propre: Enjeux et Contraintes', *Cahiers du GEMDEV*, no. 29, October, pp. 95–115.

Jung, M. (2006) 'Host Country Attractiveness for CDM Non-Sink Projects', *Energy Policy*, vol. 34, no. 15, pp. 2173–2184.

Krasner, S.D. (1983) 'Structural Causes and Regime Consequence: Regimes As Intervening Variables', in Krasner, S. (ed.) *International Regimes*, Ithaca, NY: Cornell University.

Krechowicz, D. and Fernando, H. (2009) *Emerging Risks: Impact of Key Environmental Trends in Emerging Asia*, Washington, DC: World Resources Institute and International Finance Corporation.

Lacour, P. (2012) *Quantifier le Contenu Environnemental des Relations Economiques entre le Japon et la Chine: Analyse de Trios Canaux de Transferts de Technologies Vertes*, Thèse de Doctorat pour l'Obtention du grade de Docteur de l'Université de Grenoble, Spécialité Sciences Economiques.

Lacour, P. and Simon, J.C. (2012) 'Quelle Intégration des Pays en Développement dans le Régime Climatique? Le Mécanisme pour un Développement Propre en Asie', *Développement Durable et Territoire*, vol. 3, no. 3, December, online: http://developpementdurable.revues.org/9492 (accessed 6 March 2013).

Maosheng, D. and Haites, E. (2006) 'Implementing the Clean Development Mechanism in China', *International Review for Environmental Strategies*, vol. 6, no. 1, pp. 153–168.

Meunié, A. (2004) 'Quelles Règles de Partage de la Charge pour la Réduction des Emissions de Gaz à Effet de Serre? L'Intégration des Pays en Développement dans la Lutte contre le Changement Climatique et Etude de Cas de la Chine', Contribution at the Conference *La Mondialisation contre le Développement?*, organised by C3ED, 10–11 June.

Meunié, A. (2009) 'Dynamique et Régulation des Emissions de CO₂ en Chine', *Economie Appliquée*, vol. 62, no. 1, pp. 133–168.

Meunié, A. and Quenault, B. (2007) 'Le Financement du Développement Durable', *Revue Tiers-Monde*, vol. 4, no. 192, December, pp. 853–869.

NCCCC (2005) *Measures for Operation and Management of Clean Development Mechanism Project*, National Coordination Committee on Climate Change, online: http://cdm.ccchina.hov.cn/english/NewsInfo.asp?NewsId=905 (accessed 5 March 2013).

NDRC (2006) *The 11th Five-Year Plan: Targets, Paths and Policy Orientation*, People's Republic of China: Ma Kai Minister, National Development and Reform Commission, 19 March.

NDRC (2007) *China's National Climate Change Programme*, People's Republic of China: National Development and Reform Commission, June.

Nguyen, N.T. *et al.* (2010) 'Improving the Clean Development Mechanism Post-2012: A Developing Country Perspective', *Carbon and Climate Law Review*, vol. 7, no. 4, pp. 76–85.

Nygard, J. *et al.* (2004) *Clean Development Mechanism in China: Taking a Proactive and Sustainable Approach*, The World Bank, The Chinese Ministry of Science and Technology, Federal Ministry for Economic Cooperation and Development, 2nd edition, no. 30254, September, online: http://www-wds.worldbank.org/external/default/WDSContentServer/WDSP/IB/2004/12/14/000090341_20041214100649/Rendered/PDF/302450CHA0cdm1china.pdf (accessed 6 March 2013).

OECD (2009) *Eco-Innovation Policies in the People's Republic of China*, Paris: Environment Directorate, Organisation of Economic Co-operation and Development.

Organisation Internationale de la Francophonie (2005) *Onzième Session de la Conférence des Parties de la Convention Cadre des Nations-Unies sur les Changements Climatiques* (CdP 11) *et la Première Session de la Réunion des Parties du Protocole de Kyoto (RdP 1)*, Montréal, Canada, 28 November–9 December.

Reddy, B.S. and Assenza, G.B. (2009) 'The Great Climate Debate', *Energy Policy*, vol. 37, no. 9, pp. 2997–3008.

Schroeder, M. (2009) 'Utilizing the Clean Development Mechanism for the Deployment of Renewable Energies in China', *Applied Energy*, vol. 86, no. 2, pp. 237–242.

Shuang, Z. (2005) *CDM Implementation in China*, Energy Research Institute, National Development and Reform Commission China, 23–25 March, Japanonline: http://www.meti.go.jp/policy/energy_environment/global_warming/pdf/china(dna).pdf (accessed 6 March 2013).

Szymanski, T. (2002) 'The Clean Development Mechanism in China', *The China Business Review*, vol. 29, no. 6, November–December, pp. 26–31.

Teng, F. and Zhang, X. (2010) 'Clean Development Mechanism Practice in China: Current Status and Possibilities for Future Regime', *Energy*, vol. 35, no. 11, pp. 4328–4335.

UNCTAD (2008) *World Investment Report: Transnational Corporations and the Infrastructure Challenge,* New York and Geneva: United Nations Conference on Trade and Development.

UNEP (2000) *Clean Development Mechanism: Introduction to the CDM*, Roskide: UNEP Risoe Center, UNEP Collaborating Centre on Energy and Environment.

UNEP (2011) *CDM Project Distribution within Host Countries by Region and Type*, UNEP Riose Center, July, online: http://cdmpipeline.org/publications/CDMStatesAndProvinces.xls (accessed 5 March 2013).

UNEP (2012) *CDM Pipeline 2012*, UNEP Risoe Center, September, online: http://cdmpipeline.org/ (accessed 5 March 2013).

UNFCCC (2010) *The Contribution of the Clean Development Mechanism under the Kyoto Protocol to Technology Transfer*, online: http://cdm.unfccc.int/Reference/Reports/TTreport/TTrep10.pdf (accessed 5 March 2013).

UNFCCC (2012) 'Clean Development Mechanism', available online at http://cdm.unfccc.int (accessed 1 September 2012).

Vieillefosse, A. (2006) 'Que Faire Après Kyoto? Les Principaux Enjeux', *Revue d'Economie Financière*, vol. 2, no. 83, March, pp. 77–90.

Wang, B. (2010) 'Can CDM Bring Technology Transfer to China? – An Empirical Study of Technology Transfer in China's CDM Projects', *Energy Policy*, vol. 38, no. 5, May, pp. 2572–2585.

Wanko, H. and Smida, S. (2001) 'Problématique du Mécanisme de Développement Propre et Stratégie de Développement Durable pour les PVD', International Conference *Mondialisation, Energie, Environnement*, Paris, 10–13 June.

Winkelman, A.G. and Moore, M.R. (2011) 'Explaining the Differential Distribution of Clean Development Mechanism Projects across Host Countries', *Energy Policy*, vol. 39, no 3, March, pp. 1132–1143.

10 Does the right hand know what the left hand is doing?

Similar problem, opposing remedies – a comparison of the Montreal Protocol and Kyoto Protocol's Clean Development Mechanism

Thomas Grammig

The overlap between the Montreal Protocol and the Kyoto Protocol: is this really a problem?

The Montreal Protocol on Substances that Deplete the Ozone Layer, in short, the Montreal Protocol (MP), is a protocol to the Vienna Convention for the Protection of the Ozone Layer: it is designed to protect the Earth's ozone layer by phasing out the production of numerous substances responsible for ozone depletion. The MP entered into force in January 1989 and is considered the most successful international environmental treaty (Oberthür 2001: 358).[1] Adopted in Kyoto in December 1997 and in force since February 2005, the Kyoto Protocol complements the United Nations Framework Convention on Climate Change (UNFCCC) by setting obligations for industrialised countries to reduce their emissions of greenhouse gases (GHG), thus fostering the UNFCCC's goal of achieving the 'stabilisation of greenhouse gas concentrations in the atmosphere at a level that would prevent dangerous anthropogenic interference with the climate system' (Mintzer and Leonard 1994).

The Montreal Protocol (MP) and the Kyoto Protocol (KP) are led by different actors in separate processes. They have developed an institutional overlap because both deal with chemicals used for the same purposes and in the same machines, for example for air conditioning. The policies and methods conceived by the two Conventions to support the substitution of these chemicals imply different methodologies and funding criteria, which have led to dissimilar results. Neither the Montreal nor the Kyoto Protocol has managed to address their overlap. While the MP funds the replacement of hydrochlorofluorocarbons (HCFCs), the KP finances the replacement of hydrofluorocarbons (HFCs). The chapter demonstrates that this division between HCFCs and HFCs leads to significant overlaps between the MP and the KP, and that the inertia of both regimes as well as diverging interests among and between the countries forming part of the Group of 77 (G-77) and the Organisation for Economic Co-operation and Development (OECD) make it unlikely that the overlap or a reduction of its negative effects is addressed.

As a comparative assessment of the KP and the MP is difficult, and none has been published so far, this chapter explores the perspective of the recipient side (companies) as a basis for such an assessment. Since both the MP and the KP seek to accelerate technical change, the concept of *technological trajectories* from Schumpeterian or evolutionary economics is used to tackle the overlap and the resulting lack of impact.

What has this problem got to do with 'resilience', the main issue of this book? Refrigerators and air conditioners (ACs) can partially and locally enhance resilience in coping with heatwaves; but their increasing use for general convenience by upper and middle classes dwarfs the potential resilience benefits and contributes significantly to global warming. Between 1993 and 2009, the number of ACs in US households increased from 64 to 100 million; but in China, 50 million units were sold in 2010 alone (Cox 2012). Chinese manufacturers of ACs account for 80 per cent of the global market (BSRIA market research). HCFC-22 from ACs produced in China is the largest single part of the projected 0.8 Gt CO_2e of HCFCs in 2015 (IPCC 2005). Phasing out HCFC-22 is a rare technology-based mitigation that can reduce the impact of the expanding consumption of air conditioning. The driver behind the inappropriateness of the current HCFC-22 projects is the combination of the double phase-out agreed for the MP in 2007 and China's increasing share in the respective global trade. This mitigation is barred at the moment; to attain significant resilience impacts, and faster, would require halting the MP's inertia, redesigning its tools, and addressing the overlap with the KP.

This chapter briefly describes the MP's operation and looks at the implications of its extension to dealing with HCFCs using the example of Sri Lanka; the subsequent assessment focuses on the direct industrial and technical conditions irrespective of the negotiations that took place (which is outside the focus of this discussion). Similarly, the general operation of the KP is reviewed in order to understand the application of the KP to HFCs that has occurred until today; the description is not intended to evaluate the KP, as such, but rather to show what motivates companies to utilise the KP mechanism and to assess from their perspective the strength of the incentives that the KP offers for HFC replacement. From this empirical basis, four types of overlaps illustrate the metaphorical comparison of the MP as a 'watering can' and the KP as offering 'carrots'. The reason for the institutional overlaps is not the companies or the politics, but the fact that HCFCs and HFCs are used for the same technical purposes. The chapter concludes with a future perspective, briefly analysing the current proposal of the World Bank and the US to extend the MP for a second time, to HFCs, as path dependent – and proposes to use *innovation economics* to learn from experience and increase the effectiveness of funding by better separating and targeting the use of the MP and the KP.

The technical problem: HFCs and HCFCs: a comparison

When comparing HFCs and HCFCs, problems arising from the overlap between MP and KP become clear. Most HCFCs and HFCs are used for the same purposes, mainly in refrigerators, ACs, and other appliances for cooling. Amongst the different

Table 10.1 Comparison of gases overlapping KP and MP

Factors	HFC-134a	HCFC-22
Contained in refrigerators, air conditioners (AC), and other electrical appliances for cooling	yes	yes
Estimated quantities used per year in tonnes	~100.000	~100.000
Global emissions estimated for 2015	1.15 Gt CO_2e[1]	0.8 Gt CO_2e
Global warming potential (GWP) compared to CO^2	1,410 times	1,780 times
Increase in concentration in the atmosphere 1998–2005	27 %	38 %
Replacements/substitutes	Hydrocarbons, NH_3, CO_2	
GWP	1 to 5	

Source: Based on data from IPCC 2005, SPM-4.
Note
1 Gigatonnes of carbon dioxide equivalent.

HFCs and HCFCs, only two, HFC-134a and HCFC-22, are important for climate change because only they are annually used in large quantities (see Table 10.1). Both HFC-134a and HCFC-22 were first introduced as replacements for ozone-depleting chlorofluorocarbons (CFCs) and spread rapidly in the 1990s when the 'ozone hole' was an urgent problem and CFC had to be replaced as fast as possible.

One difference between HFC-134a and HCFC-22 is, however, relevant for the division between MP and KP: HFC-134a has no effect on the atmosphere's ozone layer, while HCFC-22 has an 'ozone-depleting potential' (ODP) of 5 per cent compared to CFCs. Because of this difference, parties to the MP claimed and succeeded in justifying the inclusion of HCFCs in the MP in 2007 (Figure 10.1).

ACs are a particular problem in terms of resilience because of the negative feedback loop (the demand for air conditioning rises with average temperatures) and the high sensitivity of demand to economic growth.[2] Eighty per cent of global AC sales are produced by Chinese manufacturers and contain HCFC-22.[3] By replacing HCFCs and HFCs, GHG emissions could be decreased significantly without reducing the use of ACs because their substitutes[4] have a Global Warming Potential (GWP) between 1 and 5, compared to 1,410 and 1,780 of HCFCs and HFCs, respectively (see Table 10.1). There are no differences in the thermal efficiency of the substances since a high-efficiency AC that uses HFC-134a is as efficient as a high-efficiency AC that uses HCFC-22; all of these chemicals cover the whole range of products from the highest to the lowest thermal efficiency, depending on the appliance price and quality of manufacturing.

The Montreal Protocol: how ozone-depleting substances are regulated

Since 1992, the MP has funded investments that replace ozone-depleting substances (ODS) with alternative chemicals which do not harm the ozone layer,

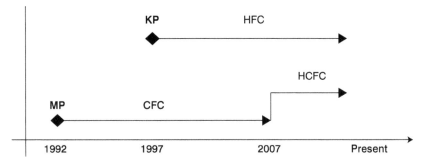

Figure 10.1 Conventions and eligible gases

focusing on CFC-11 and CFC-12 (used mainly in refrigeration). Other ODS, such as halon or methylbromide, played a much smaller role. Developing countries agreed to phase out all CFCs by 2010 if all conversions of CFC being used were funded. Thus, the MP made OECD countries pay proportionally to their GDP for the replacement of CFCs in developing countries, as those ODS had been produced by OECD-based companies such as DuPont, Dow, ICI, Atochem, and Hoechst. So far, the MP has disbursed US$2.6 billion through the Multilateral Fund (MLF), the financial institution of the MP established in 1991. In OECD countries, CFCs were replaced by 1995. Most developing countries completed their phase-out by 2008, ahead of the agreed 2010 target. Figure 10.2 illustrates how rapidly the total global production of CFCs was decreased. On this basis, the MP is considered as the single most efficient environmental treaty.

After eliminating CFCs in all developing countries, the MP was extended to HCFCs at the 19th Meeting of the Parties to the MP, in 2007. Due to an institutional path dependency and bureaucratic inertia in the triangle of the MLF, Implementing Agencies (IAs), and ministries of environment, the same practice applied by the MLF for CFC was maintained for HCFC phase-out.

As HCFC-22 is cheap and can be used to refill existing CFC-using equipment, it was considered a quick remedy in 1992, despite its small ozone depletion effect. Fifteen years later, this was reversed and it was agreed to extend the operation of the MLF to HCFCs and fund their replacement. This 'double phase-out' had previously been rejected by some parties to the MP as absurd: i.e. to first fund the introduction of HCFC-22 in order to replace CFCs, and, since 2007, to fund the phasing out of HCFC-22 in order to switch to alternatives with zero ozone depletion and zero GWP. While the MLF paid for a problem originating in OECD countries (CFC producers), it now pays for getting rid of HCFC-22, of which 80 per cent come from China (in 2012, China produced 353 ktonnes HCFC-22, all OECD countries 90 ktonnes; McCulloch 2010), thus creating an unforeseen regional bias in the MLF in favour of China. But why did this happen, and why is the disbursement procedure via the MLF (proposals, evaluation, controlling) maintained for HCFC-22 without assessing the technical and economic differences between CFC and HCFC-22? To shed some light on this question, the key aspects of the MLF operation as they were applied for CFC and continue to be employed

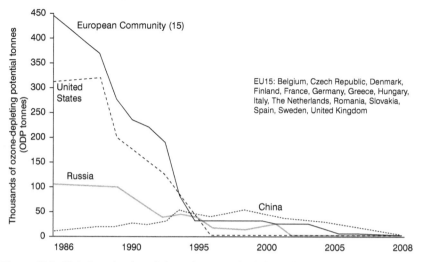

Figure 10.2 Global production of the main ozone-depleting substances

Source: UNEP, Vital Ozone Graphics 2.0 http://www.grida.no/publications/vg/ozone2/

for HCFCs are briefly analysed. Privileging the analysis of the implementation side over the negotiation side of a climate convention requires justification, but, in this chapter, it is simply taken as a premise. The following description of the HCFC project implementation suggests that therein lies the reasons for this continuity from CFCs to HCFCs ('regime inertia'), an argument which is then further strengthened by describing the overlap between MLF and KP projects.

The multilateral fund: how funds are distributed and managed

What was thought to be a strength, i.e. the possibility to cover the so-called incremental costs,[5] has actually been a weakness of the MP: the concept was never put into practice. For HCFCs, and before them CFCs, MLF funding is available only in relation to the volume of the chemicals used, irrespective of the costs/benefits occurring at the user's side. The MLF has funded some 30 project types in all developing countries; for example, maintenance of refrigerators, recovery of CFC from chillers, and replacing CFC as an insulation foam blowing agent. In total, 6,104 individual projects were approved and realised (UNEP 2010a). The same blueprints were used in all developing countries by the four IAs: the World Bank, the United Nations Development Programme (UNDP), the United Nations Environment Programme (UNEP), and the United Nations Industrial Development Organization (UNIDO). These four institutions have the right to write project proposals to the MLF and submit them on behalf of developing countries, even more so as most of the bilateral IAs, in particular, public development agencies (DFID, CIDA, United States Agency for International Development (USAID)), stopped operating in this arena after 2000. Thus, four UN agencies reproduce the same project blueprints in all developing countries.[6]

The principle of *incremental cost* was chosen to assure the effective use of funds. The MLF intended to evaluate what investments would happen in a *business-as-usual* scenario, i.e. with the use of ODS, and then in comparison to define the 'incremental' cost of an investment that would replace CFC by non-ODS. The MLF never managed to operationalise such an economic assessment because it was analytically impossible to disentangle product quality, product diversity, and raw material prices involved in an investment in new refrigeration equipment, not in industry, commerce, nor in other sectors.[7] Instead of incremental costs, cost factors of 'US$ per kg ODS replaced' used to allocate these funds were considered the only realistic option. Once the consumption of CFCs by a country was defined, the funding available was non-negotiable. For CFCs, the cost factors were agreed in 1995 (UNEP 1995) and have not been changed since.

These cost factors have been maintained across all economic sectors, countries and, most importantly, all technologies: whether funds were provided for small workshops in Lesotho replacing CFC in the refrigerant circuit of refrigerators or for ACs in luxury hotels in Mauritius, US$13.7/kg of CFC replaced were spent for all possible activities in the domestic refrigeration sector. US$15.2/kg was used for the commercial sector.[8] No matter what the economic context, what skill level the technicians required, or what growth prospects existed, all investments were treated with either the domestic or the commercial cost factor, declaring the reduction of complexity to only two cost figures as unavoidable. The economies of scale inherent in refrigeration technologies translated into large profits for companies, which received subsidies for the purchase of new production machines they would otherwise have financed themselves; on the contrary, small companies were offered too little funds so that they could not invest in new technologies, and in some cases they had to close down. UNIDO stated that phase-out implies substantially increased operating costs for one CFC-replacing company, but cost savings for another such company (UNIDO 2009: 187) in the same country. So they were the only IA that admitted publicly the key deficiency of the MLF disbursement approach – the use of only two cost factors instead of the compensation of the actual incremental cost.

For HCFC-22, all foam is treated as one category, so even less differentiation than for CFC is applied, and this after two and a half years of negotiation following the 2007 decision by the parties (HCFC phase-out in the foam sector): 'Incremental operating costs for projects in the foam sector will be considered at US $1.60/metric kg for HCFC-141b and US $1.40/metric kg for HCFC-142b consumption to be phased out at the manufacturing enterprise' and (HCFC phase-out in the refrigeration and air-conditioning sector) 'Incremental operating costs for projects in the air conditioning sub-sector will be considered at US $6.30/metric kg of HCFC consumption to be phased out at the manufacturing enterprise.'

Neither UNEP, the MLF, nor any other institution or party to the MP has, to date, published an economic assessment of why US$6.3/kg HCFC-22 is suitable, for example when comparing costs of a cooler using HCFC-22 to costs of a cooler operating with a non-HCFC substance. It is surprising that the various assessments were neither scrutinised nor any kind of controversy arose regarding these issues.

As MP insiders admit off the record, the factor was determined by dividing the funding likely to become available by the total volume of HCFC-22 consumed in developing countries.[9] There is only one cost factor for HCFC-22 in refrigeration because there was only one for CFC in refrigeration. This oversimplification was weak in 1992 and was still so in 2007.[10]

The main intention of this introduction into the MLF is that the two key aspects, which were developed for CFCs, are now being applied in the same manner for HCFC-22: the role of the IAs and the uniform cost factors per kg. As this chapter focuses on the direct industrial and technical outcomes, it does not address the negotiations between MP parties.

The HCFC phase-out management plan: the Sri Lanka example

The HCFC-22 phase-out management plan (HPMP) for Sri Lanka, prepared by UNDP and adopted at the 26th Meeting of the MLF ExCom in November 2010, is analysed here as a typical and representative example of its inadequacy in the local context (UNEP 2010b). In 2009, 212 tonnes of HCFC-22 were used, 195 tonnes in residential and 12 tonnes in industrial ACs. Regnis and Metecno are the two manufacturers using HCFC-22. As 47 per cent of Regnis is owned locally, it gets MLF funds, whereas Metecno, being 100 per cent Italian, cannot get funds. Regnis operates two production lines, one with cyclopentane,[11] the other with HCFC-22 as foam blowing agents. On behalf of Sri Lanka, UNDP requested US$237,560 to support Regnis in the conversion of the second line also to cyclopentane, to which the MLF responded as follows:

> Based on this review of the proposal for the conversion of Regnis, the [MLF] Secretariat advised UNDP that the cost for converting to cyclopentane for an enterprise with consumption below 30 tonnes would require counterpart funding, ranging from 50 to 90 per cent which might be economically difficult for the country.
>
> Following discussions, UNDP revised the proposal and came up with two technology options that could be used by the enterprise: These are cyclopentane and methyl formate. UNDP advised that the enterprise had been briefed on Multilateral Fund eligibility and funding criteria and, accordingly, the requirement for counterpart funding. It mentioned that the enterprise is financially sound and could cover the difference required in the investment either by retrofitting existing equipment, and will decide whether to invest in completely new equipment and when. The [MLF] Secretariat and UNDP agreed on the final amount of US $18,866 plus support costs for the investment project.
>
> (UNEP 2010b: 11)

The reduction in MLF funding for the only Sri Lankan HCFC-using company from US$237,560 to US$18,866 ignored the economics of Regnis' investment and only reflected MLF disbursement rules and its country investment criteria. The

MLF response cited UNDP as 'mentioning' that Regnis was financially sound, which is a coded expression that the MLF trusts UNDP to judge whether Regnis can use the funds and replace the HCFCs. Neither the UNDP proposal nor the MLF's response mentioned that, in 1997, Regnis had received US$265,917 from the MLF to shift one line from CFC-11 to cyclopentane in foam, from CFC-12 to HFC-134a as a refrigerant (project SRL/ REF/17/INV/06); and Regnis changed the second line to HCFC-22 with its own funds, not knowing that this would make the company eligible for new funds 12 years later. Without assembling more such cases, this one illustrates the importance of the relations between IAs and MLF, and we assume that Regnis is typical for funding eligibility for HCFC-using companies in most of the HPMPs.

Eighty-eight per cent of all HCFCs in Sri Lanka are used to service residential ACs, refilling the refrigerant that slowly escapes during normal usage. In many HPMPs, AC maintenance constitutes the largest part. Two options are evident: first, give incentives for households to replace their old ACs with new ones which run without HCFC-22; second, assist 6,500 formally trained technicians and 5,000 informal sector technicians (UNEP 2010b: 4) in Sri Lanka through training and provide them with HCFC-22 recovery equipment and/or leakage detectors to reduce the HCFC-22 seeping from the ACs. As part of the CFC phase-out plan, 3,700 technicians did receive training in the 1990s. Now, as part of the 1.6 million $ HPMP, US$428,000 is planned for recovery equipment, US$302,000 for training, and US$137,000 for retrofit incentives (these are the largest budget items). Recovery of HCFC-22 can be done with the same vacuum pump equipment as for CFCs, so those 3,700 who have learned it before can continue to use the same pumps for HCFC-22 (and HFC-134a). To know what these 3,700 persons are doing now with the recovery machines and the acquired skills would be a necessary basis for a decision on what to fund in future. However, as seen in the case for Regnis above, the actual outcomes of earlier CFC phase-out projects are not taken into account in the design and implementation of HCFC phase-out projects.

Criticism of the MLF and conclusions with respect to HCFC-22

Several assessments of UNEP's Ozone Secretariat and the MLF have come to the conclusion that these are weak institutions which are unable to shape the ozone regime or to reform the institutions (Bauer 2007: 10), contributing only to regime maintenance. Bauer clearly reveals the asymmetries in the triangle of the MLF, the ministries of environment in host countries, and the IAs that have grown over the years. The focus of the analysis is on the outcome of MLF funding, i.e. the results achieved in the industries concerned, not what the MP parties (might have) intended. The project blueprints, used for CFCs in all developing countries, are being reproduced for HCFCs in all developing countries, and the roles of the IAs and the uniform cost factors are also the same, as explained above.

The Sri Lankan HPMP (the Regnis case and AC maintenance) illustrates that the allocation of MLF funds took precedence over the concern for the effectiveness of investments for the phasing out of HCFCs, as was previously the case for CFCs. It is plausible that, depending on environmental policy and governance, MLF funds can be highly effective in some developing countries because the ministry of environment makes good use of the IAs, although the approach can be prone to corruption in other countries. The institutional inertia of the MP persists and UNDP, UNEP, UNIDO, and the World Bank continue to compete intensely with each other to guide ministries of environment on drawing MLF funds for HCFC-22 replacement. The business interests of the IAs also seem the most plausible explanation for why no questions about the differences between CFCs and HCFCs are asked and why the changes in geography, equipment, and economics remain unaddressed. The MLF needed and created a shortcut around the 'incremental cost' issue and funds were spent on volume of ODS, ignoring the recipients' concerns (admitted among the IAs only by UNIDO).

Before returning to Regnis and similar companies (see below), the KP is briefly described. Much more detail about the Sri Lankan case would be needed to understand the exact role of UNDP and the results this HPMP achieves; however, this case suffices to illustrate the interactions between the MLF funding and that of the KP. Since the HCFC replacements funded by the MLF and the HFC replacements funded by the KP take place in the same sector, i.e. refrigeration, the comparison of the two funding methods and their overlap leads to a bigger picture where new solutions become evident. In this bigger picture, the technical change in HCFC out-phasing can be characterised as a *scale intensive trajectory* of innovation.

The KP's Clean Development Mechanism

The Clean Development Mechanism (CDM)[12] relies on OECD countries to create market demand for emission reductions realised in developing countries, i.e. the trade part of a cap-and-trade system. The European Emissions Trading System (EU ETS) regulates the 11,000 largest energy consuming plants in Europe. Each of them decides whether to reduce their own emissions or purchase Certified Emission Reductions (CERs) in developing countries. The EU decides the cap, thereby quantifying a goal of X million tons of allowed CO_2 emissions. Companies choose to reduce their own emissions or pay for CERs, which are issued per 1 ton of CO_2 emissions avoided in developing countries.

Participation in the CDM varies greatly amongst buyers and sellers of CERs. German companies are less active than UK companies, reflecting a preference for in-house emission reductions instead of buying CERs from abroad. Chinese companies account for 62 per cent of all CER sellers worldwide. Least-developed countries (LDCs) have few CDM projects because they currently have little CO_2 emissions to reduce. After 2005, when all rules were in place (from the so-called Marrakesh Accord), primary investment in CDM projects amounted to US$3–6 billion/year. Until 2012, the KP secretariat has issued 1 billion CERs in total, the underlying investment in CDM projects for creating these CERs amounts to more than US$215 billion.[13] The CDM is bigger (in US$ by a factor of 80), more sophisticated and fine-tuned, but also more costly and challenging to steer than the MP, especially because the MLF's cost factors are applied uniformly, whereas the CDM only functions when private companies choose to act.

The national differences illustrate the market mechanism. The KP sets commercial conditions for companies, who then shape the direction and dynamics of the market. The CDM operates through bottom-up procedures: each CDM project applies so-called methodologies, which can be proposed by anybody, to calculate the CO_2 reduction achieved (thus the CERs). Some 400 methodologies, ranging from power plants to charcoal stoves and composting, have been proposed; the CDM Executive Board approved 200 of them as the accounting rules for CDM projects. UNEP/Risø has currently calculated 8,000 CDM projects worldwide. Most methodologies are developed for the commercial interests of carbon investors, such as EcoSecurities, Camco, Mitsubishi, or equipment suppliers of the most efficient turbines, boilers, photovoltaic (PV) cells, light bulbs, etc. Other methodologies are developed for policy reasons by the World Bank, NGOs, universities, and the KP secretariat itself. The assessment of the proposed methodologies is based on their environmental integrity, irrespective of the commercial or policy interests involved, and all inputs to the assessments are publicly disclosed.[14]

While the merits of the CDM are hotly debated, its role in facilitating renewable energy expansion in a variety of ways is generally accepted. It is rather impressive that CDM projects make up 80 per cent of the total 133 gigawatt wind and hydropower installed in China over the past 10 years.[15] Another key effect of the CDM is the transmission of a price signal for CO_2 within otherwise separated markets (e.g. small rural hydropower and large supercritical coal power stations), creating overall efficiency gains in allocating investment amongst power plants, sectors, and countries and involving new actors: in 2005, governmental funds dominated the CDM; in 2006, 'carbon boutiques' blossomed which subsequently merged and winners such as EcoSecurities, First Climate, and MGM attracted investors like JP Morgan, Barclays, and BP in 2007. By 2010, a substantial share of CDM business was vertically integrated into large traders of fossil fuels, like Vitol and Mercuria. The commercial judgement of market actors determines the focus of CER origins.

This introduction to the CDM and the nature and evolution of the market trends is a necessary basis to consider the particular role of CDM for HFCs. As previously mentioned, only HFC-134a is important: it can be replaced with the same substances as HCFC-22, has a similarly high GWP, and was used by the MLF to replace CFCs in the 1990s.

CDM project development to date for HFC gases under Kyoto

Because of their high GWP, all HFC gases are eligible under the current Kyoto rules (KP's Annex A). HFC-134a is the most important HFC, used in half of all household refrigerators worldwide and in many other types of refrigeration equipment. Hence, the four CDM methodologies approved by the KP so far all target HFC-134a:

- AMS-III.N Avoidance of HFC emissions in rigid Polyurethane Foam (PUR) manufacturing;
- AMS-III.X Energy Efficiency and HFC-134a Recovery in Residential Refrigerators;
- AMS-III.AB Avoidance of HFC emissions in Stand-alone Commercial Refrigeration Cabinets;
- AM0071 Manufacturing and servicing of domestic refrigeration appliances using a low GWP refrigerant.

AMS-III.N was developed in 2006 by Acme Tele, a globally operating Indian corporation that produces PUR panels, mainly for telecommunication infrastructure and water technology. The first version of III.N (submitted as SSC_80) proposed investment in foam production using pentane[16] as a blowing agent for the foam instead of HFC-134a; higher costs would stem from the import of European equipment to address its inflammability. Soon, competitors requested methodological changes to include integral skin foam in III.N, and then to also apply this to old plants. The Indian firm Jindal stated in its CDM documentation that the additional cost of shifting to pentane was $75,000 with an annual yield of CER 15,000.[17] Then, Metecno requested to expand III.N to its production which uses HCFC-141b (SSC_408), submitting a statement from the Indian Polyurethane Association that listed large PUR manufacturers in India. This illustrates how a company seeking to get a CDM methodology approved uses industrial associations and similarly neutral sources of data. Metecno argued that it could opt for HFC-134a, in case the baseline of III.N would be applicable, but it should not be punished for having moved to HCFC-141b, since both were recommended by the MP in former times. This demand was rejected because 'hypothetical baselines are not appropriate' under Kyoto rules.

The complex process of methodology submission and approval, only briefly described here, depends on innovating companies' investment in costly 'first mover' learning, especially to find out how the overlaps between the MP and the KP play out for a particular application of HFCs. The companies mentioned had the same technology options and chose particular foaming equipment often based on price and positioning in the Indian foam market, while the blowing agent chemical was a minor issue before the CDM appeared. Four of seven large Indian companies invested in developing CDM projects. Without knowing how these four evaluate their investment decisions,[18] it is plausible to assume that CDM projects respond to competition from lower production costs in this country, among those types of companies and for these products. No foam company outside India has, so far, engaged in the CDM.

The second HFC-134a methodology, AMS-III.X, was developed by Bosch/ Siemens Hausgeräte (BSH) and the German development agency Gesellschaft für Technische Zusammenarbeit (GTZ, recently renamed to Gesellschaft für Internationale Zusammenarbeit, GIZ). While BSH tends to dominate the upper price range for households appliances, it managed to gain market share in Brazil by selling its top efficient (class A+++) refrigerators to utility companies for distribution to households in Brazilian slums.[19] The author designed this methodology and worked on this co-operation as GIZ wanted to create pro-poor CDM projects with an easy-to-use methodology for low-income households. The older and the less well-maintained refrigerators are, the more they leak refrigerants (HFC-134a) into the atmosphere, thus poverty multiplies the environmental impact of refrigerators. Once the Eletropaulo CDM project is finally approved and registered,[20] other utilities will hopefully follow, including similar efforts of BSH through utility companies in other countries, for example China and India.

Finally, AMS-III.AB was developed by a user of refrigeration equipment, Unilever India, which owns hundreds of thousands of ice-cream selling cabinets that offer ice cream in shops. Unilever has replaced the HFC-134a refrigerant with isobutene (GWP 4 instead of 1,410), while similar companies (e.g. Coca-Cola) still use HFC-134a in vending machines. Unilever has no economic interest in CDM projects based on AMS-III.AB because it is a very small part of the cabinets' costs, but is motivated to improve its ecological image for marketing and public relations purposes.

Conclusions on the CDM projects for HFC gases

Overall, four CDM methodologies and subsequent projects have appeared in particular circumstances: Acme Tele, BSH, and Unilever are pursing specific commercial objectives and use CDM as a competitive tool. To judge whether CDM effectively reduces HFC emissions, the main questions to be answered are (1) whether the potential income from CDM can change investment decisions; and (2) do others follow the first movers? Jindal's additional cost for pentane is US$75,000, while income from the respective 15,000 CER/year (at US$8/CER, discounted at 10 per cent) has a net present value of US$802,000 (from a total investment of about US$1–1.5 million). Hence, the incentive to replace HFC-134a is considerable and should be so for the remaining 260 PUR manufacturers in India and in other countries.

Few companies, all technology leaders (in India, Germany, and South Korea), make use of CDM for their commercial strategies. The fact that leaders get the biggest incentive is intrinsic to the CDM.[21] The market character and bottom-up orientation of CDM are evident in CDM projects for HFC substitution, as is the steep learning curve for first movers to establish methodologies. Very different CDM types – steel furnaces or power plant equipment – show similar patterns. The potential income from CERs stimulates the identification of the most efficient emission reductions, but only a few companies are presently ready to invest in the preparation of a CDM project. Because of the CDM's bottom-up procedures, the evidence from these four cases can be interpreted with more certainty than the HCFC projects in the MP, where a representative example (Sri Lanka) had to be selected. To assess the CDM, HFC projects undertaken by companies, such as Jindal, Acme Tele, Metecno, BSH, and Unilever, offer a good basis.

Current overlaps between the KP and the MP for HCFCs and HFCs

Following their previous logic, both environmental regimes were extended, MP to HCFCs and UNFCCC-KP to HFCs. Oberthür *et al.* (2011: 138) asserts that regimes can pass each other like ocean liners at night, ignoring each other, blinded by their own light. For the MP, what worked for CFC is continued without acknowledging lessons learned and not putting them into practice. UN IAs shape HCFC projects so that they fit these MP rules. For the KP, few companies have taken the risk, so far, and the bottom-up structure of the CDM leads innovative companies to shape the methodologies. The overlap between the KP and the MP arises out of the substitutability of HFC-134a and HCFC-22 and their use in the same sector. As this has always been evident, the question is: Why was this overlap allowed to happen? One answer may stem from the assessment of each regime's coherence in order to see whether the respective extension to HCFCs and HFCs was compelling.

The consideration of the direct industrial and technical context and analysis of the type of overlaps between the MP and the KP that occur reveal just how counterproductive the overlap is in practice. While those working in the regimes (secretariat staff, etc.) set their own rules, the companies are in a different position of knowledge; from their perspective, four types of overlaps between the KP and the MP are clear (from the policy side there are several more):

1   when HFCs and HCFCs are alternatives for use in new installations (in industrial plants, like Regnis, or for households, such as for BSH);
2   where the MP and the KP rules apply differently to competing companies (Regnis versus Metecno);
3   when an HCFC is contained in the foam and an HFC is the refrigerant, appliances physically contain both MP and KP impacts, as was the case for both Regnis and BSH;
4   overlaps over time, for example when refrigerator manufacturers who replaced both HFCs and HCFCs 10 to 15 years ago are affected as the MP or KP created new incentives that change these options (e.g. BSH).

These four overlaps are strengthened or weakened depending on the decision-making of the company. Regnis changed its second line to HCFC-22 on its own and used MLF funds for the more expensive switch to cyclopentane (first overlap). Being excluded from the MLF, unlike Regnis, Metecno in India tried the CDM (second overlap). Metecno's competitors pursue CDM projects even though some of them are eligible for MLF funding in India. When doing so, they gauge their confidence in the national ministry's HPMP and compare it to the regulatory risks in the CDM and the uncertain price for CERs (similarly BSH's Indian competitors). Companies that use HFCs and HCFCs, such as Regnis, can see eligibility criteria as arbitrary and perhaps choose to ignore the MP and the KP rules as an unpredictable *force majeure*, reducing their influence in this case. Opinions about the MP and the KP among competitors can create strong herd effects, more than the technology itself, which is explained when addressing the issue of *innovation trajectories*.

Overlaps are specific to industry sectors. Refrigerator production implies other overlaps of the KP and the MP beyond insulation foam. In Latin America, Southeast Asia, and Africa, many companies probably wait for MLF funds before investing: in a country where these companies are the majority, the respective ministry of environment and co-operating IAs define the speed and orientation of technical change when deciding what projects to propose to the MLF. For the MP, costs and benefits differ more amongst companies than countries. The MP can be characterised as a crude watering-can distributing funds amongst countries, ignoring differences between companies and technologies. For the MP's extension to HCFCs, these differences are bigger than before for the CFCs.

In contrast, the CDM rules of the KP address these differences in the definition of 'business as usual' and 'additionality' that each project proposal must demonstrate for the particular case. Each CDM project is assessed for its financial and technological merits. The KP creates 'carrots', i.e. incentives that so far seem insufficient for HFC phasing-out for most companies in most countries. This insufficiency increases when companies choose to wait for the funds the MP will make available for HCFC phase-out (HPMPs). *Watering-can* versus *carrots* seems to be the clearest and best-fitting metaphor for the overlap or trade-off between the KP and the MP.

Regimes ignoring each other as described by Oberthür's (2011: 138) 'ocean liners at night' metaphor is an issue when the overlaps result from country differences, since both regimes must apply to all countries. Both the KP and the MP have created voluminous documentation[22] on scientific aspects, but nowhere are the KP and the MP projects' results assessed and the observable overlaps evaluated. This mutual ignorance is, however, entirely avoidable when overlaps result from technology and company conditions: both MP and KP rules can differentiate for reasons related to technology, products, and business economics. Most of this ignorance appears to be related to the habits of the 'community of experts', who, for example, continue to deal with HCFCs as they dealt before with CFCs. CDM methodologies can address the overlaps and include criteria (eligibility, baseline, additionality) for past MP funding decisions. To sum up:

- Overlaps in HFCs and HCFCs are not reflected in KP and MP rules.
- Overlaps are variable, but treatable with criteria already applied by CDM.
- The KP is weakened by the MP because companies anticipate the impact of MLF funds available to their competitors.

The four overlap types – which were distinguished through the analysis of the Sri Lankan HPMP and four CDM methodology efforts – are considerable and reconfirm the 'blanket' continuation of the MP's blueprints for HCFCs, rendering the watering-can more diffuse than it was for CFCs. The IAs could counter this by referring in a particular HPMP to all companies that use or could use HCFCs in a particular country. So far, this has not occurred. The outright continuation of MP blueprints for HCFCs and the inability to address the identified overlaps (despite the voluminous studies) between HCFC phase-out and CDM projects for HFC substitution confirm the ocean liner metaphor.

How to overcome institutional overlaps: ideas for the future

At present, no proposal from any party to the KP or the MP addresses the described overlap, and the overlaps continue to be ignored. Only three proposals to extend the MP a second time have been presented: the first (in 2007) was to add HCFCs to the gases for whose replacement the MLF pays, the second would be to also add HFCs to the MLF gases entitled to get support for phase out; this extension would enhance the overlap between MP and KP. Strikingly, none of the existing proposals, so far, refers to advantages and disadvantages of the MP and the KP or to their outcomes: again, a class of chemicals is simply tackled as a class and the context of the users is not analysed, thus illustrating the regimes' inertia and the significance of HFCs which prompts quick action.

First, as shown in Figure 10.3, the World Bank has proposed to unilaterally assemble the funding mechanisms in a top-down manner In this scenario, each country would get an overall programme, combining three and more sources of funding to pay for replacing equipment that uses HCFCs.

This proposal has the advantage of being faster than bottom-up approaches. However, it does not address the incompatible aspects, for example the determination of MLF funds according to the volume of HCFCs used versus CDM, where income is related to CER volume and price. To obtain the MLF, GEF funds, and the CDM incomes, the responsible entity would have to act beyond and outside the current MLF, GEF, and CDM rules – an implausible solution (especially for the World Bank). The Meeting of the Parties of the MP has not yet put this proposal on its agenda.

A second proposal (by the US, together with Canada and Mexico – UNEP 2010c) is to leave HFC gases in the KP for now, while, at the same time, spending MLF funds on HFC substitutions. This proposal has reappeared at several Meetings of the Parties, where it was rejected, in particular by China and India, most likely to defend the existing KP regime.

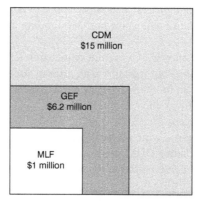

Figure 10.3 The World Bank's proposal combining the Kyoto and Montreal Protocols

Source: 'Leveraging Support for HCFC Phase-out: Opportunities and Modalities for Pursuing Linkages with the Climate Change Agenda', World Bank, 28th OEWG, 2008. Available at http://siteresources. worldbank.org/INTMP/Resources/HCFCflyer_June2010.pdf?&resourceurlname=HCFCflyer_ June2010.pdf (accessed Oct 2011).

As a third option, Micronesia has proposed a different inclusion of HFCs into the MP, with a more aggressive phase-out schedule until 2030 (UNEP 2010d) to reach the quantitative goals five years earlier than the US proposal. The US and Micronesian proposals maintain the co-existence of conflicting regimes while addressing HFCs with the same MLF funding approach used for CFCs. This implies a repeat of the regime inertia that extended the MP to HCFCs for a second time by including HFCs.

An approach that harnesses general technical change for the replacement of HFCs and HCFCs is worth exploring. As in other climate policy, the sociology of actors (companies) and a typology of behaviour (co-operation between companies) allow for defining new ways for using funds. Since none of the above-mentioned proposals addresses the outcomes of the KP or MP, the variation in HFC and HCFC use among regions, or the MP–KP overlaps, the proposals, and their underlying policy motivations, are sidelined in favour of examining the missing elements: criteria related to innovation might lead to the identification of new policy elements that the physical parameters (volumes of consumption and production of GHG) do not reveal. Such attempts to move beyond the 'project-by-project' accounting are frequent and in the CDM policy debate these are subsumed as 'Nationally Appropriate Mitigation Actions' (www.namadatabase.org).[23] No such actions have been developed for HFCs or HCFCs.

Industry context for HFC and HCFC uses: what to learn for KP and MP

The limits visible in the MP are mostly intrinsic to the MLF rules, and the limits visible in the KP reflect that few leading companies engage in it. We now suggest assessing the industry context to define lessons for overcoming these limits in KP and those in MP. That this is rather easy adds to our suspicion that the three proposals are motivated by MP insider interests. HCFC use is dominated by ACs, i.e. a mass consumer market with a small number of large corporations, competing with thousands of different models, frequent new designs, and 'cut-throat profit margins'. In this context of a mass of consumers and a few huge suppliers, the most effective way to phase-out HCFC-22 is to include it in the corporations' normal course of innovation. China's Haier or Greee, America's Whirlpool or Maytag, and South Korean, German, Mexican, and Brazilian multinationals are beyond an individual government's reach. Only three of these engaged in the CDM; namely BSH, Samsung, and LG. A key aspect is a principal–agent problem:[24] households' preferences are limited to the ACs available in a shop and their preferences are only one part of the multinationals' strategies. At present, the main driving force is the energy labels in Europe or Japan that lead to a succession of innovations. But in the absence of labels in developing countries, multinationals keep offering their low-efficiency appliances since the profit margins are higher than with new, more efficient appliances.

The context of HFC usage is quite different, as most HFCs are used by a limited number of larger installations, such as industrial plants or supermarkets. HFC-using equipment is manufactured by many producers in each country who specialise in certain types of customers. This is the case for HFCs as refrigerants (e.g. in chillers) and for HFCs as blowing agents in foam blowing machines, where the mostly medium-sized companies are quite technology-oriented, use patent protection, and produce a limited number of units per batch or model, using skilled craftsmen instead of automation.

HFC and HCFC technologies as types of innovation

The different industry context of HCFCs and HFCs corresponds to innovation types. A broad school of Schumpeterian economics is nowadays applied to design innovation policy, R&D strategies, and research funding criteria (even theories about transition to sustainability). Nelson and Winter's (1982) 'An Evolutionary Theory of Economic Change' and Dosi's (1983) 'Technological paradigms and technological trajectories' are the starting points of the renewal of Schumpeterian analysis. Some call it the 'Sussex-Yale-Stanford-synthesis' (Dosi *et al.* 2006: 1450), referring to the universities where the most influential researchers are located. Their common denominator is that firms acquire technology capacity which predetermines their R&D and future products. The organisational properties of firms, how they scan information, hire people, reward them, test products, and capture competitive advantages, together create certain *trajectories*. Computers, drugs, plastics, airplanes, as well as 'white' consumer goods are prominent industrial sectors where research reveals how successful firms copy these organisational tools from each other. The OECD secretariat is a proponent of this school of *industrial economics* and translates it into influential economic policy. The rediscovery of the importance of institutional issues is visible in many fields of economics.

HCFC- and HFC-related technologies are the product of recent industrial innovations, and the companies who invented HCFCs and HFCs are standard objects of analysis. A popular innovation typology was produced by Keith Pavitt at Science Policy Research Unit (SPRU) at Sussex University (Table 10.2).

Pavitt used large databases of patents to define four *trajectories* for innovation (the rows). The columns are the major aspects of these trajectories which together distinguish them. 'Typical products' are the sectors where the trajectories appear most often. 'Innovation drivers' are the key decision makers: who or what maintains or changes the trajectory.

What does this description of technological trajectories imply for both the analysis of KP and the MP regarding HCFCs and HFCs? In many cases, HFCs are in a specialised supplier trajectory (bottom row of Table 10.2) and innovation happens when suppliers agree with important customers to pursue alternatives. This is also adequate because alternatives to HFC-134a as refrigerants require new skills amongst the users, for example when chillers using HFC-134a are replaced with chillers using ammonia or CO_2 as refrigerant, for which equipment suppliers also provide training and information. HFC-134a phase-out efforts can target specialised suppliers' ability to provide such training and information. Often, industry associations provide neutral, trusted platforms that facilitate co-ordination; this is a function that the MLF is more suitable to fund than the

Table 10.2 Trajectories of technical change

Definition	Source of technology	Trajectory for innovation	Typical products	Innovation drivers	CDM barriers
Science based	R&D laboratory	Synergetic new products	Electronics, chemicals	Scientists, patents	Additionality
Scale intensive	Production engineering and specialised suppliers	Efficient and complex production and related products	Basic materials, durable consumer goods	Political power	Baseline is policy
Information intensive	Software/ systems department and specialised suppliers	Efficient (and complex) information processing, and related products	Financial services, retailing	Marketing, advertising	Monitoring
Specialised suppliers	Small-firm design and large-scale users	Improved specialised producers, goods	Machinery, instruments, speciality chemicals, software	Techno-economic paradigms	Integrated systems, 'conserva-tiveness'

Source: Adapted from Pavitt 1984: 354; 1992: 216.

CDM. In this case, the relation between ministries of environment and IAs can be effective. The MLF would define how chiller suppliers and operators exchange information and how specialised suppliers can be paid for enabling operators to acquire skills for managing alternatives to HFC-134a. Metecno's above-mentioned use of the Indian PUR industry association statement is an example in this respect. HFC phase-out is effective when pursued by a neutral industry body that helps specialised suppliers and their customers to co-operate. Rather than funding individual HFC-using companies at the discretion of the co-operation between IAs and the national environment ministries, the MLF would pay for enabling information services to replace HFC uses.

HCFCs are in a scale-intensive trajectory (second row in Table 10.2) because ACs are produced in automated production lines. With 100,000–1,000,000 units manufactured each year, multinational corporations pursue elaborate marketing strategies. The MP instruments are not adequate because the corporations are beyond government control and their competition for low profit margins cannot be influenced by funding based on uniform cost factors. Neither the KP nor the MP can be seen as regimes where political power is built up to affect large systems. Multinational companies cannot be encouraged to undertake CDM projects where income is derived from CER sales, nor by the funds available from the MLF itself. Mass-producing multinational companies can easily replace all HFC-22 in ACs with alternatives, as refrigerant choice is a minor issue to them at irrelevant additional cost. It is mainly a question of how to assure that all competitors do it at the same time. The innovation process in ACs (as in many household appliances) can be influenced by measures that address the scale intensity of production. In the literature on CDM policy, this is often done by referring to the role of the Designated National Authorities (DNAs), the governmental authority that must formally approve each CDM project and can define country-specific sustainability criteria and standardised baselines. Cement production is an example of a scale-intensive trajectory where DNAs play a role in defining technical change criteria for CDM.

The striking differences in trajectories between HFCs and HCFCs suggest different change projects from the criteria used at present by the MP and the KP. The trajectories are not direct outcomes of project activities but they clearly distinguish types of project activities.[25] If, as suggested, DNAs define CDM criteria in mass production of ACs, and the MLF were to fund specialised supplier–client support for HFC substitution, decisions in companies like Regnis and Metecno would be differently affected and the current overlaps would change radically. Enhancing technical change has always been part of the MP and the KP, but regulations have only sometimes used the criterion of company size. Trajectories distinguish decision making in companies, especially regarding their co-operation with their clients and customers, whereas, until now, the KP and the MP only reflected companies' volume of HFC and HCFC consumption. The evidence for the difficulties for companies to use phase-out funding for HCFC-22 and HFC-134a, as described above, underlines the scope for harnessing technical change in the companies' own innovation efforts. This observation may seem straightforward, but it merits further examination as companies (e.g. Metecno) face real problems in using the present MP and KP regulations to redefine MP and KP projects according to technological trajectories.

Conclusions

Although two chemicals, HFC-134a and HCFC-22 (which are actually being phased out), are significant contributors to global warming, their production continues to increase, even though replacements for all uses of both have been tested and applied in some countries! The MLF applies funding criteria for substituting HCFC-22 that create conflicts with the CDM methodologies for HFC-134a replacement. The division of HCFCs and HFCs between the MP and the KP seems set to continue, ignoring the fact that both chemicals are used for the same purposes and that the co-existence of different methods and criteria is by itself counterproductive. The current proposals for changing the division between the MP and the KP are blocked and none of these appears to have taken any lessons from current HFC and HCFC projects. This chapter uncovered three manifestations of regime inertia: the outright continuation (project blueprints, uniform cost factors, role of IAs, absence of lessons learned especially for AC maintenance) of the MLF for HCFCs, the ignorance of the overlaps between the MP and the KP, and the lack of sophistication of the current proposals to extend the MLF a second time.

The MP inertia is an expression of bureaucratic reproduction in the triangle composed by the MLF, ministries of environment, and IAs, probably including 'donor dynamics' amongst the OECD governments providing MLF funds. Regime theory[26] distinguishes inertia from different sources:

- cognitive factors in the expert community;
- economic power of chemical companies;
- arena interactions around the MLF; and
- control of solutions by insiders.

This chapter points to the last source since the inadequacies of the HCFC-22 projects are so evident and do not suggest a gap between policy and practice, as in many development areas. The division between HFCs under the KP and HCFCs under the MP makes mutual disregard the easy solution, especially as regional differences in the use of foam and refrigerants lead to a redistribution of costs and benefits between countries, which is not reflected in the decision-making bodies of each regime.

Based on the example of Sri Lanka for the MLF's HCFC phase-out and four types of CDM methodologies for HFC phase-out, four types of overlaps have been defined, which are important when considering the MLF and CDM allocation criteria from the perspective of the affected companies. The methodologies and funding criteria of the MLF and the CDM themselves contain the parameters which shape their overlaps. Some companies that invest in new equipment chose between MLF and CDM support, others received MLF funds in the past and now develop CDM projects, and yet others are excluded from both. Currently, the rules of the KP and the MP do not reflect each other. Irrespective of the unjustifiably ineffective division of the gases between these two institutions, an efficient and effective use of funds would require CDM methodologies to include criteria about past MLF funding and refer to MLF subsidies, and the distribution of MLF funds can reflect the CDM projects that appear in a sector and country. The KP implementation and the creation of CDM projects are hampered more by the companies waiting for MLF funds, than the MP is affected by the KP. Both could benefit significantly by aligning rules for the phase-outs of HFCs and HCFCs. A comparative assessment of the MP and the KP is feasible when both are approached from the perspective of the companies, from their direct technical and industrial conditions, to which this analysis intends to make a contribution.

A preferable alternative to aligning the MLF and CDM regulation would be to redefine both in light of the general technical change occurring in the sectors where HFC-134a and HCFC-22 are used, for example by learning from the economics of innovation (as pursued in SPRU at Sussex University) for revised funding criteria: technological trajectories indicate that HFCs would be better addressed by the MP than by the KP, especially if the MLF gave funds to neutral industry association activities.[27] The innovative character of HFC substitution should be effectively addressed by MLF means, abandoning the blueprints formerly used for CFCs. Alternative replacement activities, specific to technological trajectories, can be defined.

The overlaps between the MP and the CDM are profound and visibly counterproductive. The rejection of the three current reform proposals (from the World Bank, the US, and Micronesia) by China could be influenced if (Chinese) AC exporters received other support than the one foreseen by the current HPMP for China; addressing the innovation character might lead to a call for change in MLF implementation. Orienting MLF projects towards specialised suppliers' relations with key customers and CDM projects to scale-intensive mass-producers would require more efforts in project definition, but the companies concerned may well decide that such projects are much closer to their own objectives and efforts. Finally, the phasing out of HCFC-22 is a technology-based mitigation that reduces the impact of the expanding consumption of AC. The driver behind the inappropriateness of the current HCFC-22 projects is the combination of the double phase-out agreed by the MP in 2007 and China's increasing share within the respective global trade. This mitigation is currently barred. To attain significant resilience impacts faster would require addressing the MP's inertia and redesigning its tools. If combined with energy efficiency and efforts to advance sustainable buildings and city planning, this could contribute to allowing the use of ACs to cope with increased heatwaves, where necessary, at a lower environmental impact.

Notes

1　'Perhaps the single most successful international agreement to date has been the Montreal Protocol' – Kofi Annan, Former Secretary General of the United Nations, http://www.theozonehole.com/montreal.htm (accessed 22 February 2013).
2　For example, in peak summer times in the Gulf States, ACs are responsible for the exceptionally high daily load variation in the electricity grid of 20 per cent (Lennox 1996).
3　http://www.bsria.co.uk/ (accessed 22 February 2013).
4　Most replacements are simple hydrocarbons, mainly isobutane and cyclopentane. Large cooling units also use NH_3 and CO_2. There are no technical or economic barriers for any of these replacements. The same simple hydrocarbons are also used in CDM projects to replace HFC-134a. For example, Regnis replaces HCFC-22 with cyclopentane with the MP, while Acme Tele substitutes HFC-134a with pentane as a CDM.
5　Cost difference between technology with and technology without CFC use.
6　As the host countries can choose the IA that best suits their own interests, competition between IAs is intense. This particular 'nature' of competition amongst only four UN agencies deserves scrutiny and at least an effort to document the selection processes and their results. Until December 2009, these investment projects amounted to 292 million $ (UNDP), 224 million $ (UNIDO), 317 million $ (World Bank), and 13 million $ (UNEP) (UNEP 2010a). In most countries, the same IA that formerly ran the CFC projects now sets up HCFC projects.
7　Incremental cost unavoidably also involves subjective factors and these require a suitable process to approximate companies' decision criteria. In the KP, it was also not possible to define investment analysis, even the World Bank refused to propose a general approach while the KP Secretariat tried several routes and still maintains this goal (World Bank 2011).
8　UNEP/OzL.Pro/ExCom/16/20, p. 8.

9   Elaborate projections by ICF for the World Bank estimated 573,000 tonnes HCFC-22 in all developing countries in 2015. ICF International (2007) confronted a lower HCFC-22 projection prepared by the Chinese Ministry of the Environment on which the author had been advising the ministry while working for GTZ-Proklima (UNEP/OzL. Pro/ExCom/51/Inf.3 of 19 February 2007). These projections were discussed at the 19th MP Meeting of the Parties (September 2007).

10 The MLF's evaluation studies contain evidence of compliance with MLF regulation; http://www.multilateralfund.org/Evaluation/evaluationlibrary/default.aspx (accessed 26 April 2013).

11 Cyclopentane has been used as a blowing agent for polyurethane foam (PUR) for 20 years and was always available for PUR producers willing to invest more in their machinery. Cyclopentane is typical of the simple hydrocarbons that can replace most HCFC-22 and HFC-134a.

12 The two other mechanisms of the KP, joint implementation and trading between countries, are smaller in volume and impact.

13 http://unfccc.int/resource/docs/2012/cmp8/eng/03p01.pdf (accessed October 2011).

14 http://cdm.unfccc.int/methodologies/index.html (accessed October 2011).

15 http://cdm.unfccc.int/methodologies/index.html (accessed October 2011).

16 Another frequently used simple hydrocarbon, slightly different from cyclopentane used in Regnis.

17 All CDM documentation is public (websites listed below). This information can be found in cdm.unfccc.int/filestorage/2/B/Z/2BZITP5A6XUYLG OCSDM34EF01KRHQ8/PDD_Manufacture%20of%20Polyurethane. pdf?t=YnN8bWVlZHVwfDBXosiQo1R-V2hkYfETGzHj (accessed October 2011).

18 The four are 'unilateral' CDM because, unlike most other CDM projects, the manufacturers kept the CERs to be sold at a later stage, thus betting on increases in international carbon prices. The decision to sell the CERS is the CDM project owner's as CDM regulations only contain rules until the point in time when the CERs are issued to the project owner.

19 Utilities' services to Favelas (slums) are more a political than a commercial matter and probably utilities follow their political masters (being owned by the state) or perhaps they attempt to reduce their technical or operational problems in Favelas.

20 http://cdm.unfccc.int/Projects/Validation/DB/ ZYPV9HFM96AGO7TCT1VPA776H6G35O/view.html (accessed October 2011).

21 The World Bank (with AM0060) and GTZ are the only public policy-oriented institutions to wade into the CDM for HFCs and they decided against expanding on their first methodology-making success for unrelated reasons. For GTZ, it was the only successful effort ever to produce a CDM methodology and this reflects only the difficulties in GTZ of creating a policy and has nothing to do with HFCs or the MP.

22 See http://ozone.unep.org/Meeting_Documents/dialogue_on_high_GWP/index. shtml; http://unfccc.int/methods_and_science/other_methodological_issues/ interactions_with_ozone_layer/items/522.php;   http://cdm.unfccc.int/about/hcfc22/ index.html (accessed October 2011).

23 In addition to the lack of new ideas, other reasons why the KP and the MP implementations are stuck could be found as well.

24 Average end-users pay the electricity bill but their cash preferences reduce their choices (IEA 2007).

25 Exceptional and atypical HFCs are in scale-intensive trajectories and exceptional HCFCs in a specialised supplier trajectory. When industry context factors are addressed in full, it will also be necessary to stop treating HFCs and HCFCs as homogeneous groups.

26 For the MP in particular, see Haas (2005).

27 Totally unlike CFC phase-out where the producers were all OECD-based chemical corporations.

References

Bauer, S. (2007) 'The Ozone Secretariat', *Global Governance Working Paper*, no. 28, online: http://www.glogov.org (accessed 4 March 2013).

BSRIA (n.d.) 'BSRIA' available online at www.bsria.co.uk (accessed 22 February 2013).

Cox, S. (2012) 'Cooling a Warming Plant: A Global Air Conditioning Surge', *environment 360*, Yale University, online: http://e360.yale.edu/feature/cooling_a_warming_planet_a_global_air_conditioning_surge/2550/ (accessed 1 August 2012).

Dosi, G. (1982) 'Technological Paradigms and Technological Trajectories', *Research Policy*, vol. 11, pp. 147–162

Dosi, G., Llerena, P. and Sylos, M. (2006) 'The Relationships Between Science, Technology and Their Industrial Exploitation: An Illustration Through the Myths and Realities of the So-Called "European Paradox"', *Research Policy*, no. 35, pp. 1450–1464.

Haas, P.M. (2005) 'International Institutions and Social Learning in the Management of Global Environmental Risks', *Policy Studies Journal*, vol. 28, no. 3, pp. 558–575.

ICF International (2007) *Assessment of HCFC-Based Air Conditioning Equipment and Emerging Alternative Technologies*, Washington, DC: World Bank Montreal Protocol Operations.

IEA (2007) *Mind the Gap: Quantifying Principal-Agent Problems in Energy Efficiency*, Paris: OECD/IEA.

IPCC (2005) *IPCC/TEAP Special Report: Safeguarding the Ozone Layer and the Global Climate System*, Geneva: IPCC.

Lennox, F.H. (1996) 'Optimizing Power and Water Production under Gulf Conditions', *Desalination and Water Reuse*, vol. 6, no. 3, pp. 32–39.

McCulloch, A. (2010) *Incineration of HFC-23 Waste Streams for Abatement of Emissions from HCFC-22 Production: A Review of Scientific, Technical and Economic Aspects*, Prepared for the UNFCCC, online: http://cdm.unfccc.int/methodologies/Background_240305.pdf (accessed 1 October 2011).

Mintzer, M. and Leonard, J.A. (1994) *Negotiation Climate Change: The Inside Story of the Rio Convention*, Cambridge: Cambridge University Press.

Oberthür, S. (2001) 'Linkages between the Montreal and Kyoto Protocols – enhancing synergies between protecting the ozone layer and the global climate', *International Environmental Agreements*, vol. 1, no. 3, pp. 357–377, doi 10.1023/A:1011535823228 (accessed 22 February 2013).

Oberthür, S., Dupont, C. and Matsumoto, Y. (2011) 'Managing Policy Contradictions between the Montreal and Kyoto Protocols', in Oberthür, S. and Stokke, O. (eds.) *Managing Institutional Complexity: Regime Interplay and Global Environmental Change*, Cambridge, MA: MIT.

Nelson, R. and Winter, S.G. (1982) *An Evolutionary Theory of Economic Change*, Cambridge MA: Belknap Press.

Pavitt, K. (1984) 'Sectoral Patterns of Technical Change: Towards a Taxonomy and a Theory', *Research Policy*, vol. 13, pp. 343–373.

Pavitt, K. (1992) 'Some Foundations for a Theory of the Large Innovating Firm', in Dosi, G., Giannetti, R. and Toninelli, P.A. (eds) *Technology and Enterprise in a Historical Perspective*, Oxford: Clarendon Press, pp. 212–228.

UNEP (1995) *Report of the Sixteenth Meeting of the ExCom of the MLF.* Available online at http://www.multilateralfund.org/MeetingsandDocuments/meetingsarchive/reports/English/1/1620.pdf,

UNEP (2010a) *Consolidated Progress Report as at 31 December 2009*, UNEP 61st Meeting of ExCom to the MLF. UNEP/OzL.Pro/ExCom/61/13,

UNEP (2010b) 'Project Proposal: Sri Lanka', UNEP 62nd Meeting of the ExCom to the MLF. UNEP/Ozl.Pro/Ecom/62/48.

UNEP (2010c) 'Proposed amendment to the Montreal Protocol (submitted jointly by Canada, Mexico and the USA)' UNEP 22nd Meeting of the Parties to the Montreal Protocol. UNEP/Ozl.Pro/22/5.

UNEP (2010d) 'Proposed amendment to the Montreal Protocol (submitted by Micronesia)' UNEP 22nd Meeting of the Parties to the Montreal Protocol. UNEP/Ozl.Pro/22/6.

UNIDO (2009) *Preparing for HCFC Phase-Out: Fundamentals of Uses, Alternatives, Implications and Funding for Article 5 Countries,* Vienna, online: www.unido.org/fileadmin/user_media/Publications/Pub_free/Preparing_for_HCFC_phaseout.pdf (accessed 1 October 2011).

World Bank (2011) *Response to the EB Call for Public Inputs at its 58th Meeting Regarding the Draft Revised Guidelines on the Assessment of Investment Analysis,* online: http://cdm.unfccc.int/public_inputs/2010/guid_inv/cfi/7E0AJBWKV7B8ZWGXZ4VQ1E3S 2IJTGD (accessed 1 October 2011).

UNFCCC CDM documentation

Home page http://cdm.unfccc.int

Acme Tele http://cdm.unfccc.int/UserManagement/FileStorage/AM_CLAR_3RUTIXDU H9CWTOBRBHF06Y60TRYYJ3

Jindal http://cdm.unfccc.int/UserManagement/FileStorage/2BZITP5A6XUYLGOCSDM 34EF01KRHQ8

Lloyds Insulations Ltd http://www.netinform.net/KE/files/pdf/LLOYDS_PDD_ver21.pdf

Metecno http://cdm.unfccc.int/UserManagement/FileStorage/ SO6GWVQ7IR9BPLYUNFM318DZXCTK4J

Rinac http://cdm.unfccc.int/filestorage/O/8/K/ O8KABVYMPCFSL4H1J9Z0G2DX3W7I6T/PDD%20Version%201.pdf?t=S1l8bHJi MTYwfDBRqdLevIouswySFAoPNLj2

Montreal Protocol documentation

http://www.afeas.org
http://www.multilateralfund.org
http://ozone.unep.org
http://www.teap.org

11 Interregional climate cooperation

EU–China relations as a success story?

Astrid Carrapatoso and Mareike Well

EU–China cooperation on climate change: setting the stage

The cooperation between the European Union (EU) and China on climate change issues significantly contributes to global efforts on climate-resilient development (CRD). CRD refers to managing the unavoidable consequences of climate change while, at the same time, proactively changing existing political, social, and economic systems or, at least, recombining already-evolved structures (Smit and Wandel 2006; Adger *et al.* 2011). As major emitters of greenhouse gases (GHGs), the EU and China can engage in innovative and context-specific problem solving, which brings about cooperation mechanisms that are flexible, problem-oriented, and go beyond current negotiations for a single post-Kyoto treaty. This 'hybrid' or 'quasi-interregional' relationship, defined as either a strategic 'region-to-state' partnership such as EU–China relations or a cooperation in intercontinental forums like the Asia–Europe Meeting (ASEM) (Hänggi 2006: 41ff), supports CRD by providing a platform for agenda-setting, institution-building, rationalising, collective identity building, and policy diffusion, which are in addition to (soft-) balancing the classic functions of interregionalism (Dent 2004; Roloff 2006; Rüland 2010; Carrapatoso 2011). Interregional relations foster knowledge- and information-sharing and can more easily take local sensitivities into account, compared to multilateral cooperation.

The aim of this chapter is to explore the extent to which EU–China cooperation on climate change can fulfil these functions and assist in achieving CRD, with which effects, and in which ways. The so-far neglected research topic of policy diffusion in interregional partnerships is also addressed. Policy diffusion is understood as 'the spreading and melting of ideas through the communicative interactions of two collective entities' (Carrapatoso 2011: 178). According to this understanding, institution-building is a prerequisite for agenda-setting and knowledge-sharing, which, in turn, is a precondition for the assimilation of policies (ibid.).

This chapter will show that EU–China cooperation on climate change addresses these challenges, at least rhetorically, by:

- establishing common interest in climate policy and developing shared objectives backed up by strong political commitment;

- creating deliberation platforms for the exchange of knowledge, information, and best practice, thereby enabling policy diffusion;
- building joint institutions to foster political, scientific, economic, and multi-stakeholder cooperation;
- integrating various stakeholders into the policy-making process.

The key question is whether rhetoric is followed by action and if indeed EU–China cooperation is a model for a cooperative interregional relationship that increases climate resilience at local, national, regional, and global levels. On the one hand, this cooperation can provide best practice examples, such as the establishment of a joint Clean Energy Center,[1] but it can also exemplify some shortcomings that have to be remedied in order to improve the performance of both China and Europe in CRD, such as the integration of civil society actors.

This case study provides an analysis of the current structure of the EU–China climate partnership and how it can respond to local, national, and regional needs concerning climate resilience. The study thereby draws on the theoretical insights gained through research on interregionalism (see, for example, Hänggi 2006; Roloff 2006; Rüland 2010; Carrapatoso 2011) as well as on sustainable development (SD) and CRD (see, for example, Jacobs 1999; Haughton 1999; Hopwood *et al.* 2005; Jänicke and Jörgens 2007; Adger *et al.* 2011). The case of an EU–China climate dialogue is particularly significant since these partners are well-placed to act as leaders concerning the development of low-carbon economies while at the same time rendering their societies more resilient to the inevitable effects of climate change. Both regions are confronted with similar vulnerabilities, including drought, flooding, shifting agricultural zones and productivity, sea-level rise, disturbance to natural ecosystems and biodiversity loss (Darkin 2007). Moreover, the urgency of improving the adaptive capacity of the respective constituencies is recognised by both partners and is often framed as an intricate interdependence, especially on energy and security issues (Chatham House 2007: viii). By developing similar or even common policies and exchanging technical tools and know-how as well as increasing investment in research and development (R&D), capacity-building, and human mobility, the EU and China can improve their ability to predict future shocks and to enhance coping strategies as well as adaptation mechanisms (Darkin 2007).

This chapter provides an overview of the agenda-setting and institution-building functions of EU–China cooperation on climate change. As a prerequisite for policy diffusion, these sections explain the political framework conditions and outline the various deliberation platforms where the exchange of norms, ideas, and policies can occur. In a subsequent step, two salient examples of policy diffusion – the Chinese Emissions Trading Scheme (ETS) and Vehicle Emissions Standards – are discussed.

The multi-level dimension of EU–China climate cooperation

Interregionalism refers to a process in which regional actors – like regional organisations, groups of states, or individual states – cooperate in order to manage or balance relations amongst themselves in the emerging system of global governance. Initiated in the 1990s within the dynamic of a 'new regionalism' triggered by globalisation and regionalisation, interregional forums have become more numerous and specific (Hänggi 2006: 31). The SD agenda is an example of 'complex interdependencies' (Roloff 2006: 18) that require the concerted action of regions, such as Europe and Asia, by way of interregional forums.

Interregional cooperation can show a multi-level dimension, thereby offering states and regional organisations various deliberation platforms, which is the case in EU–China relations. The EU and China collaborate on two tracks: first, they regularly meet under the framework of the ASEM, which integrates the EU and its members, the Association of Southeast Asian Nations (ASEAN) and its members as well as other interested European and Asian countries such as China and Russia.[2] Second, they cooperate in the context of the EU–China Strategic Partnership, and, directly related to climate change, the China–EU Partnership on Climate Change.[3]

ASEM plays an important role in agenda-setting on climate issues. Agenda-setting in interregional relations is defined as the ability to initiate and shape public discourse for strategic, substantive, or ideational reasons and can serve as a platform for regional organisations or state coalitions to frame new global problems within the global governance architecture (Rüland 2010: 1277). Within the ASEM framework, China and the EU have worked out a common agenda on climate change which is manifest in non-binding declarations, such as the *ASEM6 Declaration on Climate Change* (ASEM 2006) and the *ASEM7 Beijing Declaration on Sustainable Development* (ASEM 2008). The summits of 2010 (ASEM8) and 2012 (ASEM9) stressed the centrality and legitimacy of the UNFCCC process (ASEM 2010, 2012b). Additionally, the ASEM Environment Ministers' Meeting provides a platform for framing environmental issues. The third meeting in 2007 focused on the question of energy, the fourth meeting in 2012 covered sustainable water and forest management (ASEM 2012a). Apart from these official forums, there are other platforms for multi-stakeholder cooperation within the Asia–Europe Foundation (ASEF 2012), such as the Asia–Europe Environment Forum (ENVforum),[4] which provides experts with the opportunity to exchange knowledge on climate change. Although ASEM offers an important platform for developing shared visions and objectives and for facilitating knowledge exchange as well as concrete bilateral cooperation, it is constrained by its informal and unbinding nature and is often restricted to rhetoric rather than action. The development of tangible cooperative frameworks and policies and their implementation occurs bilaterally or in 'region-to-state' relations, such as the Comprehensive Strategic Partnership[5] between the EU and China.

In 2005, the EU and China agreed on a Partnership on Climate Change, which aimed at intensifying cooperation in the fields of low carbon technology, energy efficiency, low carbon development, and market-based instruments (EU 2005). Especially in terms of energy issues, the EU and China are highly interdependent and have complementary needs (Chatham House 2007: viii; Holzer and Zhang 2008: 219). This is in line with Roloff's assumption that the more interdependent the regions are, the more intensive the cooperation will be, which in return also increases the potential of conflict (Roloff 2006: 26). In EU–China relations, this becomes explicit when, on the one hand, looking at the gap between the EU's normative claims and its economic interests (Hackenesch and Ling 2009), and, on the other hand, China's perception of the EU putting inappropriate normative pressure on the government (Fox and Godement 2009). In sum, this hybrid interregional relationship (Rüland 2010: 1272) deepens the common agenda on climate change and transcends it into joint institutions that are capable of tangible action. By establishing trust, transparency, and predictability, institutionalised cooperation is conducive to the diffusion of environmental policy innovations between Asia and Europe.

Setting the agenda in EU–China relations on climate change: political framework conditions

The EU and China have maintained diplomatic relations since 1975 and have established more than 50 bilateral dialogues. The annual EU–China Summit is the major forum for political leaders where common issues are discussed. In addition, there is the High-Level Economic and Trade Dialogue (2007), the Strategic Dialogue (2010), the High-Level People-to-People Dialogue (2012), and the EU–China High-Level Energy Meeting (2012).[6] All of these high-level forums have integrated SD, the environment, and climate change into their agendas.[7]

A major focus has been on trade relations since the establishment of the free trade agreement in 1985. In 2003, the partners upgraded their relation to a Comprehensive Strategic Partnership, which was followed by a communication entitled 'EU–China: closer partners, growing responsibilities' in October 2006 and a policy paper on trade aiming for a close and comprehensive partnership with China (EC 2006). The importance of EU–China relations became explicit in China's white paper on its foreign relations to the EU (Information Office of the State Council of the People's Republic of China 2003), which was the first white paper on relations with a specific partner. In the same year, discussions on environmental policy were institutionalised through the EU–China Environment Dialogue. Further dialogues followed, such as the Bilateral Cooperation Mechanism on Forests (BCM; established in 2009) and the ongoing dialogue between the Directorate General for Climate Action (CLIMA) and the Chinese government. In January 2007, negotiations were launched on a new EU–China partnership and cooperation agreement (EU 2012b). Central to this direct dialogue is the 2005 China–EU Partnership on Climate Change, which was established at the 2005 EU–China Summit and laid down in the *The EU and China Partnership on Climate Change* (EU 2005), which is regulated by the 2006 *China–EU Partnership on Climate Change Rolling Work Plan* (PRC 2006). The focus of the partnership is on new technologies for 'clean' energy, such as the development of low emission carbon technology based on carbon capture and storage (CCS), but energy efficiency, energy conservation, and renewable energies are also covered (EU 2005). Two work plans regulate the partnership:

the 'China–EU Action Plan on Clean Coal' and the 'China–EU Action Plan on Energy Efficiency and Renewable Energies' (ibid.). The *The EU and China Partnership on Climate Change* lays down 11 common principles, which include having the support of the UNFCCC process and Kyoto Protocol, dialogue on climate change policy models, cooperation to enhance the energy efficiency of the respective economies, cooperation on developing low carbon economies, as well as technical cooperation on energy efficiency and renewable energy. Until 2020, the partners aim to develop a near-zero emissions coal technology through CCS and reduce the cost of energy technology. Additionally, they have agreed to reinforce the Clean Development Mechanism (CDM), enhance cooperation concerning adaptation, and pursue cooperation in R&D. By increasing personal and knowledge exchange, capacity-building, and establishing common publicity, they aim to strengthen their joint institutions (ibid.).

The *Joint Declaration* exemplifies the extent to which agenda-setting is a core function of interregionalism. This paper goes beyond general declarations of intent by detailing potential areas of cooperation and concrete goals, such as the development of CCS technology until 2020. Rhetorically, the convergence in environmental issues is being stressed and framed as necessary due to the interdependence of the partners, especially in energy and trade relations (ibid.). It is remarkable that the most detailed rhetoric and agreements, by means of the respective Action Plans, are found in renewable energies, which reflects a strong mutual interest in this area. This shows how agenda-setting that is followed by tangible action plans and joint institutions is by no means redundant since this kind of cooperation cannot be found within ASEM or other forums. For this case, the alleged redundancy of hybrid interregional forums and the putative institutional overlap (Rüland 2012: 266) can be ruled out since EU–China cooperation does not copy but actually goes beyond and complements projects within ASEM.

This pattern of a gradual deepening of the cooperation and diversification and specification of the agenda can be traced in more detail. In 2006, the European Commission published the report *EU–China: Closer Partners, Growing Responsibilities* (EC 2006), which details the joint challenges concerning SD and energy supply. With respect to institution-building, a positive trend can also be observed: in 2007, the partners began negotiating the Partnership and Cooperation Agreement, which would upgrade and expand the issues of the 1985 trade agreement. While focusing on trade issues, the negotiations also included SD aspects. The European Commission, for example, advocated for a systematic Trade Sustainability Impact Assessment. The Commission's published report is designed to inform and orient Chinese diplomats as well as civil society stakeholders in China and the EU (EC 2009). This exemplifies an increasing political will to transform the detailed agenda into efficient joint institutions. This development can be observed especially in energy issues, which constitute a decisive focus of institution-building. An example of this trend is the biannual ENER-MOST Energy Conferences, which are alternately hosted in Brussels and China and organised by the Chinese Ministry of Science and Technology (MOST) and the Directorate General (DG) Energy.[8] These conferences offer a platform for Chinese and European energy companies to meet.[9] Additionally, in the course of the EU–China Summit 2005, the partners initiated the EC–China Energy Dialogue, which focuses on the exchange, on an administrative level, of information, knowledge, and experience between the European Commission National Development and China's Reform Commission (NDRC). In this context, two working groups on energy and transport were formed. The aims and structure of the dialogue are detailed in the *Memorandum of Understanding* (EC 2005). Since its first meeting in 2006 and the establishment of the Chinese National Energy Administration (NEA), cooperation within the energy field has markedly increased. The most recent energy dialogue in July 2011 was conducted at the ministerial level for the first time, chaired by the EU's commissioner for energy, Günther Oettinger, and Zhang Guobao from the NEA (EC 2008).

Platforms of diffusion: institution-building in EU–China climate cooperation

The previous section illustrated the institutionalised dialogue platforms that already exist at the political high level. The summits and diverse dialogue forums show a clear agenda-setting function and trigger further institution-building on other levels, such as scientific, civil society, private sector, city-to-city, or multi-stakeholder cooperation. The above-outlined cooperation framework demonstrates the importance of energy cooperation, both in the promotion of clean energy technology as well as energy efficiency. Further climate-related cooperation takes place in the context of sustainable urban planning. Interregional municipal relations are thus becoming increasingly important, which was emphasised through the *Joint Declaration on the EU–China Partnership on Urbanisation* on 3 May 2012 (EC 2012b). This was followed by the first EU–China Mayors' Forum in September 2012.[10] A further area of intensified cooperation is market-based instruments, such as the CDM and ETS. In 2011, the Chinese government launched pilot projects in eight cities and five provinces to test various ETSs, including the EU model (Reuters 2011). On 20 September 2012, the EU and China signed a financing agreement to assist China in the design and implementation of its own ETS (EU 2012c). The following sections overview the institutions in the above-mentioned areas and discuss their effects with regard to policy diffusion.

Low carbon development, clean energy, and energy efficiency

The scientific cooperation projects between China and the EU are an important channel for interaction on clean energy and low carbon development and serve as important triggers for policy diffusion. The importance that both partners attribute to this type of cooperation reflects both China's scientific approach to development and the EU's interest in job creation and economic benefits through innovation, as well as the recognition of science as a way to reinforce external relations.[11]

Prominent joint institutions are the Europe-China Clean Energy Centre (EC2) in Beijing as well as the China–EU Institute for Clean and Renewable Energy

(ICARE) in Wuhan (EU 2012b). ICARE is a joint education institute[12] that intends to 'fill up the gap between China's priority in battling against climate change by adopting clean and renewable energy and the lack of a critical mass of Chinese engineers in these new technologies' (Delegation of the EU to China 2012a). EC2 was founded in 2010 by the European Commission, the NEA, and the Chinese Chamber of Commerce and is supported by the Italian Ministry of the Environment. The centre functions as a joint research body focusing on policy advice, technological cooperation, capacity-building, and awareness-raising.[13] During its five years of operation, it has been concerned with energy policy strategies and technical cooperation in CCS, sustainable biofuels, renewable energy sources, energy efficiency, and efficient dissemination methods. Events like the 'EC2 Sharing Event – Designing Integrated Demonstration Zones in China: What works? Lessons from the European experience'[14] and the 'EC2 EURUMQI Demo Zone Sharing Event – Sustainable Energy Action Plans in Europe: Good practices and lessons learnt'[15] provide a platform for knowledge exchange and may subsequently spark policy alignment.

The second issue that is taken very seriously in terms of creating bilateral institutions is the development of near-zero emissions coal technologies (Dai and Diao 2011: 262). To assist China on its way to an energy efficient economy, the EU and China cooperate to develop and disseminate Near-Zero Emissions Coal (NZEC) technologies. The EU–China NZEC agreement was signed at the 2005 EU–China Summit and is part of the EU–China Partnership on Climate Change. The project is subdivided into three phases, which has an overall goal to build a CCS demonstration plant in China by 2020 (EC 2010). This project is marked by a detailed work plan and schedule and has a relatively binding character. It is a clear example of how good intentions have been transformed into joint institutions and concrete cooperation projects.

The Environmental Governance Programme[16] has a broader portfolio and generally strives to improve China's environmental governance performance. In addition to strengthening initiatives against environmental degradation in China, involving the public, and enhancing legal assistance for compensation claims, it also aims to create business incentives for environmentally friendly technologies (Dimas 2008).

In addition to the above-mentioned institutions, a multitude of specific joint research projects are funded through the EU F6 (2002–2006) and FP7 (2007–2013) framework programmes. Climate- and energy-related projects within the FP6 and FP7 frameworks include (Scott 2009: 214):[17]

- Assessing European Capacity for Geological Storage of Carbon Dioxide (EUGeoCapacity) (2006–2008);
- Monitoring and Verification of Enhanced Coalbed Methane (MOVECBM) (2006–2008);
- Development of Co-firing Power Generation Market Opportunities to Enhance the EU Biomass Sector Through International Cooperation with China (CH-EU-BIO) (2006–2008);

- Cooperation Action with CCS China–EU (COACH) (2006–2009);
- Full Costs of Climate Change (CLIMATECOST) (2009–2011);
- Land–Atmosphere Interactions in China (LAIC) (2009–2011);
- Carbon Capture and Hydrogen Production with Membranes (CACHET II) (2010–2012);
- EU–China Cooperation for Liquid Fuels from Biomass Pyrolysis (ECOFUEL) (2010–2014);
- Greenhouse Gas Recovery from Coal Mines and Unmineable Coalbeds and Conversion to Energy (GHG2E) (2011–2015).

These cooperation projects are examples of issue-specific institutions and demonstrate how interregionalism can go beyond 'contingent broadband multi-purpose institutions' (Rüland 2010: 1280) and thereby contribute to meaningful and effective cooperation.

Sustainable urban planning

During the last EU–China Summit in February 2012, the *Partnership on Sustainable Urbanisation* was initiated (EU and PRC 2012a, 2012b).[18] This project draws on previous experience in urban development in the context of the Asia-Urbs (2003–2006) and Asia-Pro-Eco (2005–2009) programmes and incorporates cooperation concerning urban planning, energy supply and management in cities, the development of 'green digital cities', urban mobility, water and air quality, waste management, and the social inclusion of migrants in cities. The agenda also included practical cooperation in the development and commercial transfer of green technologies and energy efficiency in cities. This urbanisation partnership has been designed together with the first EU–China Mayors' Forum.[19]

Various research and professional training projects are currently in place, including:

- Sustainable Urbanisation in China Historical and Comparative Perspectives, Mega-trends towards 2050 (URBACHINA) (2011–2014): analysis of China's urbanisation trends; identification of core aspects of urban sustainability;[20]
- Switch Asia – Energy Efficient Building Training Project: convert to more sustainable production and consumption patterns; develop energy-saving strategies in the Chinese construction industry[21];
- Urban Reduction of GHG Emissions in China and Europe (URGENCHE) (2011–2014);[22] development of a methodological framework to assess alternative GHG emission reduction policies for health and well-being, thereby considering GHG emission reduction in the policy fields of energy and transport.

Cooperation in sustainable urban planning illustrates the importance of agenda-setting on the political level followed by tangible action in terms of further institution-building and the implementation of concrete projects. Again, science plays a vital role in this respect and demonstrates the strong belief in technological innovation through knowledge exchange. Given that the Partnership on Sustainable Urbanisation and the EU–China Mayors' Forum are recent initiatives, the effects with regard to policy diffusion remain to be seen. In any case, they show the importance of cities and municipalities in the implementation of climate-related policy goals and their contribution to CRD.

Market-based instruments: CDM and ETS

In July 2011, the Chinese government announced the development of an ETS enabling eight cities and five provinces to trade emission reduction certificates, which is to become operational in 2013 (Reuters 2011). One of the first regulated ETS is being set up in Wuhan and is based on a cap for carbon emissions for the local firms. At present, this project is under-equipped concerning financing and staff and will have to improve its capacities to be successful (Ivanova 2012). In addition to these regulated ETS pilots, China has witnessed the rapid establishment of voluntary climate, carbon, and environment 'exchanges'. In 2008 and 2009, the China Clean Development Mechanism Fund and Management Centre, the Tianjin Climate Exchange (TCX), the China Beijing Environment Exchange (CBEEX), and the Shanghai Environment and Energy Exchange (SEEEX) were established. In 2010, the Shenzhen Environment Exchange was established. Although officially not state-owned, these exchanges are all government-backed and indicate the emergence of a national strategy to develop a carbon trading infrastructure (Han *et al.* 2012: 52). Following these pilot projects, a comprehensive Chinese ETS is planned for 2015 (Tianbao 2012: 55); its design will likely take account of the European experience with emissions trading, keeping both the success and the criticism of the EU ETS in mind (ibid: 19). Concerning the allocation of emission credits, Tianbao indicates that China's nationwide ETS would, once implemented, function according to the EU's example:

> Different regions would allocate all allowances free of charge by 2015. When a national ETS is set up, China would allocate one part of the allowances free of charge and the ratios of allowances free of charge would be gradually reduced until all allowances are auctioned. Auctioning of allowances will become the basic principle for allocation.
>
> (Ibid.: 80)

China has already gained experience in carbon trading through CDM projects. Since the implementation of the CDM, China has become the most important recipient country for these projects. In March 2012, 47 per cent out of a total of 3,933 CDM projects were carried out in China (UNFCCC 2012), marking substantial cooperation with the EU. During 2007–2010, CDM implementation was supported by the EU–China Facilitation Project,[23] which established the CDM as a central pillar of SD in China (Delegation of the EU to China 2010).[24] China's comparatively high commitment in the CDM and thus its first encounter with carbon trading may have had an effect on the establishment of a Chinese ETS in terms of adaptive learning. Han *et al.* (2012: 5) point to the fact that European governments have promoted the uptake of market-based instruments. Chinese delegations have subsequently visited European governments and private sector constituents in the EU ETS on fact-finding missions, thereby influencing the Chinese stance and knowledge regarding emissions trading. One recent example of knowledge exchange is the 'Sino-Europe Carbon Emission Trading Roundtable' in Wuhan, which facilitated the exchange of expert opinions and was targeted at policy makers and the designers of the ETS in Hubei Province (E3G 2012). Han *et al.* also argue that expertise on ETS implementation is urgently needed:

> Even if a carbon market were effectively set up in China at this point, traditional corporate behaviour and resistance could prevent any substantial trading from taking place. ... Lessons learned by Chinese entities while operating in the CDM market might be only loosely transferrable to managing emissions for compliance purposes underneath a cap. International support and advice will be critical.
>
> (Ibid.: xxiii)

Concerning the Guangdong ETS (GD ETS), one of the pilot trading schemes, the Guangdong Provincial Government is researching the implementation plan for its ETS and in this vein 'will be looking at every aspect of the EU ETS for lessons they can apply locally, including modelling to set emissions targets, analysing impacts on sectors and deciding on allocation methods ... legal frameworks and GHG measurement, reporting and verification (MRV) principles' (ibid.: 24). The GD ETS might also become similar to the EU ETS since it will possibly trade CERs, analogous to those now traded within the EU ETS and will eventually even be able to link to other trading systems worldwide, such as the EU ETS (ibid.: 27). During the 15th EU–China Summit, for example, the partners started negotiating the possibilities for cooperation in emissions trading.[25]

The effects of joint agenda-setting and institution-building: policy diffusion as a result?

Considering the diversity of cooperative arrangements that have led to a detailed agenda and joint institutions, it is timely to ask whether 'quantity [is] equivalent to a qualitative change in international politics ... Is there a noteworthy change in cooperative relations through the emergence of interregionalism? ... Does interregionalism matter?' (Roloff 2006: 18). These are valid questions concerning the construction of a cooperative interregionalism as a contribution to making communities more resilient to climate change. The fact that China voluntarily adopts innovations in environmental policy that are similar to European standards and the subsequent emergence of a low-carbon, energy efficient economy points to a qualitative shift in global environmental governance. The relationship between the EU and China is increasingly marked by cooperation in specific issue areas that is mutually beneficial. The fact that interdependence leads to cooperation is, in fact, a recent development and not self-evident. If interregionalism is inducing more cooperative behavior in international relations, these kind of forums are significant, even if they lack a legal foundation and binding agreements.

The previous sections illustrated how the interregional level offers an institutionalised setting for formal and informal social interaction and thereby helps to build trust and mutual understanding. This section discusses how the shared (professional) norms, a joint interest in problem solving as well as similar characteristics of the involved actors facilitate the learning process (Newig *et al.* 2010: 30), which can then result in the diffusion of innovative and pragmatic policies in the above-mentioned policy fields. Tews defines policy diffusion as 'the spreading of innovations due to communication instead of hierarchy and/or collective decision-making between actors across national borders' (Tews 2006: 229). According to her, three factors determine policy diffusion: national, inter- and transnational factors, and innovation characteristics. In this sense, interregional relations between the EU and China can be regarded as both an inter- and a transnational factor. This means that the degree of the cooperation determines the degree or likelihood of policy diffusion. The political feasibility, the national responsiveness to the innovations, and the localisation of foreign ideas influence the probability of diffusion at the national level. Building congruence between existing practices and values in China with EU policy innovations is crucial to the national responsiveness (Acharya 2009: 15). This means that policy diffusion is likely in areas where Chinese authorities can benefit from European experiences and know-how on policy integration, which is the case in emissions trading, energy efficiency, and standard-setting procedures. Heinze (2011) provides an overview of the abundant literature on diffusion mechanisms from which he derives that, firstly, diffusion mechanisms refer to rationalist reasoning based on instrumental considerations of actors, or on constructivist arguments, such as norms and rule-driven actors. Secondly, causal mechanisms can be differentiated according to their impact on public choice; namely, if they have a direct effect on the belief system of actors or if they influence the structural conditions for decision making. Taking these differentiations into account, Heinze proposes four classes of causal mechanisms in the current state of the art: emulation, learning, socialisation, and externalities (Ibid.: 7). The latter mechanism is characterised by creating positive or negative incentives for the adoption of policies, thereby manipulating utility calculations of policy makers. Externalities put adaptive pressure on policy makers by altering the material payoff structure associated with a specific policy (Heinze 2011: 17). Börzel and Risse add coercion and persuasion (Börzel and Risse 2009: 9). The examples show how adaptive learning and emulation are more probable processes than complex learning. Changing incentives rather than bringing about changes in the belief system has led to a change in behavior. Fox and Godement share this rather sceptical view on Europe's leverage in China's energy policy, indicating that China limits the joint successes to the development in which it is anyway in conformance: 'The EU's leverage as a fellow energy consumer is limited and has shown results only when governments or companies have proved willing to invest financial resources, such as the EU–China energy centre or the numerous joint ventures across China' (Fox and Godemont 2009: 44).

The following sections discuss the question of whether cooperation in the fields of energy efficiency and emissions trading show effects of policy diffusion. Due to the existing cooperation between the EU and China, the clustering of policy innovations during 2000–2008 and the similarity of the targeted goals and schedules can be interpreted as a case of diffusion of energy goals from the EU to China (Carrapatoso 2011: 191). The indicators of policy diffusion in interregional relations are the timing of adoptions of policy innovations (Elkins and Simmons 2005) and the similarity of the policies adopted (Jetschke 2010: 17). The two chosen examples – the Chinese ETS and Vehicle Emissions Standards – are salient with regard to timing and similarity and show the policy effects of continuously deepening EU–China relations.

The Chinese ETS

The previous section on market-based instruments showed a trend to design the Chinese ETS according to the EU model. But what drives the Chinese emulation of the EU ETS? There are both national and inter/transnational factors influencing this kind of behavior. Domestically, in the 11th Five Year Plan (FYP), there has been a shift towards the use of market-based instruments to reduce cost and increase efficiency to reach carbon- and energy-intensity goals, in contrast to the reliance on administrative and political measures as promoted in the 10th FYP. At a global level, the financial potential of new carbon markets, the possible integration into existing ETS, the unclear future of the CDM, as well as the possible emergence of a 'new market mechanism' from the international climate negotiations provide strong incentives for China to set up a domestic carbon trading system (Han *et al.* 2012: 50) This combination of internal and external factors influencing China can be described with the concept of externalities as a type of policy diffusion mechanism.

In the present case, the externalities that put adaptive pressure on policy makers include the growth of regional carbon markets and the subsiding relevance of the CDM (Han *et al.* 2012: 9, 16, 34). The relevant concept here, within the wider idea of externalities, relates to cooperative advantages as drivers of innovation. Cooperative advantages arise from compatible policies and common standards (Heinze 2011: 18). The EU has installed itself as a front-runner in emissions trading and thereby provides model policies that can be tested in other jurisdictions. Since the target is to eventually link with other regional ETS, the EU provides an incentive for China to invest in this kind of market-based mechanism. This is supported by technical assistance and the sharing of knowledge during the numerous fact-finding missions between the Chinese and European governments. The emulation of the EU ETS design, such as the trade with CERs to eventually link with the EU ETS, shows that the goal of the emerging Chinese ETS is to be eventually compatible with the EU ETS and thereby to benefit from cooperative advantages. The mutual interest in emissions trading as a cooperative advantage was also expressed at the 14th EU–China Summit. In the Joint Press Statement, the two sides 'agreed to further intensify practical cooperation on issues with common concerns. ... [and] agreed to continue to explore the possibilities of conducting practical cooperation on the Emission Trading System' (EU and PRC 2012a).

Vehicle Emissions Standards

It is evident that Chinese national Vehicle Emissions Standards have been modelled on European standards.[26] China II fuel (low sulfur diesel fuel, sulfur ≤ 500 ppm) was implemented nationwide in 2004. This was followed by China III fuel (sulfur ≤ 350 ppm) in 2011. China IV fuel (sulfur ≤ 50 ppm) became available in Beijing (2008) and Shanghai (2009), and Beijing adopted China V fuel (sulfur ≤ 10 ppm) in 2012. The Chinese standards on low-sulfur fuel are identical to those in Europe. Euro II was adopted in 1996, Euro III in 2000, and Euro IV in 2005.[27] The nationwide implementation of the China IV standard, which was due to become operational in 2011, has been delayed; in January 2012, the deadline was again postponed until July 2013 (Watts 2012). The recent smog alarm in Beijing once again illustrates the pressing need for such measures (Branigan 2013). Since the implementation is still pending, the Chinese government's pledge to tighten control of air pollution has become less credible, thereby undermining a central pillar for smog reduction. According to environmental scientists, this shows how public health concerns are less of a priority than the economic interests of state-owned oil companies such as PetroChina and Sinopec (ibid.), although these companies are able to comply with stricter standards as the Beijing example shows.

Lessons learned and conclusions

In assessing the influence of EU–China relations on Chinese climate policy making, it should be noted that 'a significant reorientation of the Chinese leadership's perspective on energy and environmental policy was well underway before the EU began prioritising the issue of climate change in its bilateral relations with China from 2005 onwards' (Torney 2012: 14). The major policy shift in China has consequently been influenced by domestic developments. A general new thinking regarding sustainability on the part of Chinese political leaders, which has offered the EU a window of opportunity for interregional climate cooperation, is also a factor. However, it is important to clarify that new policies and norms must resonate with pre-existing ideas, interests, and concepts – and only where there is an interest- and/or norm-based overlap does policy diffusion become likely (Carrapatoso 2011; Torney 2012).

What are the results of the above-mentioned 'window of opportunity'? In the framework of interregional dialogue, the EU and China have developed a common agenda on climate change issues and have transformed this agenda into joint institutions. The establishment of an institutionalised setting for formal and informal social interaction has helped to build trust as well as mutual understanding. It functions as the basis for convergence of interests, policy objectives, and concrete policy design. This has been the result of institution-building and agenda-setting on multiple levels of interaction. In EU–China relations, high-level and political, scientific, multi-stakeholder, private sector, city-to-city as well as civil society cooperation mutually reinforce each other and foster adaptive learning, which leads to the diffusion of innovative and pragmatic policies. Examples include the development of a Chinese ETS and the adoption of Vehicle Emissions Standards modelled on European standards. There was also intensified dialogue on the Chinese Renewable Energy Law (Torney 2012). Further intensified cooperation includes renewable energies, urban planning, and joint research projects in policy fields of mutual interest. These are examples of how political commitment and expected gains have led to tangible action within the interregional dialogue.

As argued in Part I of this volume, CRD should move beyond the separation between mitigation and adaptation, as both policies are pursued in parallel and influence each other. In EU–China relations, the focus on GHG emission reductions through renewable energy and energy efficiency policies as well as emissions trading is, on the one hand, the expression of pragmatic policy making that concentrates on a feasible joint policy agenda, which, in turn, creates a win–win solution in terms of environmental and economic benefits. On the other hand, this type of cooperation includes the potential to render both regions more resilient if ambitious policies are effectively implemented 'on the ground' and, at the same time, allow for a bottom-up process in two ways: firstly, in the sense of creating feedback loops to top-down climate policies, thus providing input on which measures work and are successfully implemented or not; secondly, in allowing ambitious policy making and implementation on local levels to become nationwide standards, given that they are transferable to other local conditions. Such measures, however, must be actively promoted on the national level and can only marginally be influenced by interregional relations.

Policy diffusion in EU–China relations can be traced in terms of timing and similarities of policies (e.g. ETS, emission and energy efficiency standards) but by no means rule out other domestic and international influence factors in designing new policies. Whether new policies have been (ecologically) effective and, consequently, whether interregional relations have a long-term impact in this respect is difficult to assess. In any case, the multi-level dimension of EU–China cooperation amply displays its management function by establishing common positions on climate policy, creating an institutionalised dialogue to foster knowledge exchange and mutual learning, building effective joint institutions, and integrating a multitude of actors into the process. In particular the China–EU Partnership on Climate Change is a best practice example for the management of climate change since the partners engage in effective knowledge exchange, issue-specific institutions, and problem-oriented policy solutions. It does not support the often-asserted pitfalls of an 'interregional interlocking trap' (Roloff 2006: 18) or of 'contingent broadband multi-purpose institutions' (Rüland 2010: 1280) because this partnership follows a specific and goal-oriented agenda.

In addition to managing and tackling the effects of climate change, CRD refers to the ability to proactively change existing political, social, and economic systems or, at least, recombining already-evolved structures (Smit and Wandel 2006; Adger *et al.* 2011). Interregional relations are not meant to generate systems change. But they can assist in raising awareness of the systemic problems in achieving CRD: firstly, by using existing structures such as ASEM and the EU–China Comprehensive Partnership to foster policy integration, and, secondly, by triggering a learning process leading to new sustainability and resilience-oriented policies and structures, such as the China–EU Partnership on Climate Change or the numerous specific high-level meetings (such as on economic, trade, energy, or strategic issues) and people-to-people contacts. The deepening, diversification, and specification of EU–China cooperation and the integration of climate change issues in all cooperation areas shows the ability to manage climate change by recombining existing political structures and, to some extent, changing them. A good example of changing structures are joint research institutions on renewable energy, such as EC2 and ICARE; the cooperation on NZEC technologies, such as the EU–China NZEC Agreement; as well as inter-communal linkages between the regions to cooperate on sustainable urban planning, such as the Partnership on Sustainable Urbanisation and the EU–China Mayors' Forum.

Furthermore, the analysed examples of policy diffusion show how interregional relations can set off CRD by addressing existing economic and regulatory structures. A shift towards market-based instruments, such as carbon trading (CDM, ETS), has altered the business opportunities and investment behaviour concerning 'green' technologies in both China and the EU. Given the structure of existing carbon trade, its problems with regard to an oversupply of CO_2 reduction certificates, falling prices, and uncertainties with respect to the future of carbon trade, its contribution to CRD remains to be seen. The second example of policy diffusion, Vehicle Emissions Standards in China that are modelled on European standards, shows how the regulatory structure in China has changed, thereby creating the basis for tackling air pollution and GHG emissions. However, the implementation of this measure is still pending.

The above-mentioned examples illustrate, however, just a fraction of the cooperation taking place between the EU and China, and due to their inherent problems are not necessarily representative of the general effects of this cooperation. The diversity of institutional dialogues and projects show that EU–China relations go beyond current negotiations for a single post-Kyoto treaty. The merit of these relations lies in their ability to balance the deficits of delayed and deficient action of the UNFCCC process. Tangible projects, practical cooperation, and the diffusion and subsequent streamlining of environmental policies between the EU and China are a key building block for the development of low-emission economies as well as for CRD. Local sensitivities are necessarily taken into account, since only by building congruence between the political culture, existing values, and practices in China with the EU policy innovations, a responsiveness to new approaches is thinkable (Acharya 2009: 15).

It can be assumed that the energy sector will remain the 'strategic key' of EU–China cooperation (Scott 2009: 221) in the future. Complementary needs, economic interdependence, expected gains, and improved bargaining positions in the international climate negotiations act as strong incentives and guarantee for a high 'diffusability' (Tews 2006: 249) of energy policies. Moreover, energy cooperation is attractive for several reasons: a focus on technical cooperation projects as opposed to normative politics of conditionality, increased investments that benefit both sides, the rather limited maturity of engagements, and the compatibility of existing governance structures (Carrapatoso 2011: 194; Chatham House 2007: viii; Holzer and Zhang 2008: 219; Scott 2009: 221; Moore 2011: 147–157). This has facilitated the exchange of knowledge and the development and deployment of technologies which has, in turn, increased expertise and the ability on both sides to implement adaptation and mitigation policy tools. As the EU and China also collaborated on the Chinese energy sector reform, this could serve as a good example to show how economic and regulatory structures can be fundamentally changed if there is strong political will and the readiness to achieve this through cooperation with both internal and external actors.

However, there are also some shortcomings and lessons to be learned for the future. Since EU–China relations are marked by the incentive-driven focus on energy, the cooperation cannot yet be described as holistic in the sense of CRD. What it lacks is the commitment to engage in areas that do not yield economic benefits on a short-term basis. Also, in order to enable the construction of a local agenda that captures the needs of communities, an efficient means to include civil society in the agenda-setting and decision-making process is needed. This can potentially take its roots in the High-Level People-to-People Dialogue. To date this mechanism is, however, not powerful enough to enhance the accountability of and social inclusion into the interregional relationship. This shows that the EU–China cooperation lacks the ability to proactively change existing social structures related to the management of climate change. There is a persistent reluctance to grant civil society access to agenda-setting and policy making in the interregional relationship. This is related to the fact that changing incentives rather than bringing about changes in the general belief system has led to a behavioural change, which is again limited to the technical and relatively uncontentious field of energy issues. This limitation is also a result of taking national sensitivities into account to a degree that can be described as a 'reverse conditionality' (Wood 2011: 254). The EU has both a pragmatic and normative climate and environmental agenda, which it seeks to follow in its external relations. However, China forces the EU to accept its own preferences, which is particularly evident in energy issues. Although the interregional dialogue has created numerous programmes that integrate SD and climate change concerns, the only tangible projects are on energy issues, which conform with Chinese interests and oppose the EU's normative and more holistic agenda (Fox and Godemont 2009: 35).

In order to manage the consequences of climate change and effectively change political, economic, and social structures in EU–China relations, tangible follow-up action outside the narrow area of energy is still needed. Also, communities at the local level need to be linked to the (inter)regional level, and civil society organisations should be granted access to agenda-setting and policy making. The newly established approach to participative governance in interregional relations, the creation of a High-Level People-to-People Dialogue, has yet to prove its usefulness, might actually marginalise some societal groups, and does not necessarily guarantee a change towards more participatory approaches in interregional climate governance.

Notes

1　For further information, see the website of the Europe-China Clean Energy Centre (EC2), http://www.ec2.org.cn (accessed 03.01.2013).
2　For a full list of members, see the website of ASEM, http://www.aseminfoboard.org/members.html (accessed 03.01.2013).
3　For an overview of EU–China relations, see the website of the Delegation of the European Union to China, http://eeas.europa.eu/delegations/china/eu_china/political_relations/index_en.htm (accessed 03.01.2013).
4　For further information on the ENVforum, see http://www.asef.org/index.php/projects/programmes/517-asia-europe-environment-forum-%28envforum%29 (accessed 03.01.2013).
5　For more detailed information on this partnership, see Council of the EU (2012) *Joint Press Communiqué – 15th EU–China Summit: Towards a Stronger EU–China Comprehensive Strategic Partnership*, http://europa.eu/rapid/press-release_MEMO-12-693_en.htm (accessed 03.01.2013).
6　In addition to a short background on EU–China Relations, this Memo 12/684 entitled 'EU Relations with China' offers a concise overview of the most recent EU–China Summit on 20 September 2012. The cooperation on clean energy as well as sustainable urban planning was emphasized. See EU (2012b); EU and PRC 2012c. For further information on the EU–China High-Level Energy meeting, see EC (n.d. a).
7　For a brief overview of environmental cooperation between the EU and China, see EC (2012a).
8　Prior to the restructuring of the EC in 2010, DG Transport and Energy (TREN) was responsible for the organisation of the conferences. The DGs were divided into DG Transport (Commissioner Siim Kallas) and DG Energy (Commissioner Günther Oettinger). For a press release on the restructuring, see EU (2010).
9　For more detailed information on the energy conferences, see EC (n.d. b).
10　For detailed information on the first meeting, see http://www.euchinamayorsforum.eu/home.html (accessed 07.01.2013).
11　These interests and understandings were confirmed at the launch of the China–EU Science and Technology Year in 2007; for further information, see EC (2007).
12　For further information on ICARE and its history, see the institute's website http://icare.hust.edu.cn/en/ (accessed 08.01.2013).
13　For further information on EC2, see EC2 (2012a).
14　For a brief outline of the event, see EC2 (2012b).
15　For a brief outline of the event, see EC2 (2012c).
16　For a detailed outline of the programme, see the official website http://www.ecegp.com/index_en.asp (accessed 08.01.2013).
17　In addition to the listing by Scott 2009, there is detailed information on the various projects available at the Community Research and Development Information Service (CORDIS), http://cordis.europa.eu (accessed 08.01.2013); please note that the projects mentioned present a random sample by the authors to illustrate joint research activities.

18 The declaration was also mentioned in the joint press communiqué, paragraph 24; see Council of the European Union (2012).
19 For more detailed information on the EU–China Mayors' Forum, see the official website http://www.euchinamayorsforum.eu/home.html; further information on the implementation of the partnership, see Delegation of the EU to China (2012b).
20 More information is provided on the project's official website, http://www.urbachina.eu (accessed 08.01.2013).
21 For more information, see http://www.train-the-trainers.net/; for more general Information about the Switch Asia project, see http://www.switch-asia.eu (accessed 08.01.2013).
22 More information is available from the project's website http://www.urgenche.eu/project/ (accessed 08.01.2013).
23 For a brief outline of the project, see Europeaid (n.d.).
24 For more information about the CDM, see also the contribution by Pauline Lacour and Jean-Christophe Simon in this book.
25 For further information, see Council of the European Union (2012).
26 See also *Country Strategy Paper China 2007–2013*, http://eeas.europa.eu/delegations/china/eu_china/development_cooperation/index_en.htm (accessed 11.02.2013).
27 For more information on fuel standards, see European Parliament and Council of the European Union (1998, 2009); Xinhua (2012); *China Daily Mail* (2012).

References

Acharya, A. (2009) *Whose Ideas Matter: Agency and Power in Asian Regionalism*, Ithaca, NY and London: Cornell University Press.

Adger, W.N. *et al.* (2011) 'Resilience Implications of Policy Responses to Climate Change', *Wiley Interdisciplinary Reviews: Climate Change*, vol. 2, no. 5, pp. 757–766.

ASEF (2012) *Asia–Europe Environment Forum. Overview*, online: http://www.asef.org/index.php/projects/programmes/517-asia-europe-environment-forum-%28envforum%29 (accessed 04.10.2012).

ASEM (2006) *ASEM6 Declaration on Climate Change*, Helsinki, online: http://www.asem6.fi/NEWS_AND_DOCUMENTS/EN_GB/1157981028054/INDEX.HTM (accessed 04.10.2012).

ASEM (2008) *Beijing Declaration on Sustainable Development*, Beijing, online: http://www.asem7.cn/download/bdsd.pdf (accessed 04.10.2012).

ASEM (2010) *Chair's Statement and Brussels Declaration*, Brussels, online: http://www.asem8.be/asem-8-chairs-statement-and-brussels-declaration (accessed 04.10.2012).

ASEM (2012a) *4th ASEM Environment Ministers' Meeting*, online: http://www.aseminfoboard.org/upcoming-events/event/345-4th-asem-environmentministers-meeting.html (accessed 04.10.2012).

ASEM (2012b) *Vientiane Declaration on Strengthening Partnership for Peace and Development*, online: http://www.aseminfoboard.org/upcoming-events/event/344-asem-9summit.html (accessed 01.12.2012).

Börzel, T. and Risse, T. (2009) 'The Transformative Power of Europe. The European Union and the Diffusion of Ideas', *KFG Working Paper*, no. 1, Berlin: FU Berlin, online: http://www.polsoz.fuBerlin.de/en/v/transformeurope/publications/working_paper/WP_1_Juni_Boerzel_Risse.pdf (accessed 11.02.2013).

Branigan, T. (2013) *Beijing Smog Continues as Chinese State Media Urge More Action*, online: http://www.guardian.co.uk/world/2013/jan/14/beijing-smog-continues-media-action (accessed 23.01.2013).

Brown, K. (2011) 'Rethinking Progress in a Warming World: Interrogating Climate Resilient Development', discussion paper for the conference 'Rethinking Development in an Age of Scarcity and Uncertainty. New Voices, Values and Alliances for an Increased Resilience', University of York, 19–22 September 2011.

Carrapatoso, A. (2011) 'Climate Policy Diffusion: Interregional Dialogue in EU–China Relations', *Global Change, Peace and Security*, vol. 23, no. 2, pp. 177–194.

Chatham House (2007) *Changing Climates: Interdependencies on Energy and Climate Security for China and Europe*, London: Royal Institute for International Affairs.

China Daily Mail (2012) 'New Standards for Fuel to Reduce Pollution in City', online: http://china.org.cn/environment/2012-05/18/content_25413627.htm (accessed 23.01.2013).

Council of the European Union (2012) Joint Press Communiqué 15th EU–China Summit. Towards a Stronger EU–China Comprehensive Strategic Partnership, online: http://www.consilium.europa.eu/uedocs/cms_Data/docs/pressdata/en/ec/132507.pdf (accessed 10.01.2013).

Dai, X. and Diao, Z. (2011) 'Towards a New World Order for Climate Change. China and the European Union's Leadership Ambition', in Wurzel, R. and Connelly, J. (ed.) *The European Union as a Leader in International Climate Change Politics*, London and New York: Routledge, pp. 252–268.

Darkin, B. (2007) 'The Road to Climate Resilience', *China Dialogue*, 13 November, online: http://www.chinadialogue.net/article/show/single/en/1475-The-road-to-climate-resilience (accessed 04.10.2012).

Delegation of the EU to China (2010) *EU China CDM Facilitation Project*, online: http://eeas.europa.eu/delegations/china/documents/projects/1_euchina_cdm_facilitation_project_fiche.pdf (accessed 04.10.2012).

Delegation of the EU to China (2012a) *Project Fiche EU–China Institute for Clean and Renewable Energy*, online: http://eeas.europa.eu/delegations/china/projects/list_of_projects/20141_en.htm (accessed 04.10.2012).

Delegation of the EU to China (2012b) *Action Fiche for the Eco-Urbanisation Project with Chinese Mayors*, online: http://eeas.europa.eu/delegations/china/documents/eu_china/sustainable_urbanisaion/action_fiche_eu_china_low-carbon_and_environmental_sustainability_programme.pdf (accessed 07.02.2013).

Dent, C. (2004) 'The Asia–Europe Meeting and Interregionalism: Towards a Theory of Multilateral Utility', *Asian Survey*, vol. 44, no. 2, pp. 213–236.

Dimas, S. (2008) *Environmental Governance: Why Does It Matter for the EU and China?*, EU China Environmental Governance Workshop, Beijing, online: http://www.euchinapdsf.org/WebSite/eu/UpFile/2008/2008514102515599.pdf (accessed 20.03.2012).

EC (n.d. a) *First EU–China High-Level Meeting on Energy*, online: http://ec.europa.eu/commission_20102014/oettinger/headlines/news/2012/05/20120503_de.htm (accessed 07.01.2013).

EC (n.d. b) *Biannual Energy Conferences*, online: http://ec.europa.eu/energy/international/bilateral_cooperation/china/biannual_conference_en.htm (accessed 04.01.2013).

EC (n.d. c) *EC-China Energy Dialogue*, online: http://ec.europa.eu/energy/international/bilateral_cooperation/china/dialogue_en.htm or http://ec.europa.eu/energy/international/bilateral_cooperation/china/doc/dialogue/2005mou_eu_china_energy_transport_strategies.pdf (accessed 04.01.2013).

EC (2005) *EU–China Dialogue on Energy and Transport Strategies: Memorandum of Understanding*, Beijing, online: http://ec.europa.eu/energy/international/bilateral_

cooperation/china/doc/dialogue/2005mou_eu_china_energy_transport_strategies.pdf (accessed 05.04.2012).

EC (2006) *EU–China: Closer Partners Growing Responsibilities,* Brussels, online: http:// eurlex.europa.eu/LexUriServ/LexUriServ.do?uri=COM:2006:0631:FIN:EN:PDF (accessed 04.10.2012).

EC (2007) *China–EU Science and Technology Year,* online: http://ec.europa.eu/research/ iscp/ EU–China /about_en.html (accessed 04.01.2013).

EC (2008) *The 7th EU–China Energy Conference,* Brussels, online: http://ec.europa. eu/energy/international/bilateral_cooperation/china/conference7_en.htm (accessed 10.04.2012).

EC (2009) *Commission Position Paper on the Trade Sustainability Impact Assessment of the Negotiations of a Partnership and Cooperation Agreement between the EU and China,* Brussels, online: http://trade.ec.europa.eu/doclib/docs/2009/february/ tradoc_142373.pdf (accessed 15.3.2012).

EC (2010) *China–EU Near Zero Emission Coal,* Brussels, online: www.ec.europa.eu/ clima/dossiers/nzec/index_en.htm (accessed: 04.10.2012).

EC (2012a) *General Co-operation with China,* online: http://ec.europa.eu/environment/ international_issues/relations_china_en.htm (accessed 07.01.2013).

EC (2012b) *Joint Declaration on the EU–China Partnership on Urbanisation,* online: http://ec.europa.eu/energy/international/bilateral_cooperation/china/doc/20120503_ eu_china_joint_declaration_urbanisation_en.pdf (accessed 07.01.2013).

EC2 (2012a) *Know More About EC2,* online: www.ec2.org.cn/about-us (accessed 08.01.2013).

EC2 (2012b) *EC2 Sharing Event*: *Designing Integrated Demonstrations Zones,* online: http:// www.ec2.org.cn/en/events/ec2-sharing-event-designing-integrated-demonstrationzones- china-what-works-lessons-european (accessed 08.01.2013).

EC2 (2012c) *EC2 EURUMQI Demo Zone Sharing Event – Sustainable Energy Action Plans in Europe: Good Practices and Lessons Learnt,* online: http://www.ec2.org. cn/en/events/ec2eurumqi-demo-zone-sharing-event-sustainable-energy-action-plans- europe-good-practicesand (accessed 08.01.2013).

Elkins, Z. and Simmons, B. (2005) 'On Waves, Clusters, and Diffusion: A Conceptual Framework', *Annals of the American Academy of Political and Social Science,* no. 598, pp. 33–51.

EU (2005) *EU and China Partnership on Climate Change,* MEMO/05/298, Brussels, online: http://europa.eu/rapid/press-release_MEMO-05-298_en.htm (accessed 04.01.2013).

EU (2010) *Commission Creates Two New Directorates-General for Energy and Climate Action,* online: http://europa.eu/rapid/press-release_IP-10-164_en.htm?locale=en (accessed 04.01.2013).

EU (2012a) *4th EU–China Policy Dialogue on the Environment,* Minutes of the Meeting between Mr. Janez Potoncik and Mr. Zhou Shengxian, Brussels, online: http:// ec.europa.eu/environment/international_issues/pdf/china/signed_minutes_08FEB212. pdf (accessed 20.03.2012).

EU (2012b) *EU Relations with China,* online: http://europa.eu/rapid/press-release_ MEMO12-684_en.htm (accessed 07.01.2013).

EU (2012c) *The European Union and China Join Forces to Address Environment, Urbanisation and Climate Change Challenges,* online: http://europa.eu/rapid/press- release_IP-12-989_en.htm (accessed 07.01.2013).

EU External Action Service (2012) Information Note. Subject: *Sectoral Cooperation Between the EU and China*, Brussels, online: http://eeas.europa.eu/china/docs/sectoraldialogues_en.pdf (accessed 20.03.2012).

EU and PRC (2012a) *Joint Declaration on the EU–China Partnership on Urbanisation*, Brussels, online: http://eeas.europa.eu/delegations/china/documents/eu_china/sustainable_urbanisation/EU-China_joint_declaration_urbanisation_partnership-signed-en.pdf (accessed 08.01.2013).

EU and PRC (2012b) *Joint Press Communiqué of the 14th EU–China Summit*, MEMO 12/103, Beijing, online: http://europa.eu/rapid/pressReleasesAction.do?reference=MEMO/12/103 (accessed 05.04.2012).

EU and PRC (2012c) *Joint Declaration on the First Round of the EU–China High-Level People-to-People-Dialogue*, online: http://ec.europa.eu/education/externalrelationprogrammes/doc/china/joint12_en.pdf (accessed 05.04.2012).

Europeaid (n.d.) *EU–China CDM Faciliation Project*, online: http://ec.europa.eu/europeaid/documents/case-studies/china_environment_cdm-facilitation-project_en.pdf (accessed 08.01.2013).

European Parliament and Council of the European Union (1998) *Directive 98/70/EC of the European Parliament and of the Council of 13 October 1998 Relating to the Quality of Petrol and Diesel Fuels and Amending Council Directive 93/12/EEC*, online: http://eur-lex.europa.eu/LexUriServ/LexUriServ.do?uri=OJ:L:1998:350:0058:0067:EN:PDF (accessed 23.01.2013).

European Parliament and Council of the European Union (2009) *Directive 2009/30/EC of the European Parliament and the Council of 23 April 2009 Amending Directive 98/70/EC as Regards the Specification of Petrol, Diesel and Gas-Oil and Introducing a Mechanism to Monitor and Reduce Greenhouse Gas Emissions and Amending Council Directive 1999/32/EC as Regards the Specification of Fuel Used by Inland Waterway Vessels and Repealing Directive 93/12/EEC*, http://eurlex.europa.eu/LexUriServ/LexUriServ.do?uri=OJ:L:2009:140:0088:0113:EN:PDF (accessed 23.01.2013).

E3G (2012) *Wuhan Carbon Trading Roundtable Summary Report*, online: http://www.e3g.org/images/uploads/E3G_Wuhan_ETS_Roundtable_Summary_Report.pdf (accessed 04.10.2012).

Fox, J. and Godemont, F. (2009) *A Power Audit of EU–China Relations*, London: European Council of Foreign Relations.

Hackenesch, C. and Ling, J. (2009) 'Schwierige Partner', *Zeit Online*, 2 June, online: http://www.zeit.de/online/2009/23/china-europa (accessed 07.02. 2013).

Han, G., Olsson, M., Hallding, K. and Lunsford, D. (2012) 'China's Carbon Emission Trading: An Overview of Current Development', *FORES Study*, no. 1, pp. 1–59.

Hänggi, H. (2006) 'Interregionalism as a Multifaceted Phenomenon. In Search of a Typology', in Hänggi, H., Roloff, R. and Rüland, J. (eds) *Interregionalism and International Relations*, London and New York: Routledge, pp. 31–63.

Haughton, G. (1999) 'Environmental Justice and the Sustainable City', *Journal of Planning, Education and Research*, March, vol. 18, pp. 233–243.

Heinze, T. (2011) 'Mechanism-Based Thinking on Policy Diffusion. A Review of Current Approaches in Political Science', *KFG Working Paper*, no. 34, pp. 5–32.

Holzer, C. and Zhang, H. (2008) 'The Potentials and Limits of China–EU Cooperation on Climate Change and Energy Security', *Asia Europe Journal*, vol. 6, pp. 217–227.

Hopwood, B., Mellor, M. and O'Brien, G. (2005) 'Sustainable Development: Mapping Different Approaches', *Sustainable Development*, vol. 13, no. 1, pp. 38–52.

Information Office of the State Council of the People's Republic of China (2003) *China's EU Policy Paper*, Beijing, online: http://www.china.org.cn/e-white/20050817/index. htm (accessed 10.04.2012).

Ivanova, D. (2012) *China's Pioneering Carbon Exchange Scheme Faces Challenges*, Carbon Investments 12 March, online: http://www.carbon-investments.co.uk/china-carbon-exchange-scheme-faces-challenges.php (accessed 04.10.2012).

Jacobs, M. (1999) 'Sustainable Development as a Contested Concept', in Dobson, A. (ed.) *Fairness and Futurity: Essays on Environmental Sustainability and Social Justice*, Oxford: Oxford University Press, pp. 21–45.

Jänicke, M. and Jörgens, H. (2007) *New Approaches to Environmental Governance*, online: http://foper.sfb.rs/pdf/JanickeJorgens.pdf (accessed 19.02.2013).

Jetschke, A. (2010) 'Do Regional Organizations Travel? European Integration, Diffusion and the Case of ASEAN', *KFG Working Paper*, no. 17, pp. 1–28.

Moore, S. (2011) 'Strategic Imperative? Reading China's Climate Policy in Terms of Core Interests', *Global Change, Peace and Security*, vol. 23, no. 2, pp. 147–157.

Newig, J., Günther, D. and Pahl-Wostl, C. (2010) 'Synapses in the Network: Learning in Governance Networks in the Context of Environmental Management', *Ecology and Society*, vol. 15, no. 4, online: http://www.ecologyandsociety.org/vol15/iss4/art24/ (accessed 11.02.2013).

Oberthür, S. and Roche Kelly, C. (2008) 'EU Leadership in International Climate Policy: Achievements and Challenges', *The International Spectator*, vol. 43, no. 3, pp. 35–50.

PRC (2006) *China–EU Partnership on Climate Change Rolling Work Plan*, Beijing, online: http://www.fmprc.gov.cn/eng/wjb/zzjg/tyfls/tfsxw/t283051.htm (accessed 10.04.2012).

Reuters (2011) *China to Pilot Carbon Emission Exchange: Report*, 17 July, online: http://www.reuters.com/article/2011/07/17/us-china-emmission-idUSTRE76G0PI20110717 (accessed 04.10.2012).

Roloff, R. (2006) 'Interregionalism in Theoretical Perspective. State of the Art', in Hänggi, H., Roloff, R. and Rüland, J. (2006) *Interregionalism and International Relations*, London and New York: Routledge, pp. 17–31.

Rüland, J. (2010) 'Balancers, Multilateral Utilities or Regional Identity Builders? International Relations and the Study of Interregionalism', *Journal of European Public Policy*, vol. 17, no. 8, pp. 1271–1283.

Rüland, J. (2012) 'The Rise of "Diminished Multilateralism". East Asian and European Forum Shopping in Global Governance', *Asia Europe Journal*, vol. 9, pp. 255–270.

Scott, D. (2009) 'Environmental Relations as a "Strategic Key" in EU–China Relations', *Asia Europe Journal*, vol. 7, pp. 211–234.

Smit, B. and Wandel, J. (2006) 'Adaptation, Adaptive Capacity and Vulnerability', *Global Environmental Change*, vol. 16, no. 3, pp. 282–292.

Tews, K. (2006) 'The Diffusion of Environmental Policy Innovations', in Winter, G. (ed.) *Multilevel Governance of Global Environmental Change*, Cambridge: Cambridge University Press, pp. 227–254.

Tianbao, Qin (2012) *Climate Change and Emission Trading Systems (ETS): China's Perspective and International Experiences*, KAS-Schriftenreihe CHINA, no. 43, Shanghai.

Torney, D. (2012) 'Assessing EU Leadership on Climate Change. The Limits of Diffusion in EU Relations with China', *KFG Working Paper*, no. 46, Berlin: FU Berlin, online: http://www.polsoz.fu-berlin.de/en/v/transformeurope/publications/working_paper/WP_46_Torney.pdf (accessed 11.02.2013).

UNFCCC (2012) *Registered Project Activities by Host party*, Bonn, online: http://cdm. unfccc.int/Statistics/Registration/NumOfRegisteredProjByHostPartiesPieChart.html (accessed 31.3.2012).

Watts, J. (2012) 'China Quietly Shelves New Diesel Emission Standards', *The Guardian Environment Blog*, 1 February, online: http://www.guardian.co.uk/environment/ blog/2012/feb/01/china-shelves-plan-diesel-emissions, (accessed 23.3.2012).

Wood, S. (2011) 'Pragmatic Power Europe?', *Cooperation and Conflict*, vol. 46, no. 2, pp. 242–261.

Xinhua (2012) *Beijing to Implement Stricter Fuel Standards*, online: http://www.china.org. cn/environment/2012-05/19/content_25422404.htm (accessed 23.01.2013).

12 How to bypass multilateral gridlocks

Resilient climate change management and efficient multi-level climate politics

Edith Kürzinger

Since 1996, when I stopped being a negotiator of the UNFCCC for Germany, I have followed the unsatisfactory progress of the negotiations from the distance of a consultant and coach of diverse stakeholders in Africa, Asia, Latin America, and Europe on resource efficiency (RE) and sustainable development (SD) issues. When meeting colleagues from the 'system' I saw their increasing frustration, but also resistance to openly express criticism, and finally an attitude of defending the job, peers, and the process of the UNFCCC 'silo'. In what follows, I want to share my ideas and reflections on climate change (CC) management from the perspective of 'change management'[1] and 'organisational development', hoping that this view from an 'outsider' adds value to the discussion on the international climate regime (ICR) and contributes to evolving the concept and implementation of climate-resilient development (CRD).

So far, the CC topic/problem has been mostly looked at from a *climate* perspective, with the involvement of and reliance on all kinds of climate experts with a narrow 'climate' view on CC. However, the gridlock of the negotiation process and the poor progress in real mitigation and adaptation in most places requires, in my perception, an urgent shift of focus to the *change* aspect of CC and a broader, CRD perspective. This also involves addressing, in more detail, the 'how' of the process, for example the 'politics', a perspective that has been either neglected or considered of secondary importance compared to 'policy' (Bodansky 2007). By looking at the change side of CC management, this chapter will elaborate:

- why the UNFCCC has not reached its objectives and is (for the time being) a 'dead horse' (as seen through a change management perspective);
- why and how new energy can be created by dismounting, doing things differently, and changing track to do the right things (Argyris and Schön 1978);[2]
- which alternative approaches could offer common ground and effectively promote CRD.

The lore of the Dakota Indians advises: 'If you notice that you are riding a dead horse, dismount!!!'

The horse (UNFCCC process) is dead: why more of the same does not make sense

Complex problem – coarse tools: the limiting factor of 'UN bureaucracy'

The experience with the Montreal Protocol (MP) has shown that relatively quick success in dealing with an environmental problem can be reached even multilaterally, if (1) its impact is tangible enough to create a joint interest amongst different stakeholders and make concrete action a high priority; (2) the number of problem-causing substances is limited and a general consensus on a few technological options is easily achievable; (3) the need for action lies only with industrialised countries who are also willing and able to cover the (incremental) costs (Benedick 1998; Chapter 10). However, this seems to be an exception and not the rule for multilateral environmental treaties. Rayner (2011) argues that the UNFCCC, especially the Kyoto Protocol (KP), was misled in its design by drawing on experiences such as the MP, the Strategic Arms Reduction Treaty (START), and the US Acid Rain Programme. He considers these unsuitable, as the CC issue is a complex of multifaceted, supra-sectorial, and transnational problems with diverse, only partially known or disputed cause–effect relationships at different levels (local, national, regional, global), with intra-generational and trans-generational impact on conflicting interest groups; for its resolution, a road to transformational change needs to be developed step by step under imperfect information that finally would lead to SD: a tremendous task for which the UN(FCCC) negotiation bureaucracy has proven an inadequate mechanism, as it does not provide a working environment[3] conducive to substantial (measurable) cost-efficient results:

- The consensus principle of the UN leads to decisions that do not reflect best performance, contrary to what happens, for example in sports or economic competition, where the winner or best price or product sets the pace; instead, the UNFCCC produces a 'lowest common denominator', resulting from a sequence of consensus processes (see Figure 12.1; Rayner 2011: 617; Abbott 2013: 3).
- The combination of the consensus principle and the concentration on achieving legally binding agreements between the main actors (e.g. OECD countries; emerging economies) has not led to ambitious reduction targets, and groups interested in a fast track (e.g. EU/OECD countries, Alliance of Small Island States (AOSIS)) could not overcome the logjams.
- The concept of 'developing' and 'developed' countries still prevalent in the UN system;[4] the respective language of involved actors is based on a crude, outdated North–South logic and a relic from times when the 'catch-up-industrialisation' concept prevailed that considered economies as 'developed' if industry's share in gross domestic product (GDP) exceeded a certain level.[5] Since the UN Conference on Environment and Development (UNCED; 1992), this concept has been replaced, at least in theory, by SD; according to its guiding principles for economic, environmental, and social sustainability

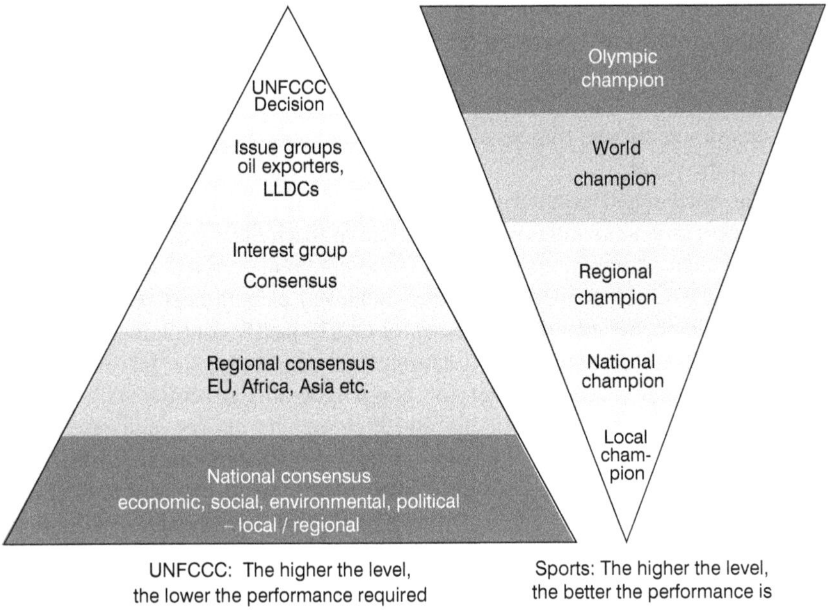
UNFCCC Decision
Issue groups oil exporters, LLDCs
Interest group Consensus
Regional consensus EU, Africa, Asia etc.
National consensus economic, social, environmental, political – local / regional
Olympic champion
World champion
Regional champion
National champion
Local cham-pion
UNFCCC: The higher the level, the lower the performance required
Sports: The higher the level, the better the performance is

Figure 12.1 Consensus levels leading to lowest common denominator results in UN

in all types of developing as well as industrialised societies, no 'industrialised' country (the term best substituting 'developed') has reached sustainability nor can as yet provide a reasonable road map to SD (see Chapter 2).[6]

- UNFCCC delegates are mostly government officials from capitals, poorly trained in negotiation techniques, representing the interests of electorates or, more often than not, of poorly legitimised or authoritarian regimes: this makes UN bodies act according to (conflicting) individual country and group interests and not in the 'general interest of humankind'. This unrealistic 'wishful thinking' is recurrently criticised: by climate scientists (e.g. WBGU 2011), who see that time is running out for keeping CC to a manageable dimension, and who cannot understand why politicians are not acting accordingly; by NGOs, often not clearly mandated, who demand a 'just world' (Baer *et al.* 2008) from a body that is not a 'global independent actor'; by countries under particular threat from CC (e.g. within AOSIS); and by governments that use their poor citizens as bargaining chips for repeating stereotypical demands for a general North–South transfer of finance and technology, from which their poor would benefit the least.
- The periodic diplomatic negotiation rounds, for example Conferences of the Parties (CoP), usually called 'climate summits', have increasingly turned into 'public events' (e.g. in Copenhagen, 2009): the unmanageable and climate-unfriendly number of 'participants' did not contribute to better results but rather to emissions (UNFCCC 2006: 4).

- Ineffective working methods (e.g. long general speeches in plenary sessions; poorly trained and prepared delegates; limited use of modern visualisation, communication, negotiation, and evaluation techniques) consume (nearly unlimited) session time and budget and produce too little output: the incentive structure increased this 'mountain which labours and brings forth a mouse' over the years.
- The open-ended process lacks clear SMART[7] objectives and measurable success indicators; otherwise, the failure to reach the aspired legally binding agreement on emissions reduction could not be interpreted as a 'success' by bringing up unintended side effects achieved at high cost (e.g. intensified policy dialogue, general awareness for CC) to justify continuing this track.
- The ICR is based on incorrect assumptions concerning the involved actors: (1) frequently, delegates act for non-democratic governments;[8] (2) they mostly represent urban middle- and high-income classes, and often know little about the (rural) poor already struggling with autonomous adaptation to CC and weak performance of local authorities; (3) well-intentioned UNFCCC enthusiasts from environment ministries prevail, usually acting as national focal points and managing funds of UNFCCC mechanisms (see Chapter 4); (4) delegates often lack know-how on the range of policy and technical aspects discussed in the various scientific communities; in particular, in least developed countries (LDCs) they are typically generalists working in small missions.
- The UNFCCC process is mostly about 'what should be done' (often than not, by others!) and little about 'how it can be done' (by oneself). Many delegates and their institutions lack the capabilities to implement the bottom-up strategies nicely drafted in decisions, for example by making other (more powerful) ministries co-operate or take action, managing genuine stakeholder dialogues, or designing appropriate support to local target groups (e.g. on agricultural issues, corruption of local authorities, competences of NGOs, etc.). Therefore, decisions on, for example, a greenhouse gas (GHG) inventory or a National Plan for Adaptation (NAPA) often ignore feasibility issues (do parties really have the capacity to draft another of the many plans or manage a stakeholder dialogue that merits this term?) and avoid conflict with national sovereignty.
- Since the progress of the political negotiations on the main issue, targets and timetables for GHG reduction, has been poor, the UNFCCC system seems to occupy idle time and resources with hustle and heavy institution-building on two primarily instrumental issues: finance and technology. The financial mechanisms are not only frequently used to co-opt opponents into the process (e.g. emerging economies: Clean Development Mechanism (CDM); LDCs: Adaptation Fund), they also consumed enormous resources to 're-invent' a new Global Environment Facility (GEF) named Green Climate Fund (GCF): the technical outcome will probably not improve as political considerations of funding will be more pronounced; the UN principle 'one country one vote' usually leads to a watering can disbursement. The deliberations on

technology transfer with reference to Article 4.5 of the UNFCCC seem to have gained speed: instead of discussing production patterns more profoundly, a complex Climate Technology Centre (CTC)[9] structure is envisaged to meet well-known, but often unrealistic demands of LDCs, for example making technologies public domain and free of patents, creating a technology platform for LDCs, etc., which is still less obvious in the era of generalised Internet access.[10] While refused by OECD countries at the time of CoP 1 in Berlin in 1995, some donor agencies (e.g. Germany's GIZ) are now willing to use the new funds in co-operation with UNEP (UNEP 2012), getting another financial injection for its moderately successful Cleaner Production Centres (van Berkel 2011).

The 'poor politics' of the failed top-down 'policy approach' (to legally binding agreements): the need for realistic and bottom-up thinking

Focused on the negotiation of legally binding, absolute targets and timetables for CO_2 emission reductions, the UNFCCC process adopted a problem-based, comprehensive, top-down policy approach: results are expected to be achieved by national policies, deducting binding, absolute targets from historical emissions, and fostering the ambitious aim of limiting temperature increase to 2°C. This intellectually convincing 'good' policy allows for flexibility in the choice of implementation instruments; but it is, at the same time, 'bad' politics, in the words of Bodansky (2007), as the obstacles to such an agreement make it very unlikely to happen.

The gridlocked negotiations confirm the shortcomings of this approach: (1) two of the major actors, the US and China (and India) (Bodansky 2007: 61f), have structural problems with a legally binding international agreement as it could encroach on national sovereignty; (2) the fear of free-riders leads to an attitude of binding one's own agreement on targets and timetables to the previous agreement of others, unlike in other areas where a difference in pace is accepted: hence, to blocking or retarding coalitions for different reasons. As both obstacles will persist, the 'positive thinking approach' of environment ministries on the achievement of a substantive post-Kyoto agreement before 2015 is not realistic.

Two key factors hamper making the best out of this 'good' policy approach. Most importantly, too many actors obstruct the results: as UN negotiation processes are open to all members (195; 165 signatories of the UNFCCC (UNFCCC n.d.)), a large number are neither deeply involved in the problems (e.g. emissions) nor in the solutions (not proposing own action and funds), but have the right to intervene at any moment, complicating the negotiations, while causing costs (e.g. travel costs for developing country representatives, conference costs). The chosen open-endedness of the process (as many parties, as long as it takes) contradicts the urgency of the problem, which, in turn, is used for insisting on the approach of a 'legally binding agreement': this sounds very much like circular reasoning. To avoid 'many cooks spoiling the broth', it is recommended to restrict negotiation to those (~20–25) countries responsible for 80 per cent of total GHG emissions, and those willing to take on commitments.

Another key factor driving poor outcomes is the limitation to one form of commitment (i.e. absolute targets, fixed timetables), which could be addressed through more flexibility in commitments, for example also using indexed targets, taxes, efficiency standards, etc., which would reflect 'not ideal policy, but rather less than ideal politics' (Rayner 2011: 65), but bring energy into the system.

To fundamentally address the shortcomings of the current strategy, an alternative flexible bottom-up approach is more promising that builds on 'what is already going on' (Bodansky 2007: 63f). Rayner (2011: 617) calls this a 'clumsy approach' which prioritises the 'direction of the travel' over 'targets and timetables' and abandons the claim that mitigation requires a universal framework. Such a bottom-up approach would apply the subsidiarity principle by addressing problems at the lowest possible level (where they usually originate): such a flexible process would contribute to minimising global warming and to fundamentally shift, for example, energy and land use, notwithstanding the wide range of distinctive measures resulting from different institutional, technical, economic, and political capacities. The issues left to be tackled at the international stage – after tapping the potential of the local, regional, and national levels, including by co-operation at these levels – would prove to be fewer than the present managers of the UNFCCC process claim.

Such a bottom-up process would better address the necessary modification of many elements of a socio-economic system to cope with CC and move towards CRD: through a change of policy framework, resource prices, user rights, production and consumption patterns, and social and individual behaviour for which there is no 'solution', even less at the global level; it requires a long change process steered by actors working proactively on climate management issues on all levels in most countries.

Another element of the bottom-up proposal and its contribution to 'speed up the travel' (Rayner 2011: 617) is that adaptation might come first: not as an alternative to mitigation, and only exceptionally financed by external resources, but as a means to create real, immediate, and visible benefits for affected populations. As it is up to national, and even regional and local administrations, for example 'to revise and implement zoning, planning and building regulations and invest in infrastructure in ways that drastically reduce vulnerability to CC in the short and medium term', no international negotiations are needed; intelligently mixed bottom-up adaptation and cost-effective mitigation can create local ownership. This is also relevant for industrialised countries (Martens and Chang 2010; Nicholls and Kebede 2012): Moreno (2010: 41f) shows the usefulness of stakeholders' involvement when analysing tourism's vulnerability and developing adaptation (and mitigation) measures bottom up. The untapped potential for the implementation of subsidiarity is also evident in the controversy about centralised or decentralised energy systems following the phase out of nuclear energy in Germany (see Chapter 2; Morris 2013).

The implementation of this approach is only feasible if some change in mindsets and practice within the UNFCCC system can be evolved. Firstly, the separation between 'mitigation (countries)', i.e. the main emitters, and 'adaptation (countries)', i.e. those with little (but sometimes quickly increasing) emissions, but a high vulnerability, needs to be mentally and institutionally overcome. All parties are affected by CC (e.g. hurricanes) and must manage some sort of adaptation, not only 'vulnerable' countries (Horstmann and Scholz 2011); all countries contribute through unsustainable development models to global warming and the need for adaptation: if not by GHG emissions from fossil fuels, then by diminished sink capacities, deforestation, loss of organic matter and CO_2 storage capacity from soil-depleting agricultural practices (Hoffmann 2011), resource use beyond ecosystems' carrying capacity, or destruction of coastal zone ecosystems. The respective weakening of adaptation options and local livelihoods falls under the responsibility of the respective national governments (see Chapters 5 and 6).

Secondly, the 'recipient attitude' of many 'adaptation country' representatives, 'milking the cow UNFCCC' by only accepting responsibility for undertaking adaptation measures if fully fledged financing is provided is unrealistic in view of the available funds, and unjustifiable: sustainable management of natural resources, sound coastal zone and risk management, etc., are 'no regret measures' (measures which make sense under any circumstances, and are usually profitable) that are in the self-interest of their (local) population and should usually be part of the standard tasks of national policy. In addition, development co-operation projects are already taking up such issues (as shown in Chapters 4, 5, and 6). This strategic change, starting with tangible adaptation, is only feasible if own means and efforts are mobilised, and combined adaptation and mitigation is integrated with a CDR perspective.

The UNFCCC self-referential system: 'Are we really doing the right things?'

As pointed out in Chapter 2, the UNFCCC process is, to a large extent, a self-referential system (Luhmann 1990; Teubner 1992: 95). The following factors hamper continuous learning, reflection, and communication with the external environment:

- The UNFCCC 'labyrinth' builds up a large number of involved public and private actors and institutions: NGOs and lobbyists of all stripes get a forum for their views at side events; development co-operation agencies grow by opportunistically adding a considerable budget to their portfolios (e.g. GIZ 2012a: 12f; 21);[11] environment policy representatives, who (even in Germany) mostly play a modest role in the Cabinet, are happy to be part of the international 'saving the climate' community, 'escaping' less appealing national issues and counting on own money for 'co-operation projects'.[12] Thus, losing the UNFCCC forum would have major implications for many of the currently involved actors.
- No effective mechanisms for self-reflection and external evaluation, as well as continuous learning, are in place, similar to the official development assistance (ODA) system[13] (individual systems by country and/or institution),[14] OECD Development Assistance Committee (DAC) peer reviews.[15] No critical and

comprehensive assessment of meetings is undertaken, asking 'what was good (+), could have been better (-), or was missing (0)', i.e. what progress was made, or not (and why), and what to do differently. Regular external support could help to formulate SMART objectives, improve process monitoring and put an end to diplomats' habit of declaring any outcome a success and deferring open questions unnoticed to future negotiations.

- UNFCCC has turned into a weird mixture of a 'political negotiation process' and a sort of 'technical implementing agency' for CC activities: the policy level has to be seconded by a well-staffed secretariat facilitating the negotiation process; with the mushrooming of bodies and working groups and increased funding, UNFCCC crosses the border to project implementation, but without the publicly scrutinised planning, monitoring, and evaluation structures applied e.g. by the ODA system. Does anybody really have control of this evolving system? Or a precise idea about the impact and outcome of additional instruments such as National Appropriate Mitigation Actions (NAMAs) (Würtenberger 2012; Yim 2013)? Even though seconded by nice tools (Lacy *et al.* 2012), these still follow a supply-driven top-down approach.
- Provided with 'own funds', for example through the GCF, disbursed according to criteria elaborated within the UNFCCC process, the 'climate silo' (Stone 2004; Lencioni 2006) becomes more independent, increasing the risks of institutional overlap with ODA structures through 'lighthouse projects' which are already common practice in development co-operation (e.g. energy-efficient stoves, solar pumps and lighting) (UNFCCC 2012[16]).

These issues are crucial for cost-effectiveness, even though the costs of the process never seem to be a problem: more concern for costs could trigger efficiency and prioritisation, for example in response to the question 'is the UNFCCC still doing the right things?' The insistence on a legally binding general agreement can also be taken as an indicator for the absence of a learning and evaluation mechanism and the conceptual trap in which the UNFCCC silo is locked (Marshall *et al.* 2011: 14–15): the way in which actors think (leaving out field experience) and create knowledge (in the 'spaceship' of air-conditioned conference rooms) limit the capacity to check its relevance for the 'real' world and step out of the box to acquire new perspectives. Global emissions, for example, may be looked at in a different way, i.e. not as the problem, but as the ultimate symptom of the (root) causes of CC: the unsustainable production and consumption patterns everywhere. The absence of such considerations indicates UNFCCC's distance to the SD concept: SD implies a profound reflection on the feasibility of the industrial growth society model, on rebound effects[17] (UNEP 2011: 259) which counteract partial decoupling of growth from resource use, and on technology transfer from industrialised countries as the panacea to CC. Answering the question of why the multitude of lighthouse projects are never scaled up could be a first step in the direction of a CRD approach.

The absence of progress also indicates a lack of energy in the UNFCCC system. The injection of money (GCF) will enhance the economic concerns of vested interest groups, increasing resistance to critical reflection, learning, and an eventual change of course. As long as the components of a system remain the same (the stakeholders and their interests), whatever additional structure, they can only produce similar outcomes.

Climate silo versus development co-operation: nobody wants to miss the CC 'train'

In addition to the institutions forming part of the expanding UNFCCC labyrinth, practically all ODA institutions undertake climate-related action: either by 'climate-proofing' of projects through a bureaucratic procedure, integrating CC issues into 'normal' development co-operation aiming at SD and poverty eradication, or as implementing agencies (IAs) for projects funded by the 'CC complex' (e.g. GIZ 2012a: 12). The risk of overlap, duplication, and even crowding-out is high. Conceptually, three options seem to exist:

1. Separate CC matters from the ODA business, which would lose importance, influence, and the opportunity to put to use for CC action the vast know-how and capabilities regarding development issues; in view of developing countries' interest in receiving the full 0.7 per cent GDP as ODA (even though not realistic, and eventually not necessary), and the lack of implementation capacity of actors from the environment silo, this is unlikely and inadvisable (errors would be repeated, but by others).
2. Display the socio-economic or pro-poor 'co-benefits' of CC action, which seems already underway (Crowe 2013; Blodgett *et al.* 2012: 27–30); this is an unclear option: if applied to private actors (e.g. CDM), the impact is limited by the chosen market approach; if applied within public projects (NAPA, NAMA), the boundary or relationship with development co-operation becomes rather blurred.
3. Mainstream CC into a joint CRD approach with ODA institutions, reinforced by CC funds, the experience of development co-operation, and the involvement of competent actors from outside the environment silo and the local levels; this could stimulate CC-related action and a profound rethinking of approaches, if looked at from a CRD perspective, instead of 'either' CC management 'or' pro-poor development.

Hence, there is a need for clarification of strategies and division of roles to ensure that (new) funds are applied efficiently and effectively, avoiding a too-narrow focus: for example on either mitigation or adaptation, on mitigation understood in a limited sense as renewable energy or just energy, or the application of mechanisms created by the UNFCCC, for example CDM, NAPA, NAMA, REDD+, for which countries lack implementation capacities and a CRD-oriented framework. The actual practice of commissioning projects to development co-operation IAs avoids the costly learning processes of climate silo actors, but enhances the economic interests of IAs to remain part of the UNFCCC silo:

existing approaches risk being reproduced (or relabeled) with new funding without critical reflection on whether these lead beyond CC management, aiming at a broader CRD strategy. It is also disputable whether IAs that explicitly pursue institutional growth (e.g. GIZ seeks to increase its turnover: GIZ 2012b[18]) can be change agents for CRD, where resilience and well-being, not growth, are the centre of attention.

However, only a combination of the CC and ODA 'worlds' can eventually lead to the development of CRD approaches, bottom up with partners, and the implementation of strategies, and not individual projects, which help to move forward in the right direction. But how can this happen? Fresh research and conceptual work is needed to answer this question. The discussions on revised MDGs and SDGs, described in Chapter 2, would be a good opportunity to take up the issue of CRD and institutional overlap. But how can this high-level exercise be turned into a bottom-up approach?

Creating energy for CC management oriented to CRD by dismounting the 'dead horse'

Taking the interests of involved actors more explicitly into account

The prevailing UN diplomatic negotiation style is often based on 'positions' repeated over and again, with the effect that key actors typically fall back to more rigid positions. According to the experience of coaching within change processes (Rock 2008; Walker 2011), the normal reaction to pressure or threat is that the body and brain will not be receptive to proposals, as they are geared to fight, freeze, or flee.

Stakeholders are often called 'egoistic' when clearly voicing their own interests; but those who claim ethical behaviour according to 'climate equity' and the 'right to development' deliberations are not interest-free either, as they align themselves with the postulations of developing countries' negotiators, adding power to these positions (Baer *et al.* 2008).

To avoid hidden agendas, the interests of negotiating parties need to be dealt with explicitly and in a productive way. Following the Harvard method, negotiation only makes sense as long as the expected results are superior to one's 'best alternative to a negotiated agreement' (BATNA) (Fisher and Ury 1981). In an interest-based 'negotiation culture', the individual BATNA would indicate the moment when it is better to walk away from negotiation, and consists of:

- a list of actions to be taken by oneself or one's interest group if no agreement is reached through negotiation;
- one's own promising ideas are developed sufficiently to serve as practical alternatives;
- these alternatives are prioritised.

The concept of principled negotiation according to the Harvard method comprises five steps:

1 Separate the people from the problem

Negotiators should consider participating parties as potential problem solvers, not as adversaries (Fisher and Ury 1981)! This excludes repeating statements on fixed positions, expressed in terms such as 'must', 'have to' in the UNFCCC process, and suggests that any ideas are assessed in view of their possible contribution to solving the problem; the question: 'What/how does this contribute to the resolution of the problem?' is often left out of sight.

2 Focus on interests, not on positions

When expressing own interests and listening carefully to understand the expressed interests (often hidden behind the positions) and trying to put oneself into the other party's shoes, common ground can be found as a start for the negotiation, thus sparing time and energy for fighting about (fixed) positions. Example: I do not make commitments now (position), because I want to avoid putting at risk my growth goals and the sovereignty over my development path (interest).

3 Invent options for mutual gains

The use of creativity techniques, like brainstorming (Buzan 1974), widens perspectives and increases chances for agreement on win–win opportunities. The generation and analysis of options should be separated from the decision about them.

4 Use 'objective' criteria for discussion and assessment of options

Using neutral criteria orients discussions towards the application of reason and logic and helps in revealing when the negotiated problem has disappeared or is reduced, by using, for example, statistics, scientific references, legal texts, recognised information, provable, eventually measurable or observable facts (photos), independent from the subjective positions of the parties. In this way, emotional battles can be avoided.

5 If an agreement can't be reached, step out of negotiation and realise the BATNA

Insisting on continuing negotiation (more of the same) where no agreement (e.g. on legally binding commitments) can be reached is a waste of energy. Principled negotiation also recommends paring down large groups as much as possible (Noble 2001: Rule 2.4). Three criteria can measure the success of a negotiation. It should: (1) produce a solid and acceptable agreement; (2) be efficient, with reasonable negotiation effort; and (3) improve, or at least not damage, the relationship between the negotiating parties.

Arguments, acts, and behaviour		Actors influencing the issue/problem	Type of contacts, communication, co-operation	Arguments, acts, and behaviour	
(Very)	Favourable			Neutral	Unfavourable
+ +	+	*Name/function*	*Description*	o	– – –

Figure 12.2 Force field analysis diagram

As the UNFCCC negotiations do not show a reasonable relationship of efforts/ costs and benefits/results, the application of the above-mentioned Step 5, implementation of BATNAs, would be an interesting, and to some extent, paradoxical, intervention.[19] Expressions that 'there is no alternative to the UNFCCC process' can indicate that negotiators have not developed a BATNA, depend on the process, and practise 'wishful thinking', instead of shaping negotiations (Michaelowna 2012; Bailer 2012). When coached professionally, parties can systematically analyse the progress regarding (their interests within) the negotiation, for example by applying methods such as 'force field analysis', and adapting their negotiation strategy accordingly (see Figure 12.2).

Treating the complex socio-political change process as a change management project

In the case of CC management, the journey to the ultimate objective is most important, as currently no blueprint for a climate-friendly model society or a clear joint vision of the future is available, beyond the agreement that the increase of global warming should be kept within the range of 2°C until end of the century compared to pre-industrial levels. The implementation of a successful change process is a complex undertaking as some of the involved actors usually prefer the status quo and resist change. Organisational development points to the need to go through predetermined steps to avoid the risk of stopping or the petering out of the process. The 'cycle of change' (Figure 12.3) based on Gestalt psychology'[20] (Matthew and Sayers 1999: Kürzinger and Miller 2009: 118) has proved to be a successful roadmap for guiding actors towards sustainable change.

Typical errors in change processes concerning the elements of the outer, substantive cycle include:

- jumping from (the supposed) recognition/understanding of the problem into the recommendation of measures, without properly analysing the causes (Step 3);
- exhausting all the energy of the parties through a too-detailed analysis of problems and their actual effects, before taking any action;

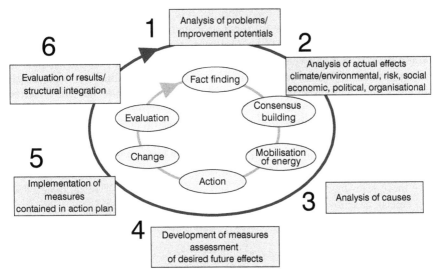

Figure 12.3 Cycle of change applied to CC management

- making either action plans for other actors (outside one's sphere of influence) or too complex plans that will never be implemented as they overstretch available energy;
- creating action plans without SMART objectives, success indicators, responsibilities, resources, i.e. lack a realistic orientation;
- finding 'culprits to blame for the problem', thus enhancing resistance to change, instead of 'objectively' analysing all possible causes (e.g. due to structure, processes, procedures, technologies, inputs, behaviour of involved persons, responsibilities, information flow, monitoring, reward system, etc.);
- not documenting the situation before – so the impact of the situation after (= results) cannot be quantified, visualised, and appreciated.

Notwithstanding the huge amount of information available, there seems to be a lack of consensus or weak common understanding of the different causes of GHG emissions. Experience has shown that a comprehensive cause analysis, which includes as many problem-related aspects as possible (technical, economic, social, and human), and the identification of root causes, makes the subsequent development of pertinent measures easy, which will, in principle, lead to the reduction or disappearance of the problem (Kürzinger and Miller 2009: 110f). An example of the negative impact of action based on limited analysis is the replacement of ozone-depleting substances (ODS) as described in Chapter 10.

The inner, more process-oriented cycle shows the necessary organisational steps to be worked through by all relevant stakeholders during each substantive step of the outer cycle. It is clear that, for example, the need to get consensus on each of the six steps, i.e. the facts, the effects, the causes, etc., makes a successful conclusion of the cycle rather impossible if too many actors with low impact on the problem, a low degree of ownership for it (e.g. 'developed countries' are the culprits and have to take the lead, not us!), and little or no contribution to the solutions are involved (e.g. US binding its own meagre contributions to China's commitments, and vice versa). The definition of the key actors and their reduction to a minimum is crucial for such a process to be successful. With increasingly larger CoPs, with everybody giving opinions, the opposite tendency can be observed.

Another aspect related to 'causes' and 'fact-finding' concerns data going beyond or below the 'country' perspective. According to Hertwich and Peters (2009: 6419), the data of the Inter-Governmental Panel on Climate Change (IPCC) is insufficient to reallocate standard emissions to the consumption activities that are more relevant for policy makers and mitigation. In their remarkable paper on emissions embedded within trade, these authors asserted that IPCC emission inventories

> do not reveal any information about what causes emissions; they only reveal that the emissions occur... Although international climate agreements may still be based around the standard IPCC emission inventory methods, the design of mitigation policy must consider the underlying drivers for emission. *Ultimately our daily consumption and production decisions drive global emissions.*

Following the steps of the cycle of change and using creativity techniques such as mind-mapping (Buzan 1974) might draw more attention to these aspects.

The term 'energy' refers to both the existing motivation and the availability of the financial, human, and organisational resources required for the implementation of a change project such as the 'successful management of climate change': for example increasing resource prices and setting efficiency-stimulating policy frameworks to modify the behaviour of major polluters and economic sectors, and organise adaptation. The term 'energy' can also be described as '*willingness and capacity for change*' for which David Gleicher has developed a very useful formula (Kürzinger and Miller 2009: 120ff; footnote 11):

$$C = f(a, b; d) > x$$

C = the energy for change
a = the degree of dissatisfaction with the status quo
b = the clear or publicly-announced desired future situation
d = the first practical steps into the direction of the desired future state (situation)
x = the 'costs' of change.

This formula suggests:

a   For change to take place (e.g. mitigation of emissions) and the necessary motivation to develop amongst relevant actors, there must be a sufficient degree of dissatisfaction with the status quo (=a); otherwise, the necessary energy for change cannot be mobilised (no pain, no change!). If pressure within the company, institution, or administration is not high enough or not perceived – for example from GHG emissions or CC – little can be moved, even if there is strong influence from scientific analysis, technical consultancy, political advocacy or pressure from NGOs, or even abundant (external) funds.

Looking at the different positions of the negotiating actors, there is no unanimous degree of dissatisfaction, or even dissatisfaction about the same aspects of CC due to:

- the interpretation of IPCC data differs depending on own interests, for example US, oil-exporting countries, emerging economies;
- the feeling of not being responsible for or not recognising the urgency of the global warming problem or its impact on oneself, in view of the historical debts of others and more urgent 'development needs';
- the perception of being a victim of CC, thus having only a partial interest: for example countries with low fossil emissions demanding financial support for adaptation;
- different aspects of dissatisfaction blocking each other, evident through finger pointing at who should act first, as in the already-cited conflict between the US and emerging economies.

b   A change process will only be successful if there is also a clear perception of the future situation after successfully implementing change (=b).

A 'joint vision' of the desired future situation has hardly been developed amongst major stakeholders, less among all parties, for a situation when GHG emissions are kept below a certain level, renewable resources are widely used, consumption and production patterns are modified, etc. (WEF 2012). Even though numerous specific examples are available on how to consume, produce, cultivate, transport, and so on with less emissions in specific situations, caring about sinks and changing to renewable resources, these are not widely accepted nor practised. Actual consumption patterns in emerging economies (rapidly increasing numbers of big cars, sport utility vehicles) and carbon-intensive technologies generated in industrialised countries do not indicate a climate-sensitive development. The structural differences between the EU and US in CC management demonstrate the lack of a joint vision for a climate-compatible society and the consensus on how to get there. The Copenhagen Accord to limit global warming to 2°C is probably too vague to trigger energy for concrete action on a large scale.

d   Only if the first successful measures (=d) are also implemented by using clear, manageable, realistic action plans, will the process move from (a) to (b), that is, the implementation of change will start and successful action will create additional energy to undertake continuous improvement by following the cycle again.

Concerning UNFCCC, to date, concrete action is too selective to be easily recognisable, or limited to CDM or 'lighthouse projects' that are not generally replicated or scaled up (see Chapter 9). On the contrary, new sources of fossil fuels and climate-negative practices, such as 'shale gas fracking', are spreading[21] (Harvey 2012; Hunt 2012) without being addressed by a negotiation system busy with illusionary reduction targets. Little energy, if at all, will be created unless the process is put onto another track, for example through creative instruments like the Yasuní–ITT initiative (Chapter 8) and by fostering a change in mindset, for example by looking at high individual emitters instead of average per capita emission data.

The assumption that the implementation needs to achieve the (often general) objectives is easily done, but is contradicted by the experience from development co-operation and organisational development: complex change processes that involve many actors with conflicting interests need facilitation or coaching (Kürzinger and Miller 2009: 109f) to be accomplished; the 'support' by (proliferating) guidelines (Lacy *et al.* 2012; Blodgett *et al.* 2012; International Renewable Energy Agency 2012) cannot substitute support for experiential learning to ensure the transfer of learning to one's own reality.

x Last but not least, change has a cost ($=x$): either material (e.g. investment) or immaterial (e.g. lasting modification of consumption habits, mobility behaviour, production patterns, information flows, co-operation, etc.). If the cost incurred by the relevant stakeholders exceeds the energy resulting from the above-mentioned factors (a), (b), and (d), then no change will happen. Usually no change takes place without a cost-sharing scheme that is acceptable to the parties involved.

Looking at the UNFCCC system, there is no general agreement on the costs and burden-sharing: referring to the 'historical debt' of industrialised countries, the self-acclaimed 'victims of CC' discard responsibility for (co-)financing (own) action; fast-growing emerging economies favour baselines that consider any investment as 'incremental costs' and CC action of low priority according to the 'development comes first' principle.

Even though the Gleicher formula of energy for change (Beckhard 1969) is not a mathematical function, conceptually, there is a major problem if the value for any of the variables is zero (when summing up the individual energy levels of the stakeholders). In view of the limited progress made and generalised frustration expressed, the UNFCCC would have to consider if and how one or several of the factors in the equation could be modified to increase the probability of implementing change.

To 'energise' the change process and reorient it towards CRD, a general moratorium with the following objectives/outcomes would be helpful to:

• assess the major factors for the lack of energy through self-assessment by the involved players and external evaluation by actors that are not part of the UNFCCC 'silo';
• determine what works well as a basis for a new UNFCCC track, for example by using methods such as Appreciative Inquiry (Haussmann and Scholz 2007);

- foster implementation of 'no regret' policies and measures by all 'willing actors', which will successfully trigger best practices and the general up-scaling of low-carbon technologies.

The way forward to climate-resilient management: changing track by changing perspectives

Stepping out of the North–South trap

The promise of more financial resources to developing countries is less realistic than ever in view of the prevailing financial crisis and acceptance problems of electorate and middle-income taxpayers: German politicians have already reacted to protests against the cost of the 'energy U-turn' by cutting subsidies for renewable energy feed-in tariffs referring to low-income households. Developing countries need to avoid a self-destructive attitude towards CC and increase ownership for their own development. Emerging economies retain untapped capacities to self-finance development (Haldenwang 2011). According to Furness *et al.* (2012), it is unclear whether the sizable (high- and) middle-income classes will play the constructive role expected of them in shaping the path to CRD. This chance will be lost if they do not provide room for the well-being of their poor population by improving income distribution and assigning emission margins (provided by industrialised countries) to the satisfaction of basic needs (access to clean energy, transport, and natural resources) and squander them by uncritically adopting industrialised countries' consumption (and production) patterns. As middle classes rise the quickest and are the biggest in countries like China and India, their chosen development paths are of utmost importance for pursuing CRD (Galli *et al.* 2012; UNDP 2013).

   Some positions that claim justice and equality for developing nations and their poor do not take the above-mentioned risk into account and apply a too narrow 'climate = emission' view, which loses sight of the broader perspective of SD to which all countries have committed themselves (Baer *et al.* 2008):

- Even though there may be a 'right to development', in a globalised world this can hardly mean getting external finance *and* a 'free pass' to repeat the (now recognised) errors already committed by others (GHG emissions), following a development path that does not apply the lessons about consumption of non-renewable resources, emissions, and alternative best practice.
- In addition, there are a number of possible criteria for distribution of emission rights: generational justice as such is undisputed; however, the Responsibility Capacity Index proposed by Baer *et al.* (2008) seems not in line with a sustainability principle (using not more resources than nature can re-create) and can invite moral hazards.

   According to Tavoni *et al.* (2012: 217; 221f), the position of 'getting the same emission rights' is not a good indicator for justice, as the interest should be a comparable welfare level, which can be achieved with less energy and emission intensity, using policies and technologies that will evolve over time into a less carbon-intensive development. As this can require less than the 'theoretical' emission rights accorded to developing regions, 'priority must be given to reducing emissions associated with any given level of human welfare' (ibid.: 222). In addition, a CRD approach needs metrics other than GDP, which does not measure well-being or sustainability but economic activity only (Waddock and McIntosh 2011: 32).

Changing perspectives: individual high emitters and embedded emissions

Chakravarty *et al.* (2009) show a way out of the 'North-offender' versus 'South-victim' discourse by changing perspective: analysing which actors contribute individually most to GHG emissions (using emission and income distribution data). Thus 'common, but differentiated responsibilities' to reduce emissions are derived from individuals' emissions, and not from aggregated national data on emissions and average per capita income. In view of available data on income distribution, it is astonishing that this has not already been considered.

These researchers propose to allocate national targets for CO_2 emissions derived from identified 'high emitters', who exceed a universal individual emission cap based on several overall emission restriction scenarios. Their most interesting findings are:

- Individual high emitters are relatively evenly distributed in four main regions: US, 270 million persons; China, 300 million; non-OECD countries minus China, 280 million; OECD minus US, 280 million.
- The results do not change much when a poverty-related component is introduced, i.e. a floor of 1t CO_2 yearly for the lowest emitters (e.g. diesel engine to provide primary lighting, TV, charging batteries; liquefied petroleum gas (LPG) for cooking, etc. where these technologies are the least cost options for poor people): mitigating emissions and covering the basic energy needs of the poor are nearly decoupled.
- The universal emission cap (of 30 Gt CO_2 in 2030) achieves equity and fairness in the sense that:
  – countries with a larger proportion of high emitters will do more for mitigation;
  – countries with similar emission profiles will have similar commitments independent of the 'developing' or 'developed' country status.
- The US and China have the highest abatement assignments.
- Africa has to take up mitigation assignments, due to South Africa's and Northern African countries' carbon intensity; the same applies for Russia and the Middle East (energy production).

Surprisingly, the recent (missing) literature does not indicate that this interesting perspective has been assimilated. Shifting the focus from the national averages of emissions to the individual level and 'high emitters' in all countries might not be appreciated by some of the emerging economies; but this can help to overcome the North–South impasse by addressing the carbon-intensive behaviour of high emitters and the underlying unsustainable consumption and production patterns in all societies, thus increasingly addressing mitigation and climate resilience everywhere.

Trade plays a major role in creating emissions (Dittrich and Bringezu 2010; Dittrich *et al*. 2012) and the role of consumers in demanding low-carbon products and services has not been sufficiently mobilised. The study of 'emissions embodied in trade' (Davis and Caldera 2010) indicates that when looking at net import and export of emissions, a certain decoupling of population and emissions will occur: readjusting emissions would add to the data for the EU, Japan, and US, and reduce those from China, Russia, India, and the Middle East.

However, to allocate the net export of emissions only to the recipient country of the products might give an undesired indication of what policies to develop in net importing countries. For example, the EU, the US, and Japan could alternatively produce quite a few of the products nowadays imported, eventually re-employing some of the unemployed workforce (official average around 10 per cent);[22] consumers could also become more critical about product quality, non-essential products, and lower social and environmental production standards in the countries of origin. The possible effects on growth, employment, income, consumption, and foreign currency generated by these exports in the countries of origin, like China and India, could be important and trigger discussions about national markets, income distribution, and even of politics.

Concerning emissions embedded in products and services, Acquaye *et al*. (2010) studied the construction sector. Embodied energy is the total energy required to produce a product (such as a building) and can represent a significant portion of the energy required throughout the lifecycle: for residential buildings up to 40 per cent (Chen *et al*. 2001); for unoccupied infrastructure, like bridges and motorways, up to 90 per cent.

Policy measures applicable in most countries comprise:

- information tools like eco-labelling schemes based on life-cycle assessment for buildings (Acquaye *et al*. 2010: 9 for US, UK, Hong Kong); after slight adaptation, these are applicable at low or no cost to new constructions, leading to savings of around 25 per cent compared to business-as-usual (BAU) scenarios (Acquaye *et al*. 2010: 11);
- regulatory tools, such as the definition of minimum standards, can save at a modest cost: 25–30 per cent of embodied energy according to a study on new apartment buildings in Ireland (Acquaye *et al*. 2010: 11); projected to the EU level, this would reduce 3.5 per cent of the total EU-27 emissions and be equivalent to saving €2 billion in carbon credits.

In China, the building sector is very important but mostly not even best available technologies (BATs) are taken into account for minimising operational emissions related to heating/cooling and powering. Generally just 'concrete carcasses' are provided for subsequent outfitting by the owners: cutting holes into the walls to install air conditioning and heating, thus creating emissions through 'energy bridges' in each room. This is light years away from ecological construction which takes into account passive heating/cooling and use of renewable energy.

The argument of eventual higher costs is unconvincing as these buildings are mostly occupied by middle- or high-income classes who can afford them; the private sector is able to incorporate climate-related costs within production costs, just aligning profit margins and payback periods with levels considered 'normal' in industrialised countries. Thus, the actual construction in emerging economies offers an important 'no regret option': to tap the huge energy (and emissions) saving potential from operation (at least 20–30 per cent), and from embodied energy (an additional 25 per cent) related to maintenance, demolition, and construction.

Guiding principles for resource use conducive to CRD

The UNFCCC process, as well as the discussion on SD, seem to have forgotten the work done in the 1990s by environmental economists (Costanza *et al.* 1997) on principles for resource use which help to 'live sustainably and well but within the material limits of a finite planet', also stating 'that we cannot grow into sustainability' (Goodland 1995: 5).

Using 'Bartletts' law' (relating to sustainability and hypotheses about the actual development path), the concept of material 'throughput' covering sources *and* sinks, and the definition of 'environmental sustainability' lead to rules for resource use (Goodland 1995: 10):

- *Output rule*: waste emissions should be kept within the assimilative capacity of the local environment.
- *Input rules*: (1) harvest rates of *renewable* resources should be kept within regenerative capacities of the respective natural system; (2) depletion rates of *non-renewable* resource inputs should be set below the rate at which renewable substitutes are developed (invention, investment). A portion of revenues from non-renewable resources should be allocated to researching sustainable substitutes.
- *Operational principles*: (1) the scale of the human economic subsystem (resultant from population, consumption per capita and technology) should be sustainable, i.e. within the carrying capacity; (2) technology development should be efficiency-increasing, not throughput-increasing; (3) renewable resources should be exploited on a sustainable basis (sustained yield, profit-optimising).

Goodland (1995: 16) also recommended applying three rules for rebuilding natural capital stocks: (1) foster the regeneration of natural capital (e.g. by allowing soils to fully regenerate); (2) relieve pressure on natural capital (e.g. by minimising pollution, waste, and resource depletion); and (3) improve efficiency

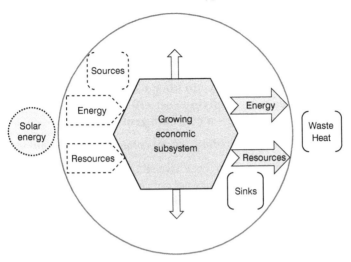

Figure 12.4 Resource use in a finite world ecosystem

Source: based on Costanza *et al.* 1997

in the use of natural capital (increased end-use efficiency, extended life cycle, durability, recyclability, and overall production efficiency).

Even though well known, this is hardly applied in practice. 'Climate-proofing' tools in development co-operation (BMU and BMZ 2011: 13, 30–31), even though a start, are far too superficial to capture the impact of projects on resource use and even less to give guidance for making these rules part of the planning and implementation process. Environmental Impact Assessments (EIAs) and Strategic Environmental Assessments (SEAs) (OECD 2012)[23] help, in this sense, to assess the impact of projects or policies that hamper or foster the application of the above-mentioned principles, but are not able to ensure their observation, especially when stakeholder dialogue, negotiations, and policy change are needed.

Notwithstanding progress regarding the use and development of renewable resources, attention is too narrowly focused on energy due to the absence of a CRD perspective: negative side effects on agriculture (Grenz *et al.* 2011) and ecosystems result from the sale of residues, which formerly enhanced the quality of topsoil, and of crops for energy generation (biofuels). Farmers can earn more income from selling biomass than practising sustainable farming; in developing countries, the scaling up of these 'energy crops' risks having a negative impact on (1) food crops, hence livelihoods, especially of the poor; (2) forests, if tropical forest is turned into palm oil plantations, for example in Malaysia; and 3) topsoil and health, for example chemical-intensive sugar cane monocultures in Brazil. There is also the risk of not fully exploiting the potential for increasing efficiency through the use of non-renewable resources, even though the Green Economy discussion and persevering work by institutions, like the World Business Council on Sustainable Development (WBCSD), to promote RE has helped to prepare the ground for a general up-scaling of respective activities in the near future, fostering SD and CRD respectively. RE is defined as 'the relation of a desired output of a process to the related resource requirement or input' (Wuppertal Institute and UBA 2008: 101).

If you can't do the necessary, do the possible (and profitable): increasing resilience by applying cost-effective 'no regret' measures on a large scale – a common ground

Generalised application of existing climate-conducive innovation

'(Nearly) Everything has already been invented, but not by everybody, and not in all places.' Unfortunately, this somewhat cynical statement is confirmed frequently when politicians, environmentalists, and development co-operation staff miss the forest for the trees, not simply up-scaling the huge number of relevant methods already available, and instead commissioning 'innovation' from consultants and scientists. A less hardware-based concept of innovation is useful to avoid this (see Figure 12.5):

- Through innovation options 1 and 2 (which might cover 50 per cent or more of any 'innovation'), developing countries will be able, with local human and financial resources, to increase resource and energy efficiency substantially and cost-effectively; this type of innovation also provides benefits for industrialised countries with low energy- and resource-efficiency levels.
- The development of new packages (option 3) needs adaptation to local conditions and learning from others' experiences, which is best achieved in co-operation with mostly (modest) technical assistance and few funds, and might cover another 30–40 per cent of innovation.
- Only innovation option 4 (invention), which is mostly sought but not very common (up to 5 per cent), requires substantial funding for development of know-how, technologies, and human resources.

It would be 'innovative', and even 'revolutionary', if outdated and uneconomic practices, such as fixed heating periods, lack of meters for charging consumers according to real consumption, and of control devices for radiators and by applying

Complexity		
2 Refinement innovations Adaptation of existing policies, management tools, technologies, experiences, to specific requirements (local conditions, target groups)	**4 New products (invention)** Develop new policies, management tools, technologies, experiences
1 Adoption innovations Apply existing policies, management tools, technologies, experiences in own context	**3 New packages (synergies)** Combination of existing policies, management tools, technologies, experiences into a new package
Creativity		

Figure 12.5 Four types of innovation

innovation type 1 measures, low or subsidised energy prices could be brought up to at least European standards. Experimenting with 'lighthouse projects' is only justifiable if they can be scaled up, thus improving BAU and avoiding the actual tendency to not fully exploit the huge potential of innovation types 1–3 even in industrialised countries.

Systemic perspective: integrating energy into a concept of RE

When talking about climate, energy consumption is generally at the centre, not taking into account that:

- direct energy use is only a fraction of total energy embedded in production and services;
- inefficient resource use also causes GHG emissions;
- only high economic saving potential (summing up energy and resource efficiency) makes change attractive for consumers and producers.

The Non-Product Output (NPO) concept helps to identify most blind spots in RE (Figure 12.6). NPO refers to 'all raw materials, water and energy (= resources) that are used in the production (or service) process, but do not end up in the final product desired by the client' (Kürzinger 2012: 54).[24]

The full costs of companies' 'blind spots', commonly representing 10 to 30 per cent (even up to 50 per cent) of production costs, are mostly overlooked as Controlling does not quantify them. By using 'NPO glasses', RE can easily be increased (1–3 measures/four-day training), and overall profit is usually raised by 1–3 per cent within six to eight months, also decreasing the respective emissions. Combining elements from Quality, Environment, and Change Management, NPO can have the forms or costs as shown in Box 12.1.

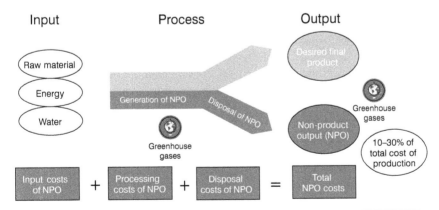

Figure 12.6 NPO: tapping the blind spots of resource efficiency

Box 12.1 Types of NPO leading to inefficient resource use

- Unqualified raw materials and all consumables
- Rejects, off-specification products (any type), and respective reprocessing (costs)
- Waste (solid, liquid, toxic, non-toxic)
- Waste water (amount, degree of contamination) = all water not contained in the final product
- Energy: all coal, steam, electricity, oil, diesel, fuel, waste heat (unless product is warm/charged)
- Emissions to air, including noise, odours, GHGs

- Losses during all handling, transport, storage
- Packaging material (unless for perfumes or similar products)
- Client reclamations and trade returns
- Losses due to lack of maintenance
- Losses due to accidents or health/environmental problems
- Virtual NPO: capacities occupied by reprocessing/machine downtimes (opportunity costs)

Figure 12.7 shows the impact on RE from a sample of 300 companies that applied the NPO concept through PREMA® training (Kürzinger 2004a, 2004b):[25]

- 85 per cent of the improvements had an impact on RE; 79 per cent direct or indirectly (related to production or transport) on GHG emissions.
- A limitation to energy efficiency would have resulted in only one fourth (22 per cent) of the results.
- Additional organisational benefits comprise optimised material flow, work processes, communication and cooperation, clear responsibilities, cleaner working place, and higher motivation.
- Safety effects included improved management of risk and chemicals, working conditions, hygiene, and compliance with legislation.

PREMA® programmes in five Chinese cities (SEPA 2004; GIZ-ZHB n.d.; GTZ n.d.) showed the enormous potential for RE: up-scaling of only three of the results, 30 per cent reduction in energy consumption, 20 per cent in water, and 8 per cent in steel consumption on average, would have a significant impact on resource consumption, GHG emissions (15 per cent less), and even price (steel). Chinese companies could finance the full training costs by a small fraction of their savings and comply with the National Cleaner Production law, as PREMA®-Environment-oriented Cost Management (EoCM®) is one of the accredited tools (Hicks and Dietmar 2007).The NPO concept itself could reinforce RE aspects of other tools such as Cleaner Production, or turn the International Organization for Standardization (ISO; management standards 14001, 9001, 8000, 22000) bottom up into a 'profitable, resource-efficient ISO' (Kürzinger 2012: 50, 57). Even in industrialised countries, this approach is important as, for example, in Germany, the average percentage of raw material costs in 2008 was 45 per cent, in general twice the share of labour cost (18 per cent) (BMU 2011: 9).

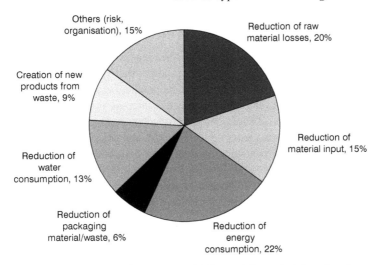

Figure 12.7 Type of PREMA® measures yielding 'triple+ wins' benefits for resource efficiency

Management improvements come first! The untapped potential of (learning by) doing things differently

The examples from the application of good practice achieved through PREMA® (Profitable Resource Efficiency Management) training in 300 companies in 22 countries and some 50 sectors also show that significant climate-friendly innovation can be triggered cost-effectively as 'no regret' through management practices improved by training and coaching programmes. Eighty per cent of the measures raised RE by improving processes and use of existing facilities; only 17 per cent needed (minor) investment in technology change, usually BAT accessible to the companies through normal market mechanisms without external support.

In the absence of maintenance, even the latest technology will not be used at its optimum. Thus, improving management is crucial for quick and 'no regret' increases in RE and reduction of emissions. Also, from an economic perspective these mostly management-induced improvements are 'no regret' measures: 25 per cent had an immediate payback, 30 per cent in less than six months, and only 13 per cent over 12 months (but under two years); regarding investment, 25 per cent needed no investment, 35 per cent less than US$1000, and only 15 per cent required US$10,000 or more. Depending on the size of the company and the measures, the annual net savings (average US$20,000 per measure) ranged from US$1000 (25 per cent) to over US$50,000 (7 per cent). A company usually implements three to five measures (up to 10) during the training and consultancy period (Kürzinger 2012: 55).

Putting one's own house in order first: top runner and sector approaches as 'no regret' on the way to CRD

Enjoying today's benefits of a globalised world requires applying the lessons from yesterday's bad practice, thus avoiding errors committed by others. The scaling up of cost-efficient 'no-regret' policies, management practices, and technologies is a must (Birkeland 2002). For developing countries, the increase in RE (including energy), and consequent reduction of emissions and production costs, provides an opportunity to increase competitiveness, leapfrog technologies and practices in using renewable resources, and reduce dependency on dwindling non-renewable resources, while reaping tangible socio-economic benefits from this interpretation of 'the joint, but differentiated responsibilities'. This also applies to industrialised countries.

From policies which have proven effective we highlight only two examples.

Top runner approaches: striving for excellence

The Top Runner Programme created in 1998 by the Japanese Ministry of Economy, Trade, and Industry (METI 2010) as part of the New Energy Conservation Law for improving energy efficiency in energy-using products addressed 21 product groups:

- The current highest efficiency rate of the products in each sub-group were taken as standard (top runner).
- This had to be achieved in a certain time frame by all producers.
- When a large proportion of the producers had reached the standard, it was adjusted to a higher level.

This approach achieved efficiency improvements of 50 to 70 per cent in a short time period. It could be replicated in most countries, eventually combined with minimum standards and/or consumer information instruments, such as product labels (Bunse *et al.* 2007) etc., and could be stepped up by expanding the energy efficiency orientation to a comprehensive RE approach.

Environmental Fiscal Reform: a sound basis for CRD

Environmental Fiscal Reform (EFR) refers to a range of taxation and pricing measures that can free up economic resources and/or generate revenues while helping to reach environmental goals. EFR's underlying rationale is to correct false price signals in the economy by using the following instruments:

- taxation of resource exploitation;
- subsidies for and taxes on products;
- taxation of environmentally harmful emissions;
- user fees and charges for disposal;
- reduction of product and other subsidies.

The implementation of EFR can have four major benefits, which are interlinked and mutually reinforcing:

1 *Environmental:* addressing environmental problems that threaten the livelihoods and health of the poor, improving the RE of all stakeholder activities, including sustainable use of natural resources;
2 *Economic*: reducing abatement costs of negative environmental impacts and generating revenues that can finance efficient and cost-effective (environmental) services;
3 *Social:* decreasing negative environmental impacts, especially on vulnerable groups, and financing access of the poor to water, sanitation, and energy; leveraging labour costs;
4 *Structural*: contributing to good governance (World Bank 2005; Cottrell *et al.* 2011).

EFR is a comprehensive 'no-regret' approach that gets the price framework right and might make costly feed-in tariffs for renewable energy unnecessary.

No-regret sector approaches for increased RE

In addition to the RE results described above by applying the NPO approach, the project on 'Carbon Footprint in Small- and Medium-Sized Enterprises (SME) in Developing Countries' (Kürzinger and Aguilar 2010; CSCP n.a.) underlined through its pilot application in Mexico's automotive sector that:

- The transport sector contributes some 20 per cent to global emissions.
- A 5 per cent reduction in assembly-related emissions would save at least 100kg of CO_2 per vehicle.
- Second tier producers (SMEs) and their RE potential had been neglected so far.
- The high potential for reducing material intensity, with the respective reduction in NPO cost and GHG emissions, can be tapped by redesigning and re-engineering parts, de-materialising and de-carbonising the automotive industry.

However, the work with SMEs also showed that the automotive sector has some features that are not conducive to easily trigger the reduction of embedded energy and resource use/NPO:

- Final assembly companies demand far-reaching disclosure of production costs from preferred SME providers and any cost savings; in the absence of a benefit-sharing approach this discourages SMEs' initiatives to increase RE.
- The final consumer has no idea about a variety of exaggerated 'quality' requirements invented by a 'luxury' sector that simply passes orders down the value chain, affecting RE: for example one specific type of grey colour

(according to the RAL colour scheme) for coated metal parts (to be installed under the bonnet).

- While global sourcing and cost-cutting were fostered by the application of the same standards, documentation methods, and management tools in the sector, these leave little room for creative 'out-of-the-box thinking'. The future will demand new approaches centring on RE and low carbon mobility.

Common ground no regrets: the possible role for UNFCCC

EFR and top runner approaches are examples of 'no-regret' measures, whose profitable and generalised application makes sense at all levels, and could be encouraged by UNFCCC through an innovative and lean 'endorsement mechanism' and specific capacity-building provided by competent ODA institutions.

The automotive industry illustrated the potential of sector-wide approaches in highly GHG emitting sectors: usually 8 to 10 main actors are responsible for at least 80 per cent of the carbon footprint of the respective sector and/or country. As the negotiation with producers at country level were not very successful (e.g. the EU), a modified UNFCCC process could help to overcome the sector's resistance to change: concise sector-specific negotiations in a small technical group at the global level could help to trigger agreements, for example on the reduction of car size, fuel consumption, and mobility concepts conducive to CRD; thus emissions saved on one side of the world by smaller and more efficient cars (e.g. the EU) would not be over-compensated by sales of carbon-intensive models on the other side (e.g. India and China).

Similar support to sector approaches makes sense for the fossil fuels-producing sectors to preserve these non-renewable resources (applying sustainability principles explained above), for example by:

- encouraging production efficiency by applying the NPO/RE concept to oil, gas, and coal extraction and processing;
- labelling of oil and gas products according to environmental impact and embedded GHG emissions to encourage consumer demand for 'greener products', for example from sources that do not flare gas or use fracking (Aitgen *et al.* 2013);
- negotiating, at global level, basic standards for 'sustainable' production and products in these sectors, including investment of part of the revenues in the development of renewable energy;
- encouraging governments to convert price benefits from decreased demand (due to higher RE) into revenues to be invested locally in CRD measures;
- considering in a systematic way how to foster measures that leave fossil fuels unexploited (see Chapter 8).

Agriculture and food production also offer opportunities to support national efforts to reduce emissions and increase availability of food by avoiding waste, for example by:

- encouraging biological/low carbon production methods;
- endorsing best practice in storage and transport to avoid harvest and post-harvest losses (Hoffmann 2011);
- communicating proven climate-resilient farming schemes;
- negotiating specific issues to overcome resistance at a national level, for example to reduce the enormous quantities of food waste from supermarkets (e.g. in the EU).

Conclusions: (how to decide) what is right in future?

An external evaluation from an organisational management vantage point (see endnote 1) by practitioners coming from outside the climate silo would be necessary to assess achievements and failures, step out of the box and acquire new perspectives. For example, global emissions should be looked at in a different way, i.e. not as the *problem*, but as the ultimate *symptom* of the (root) causes of CC: the unsustainable production and consumption patterns everywhere which would bring CC back to the larger concept of SD.

The generalised application of the described cost-effective working methods and changing focus of the ICR could lead to new paths towards CRD:

- implementation of the subsidiarity principle: developing lean political endorsement mechanisms for genuine bottom-up processes, local and national good practice, and supporting scaling up successful approaches instead of 'lighthouse projects';
- shift of attention to the negotiation of the implementation of sustainable resource use principles, starting with a few globally important emitters, such as car manufacturers, construction, fossil fuels, and the agriculture and food sectors to achieve massive application of known RE best practice and investment of part of the revenues in R&D for switching to renewable resources;
- support for scaling up low-carbon practice and strategies to generalised practice at national levels through innovative, lean mechanisms based on research and successful examples following the concept: 'think and act locally – endorse, support, and communicate internationally';
- generation of different data needed for a new orientation, for example on individual high emitters, embedded emissions, sustainability indicators: this should be fostered by a down-to-earth research programme that brings together and complements the work done over the past 20 years on these issues;
- application of the cycle of change to differently define the relevant content for the next phase of CC management, with external facilitation, mobilising the 'energy for change' to address them; this could also mean integrating some type of exposure to the real world into the ICR process, for example holding meetings near the affected target groups, under their living conditions;
- development of an effective yet lean system for systematic learning and evaluation, as well as a mechanism that avoids overlap and creates synergies

with development co-operation: this would require some concept development and research to avoid the creation of new institutions.

We do not need 'new institutions', as stated by UNDP in its recent *Human Development Report* (UNDP 2013: IV), but we need different institutions: we need to analyse which of the too many processes could be stopped in view of the meagre outcomes (on the basis of an evaluation, organisational or institutional analysis) and how the others can be improved. This should be the outcome of a 'moratorium' for profound stocktaking, reflection, and reorientation of the UNFCCC process, widening perspectives to CRD by integrating livelihoods' support with CC adaptation and mitigation at the local level, and starting to implement SD principles (e.g. of resource use).

Finally, we need to change track with respect to three essential points:

1   We cannot grow into sustainability (Goodland (1995: 5): we need to start applying rules for sustainable resource use now.
2   GDP measures economic activities, but not sustainability (Waddock and McIntosh 2011: 32): the transition from a 'green growth' BAU process towards the well-being that sustainable CRD should bring about for the majority of people requires sustainability metrics that show whether we are advancing in the right direction.
3   Finally, ' in order to think differently, we also need to engage differently with the world in practice ... we need to question the ground we stand on' (Marshall *et al.* 2011: 6).

It is a major task for all involved actors to foster a 'resilient' CC management that is open to change, with joint visions and clear objectives, cost-efficient functions and inclusive structures, effective feedback loops, and the ability to self-organise, learn, and adapt (see Chapter 2). Otherwise, we will waste the energy so much needed for advancing towards a climate-resilient sustainable development for all people.

Notes

1   'Change': make or become different (http://oxforddictionaries.com/definition/english/change); 'a continuous adaptation of (company) strategies and structures to altering frame conditions' (adapted from: http://wirtschaftslexikon.gabler.de/Stichwort-Ergebnisseite.jsp.). 'Change management' is an 'intentional', 'facilitated' (or if 'planned': project management) organisational process which supports involved actors to develop from a current, unsatisfactory state to a desired future state, maximising benefits and minimising negative change impacts and costs (own definition evolved from various sources). For change we need to think, act, learn differently, and be open to continuous open inquiry (Marshall *et al.* 2011: 7–8). Change can imply many issues: organisation, communication, co-operation, motivation, behaviour, attitudes, processes, technologies, etc.
2   Organisational learning needs three types of learning addressed by the questions: are we doing things right? (single loop learning); are we doing the right things? (double loop learning); how do we decide what is right? (triple loop learning).

3 Unfortunately, most of the arguments stemming from my own experiences are still as valid as in Kürzinger (1998).

4 A well-researched interesting article in Wikipedia http://en.wikipedia.org/wiki/ Developed_country (accessed 21.01.2013) cites on page 1 plausible sources that this term is not even a well-defined UN term, but just used for 'statistical convenience'!

5 This is an idea I also shared when participating in the German Development Institute's (GDI) research programme on 'Industrial development in advanced developing countries' like Argentina, India, Korea, and Saudi Arabia; e.g. Kürzinger (1988).

6 Poor engagement by the US to mitigate its tremendous emissions is not an example of 'development'; the global financial crisis demonstrated that even a good ranking according to the Human Development Index (HDI) does not necessarily relect a good development level (e.g. Greece 29th: http://hdrstats.undp.org/en/countries/profiles/ GRC.html (accessed 20.03.2013).

7 SMART objectives should be specific, measurable, achievable, realistic, time-bound and formulated as if already done, e.g. 'the terms of reference were applied' and not just 'elaborated' or 'will be developed'.

8 The Democracy Index of the Economist considers that less than 50 per cent of 167 states studied can be considered as democratic or semi-democratic: https://www.eiu. com/public/topical_report.aspx?campaignid=DemocracyIndex2011 and http://www. eiu.com/Handlers/WhitepaperHandler.ashx?fi=Democracy_Index_2011_Updated.pd f&mode=wp&campaignid=DemocracyIndex2011 (accessed 27.02.2013).

9 *UN Launches New Centre to Accelerate Use of Technology in Tackling Climate Change*, online: http://unep.org/newscentre/Default.aspx?DocumentID=2704&Artic leID=9418&l=en (accessed 21.03.2013).

10 As an ex-negotiator of these issues, I could hardly believe what I read on the UNFCCC website in this respect: http://unfccc.int/cooperation_and_support/technology/items/1126. php (accessed 09.03.2013).

11 Since 2008 the GIZ portfolio for environment, climate, and biodiversity has increased by a factor of 2.5, the climate portfolio by a factor of 12; acquisition of readiness funds for NAMA and GCF (Paulus 2012: 7) support 'The Path to Growth – Tapping New Markets' (GIZ 2012b: 21).

12 Since 2008, the Federal Ministry for the Environment, Nature Conservation and Nuclear Safety (BMU) can use €120 million per year for its climate projects in the frame of the International Climate Initiative; http://www.bmu-klimaschutzinitiative. de/en/results (accessed 16.03.2013).

13 *DAC Criteria for Evaluating Development Assistance*, online: http://www.oecd.org/dac/ evaluation/daccriteriaforevaluatingdevelopmentassistance.htm (accessed 18.03.2013).

14 For the latest format for project progress reviews used by GIZ see: http://www.giz.de/ de/ueber_die_giz/519.html (accessed 21.03.2013).

15 http://www.oecd.org/dac/peer-reviews/ (accessed 18.03.2013).

16 Only one of the nine projects described is in my view a real lighthouse project: 'Carbon for Water'.

17 Rebound effect: the additional consumption of resources/energy, which is facilitated by resulting decrease in resource prices and can over-compensate the achieved higher resource efficiency/product (Ullrich 2012: 12).

18 The following slogans show the institutional growth-orientation: 'Six initiatives for growth' (pp. 12–13); 'GIZ is boldly pursuing its path to growth' (p. 36); 'Business development GIZ-style' (pp. 6–7).

19 A paradox intervention refers to recommending the opposite of what the party actually wants to achieve, e.g. through a mediator. By this, the parties are prevented from doing 'more of the same', which could be very useful in situations where the resistance to change prevails or where change is blocked.

20 Gestalt: 'essence or shape of an entity's complete form'.

21 http://oilprice.com/Energy/Natural-Gas/How-the-US-Shale-Boom-Will-Change-the-World.html (accessed 21.01.2013); http://www.instituteforenergyresearch.org/energy-overview/oil-shale/ (accessed 21.01.2013); *Gas 'fracking' gets green light, The Guardian*, http://www.guardian.co.uk/environment/2012/apr/17/gas-fracking-gets-green-light, http://en.wikipedia.org/wiki/Oil_shale (accessed 21.01.2013); *How the US Shale Boom Will Change the World*: http://oilprice.com/Energy/Natural-Gas/How-the-US-Shale-Boom-Will-Change-the-World.html (last accessed 26.05.2013).
22 See International Labour Comparisons, International Unemployment Rates and Employment Indexes, Seasonally Adjusted, 2008–2012: http://www.bls.gov/ilc/intl_unemployment_rates_monthly.htm (accessed 27.02.2013).
23 See also Project Rioplus (GIZ) http://www.giz.de/Themen/de/11039.htm (accessed 21.03.2013).
24 The NPO concept is based on a method called Environmental Cost Management (Fischer *et al.* 1997) but was substantially adapted to developing countries' conditions, needs of replicability and cost-effectiveness, e.g. by group approach, and an organisational development component by German Technical Co-operation (GTZ n.d.; Kürzinger 2004a; 2012: 53f) and PREMAnet e.V. (www.premanet.net).
25 PREMA® is a modular training and consultancy method for small and medium-sized enterprises developed by GTZ and marketed by PREMAnet e.V. (www.premanet.net).

References

Abbott, K. W. (2013) *Constructing a Transnational Climate Change Regime: Bypassing and Managing States*, online: http://ssrn.com/abstract=2219554 or http://dx.doi.org/10.2139/ssrn.2219554 (accessed 25.02.2014).

Acquaye, A., Duff, A. and Badu, B. (2010) 'Embodied Emissions Abatement – A Policy Assessment using Stochastical Analysis', *Energy Policy*, vol. 10, no. 22, pp. 1–13; online: doi:101016/j.enpol.2010.10.022.; http://www.academia.edu/1430341/Embodied_emissions_abatement--A_policy_assessment_using_stochastic_analysis (accessed 27.02.2013).

Aitgen, G. *et al.* (2013) *Shale Gas: Unconventional and Unwanted – The Case against Shale Gas*, Berlin: Heinrich-Böll-Stiftung, online: http://www.boell.de/downloads/2013-02-shale-gas-report.pdf (accessed: 18.03.2013).

Argyris, C. and Schön, D. (1978) *Organizational Learning: A Theory of Action Perspective*, Reading, MA: Addison-Wesley.

Baer, P. *et al.* (2008) *The Right to Development in a Climate Constrained World: The Greenhouse Development Rights Framework*, 2nd ed., Berlin: Heinrich Böll Foundation, online: http://www.boell.de/downloads/intlpolitics/Themenpapier_GDR-2ndeEdFinal.pdf (accessed 08.03.2013).

Bailer, S. (2012) 'Strategy in the Climate Change Negotiations: Do Democracies Negotiate Differently?', *Climate Policy*, vol. 12, no. 5, pp. 534–551; online: doi: 10.1 080/14693062.2012.691224 (accessed 22.01.2013).

Beckhard, R. (1969) *Organization Development: Strategies and Models*, Reading, MA: Addison-Wesley.

Benedick, R. (2011) 'Striking a New Deal on Climate Change', *Issues in Science and Technology*, vol. 18, no. 11, pp. 71–76, online: http://connection.ebscohost.com/c/articles/5477284/striking-new-deal-climate-change (accessed: 18.03.2013).

Benedick, R. E. (1998) *Ozone Diplomacy: New Directions in Safeguarding the Planet*, Enlarged Edition, Washington, DC: Harvard University Press.

Birkeland, J. (2002) *Design for Sustainability: A Sourcebook of Integrated Eco-Logical Solutions*, London: Earthscan.

Blodgett, C. *et al*. (2012) *Nationally Appropriate Mitigation Actions: A Technical Assistance Sourcebook for Practitioners*, GIZ: Eschborn, online: http://mitigationpartnership.net/ sites/default/files/giz_nama_ta_source_book_1.0.pdf_0.pdf (accessed 18.03.2013).

BMU (Federal Ministry for Environment, Nature Conservation and Nuclear Safety) (2011) *Draft for a German Programme on Resource Efficiency (ProgRess)*, mimeo.

BMU (n.d.) *International Climate Initiative*, ICI, online: http://www.bmu-klimaschutzinitiative.de/en/news (accessed: 16.03.2103).

BMU and BMZ (2011) *Germany's International Approach to Climate Change: Spotlight on Africa*, online: http://www.bmz.de/de/publikationen/reihen/infobroschueren_flyer/ infobroschueren/Materialie209_Informationsbroschuere_01_2011.pdf (accessed 21.03.2013).

Bodansky, D. M. (2007) 'Targets and Timetables: Good Policy But Bad Politics?', *University of Georgia Research Paper Series*, no. 07-014: November, and in Aldy, J. E. and Stavins, R. N. (eds), *Architectures for Agreement: Addressing Global Climate Change in the Post-Kyoto World*, Cambridge: Cambridge University Press, pp. 57–66; online: http://ssrn.com/abstract=1033550 (accessed 22.02.2013).

Bunse, M. *et al*. (2007) *Top Runner Approach*, Report to the Environmental Office, Centre for Sustainable Consumption and Production-CSCP: Wuppertal, mimeo.

Bureau of Labor Statistics (2013) *International Unemployment Rates*, and in *Employment Indexes, Seasonally Adjusted, 2009–2013*, online: http://www.bls.gov/ilc/intl_ unemployment_rates_monthly.htm (accessed 27.02.2013).

Buzan, T. (1974) *Use Your Head*, London: BBC Books.

Chakravarty S., Chikkaturb, A., de Coninckc, H., Pacalaa, S. and Socolow, R. (2009) *Sharing Global CO2 Emission Reductions among one Billion High Emitters*, in Proceedings of the National Academy of Sciences of the United States of America, 106:29, 11884– 11888, online: http://www.pnas.org/content/106/29/11884.full, pp. 1-6 (accessed 02.03.2013); see also their reply, online: http://www.pnas.org/content/106/43/E124. full.pdf+html?sid=b3532ab3-8869-4575-9cc7-a8be60e285a9 (accessed 27.02.2013) to a critical comment by Grubler, A. and Pachauri, S. (2009) PNAS:106, 43; pp. 122–123; online: http://www.pnas.org/content/106/43/E122.full.pdf+html?sid=3b43edda-ccce-427f-87e4-ca1bba400eb6 (accessed 02.03.2013).

Chen, T. Y. *et al*. (2001) 'Analysis of Embodied Energy Use in the Residential Building of Hongkong', *Energy*, vol. 26, no. 4, pp. 323–340, online: http://www.sciencedirect.com/ science/article/pii/S0360544201000068 (accessed: 18.03.2013).

Chevalier, J. M. and Buckles, D. J. (2013) *Participatory Action Research: Theory and Methods for Engaged Inquiry*, London: Routledge, online preview: http://www. ewidgetsonline.net/dxreader/Reader.aspx?token=ec5eea20a8824590aed1499b17dc886 c&rand=865077368&buyNowLink=&page=&chapter= (accessed 20.03.2013).

Costanza, R., Cumberland, J., Daly, H., Goodland, R. and Norgaard, R. (1997) *An Introduction into Environmental Economics*, Boca Raton, FL: CRC Press LLC, online: http://books.google.de/books?id=W8IrfPJLihEC&pg=PA1&lpg=PR11&ots=udY7GV Zclt&dq=Goodland+robert&lr=&hl=de (last accessed 03.03.2013).

Cottrell, J., Schlegelmilch, K., Klarer, J. and Olearius, A. (2011) *Environmental Fiscal Reform: A Practice-Oriented Training for Policy Makers, Administration Officials, Consultants and NGO Representatives*, Training Manual for Participants, Eschborn: GIZ / Berlin: Forum Ökologisch-Soziale Marktwirtschaft (FÖS); mimeo; for public information see http:// www.bmu.de/english/ecological_industrial_policy/ecological_finacial_reform/doc/41250.php (accessed 03.03.2013).

Crowe, T. (2013) 'The Potential of the CDM to Deliver Pro-Poor Benefits', *Climate Policy*, vol. 13, no. 1, pp. 58–79; online: http://tandfonline.com/doi/abs/10.1080/ (accessed 16.03.2013).

CSCP (n.d.) *Reducing Carbon Footprints and Increasing Resource Efficiency in SME*, online: http://www.scp-centre.org/projects/basic-projects-data/04-carbon-footprints-of-smes.html (accessed 27.02.2013).

Davis, S. and Caldera, K. (2010) *Consumption-based Accounting of CO2 Emissions*, online: www.pnas.org/cgi/10.1073/pnas.0906974107, pp. 1–6 (accessed 27.02.2013).

Dittrich, M. and Bringezu, S. (2010) 'The Physical Dimension of International Trade, Part 1: Direct Global Flows between 1962 and 2005', *Ecological Economics*, vol. 69, no. 9, pp. 1838–1847, online: http://dx.doi.org/10.1016/j.ecolecon.2010.04.023 (accessed 13.02.2013).

Dittrich, M., Bringezu, S. and Schütz, H. (2012) 'The Physical Dimension of International Trade, Part 2: Indirect Global Resource Flows between 1962 and 2005', *Ecological Economics*, vol. 79, pp. 32–43, online: http://dx.doi.org/10.1016/j.ecolecon.2012.04.014 (accessed 13.02.2013).

Fischer, H. *et al.* (1997) *Umweltkostenmanagement: Kosten Senken durch Praxiserprobtes Umweltcontrolling*, München: Hanser Fachbuch.

Fischer, H. *et al.* (2004) 'Wachstums- und Beschäftigungsimpulse Rentabler Materialeinsparungen', *Wirtschaftsdienst*, no. 4, pp. 247–251.

Fisher, R. and Ury, W. L. (1981) *Getting to Yes: Negotiating Agreement without Giving In*, Boston, MA: Houghton Mifflin.

Furness, M., Scholz, I. and Guarín, A. (2012) *History Repeats? The Rise of the New Middle Classes in the Developing World*, Briefing Paper 19/2012, Bonn: GDI, online: http://www.die-gdi.de/CMS-Homepage/openwebcms3.nsf/(ynDK_contentByKey)/ANES-935EAS?Open&nav=expand:Publikationen;active:Publikationen\ANES-935EAS (accessed 03.02.2013).

Galli, A., Kitzes, J., Niccolucci, V., Wackernagel, M., Wada, Y. and Marchettini, N. (2012) 'Assessing the Global Environmental Consequences of Economic Growth through the Ecological Footprint: A Focus on China and India', *Ecological Indicators*, vol. 17, pp. 99–107, online: http://dx.doi.org/10.1016/j.ecolind.2011.04.022 (accessed 03.03.2013).

GIZ (2012a) *Company Report 2011*, Eschborn: GIZ, online: http://www.giz.de/en/downloads/giz2012-en-unternehmensbericht-2011.pdf (accessed: 15.03.2013).

GIZ (2012b) 'We're Enterprising', *GIZ Staff Magazine*, vol. 02-2012, Eschborn: GIZ.

GIZ (2013) 'Capacity Development for Environmental Fiscal Reform. A Training Seminar for Policy Makers, Administration Officials, and NGO Representatives', Eschborn, online: http://www.giz.de/Themen/de/dokumente/giz2013-en-rioplus-training-environmental-finance-reform.pdf (accessed 27.05.2013).

GIZ-ZHB (n.d.) *PREMA Facts and Case Studies: Examples of Implementation in Tianjin and Guiyang City*, Tianjin: GIZ.

Goodland, R. (1995) 'The Concept of Environmental Sustainability', *Annual Review of Ecology and Systematics*, 1995, vol. 26, pp. 1–24; online: http://www.jstor.org/discover/10.2307/2097196?uid=3737864&uid=2134&uid=4577813557&uid=4577813547&uid=2&uid=70&uid=3&uid=60&sid=21101748824457 (accessed 03.02.2013).

Grenz, J. *et al.* (2011) *Response-Inducing Sustainability Evaluation*, RISE 2.0, Bern: HAFL, online: http://www.saiplatform.org/uploads/Modules/Library/What%20is%20RISE%202.pdf (accessed: 21.03.2013).

GTZ (n.d.) *GTZ Factsheet: Profitable Environmental Management in Chinese SMEs – Striving for a Triple Win*, online: www.giz.de/eco-efficiency (accessed 15.01.2013).

GTZ-P3U (2005) *Report: PREMA® Triple Win Approach Reduces Costs and Environmental Impacts while Building Capacities to Implement Change*, mimeo, Bonn: GTZ.

GTZ-PREMAnet (2012) *EoCM® Trainer Manual*, actualised version available at info@premanet.net (www.premanet.net).

Haldenwang, C. V. (2011) *The Taxation of Non Renewable Resources in Developing Countries*, Briefing Papers 8/2011, Bonn: GDI, online: http://www.die-gdi.de/CMS-Homepage/openwebcms3_e.nsf/(ynDK_contentByKey)/ANES-8JNHC6/$FILE/AuS%208.2011.pdf (accessed 20.02.2013).

Haldenwang, C. and Iwanya, M. (2010) *Assessing the Tax Performance of Developing Countries*, Discussion Paper 20/2010, Bonn: German Development Institute, online: http://www.die-gdi.de/CMS-Homepage/openwebcms3_e.nsf/(ynDK_contentByKey)/MPHG-8CVDS3/$FILE/DP%2020.2010.pdf (accessed 09.03.2013).

Harvey, F. (2012) 'Gas "Fracking" Gets Green Light', *The Guardian*, 17 April, online: http://www.guardian.co.uk/environment/2012/apr/17/gas-fracking-gets-green-light (accessed 21.01.2013).

Haussmann, M. and Scholz, H. (2007) *Appreciative Inquiry, Learning Map No. 3*, Eichenzell: Neuland.

Hertwich, E .G. and Peters, G. (2009) 'Carbon Footprint of Nations: A Global, Trade-linked Analysis', *Environmental Science & Technology*, vol. 43, no. 16, pp. 6416–6420;,online: http://pubs.acs.org/doi/abs/10.1021/es803496a (accessed: 15.03.2013).

Hicks, C. and Dietmar, R. (2007) 'Improving Cleaner Production through the Application of Environmental Management Tools in China', *Journal of Cleaner Production*, vol. 15, no. 5, pp. 395–408, online: http://www.sciencedirect.com/science/article/pii/S0959652605002349 (accessed: 18.03.2013).

Hoffmann, U. (2011) 'Effective Ways to Overcome the Food Security Crisis through Eco-functional Intensification and Smallholder Empowerment', *Local Land & Soil News*, no. 38/39, pp. 5–9, online: http://www.bodenbuendnis.org/fileadmin/docs/infozeitung/llsn38-39-col.pdf (accessed 16.03.2013).

Horstmann, B. and Scholz, I. (2011) *Criteria for Burden-sharing and Allocation Criteria under the UN Climate Regime: Neither Fair Nor Effective*, Briefing Paper, no. 9/2011, Bonn: German Development Institute (GDI), online: http://www.die-gdi.de/CMS-Homepage/openwebcms3_e.nsf/(ynDK_contentByKey)/ANES-8K4HCM/$FILE/AuS%209.2011.pdf (accessed 09.03.2013).

Hunt, G. (2012) *How the US Shale Boom Will Change the World*, online: http://oilprice.com/Energy/Natural-Gas/How-the-US-Shale-Boom-Will-Change-the-World.html (accessed 21.01.2013).

International Renewable Energy Agency (2012) *IRENA Handbook on Renewable Energy Nationally Appropriate Mitigation Actions (NAMAs) for Policy Makers and Project Developers*, online: http://www.irena.org/menu/index.aspx?mnu=Subcat&PriMenuID=36&CatID=141&SubcatID=265 (accessed: 25.01.2013).

Jänicke, M. (2011) *Dynamic Governance of Clean Energy Markets: Lessons from Successful Cases*, IPCC Symposium, Tokyo: METI, 5 July 2011, online: http://www.gispri.or.jp/english/symposiums/images110706/Prof_Janicke.pdf (accessed: 22.03.2013).

Kunreuther, H. and Unseem, M. (2010) *Learning from Catastrophes, Strategies for Reaction and Response*, Upper Saddle River, NJ: Prentice Hall.

Kürzinger, E. (1988) 'Argentina. Blocked Development', *Occasional Papers*, vol. 94, Berlin: German Development Institute (GDI).

Kürzinger, E. (1998) 'Act Not (Only) Negotiate?! – The Three Environment Conventions Six Years after Rio', *Agriculture and Rural Development*, vol. 1, pp. 56–60.

Kürzinger, E. (2004a) 'Von Afrikas Industrie lernen. Der Fall Profitables Umweltmanagement', in Lühr, V., Kohls, A. and Kumitz, D. (eds) *Sozialwissenschaftliche Perspektiven auf Afrika*, Festschrift für Manfred Schulz, pp. 263–287, Münster: LIT.

Kürzinger, E. (2004b) 'Capacity Building for Profitable Environmental Management', *Journal of Cleaner Production*, vol. 12, no. 3, pp. 237–248; online: http://www.sciencedirect.com/science/article/pii/S0959652603000957 (accessed: 17.03.2013).

Kürzinger, E. (2012) 'Tapping Resource Efficiency Potentials in SME through Training and Consultancy Services', in Ullrich, D. (2012) *Resource Efficiency in Development Cooperation*, Eschborn: GIZ, pp. 47–58, online: http://www.giz.de/Themen/de/35799. htm (accessed 03.02.2013).

Kürzinger, E. and Aguilar, M. (2010) *Profitable Climate Friendly Management, Training Manual: Basic Module*, CSCP/PREMAnet e.V., Wuppertal: mimeo; available at info@ premanet.net.

Kürzinger, E. and Miller, J. (2009) 'Profitable Environmental Management', in Galea, C. (ed.) *Consulting for Business Sustainability*, Sheffield: Greenleaf, pp. 105–127.

Lacy, S. *et al.* (2012) *The Climate Policy Toolbox, (NAMA)*, Eschborn: GIZ, online: http://www.mitigationpartnership.net/nama-tool-steps-moving-nama-idea-towards-implementation (accessed 18.03.2013).

Lencioni, P. (2006) *Silos, Politics and Turf Wars: A Leadership Fable about Destroying the Barriers that Turn Colleagues into Competitors*, San Francisco, CA: Wiley.

Luhmann, N. (1990) 'Über systemtheoretische Grundlagen der Gesellschaftstheorie', *Deutsche Zeitschrift für Philosophie*, vol. 38, no. 3, pp. 277–284, online: http://cat.inist.fr/?aModele=afficheN&cpsidt=6129385 (accessed 16.03.2013).

Marshall, J., Coleman, G. and Reason, P. (2011) *Leadership for Sustainability: An Action Research Approach*, Sheffield: Greenleaf Publishing.

Martens, P. and Chang, C. T. (eds.) (2010) *The Social and Behavioural Aspects of Climate Change*, Sheffield: Greenleaf Publishing.

Matthew, B. and Sayers, P. (1999) 'The Application of Gestalt to Organizational Interventions in Universities', *International Journal for Academic Development*, vol. 4, no. 2, pp. 134–141, online: http://www.tandfonline.com/doi/abs/10.1080/1360144990040208 (accessed 18.03.2013).

METI (Japanese Ministry of Economy, Trade, and Industry) (2010) *Top Runner Program. Developing the World's Best Energy-Efficient Appliances*, Tokyo: METI, online: http://www.meti.go.jp/english/index.html (accessed: 13.02.2013).

Michaelowna, K. and Michaelowna, A. (2012) 'Negotiating Climate Change', *Climate Policy*, vol. 12, no. 5, pp. 527–533, online: doi: 10.1 080/14693062.2012.693393 (accessed 22.01.2013).

Moreno, A. (2010) *Climate Change Impacts: The Vulnerability of Tourism in Coastal Europe*, in Martens, P., and Chang, Ch. T. (eds.) (2010) *The Social and Behavioural Aspects of Climate Change*, Sheffield: Greenleaf. pp. 30–47.

Morris, C. (2013) *German Energy Freedom: Moving beyond Energy Independence to Energy Democracy*, Series on the German Energy Transition: 6, Washington DC: Heinrich Böll Stiftung, online: http://www.boell.org/downloads/Morris_GermanEnergyFreedom.pdf (accessed 09.03.2013).

Nicholls, R. and Kebede, A. S. (2012) 'Indirect Impacts of Coastal Climate Change and Sea-Level Rise: The UK Example', *Climate Policy*, vol. 12 (suppl 1), pp. 28–52, online: doi:10.1080/14693062.2012.728792, 05.02.2013 (accessed 15.02.2013).

Noble, T. (2001) *Improving Negotiation Skills: Rules for Master Negotiators*, online: http://www.tnoble.com/Articles1.shtml (accessed 29.03.2011).

OECD (2012), *Strategic Environmental Assessment in Development Practice: A Review of Recent Experience*, OECD Publishing, online: doi: 10.1787/9789264166745-en (accessed: 21.03.2013).

Paulus, S. (2012) *Opening Speech: Environment and Climate Expert Conference*, online: in German: http://www.giz.de/Themen/de/dokumente/giz2012-de-fachtagung-umwelt-rede-paulus.pdf (accessed 20.03.2013).

PREMAnet and GTZ (2009) *PREMA Impact Report*, Eschborn, online: http://www. phemolabservices.com/PREMA%20in%20brief.pdf (accessed 20.03.2013).

Rayner, S. (2011) 'How to Eat an Elephant? A Bottom-up Approach to Climate Policy', *Climate Policy*, vol. 10, no. 6, pp. 615–621, online: http://dx.doi.org/10.3763/cpol.2010.0138 (accessed 25.02.2013).

Rock, D. (2008) 'SCARF: A Brain-based Model for Collaborating With and Influencing Others', *NeuroLeadership Journal*, no. 1, pp. 1–9, online: http://www.scarf360.comfiles/SCARF-NeuroleadershipArticle.pdf (accessed 16.03.2013)

Schwedersky, T. and Karkoschka, O. (eds.) (1996) *Process Monitoring Pilot Project for Natural Resource Management*, 402/96, 22e, NARMs, Tool 22, Eschborn: GTZ, online http://star-giz.de/dokumente/bib /96-1351.pdf (accessed 18.03.2013).

SEPA (2004) *Evaluation of PREMA® applications in China*, Beijing, mimeo.

Stone, F. (2004) 'Deconstructing Silos and Supporting Collaboration', *Employment Relations Today*, vol. 31, no. 1, pp. 11–18, online: doi: 10.1002/ert.20001 or http://onlinelibrary.wiley.com/doi/10.1002/ert.20001/pdf (accessed 26.02.13).

Tavoni, M., Chakravarty, S. and Socolow, R. (2012) 'Safe vs. Fair: A Formidable Trade-off in Tackling Climate Change', *Sustainability*, vol. 4, pp. 201–226, online: doi:10.3390/su4020210; www.mdpi.com/journal/sustainability (accessed 23.01.2013).

Teubner, G. (1992) 'Die vielköpfige Hydra: Netzwerke als kollektive Akteure höherer Ordnung', in: Krohn, W. and Küppers, G. (eds) *Emergenz: Die Entstehung von Ordnung, Organisation und Bedeutung*, 2nd ed., Berlin: Suhrkamp, pp. 189–216, online: http://publikationen.ub.uni-frankfurt.de/frontdoor/index/index/docId/3898 (accessed 04.03.2013).

Ullrich, D. (2012) *Resource Efficiency in Development Cooperation*, Eschborn: GIZ, online: http://www.giz.de/Themen/de/35799.htm (accessed 03.02.2013).

UNDP (2013) *Human Development Report 2013: The Rise of the South. Human Progress in a Diverse World*, online: http://hdr.undp.org/en/reports/global/hdr2013/ (accessed 16.03.2013).

UNEP (2011) *Towards a Green Economy: Pathways to Sustainable Development and Poverty Eradication*, Nairobi, online: www.unep.org/greeneconomy (accessed 01.03.2013).

UNEP (2012) *Climate Technology Centre and Network. Proposal to Host the Climate Technology Centre*, Paris: Division of Technology, Industry and Economics, online: http://unfccc.int/files/cooperation_and_support/technology/application/pdf/main_proposal_unep.pdf (accessed 09.03.2013).

UNFCCC (2006) *GHG Emissions Inventory of the Secretariat for the Biennium 2004–2005*, online: http://unfccc.int/files/secretariat/environmental_responsibilities/application/pdf/unfccc_ghg_emissions2004-2005.pdf (accessed 08.03.2013).

UNFCCC (2012) *Momentum for Change: 2012 Lighthouse Activities*, online: http://unfccc.int/secretariat/momentum_for_change/items/7159.php (accessed 21.03.2013).

UNFCCC (n.d.) *Status of Ratification of the Convention*, online: http://unfccc.int/essential_background/convention/status_of_ratification/items/2631.php (accessed 08.03.2013).

van Berkel, R. (2011) 'Evaluation of the Global Implementation of the UNIDO-UNEP National Cleaner Production Centres (NCPC) Programme', *Clean Technologies and Environmental Policy*, vol. 13, pp. 161–175, online: link.springer.com/article/10.1007%2Fs10098-010-0276-6?LI=true#page-2 (accessed 21.03.2013).

Waddock, S. and McIntosh, M. (2011) *SEE Change: Making the Transition to a Sustainable Enterprise Economy*, Sheffield: Greenleaf.

Walker, S. (2011) *Coaching: Making them Listen*, posted on www.trainingzone.co.uk, 29 March 2011 (accessed 30.03.2011).

WBGU (German Advisory Council on Global Change) (2011) *World in Transition: A Social Contract for Sustainability*, Berlin: WBGU, online: www.bgu.de/en/flagship-reports/fr-2011-a-social-contract/ (accessed 21.03.2013).

WEF (World Economic Forum) (2012) *More with Less: Scaling Resource Efficiency and Sustainable Consumption*, Davos: WEF, online: http://www3.weforum.org/docs/IP/CO/WEF_CO_ScalingSustainableConsumptionResourceEfficiency_Report_2012.pdf (accessed 18.01.2013).

World Bank *et al.* (2005) *Environmental Fiscal Reform, What Should Be Done and How to Achieve It?*, Washington DC: World Bank.

Wuppertal Institute and UBA (Federal Environmental Office) (2008) *Resource Consumption of Germany: Indicators and Definitions*, online: http//:www.umweltdaten.de/publikationen/fpdf-l/3427.pdf (accessed 21.03.2013).

Würtenberger, L. (2012) *Financing Supported NAMAs (Nationally Appropriate Mitigation Actions)*, ECN Policy Studies, Petten-NL: ECN, online: http://mitigationpartnership.net/sites/default/files/2012_ecn_wurtenberger_financing_supported_namas.pdf (accessed 18.01.2013).

Yim Surrat, L. *et al.* (2013) *The Road to NAMAs. Global Stories of Successful Climate Actions*, Washington DC: Center for Clean Air Policy-CCAP, online: http://ccap.org/assets/The-Road-to-NAMAs_CCAP.pdf (accessed 18.01.2013).

Part IV
The way forward to climate-resilient development

13 Conclusions for research and policy agendas

Astrid Carrapatoso and Edith Kürzinger

The analyses of this book's case studies, together with its critical reflections on the concepts of sustainable development (SD) and climate-resilient development (CRD), clearly illustrate that there is no need for additional concepts or new policies. Rather, SD objectives need to be implemented in the way that they were intended but through different processes, which rely less on complex, comprehensive strategies, and more on wide-ranging, flexible, piecemeal engineering and well-reflected trial and error within an extensive use of 'windows of opportunity'. The new element – the integration of 'resilience thinking' into SD – should open the way towards more flexibility and inclusiveness, bottom-up processes, and practical stakeholder involvement; embrace a holistic view by integrating livelihoods, risk management, and climate change (CC) issues (both adaptation and mitigation); apply thinking-in-processes (i.e. combining short-term response and mid-term strategic issues, based on action-reflection cycles); and implement proactive, cross-sectorial, and multilevel change management. In order to achieve CRD, this book's authors come to the conclusion that the policy-making process should be based on:

- policy integration and subsidiarity;
- an integration of people's needs, knowledge, and bottom-up thinking;
- a livelihoods approach to better achieve climate resilience on the ground;
- experiential and context-specific learning;
- knowledge- and information-sharing through institutionalised dialogues at all levels;
- the cycle of change to avoid 'quick fixes';
- a reflection of a best alternative to negotiated agreement (BATNA) and a culture of log-frame in the UNFCCC process as well as an honest reflection on how to reform or to bypass current processes;
- creative thinking to find innovative, alternative, and/or complementary solutions to effectively design and implement CRD strategies.

Doing things 'right': policy integration and subsidiarity as core principles to achieve CRD

Lessons learned

Following the above-mentioned logic, policy integration and subsidiarity must become the core principles of CRD. When considering the lowest appropriate level for problem solving and specific opportunities, separate policy making by different policy 'silos' (like trade, energy, economy, transport, agriculture, environment, climate, adaptation/mitigation, and development policies and co-operation) makes less sense than ever, as all are influencing each other in terms of sustainability and resilience.

Advocating more policy integration is easy to say as policy coherence has been requested for many years but without much improvement in practice. Policy integration has, so far, been obstructed for many reasons, which, in the context of CC policy making, can be seen as follows:

- Vested interests of the institutional 'CC silo' (Chapters 2, 10, and 12), of sectorial ministries, in particular environment-related entities (Chapters 3 and 4), political interests (Chapters 3, 6, and 8), or bureaucracies. These interests limit the perception of problems, hamper the involvement of stakeholders, horizontally and vertically, and ignore the need to manage change processes by incorporating the relevant professional know-how (Chapters 3, 7, and 12).
- The predominantly top-down character of CC action (as opposed to bottom-up rhetoric as illustrated by the case studies in Benin, Ecuador, and Mozambique) and other related processes. Such an approach excludes local target groups' knowledge, interests, energy, and needs from the process, which would actually provide a sound basis for integrating different policies around clearly defined SMART objectives. Moreover, it does not address the root causes of vulnerability and poor livelihoods and often neglects local communities' realities.

In sum, the various chapters of this book have shown that the potential for CRD as a framework for realising a more pragmatic, flexible but holistic, bottom-up, and long-term approach still needs to be tapped.

Recommendations for policy and research

The recognition of the largely untapped potential for CRD as a new framework makes the need for policy integration and implementation of the subsidiarity principle even more urgent. The ongoing struggle of international climate negotiations for consensus-based solutions while at the same time following an overall business-as-usual economic trajectory reveals that policy integration and the need for structural reforms of both international negotiation processes and national policy making are merely rhetoric and not followed by concrete action (Chapters 2, 10, 11, and 12). Pursuing an integrated approach towards CC policy would require the revision of some policies and/or abandoning others altogether (Newell 2004: 125), and looking for synergies amongst different policy fields; this might take longer and will be resisted violently (ibid.) because of self-referential systems, silo thinking, the existence of ineffective incentive structures, and power struggles. But in the end, such an approach would transform the whole process aiming at CRD into a more efficient and effective mechanism that helps to overcome the current duplication of CC and development policies.

Resilience thinking can help to overcome existing structural inefficiencies and to seriously tackle the effects of CC by:

- applying the subsidiarity principle; obstacles can be surmounted more easily as the policy silos are less apart and the actors know each other better at lower political levels;
- analysing the root causes for vulnerability by increasingly integrating relevant empirical investigation – which are rooted in area studies,[1] i.e. research based on extensive fieldwork to develop a better understanding of local contexts, as well as action research – into the policy-making process;
- taking the needs of affected people more seriously, incorporating local knowledge and initiatives for effective problem solving on the ground and creating ownership through participatory bottom-up approaches;
- incorporating flexible mechanisms when designing policy approaches and paying more attention to effective change management by relevant actors;
- combining mitigation and adaptation as, in practice, they cannot be separated from each other;
- supporting the implementation of bottom-up approaches by integrating CC policy making, for example National Action Plans for Adaptation (NAPA) and/or Nationally Appropriate Mitigation Action (NAMA) with official development assistance (ODA) programmes, planned on the basis of field and action research.

Towards a more flexible approach: integrating people's needs and knowledge and putting bottom up into generalised practice

Lessons learned

The case studies in this book have shown that CC is an additional stressor for those actors whose livelihoods are already under pressure, especially for the poor and the rural population. To render societies more resilient to the effects of CC, this multidimensional problem has to be integrated systematically into all kinds of development activities. This implies, in turn, that a too narrow focus on CC measures financed by components of the international climate regime (ICR) needs to be replaced by a more holistic approach where synergies are sought with policies addressing SD issues, especially social and economic issues, but also using a broader definition of environmental issues.

Hence, such an approach would require, amongst other aspects, abandoning the narrow focus on energy or renewable energy projects promoted by specialists, and the downgrading of socio-economic issues to 'co-benefits of sustainable development', for example in the context of the new silver bullet of NAMA (Hänsel *et al.* 2012: 35). This also implies not adapting the design of programmes to the sectorial logic of a measurement, reporting, and verification (MRV) system which favours strictly sectorial approaches in order to more easily count emissions reduced and credits gained, instead of choosing a more natural 'household' or 'enterprise' perspective. The latter would provide a coherent framework for supporting actors in achieving tangible results when addressing CC issues by going through the full cycle of change (Chapter 12). While 'double counting' of emission reductions would be more likely in a CRD approach, as actors do not think in terms of 'sectors', it is more important to trigger action 'in the right direction' (as described in Chapter 12) than to have a perfect MRV system. The latter should support the measurement of success and impact and not be a system that fosters classic sectorial, un-holistic politics, and policy approaches. The case study from Orissa, India, in Chapter 5 provides a good example in this respect.

The adoption of an integrated CRD perspective would require nothing less than a structural change of the international policy making and consequently implementation process. Due to many vested interests and the dynamics of a self-referential system, the reform of the ICR is a challenging task and requires a shift in mindset on the part of all involved actors. A starting point would be to ask: Are we doing things right? And are we doing the right things? In which ways can we move from the currently rather sclerotic institutional set-up for tackling CC to a more flexible, participation-oriented system based on the subsidiarity principle which calls for management of problems at the lowest possible level?

Recommendations for policy and research

To achieve CRD and reduce vulnerabilities, all actors involved need to show ownership and leadership with respect to the issues they must tackle and by which they are directly affected; flexibly react to problems while also incorporating an approach of strategic planning; ensure efficient implementation as well as reflection, monitoring, revision, and adaptation of policies; and encourage co-ordination and facilitate participation. The case studies at the local level documented in this book show that a participatory approach should be based on action research and deep knowledge of the relevant area, process learning, and be oriented towards immediate action according to long-term objectives. Consequently, policies should be designed in a way that:

- more broad-based rural development and needs-based strategies become central to (climate-resilient) policy making in order to enhance rural livelihoods, i.e. combining adaptation and mitigation measures to generate and assure income from farming as well as non-farm livelihoods strategies, and adequately supporting autonomous initiatives;

- local communities are involved in all steps of the policy cycle, from agenda-setting, policy development planning, and announcement to implementation and monitoring of the change process, thereby taking local knowledge, needs, interests, and norms into account and promoting ownership at all stages, and thus avoiding the call on local populations to implement what has been developed at a higher level without their involvement;
- local capacity-building and context-specific training in a wide range of areas (from agricultural practices, to marketing of products or housing, etc.) become core elements of CRD strategies (e.g. Chapters 3 to 7) with a view to empower people to analyse, plan, monitor, and finally manage change under imperfect information;
- necessary information on CC such as meteorological data or on new agricultural practice is provided in a timely, sufficient manner using appropriate media;
- trust-building is taken seriously in order to foster mutual understanding and to avoid that CRD initiatives are compromised by partisan power plays or corruption;
- mutual learning, the use of participatory tools, and dialogue processes are actively promoted.

The empirical case studies have shown that if policies, strategies, and projects are designed and implemented 'right', we might also be prepared to do the 'right' things in terms of CRD. The urgency, potential, and willingness to modify existing structures in response to the inevitable effects of the additional stressor CC are highly visible at the local level. But the case studies in this book also make explicit that even in smaller settings, a lack of appropriate incentive structures and participation, power struggles, and ongoing fights about competencies and funds, as well as communication deficits often hinder effective problem solving – although everyone seems to know the right solutions.

Doing the right thing: enhancing climate resilience through improving livelihoods and vice versa

Lessons learned

Best practice, such as the Western Orissa Rural Livelihoods Project (WORLP) discussed in Chapter 5, can inspire more creative thinking about CRD at local, regional, and international levels. WORLP follows a participatory approach but with governmental backup, which shows that participation and governmental policies do not have to contradict each other. On the contrary, building community-based institutions and collectives to promote local ownership, while at the same time offering governmental support, seems to have worked well in this context. As a result, the project has essentially achieved its original aims to:

- reduce poverty and generate income;
- diversify livelihoods;

- sustainably manage natural resources; and
- reduce vulnerabilities and render communities more resilient to CC.

Similar insights were gained through the cross-regional study outlined in Chapter 3, which argues that improving rural livelihoods makes affected people more resilient to the inevitable effects of CC. As this also led to a better awareness of the CC problem and behavioural change, such an approach eventually also fostered mitigation efforts. In contrast to the overall positive example of the WORLP project, the authors of Chapter 3 conveyed rather mixed results regarding the effectiveness of existing policies.

Recommendations for policy and research

In general, the empirical cases documented in this book illustrate that CRD is indeed a way forward but calls for an integration of people whose livelihoods are affected, together with governmental agencies and other relevant stakeholders, including civil society and the private sector. The WORLP project, in particular, shows that in the case of watershed development, a more holistic approach towards area development and the improvement of livelihoods through a wide variety of means seems to be the way forward. Such a development model needs support structures at both the state and local levels which mutually reinforce each other. Furthermore, a plurality of institutions that implement pro-poor strategies as well as decentralised governance of natural resources through community-based institutions have so far proven to be successful in addressing CC impacts.

In this respect, Chapter 3 highlighted the positive aspects of action research and area studies as a means to understand the needs and problems of rural livelihoods, recommending that researchers should try to get information about what is happening in terms of observation and perception of CC, symptoms, and a description of what local communities have changed regarding their behaviour, if possible without explicitly referring to CC (as described in both Chapters 3 and 4). An understanding of already existing autonomous adaptation is an important basis for supporting self-help initiatives, which inherently maintain ownership and leverage the existing 'energy for change'. Such an approach is also indirectly supported by the case studies on Benin (Chapter 4) and Mozambique (Chapter 6) in that they explain how local communities deal with the effects of CC without significant support. These studies also argue that culture, values, and norms must be taken into account when designing CRD strategies, as the understanding of those aspects as well as their observance during the policy-making process significantly contributes to the success or failure of climate action.

Thinking out of the box: foster reflection, experiential- and context-specific learning

Lessons learned

The ICR acts far above reality when not taking seriously the local realities and the capacities of the implementing levels into account. As there is a heterogeneous group of experts and diplomats involved who often do not have any or, at least, not significant exposure to the livelihoods that are critically affected by CC, these actors often do not only lack the information provided by research such as that described in Chapter 3, but the rather isolated approach due to silo thinking hampers the experiential and context-specific learning needed for more flexible strategies based on the notion of resilience. This is an argument in favour of promoting a different learning culture within the UNFCCC process, as well as for applying the subsidiarity principle: a profound reflection on whether and how UNFCCC is learning (i.e. through open reflection, effective assessment, monitoring and evaluation mechanisms, as well as the documentation of failures and not only of inevitable 'successes'), and identifying what additional know-how would have to be integrated at which levels. Best practice from the local level and social science perspectives are needed in particular to apply the subsidiarity principle and to effectively address all context-specific problems at local and national levels. Furthermore, an (unlikely) agreement on legally binding emissions reduction would finally require the translation of aggregated commitments into effective measures at national and local levels. In the absence of that development, the inverse approach of implementing 'no regret' policies at the lowest possible level and scaling up action from local and national level to foster agreements at the global level is obvious, unless blinded by UNFCCC silo thinking.

In short, as argued in Chapter 12, the ICR and its related actors need to show their willingness to build up the necessary capacities to change the current system in order to move in the 'right' direction with CC management and to promote a broader CRD approach rather than waiting for an (unlikely) internationally legally binding framework for action. The same chapter argues further that (cost-) effective policies already exist, such as Environmental Fiscal Reform (EFR) to reduce subsidies that are not conducive to CRD, and top runner approaches to trigger systematic improvement of resource efficiency and tap the potential at company level to support profitable resource efficiency management behaviour (through methods such as PREMA®). A modified view of innovation that does not concentrate on lighthouse projects would also support CRD. A profound analysis of why the up-scaling of these policies and good practices has not happened so far – even though they are profitable and therefore do not need public or external finance, thus are 'no regret' approaches that make sense in any case (even for the use of renewable resources). Such an analysis would be the essential first step to think about, design, and implement CRD strategies, to follow a more integrated and flexible approach and to foster climate action on the ground with the potential for bottom-up approaches finally reflected at the international level. In any case, sustainability criteria for resource use and the rebuilding of natural capital stocks should be applied according to local and national conditions in order to enable ownership. Chapter 5 clearly demonstrates that this is a way forward towards CRD. The redirection of attention from national emissions to their causes, unsustainable production and consumption patterns, and the behaviour of high emitters in all countries, could stimulate (even at the UNFCCC level) the discussion and eventual agreement on the application of criteria for sustainable resource use (already developed 20 years ago) and infuse SD thinking into the climate silo.

In addition to training and coaching programmes for resource efficiency 'on the ground', for example in companies or in the public sector (e.g. sustainable procurement), another way to foster context-specific learning and professional training on CRD issues from the bottom up is to actively integrate a resilience perspective into educational institutions in order to train future professionals accordingly. Some lessons can be learned from Chapter 7 which describes how the College of Agriculture and Natural Resources (CANR) at the Kwame Nkrumah University of Science and Technology (KNUST) in Ghana has been promoting Integrated Natural Resource Management (INRM) in its study and research programmes and thereby providing trained professionals, as well as engaging involved stakeholders to pursue CRD objectives. While it seemed a logical step and an easy task to 'just' integrate a CRD perspective into the university, the need to overcome institutional inertia rendered the process difficult, time-consuming, and only successful over the long term. Changing traditional educational approaches requires strong leadership and strategic planning as it calls for an interdisciplinary approach and teams, modified capacity-building, institutional collaboration, and stakeholder engagement as core principles in teaching and professional training – precisely the opposite of the actual practice of narrow disciplinary and silo thinking. Involving new stakeholders makes decision making slower but, in the end, more sustainable. The most difficult problem is to modify the incentive structures for the actors involved to reward a new behaviour; in this case, interdisciplinary teamwork. It also proved to be rather difficult, but not impossible, to implement a change project in one institute or even reform the university from below, while the umbrella structure of the university continues to apply the 'old rules'.

Recommendations for policy and research

Context-specific learning can be promoted through action research as well as through training and consultancy approaches based on experiential learning methods. In this respect, it is important to know what is really happening in different contexts in terms of CC and local reactions. As most people, particularly in rural areas of developing countries, have already coped with stressors and started an autonomous adaptation process, this knowledge needs to be used as a starting point to address new and potentially more challenging stressors in future. The UNFCCC, for example, should actively take results stemming from this type of research into account as these studies have a profound scientific basis, while at the same time reflecting and analysing the existing realities of affected people. This type of research could also be an integrated part of NAPA,

NAMA, or similar programmes or projects. Through co-operation between local educational systems (e.g. engaging students to collect data), national and international research facilities, as demonstrated by Trócaire in Chapter 3, local and national (action) research and knowledge management can be improved, thus expanding the information basis in areas and of actors with high vulnerability. In addition, this type of research can trigger joint action 'on the ground', i.e. in the respective local, national, and regional contexts, which promotes CRD as shown in Chapter 3. Learning and change at the international level can be facilitated through integrating more bottom-up perspectives into the negotiation process.

Equally important is a profound reflection on and assessment of what should be dealt with and managed by the UNFCCC and what should be managed at other levels, i.e. integrating and applying the subsidiarity principle. Moreover, as Chapter 12 suggests, using management tools such as the 'cycle of change' as a roadmap for moving forward would mean that the current dissatisfaction with the status quo which can be heard all over the world but is never acknowledged in official outcomes of the climate summits, could be openly addressed by government officials in sessions moderated by professionals; the outcome of this reflection could be the starting point for an ambitious change process in all respects. This would require that all relevant actors develop a joint vision, i.e. an unambiguous perception on what the future should look like based on CRD thinking, to take stock of what actually works well or not, to plan realistic and manageable steps towards implementation of first measures, and to get an agreement on who will bear the costs (and reap the benefits). The bottom-up perspectives would have to be taken into account, and acceptable cost sharing and funding schemes for the parties involved would have to be developed using existing structures more effectively rather than creating more and more institutions. One important element of a new learning culture would be to establish a lean but effective mechanism for learning and evaluation drawing on structures available in ODA institutions or joint development of innovative instruments that foster CRD thinking.

With regard to education and professional training, Chapter 7 concludes that in order to systematically integrate an INRM or CRD perspective into a university, or even into a national educational system as such, a change of incentive structures would have to take place in all relevant institutions, rewarding interdisciplinary and integrated work looking for synergies, instead of promoting lighthouse projects, which in the end cannot be scaled up. Professional coaching programmes, which have already been implemented successfully in terms of CC management, should be more actively promoted and regularly revised and further developed instead of reinventing the wheel.

Let's talk and get started: knowledge- and information-sharing through institutionalised dialogues

Lessons learned

To facilitate the sharing of context-specific information, knowledge, and best practice, the institutionalisation of dialogue structures becomes important.

Chapter 11 illustrates what the subsidiarity principle for CC management means in practice, in the context of the inter-regional climate co-operation between the European Union (EU) and China: one element of problem solving could take place at a sub-global level where it is easier to find common ground for concrete action. EU–China climate co-operation was initiated at a high political level and, as such, is strongly focused on governmental co-operation. Nevertheless, as multi-stakeholder projects show, particularly in the fields of energy and urban planning, knowledge-sharing between private and civil society actors does occur. Despite existing deficits regarding stakeholder integration (particularly civil society) and a strong technology bias, such inter-regional dialogue platforms can facilitate climate co-operation. Establishing congruence between existing policy objectives is necessary to find common ground for enhanced co-operation based on mutual interests. As it focuses on 'windows of opportunity' rather than confronting each other with irresolvable positions deeply rooted in the respective political systems and cultures, such a type of co-operation is often more effective than multilateral co-operation. As a result, learning from each other as well as the diffusion of feasible policies and standards (e.g. on energy efficiency) is possible and co-operation results in joint (research) projects, such as the Europe-China Clean Energy Centre (EC2) and the China–EU Institute for Clean and Renewable Energy (ICARE).

However, this co-operation makes explicit that policy innovations have to resonate with pre-existing ideas and norms, which partly explains the technology bias in the EU–China co-operation and a focus on standards. But this pragmatic and (economic) incentive-based thinking neglects (normative) issues, such as distributional justice and lacks a more holistic approach, leaving aside some issues that would normally be part of a broader CRD approach. With its strong focus on energy, technology transfer, and research, the EU–China co-operation does not overcome the division between mitigation and adaptation and essentially does not take local and bottom-up perspectives into account; nevertheless, it assists China in designing policies and creating institutions that help to make the country's economic growth somewhat less carbon-intensive and a bit more energy efficient. This is a tiny step towards CC management, but still far away from CRD: this would require a critical discussion of the actual development model, especially the production and consumption patterns, which repeats the errors already made by OECD countries and adds a major burden on the climate without really establishing distributional justice in favour of (poor) people affected by CC. Looking at the problem of the European Emission Trading Scheme (ETS) and carbon trade, in general, the current debates on subsidising renewable energies in Germany and the need for policy revision because of the 'energy U-turn', it is questionable whether indiscriminate copying makes sense in countries with a completely different political and socio-economic background. The aspect of localisation, as briefly explained in Chapter 11, becomes crucial (see also Acharya 2004; Carrapatoso 2011).

Recommendations for policy and research

While inter-regional climate co-operation is certainly a step towards improved CC management, the EU–China co-operation still lacks essential features of CRD. In addition to an effective policy implementation 'on the ground', a bottom-up process is needed in which feedback loops to top-down policies can create input on the feasibility of proposed measures and in which successful local pilot actions are transferred into regional or nationwide standards. One example is the use of Environment-oriented Cost Management (a PREMA® tool) instead of a classic Cleaner Production Audit for complying with the National Cleaner Production Law, as described in Chapter 12. To move from project-based 'islands of effectiveness' to CRD strategies at different levels, the issue would have to be integrated into the national and inter-regional discussions, and both China and the EU would have to make efforts to implement learning at national levels. Inter-regional relations can only give an initial stimulus for such a momentum. Furthermore, given that, to date, concrete action is not only limited by its project-based character but also by its thematic focus on energy, tangible follow-up action outside the narrow area of energy is still needed. Here, the EU–China dialogue should integrate a resilience perspective in the co-operation and seek to integrate mitigation and adaptation processes. This could bring about win–win solutions by improving livelihoods and making them more resilient to climate stressors while at the same time continuing their co-operation on energy-related issues and technology transfer.

A closer look at EU–China relations reveals another problem, which is also relevant at the international negotiation level: the integration of stakeholders in less pluralistic, less-inclusive societies. Different perspectives on participatory approaches and the integration of a wide range of actors into the policy-making process as a substantial part of SD and CRD hampers implementation and compromises the core ideas of these two related concepts. To enable the construction of a local agenda that captures the needs of communities, an efficient means is needed to link civil society to the inter-regional level and grant access to the agenda-setting and decision-making process. This problem has been addressed through establishing a third pillar of EU–China co-operation, the EU–China High-Level People-to-People Dialogue (HPPD), in addition to two ongoing dialogues on economy and trade, and strategy. Founded in 2012, it is far from clear how the HPPD will develop, with what effects. Furthermore, being a separate dialogue branch in EU–China co-operation, it remains to be seen to what extent civil society perspectives will actually be integrated into the other two dialogues. Whether the HPPD can finally contribute to a more comprehensive approach on inter-regional CC management is thus an open question.

In the research domain, there is need for further analysis in the form of detailed case studies concerning the implementation and localisation of European policy models in China, for example the feasibility of incentive structures, like feed-in tariffs, in view of low energy prices and the low tax burden of the upper- and middle-income population, as well as the effectiveness of those policies in different national and local contexts, thereby addressing the environmental, social, and economic effects of an uncritical import of external policies. Another topic for further research involves the systematic integration of civil society into inter-regional relations in view of differing cultures of inclusiveness between the respective regions.

Avoid 'quick fixes' and ask the right questions

Lessons learned

Part III of this book focuses on how to reform and bypass inefficiencies in the ICR. Lessons learned from the local level have clearly illustrated that target groups and other stakeholders must be involved right from the beginning and throughout the steps of the 'cycle of change' (see Chapter 12). In this respect, key questions need to be asked, such as: What is the problem or the untapped opportunity, what are the effects of the actual situation and on whom, and what are the underlying (root) causes? What measures should be taken, by whom, with which effects, measured by which success indicators, and possibly in different scenarios? How can and should a specific policy be implemented? Who evaluates these policies and measures, through which indicators and documentation?[2] All these questions need to be answered from the perspective of affected people, not just from a macro policy, 'climate-only', or 'development-only' view – and consensus is necessary as well as 'energy' to move towards change. Such a change in management approach to problems or opportunities would also help to avoid 'quick fixes' in the sense of 'problem identified, measures to be taken suggested' without a proper analysis of the problem and its effects and causes. Such measures are often motivated by the urgency of a problem but, in the end, the suggested measures are often still part of the problem. Chapter 10 demonstrates the phenomenon that can be observed in the 'double phasing out' of ozone-depleting substances (ODS) (with finance from industrialised countries through the Montreal Protocol (MP)) to substances which are less ozone depleting. However, due to their global warming potential, they must now be substituted in a second round by subsidising the technological changes necessary to use less harmful substances that were already available at the time of the first phasing out of ODS (through HCFC-22 phase-out management plans, again funded through the MP as well as through the Kyoto Protocol Clean Development Mechanism (CDM) projects which replace Honeywell's HFC-134a).

Recommendations for policy and research

In view of limited financial resources, such a cost-adding mistake (despite the political rationales well explained in Chapter 10) must be avoided by clearly identifying a problem and its root causes as well as choosing measures that do not transfer the problem, but solve it. Professional support for the application of change management tools and process research on how this affects decisions, policies, and impact should be initiated.

Bearing these aspects in mind, the analyses of regional and international policies and structures (described in Part III of the book) set an example for how to search for innovative potential at a sub-global level, thus strengthening the idea of subsidiarity, and how resilience thinking could bring more creative thinking into the ICR: such studies on specific issues before taking costly decisions should be mandated by the respective mechanisms. In addition, the establishment of a culture that systematically applies self-assessment and external evaluation of processes and impact (not only of projects), as suggested above, would also make a considerable contribution in this respect.

UNFCCC: reform or bypass a self-referential system

Lessons learned

The analysis of the UNFCCC negotiation process from a change management perspective identified characteristics of a self-referential system: it absorbs financial and human resources with poor outcomes, which the members and beneficiaries of the 'UNFCCC silo' always praise as successful, especially as many actors involved appear to lack a viable alternative in the form of a BATNA. This could be explained by the lack of a 'culture of log-frame', i.e. the setting of objectives and indicators formulated according to SMART criteria (specific, measurable, achievable, realistic, time-bound, and formulated as if already done) from the start and transparent evaluation throughout and at the end of the process. Questions to be asked include: What was good, i.e. was there any kind of progress? What could have been better, i.e. is there room for improvement? What was missing or what work still needs to be done? Have the right things been done, i.e. has the whole process been assessed?

Taking a resilience perspective is hampered by the fact that most UNFCCC negotiators have never been exposed to the realities of local communities and rarely have an idea about what is happening 'on the ground'. This makes talking about sustainable solutions rather unrealistic. Chapter 12 argues that the setting determines the outcome, so by maintaining a structure, the results will be the same. In short, if the structural deficits of the current negotiation process and the UNFCCC bureaucracy are not tackled and the structure is not reformed, the results will always be the same and the process will not lead to viable solutions for all the parties involved. Getting a different outcome would require member states, stakeholders, and scientific actors to seriously engage in a reform process and explore to what extent the UNFCCC bureaucracy could be improved (e.g. through different working methods, processes, and content) and find ways to limit the problems aggravated by the incentives created through the mushrooming of new institutions and mechanisms (e.g. NAMA) within the constraint of available additional finance.

Recommendations for policy and research

Concerning the process, a timeout for careful reflection and honest scrutiny of the results and set-up through self-reflection, external assessment, and evaluation is recommended. Thus, it is advisable to initiate research programmes specifically designed for the assessment of the UNFCCC process, for example the identification of how to implement working methods, like those suggested in Chapter 12; how to create more efficient and cost-effective structures; how the subsidiarity principle could be implemented by the ICR and which working areas and policy fields should be abandoned or initiated in this perspective; what process could be used to agree on principles of resource use instead of a legally binding agreement on fixed emission reduction targets. In addition, research should be initiated to design an effective and cost-efficient system of learning and evaluation of the UNFCCC process and related bodies, including a knowledge management system that could be freely accessed by all relevant actors. Furthermore, research that considers the content (i.e. a legally binding agreement on emissions reductions) as unrealistic and inappropriate should be brought to the process, i.e. presented and discussed within the bodies, in order to stimulate critical and creative thinking regarding the appropriateness of one's own work and to yield complementary or alternative solutions to the current ICR structure. To move forward and get out of the current gridlock of international negotiations it is vital to:

- encourage a change of perspectives, and thinking that is different from the mainstream, for example avoiding the North–South trap, looking into different issues such as individual high emitters and embedded emissions;
- apply the subsidiarity principle to institute 'no regret' policies and leave resource-efficiency increasing measures to the lowest possible levels;
- concentrate on the causes behind the emissions, i.e. issues related to production and consumption patterns;
- stimulate discussion on relevant issues for resource use: for example the principles for sustainable resource use (see Chapter 12) and negotiation with major polluting sectors in this respect, for example with car manufacturers, the construction sector, and trans-boundary transport to achieve a roadmap to sustainable resource use and facilitate the switch to renewable energy sources;
- focus on a CRD perspective, i.e. moving in the right direction and not just focusing on emissions reduction, in order to achieve tangible results.

Take it or leave it: making existing mechanisms more effective or finding alternatives

Lessons learned

According to Newell *et al.* (2009: 5), we still know little about '[w]hich features of these [clean development] actors, institutions, and policy-making processes are resulting in effective outcomes in terms of climate action and development benefits, which are not, and why'. Chapter 9 addressed these questions in asking whether the CDM has triggered more ambitious climate policy making in the country where it operates. As this project-based mechanism follows a bottom-up logic by offering economic incentive structures to finance context-specific climate mitigation activities in developing countries, a contribution to CRD might be expected. The study showed that measuring the impact of the CDM on national climate policy is a challenging task, and identifying a causal relationship between the CDM and improved national climate policies is difficult. This is because CDM projects largely fit into existing national climate policies and serve already-formulated policy goals and programmes. The expectation that individual projects can trigger new policies is another important area for further investigation. In any case, existing research has shown that those countries profiting from the CDM may achieve their objectives slightly faster, and, finally, a policy revision towards more ambitious emissions reduction or energy efficiency goals might be more feasible. But this policy change has not been triggered, as yet, due to the limitations of a project-based approach (problem of up-scaling) and due to the character of the CDM as a mechanism to get 'buy in' from emerging economies with rapidly increasing emissions into the UNFCCC process, to respect commitments, and to boost the certified emissions reductions (CERs) market mechanism.

The analysis also raised critical thoughts concerning CRD and distributional justice amongst countries. Because Asian countries (especially China) are the major beneficiaries of CDM investment, which primarily follows the market-based logic of reducing emissions where they occur most and where they can be mitigated at lowest cost, the CDM discriminates against investment where the poorest and most vulnerable people to CC with low GHG emissions live. This can be considered a major flaw of the clean development system as it exacerbates the artificial separation of adaptation and mitigation, a division maintained for political and administrative reasons, and risks provoking demand for new mechanisms within the UNFCCC process from countries with low emissions: the recent activities on technology transfer may have such a component (Chapter 12). In practice, mitigation occurs in countries where adaptation is happening and vice versa, which is even illustrated by UNFCCC's own 'lighthouse projects'. Originally, mitigation projects in developing countries were attractive to foreign investors because of the CERs, i.e. carbon credits. The surplus of these credits on the global market, in addition to other factors which together lowered CER prices, made the carbon market (as argued in Chapter 2) less attractive to foreign investors. Given that the collapse of the global carbon market may render such projects less appealing and profitable, the CDM has been put into doubt, triggering current negotiations on the reform of this mechanism. Nevertheless, carbon trading is still a potentially huge market and the larger the potential for emissions reductions (such as in China), the more attractive it will be for foreign investment. Unsurprisingly, less developed countries with smaller emissions reduction potential do not benefit much from the CDM even though this mechanism could be beneficial for those countries as well, in view of the untapped potential for resource efficiency which often only differs in scale but not in nature.

Recommendations for policy and research

The CDM has the potential to integrate mitigation and adaptation, eventually making less developed countries more resilient by providing renewable energy technology, reducing dependency on fossil fuels, and eventually creating income-generating jobs: the conditions for scaling up and triggering policy change to design effective change management and related mechanisms is an important issue for policy and further research. However, because the CDM is strongly market-based, adaptation projects may become more important for less developed countries as these are increasingly part of development projects. The growing overlap of ODA and CC institutions and processes is also an issue for profound assessment if CRD is considered the long-term objective at which to aim. Because less developed countries do not enjoy much private financial flows, they ask for financial assistance from donor countries, which is not justified for projects that are profitable. But, as Newell (2004) argues, ODA is declining and financial flows are insignificant compared to those of the private sector, as observed in the CDM market. It would thus be worth exploring the relationship between CC policy-related financial flows and ODA. In any case, it is strongly recommended to better integrate CC (resource-efficiency issues) and development policies (e.g. concentrating on framework conditions), to support policy reforms such as EFR, capacity-building for resource efficiency, and the integration of local level and other stakeholder views in order to achieve CRD objectives while at the same time avoiding the implementation of contradictory policies by two still separated policy arenas. In light of the inevitable effects of CC, i.e. a need for both adaptation and mitigation, it makes sense to act on both in a coordinated way rather than building up similar, competing institutions in parallel.

Another relevant issue for current and future CC negotiations would be to consider the scope for South–South co-operation based on a North–South mechanism such as the CDM. South–South co-operation is becoming increasingly important, for example in the context of the South-South Global Assets and Technology Exchange (SS-Gate) of UNDP.[3] It facilitates knowledge exchange between countries with similar problems and local conditions. Given that emerging economies like China and Brazil are already important donor countries, South–South co-operation should play a far more prominent role in UNFCCC negotiations.

Being courageous, being different: a new mechanism to implement a climate-resilient sustainable development model through creative thinking?

Lessons learned

So, is the UNFCCC just 'gloom and doom' or is there potential for CRD and a process that stimulates creative thinking? An inspiring example in this respect is the Yasuní-ITT initiative in Ecuador, which can be viewed in the context of REDD+ negotiations. Chapter 8 shows what a different path to natural resource management (NRM) as a mitigation strategy could look like. This initiative offers an integrated approach to CC as a multifaceted problem: by transferring funds from the international community to Ecuador for leaving the oil fields in the Amazon untapped could have a positive win–win–win effect: reducing future carbon emissions by not putting fossil fuels onto the market in the first place (through this, addressing not the emissions as the outcome, but the underlying problem of fossil fuel consumption), transforming an oil-dependent economy into a low-carbon economy by redirecting financial transfers into alternative energies, fostering social development, and protecting the surrounding biodiversity through more public spending on social and environmental projects. This innovative idea also has its downsides as the actual politics in Ecuador make the transformation into a post-fossil fuel economy rather unlikely at the moment. The country in general, and the Amazon in particular, is increasingly opened for oil extraction and mining projects in order to finance social reforms.

But, the Yasuní-ITT initiative goes well beyond conventional development thinking and could make a significant contribution to CRD – if it gets the necessary governmental support; if it is done 'right' in terms of participation, distributional equity, and ownership; and if it is used as a starting point to seriously transform the economic structure of the country towards less oil-dependency and more climate resilience, 'the right thing'. And it would be one example where the UNFCCC contribution can be substituted by lower levels, making a reform project happen. It would also be an initiative in the direction of CRD: consuming less fossil fuel by putting less onto the market, thereby addressing the GHG emissions problem, by influencing production patterns and at the source.

Recommendations for policy and research

A reflection on existing development models and future options makes explicit how urgent effective change management and policy integration has become in light of already noticeable impacts and the unpredictable nature of CC, in addition to fast-evolving production and consumption patterns in both industrialised and developing countries. In this context, it is vital to understand not only where institutional as well as policy change happens at the global, regional, national, and local levels but what this means for local populations. It finally 'requires us to look not only at the activities of governments, but at the international institutions and market actors that shape so strongly the direction of national development strategies' (Newell 2004: 121). What does this mean for policy and research?

It is now the time for a stocktaking phase: Where do we stand? What has been achieved? And what hasn't? How can transformational change be approached in which areas? How can a resilience perspective be integrated into existing policy-making processes and implementation, and how can all actors move from rhetoric to action? One means of clarifying these issues could be a bigger international research programme based on (qualitative) empirical cases studies, including in the context of area studies, and action research to find out about the potential for integrating adaptation and mitigation by incorporating existing knowledge of affected people, i.e. local populations. This could provide a new information basis for more comprehensive thinking on CC management and open reflection towards a CRD perspective. An inter- and trans-disciplinary approach including universities, think tanks, NGOs, local populations, government agencies, and the private sector could be a way forward in this respect – although increased stakeholder integration can slow down the process as it requires more coordination among and between all the institutions involved. Sometimes, simply research co-operation between local and international research institutions, which aims at a longer term partnership, may be a useful undertaking.

In sum, to achieve CRD by effective change management, existing path dependencies in all CC and development related policy fields have to be explored, critically reflected and finally overcome when hampering a resilience-based approach. The call for more participation and bottom-up thinking as well as policy integration should move from mere rhetoric to action, i.e.:

- to seriously integrate results stemming from empirical case studies based on extensive field trips, action research, and area knowledge into the policy-making process and international negotiations, in order to bring about more realistic assumptions on what can and has to be done at different levels;
- to bring together scientists, practitioners, and policy makers but also affected people (in places closer to the latter actors' reality) to find common ground, common language, and joint viable solutions to follow a different path in CC management to be implemented in the respective spheres of influence;
- to honestly think about existing institutions and the way both CC and development policies are made – in what way these are suitable for triggering change in terms of appropriately and effectively implementing SD principles and following the path of CRD;
- to not shy away from giving up ineffective policies and inert and rather sclerotic institutional set-ups;
- to apply the subsidiarity principle because the best and most flexible solutions will probably be found at different levels according to respective affectedness, needs, motivation, and capacities; it is also a promising way forward to think about which level can fulfil which task and give what kind of support to which actors and the other levels.

Notes

1 A more detailed explanation of the scientific objectives and illustrative case studies can be found on the website of the University of Freiburg's Southeast Asian Area Studies project, http://www.southeastasianstudies.uni-freiburg.de/ (accessed 15.03.2013).
2 See Figure 12.4.
3 For further information, see the official website http://www.ss-gate.org/ (accessed 15.03.2013).

References

Acharya, A. (2004) 'How Ideas Spread: Whose Norms Matter? Norm Localization and Institutional Change in Asian Regionalism', *International Organization,* vol. 58, pp. 239–275.

Carrapatoso, A. (2011) 'Climate Policy Diffusion: Interregional Dialogue in EU–China Relations', *Global Change, Peace and Security*, vol. 23, no. 2, pp. 177–194.

Hänsel, G., Röser, F., Höhne, N., van Tilburg, X. and Lachlan, C. (eds) (2012) Annual Status Report on Nationally Appropriate Mitigation Actions (NAMAs), *Ecofys*, online: http://www.ecofys.com/files/files/ecn_ecofys_mitigation-momentum-annual-status-report_2012.pdf (accessed 14.03.2013).

Newell, P. (2004) 'Climate Change and Development: A Tale of Two Crises', *IDS Bulletin,* vol. 35, no. 3, pp. 120–126.

Newell, P., Jenner, N. and Baker, L. (2009) 'Governing Clean Development: A Framework for Analysis', GCD Working Paper, no. 001, March, online: http://tyndall.ac.uk/sites/default/files/GCD_WorkingPaper001.pdf (accessed 12.03.2013).

Index

Note numbers are indicated by '*n*' following page numbers.